Transitions to School - Interna
Research, Policy and Practice

D1589129

International Perspectives on Early Childhood Education and Development

Volume 9

Series Editors

Professor Marilyn Fleer, *Monash University, Australia*
Professor Ingrid Pramling Samuelsson, *Gothenburg University, Sweden*

Editorial Board

Early childhood education in many countries has been built upon a strong tradition of a materially rich and active play-based pedagogy and environment. Yet what has become visible within the profession, is essentially a Western view of childhood preschool education and school education.

It is timely that a series of books be published which present a broader view of early childhood education. This series, seeks to provide an international perspective on early childhood education. In particular, the books published in this series will:

- Examine how learning is organized across a range of cultures, particularly Indigenous communities
- Make visible a range of ways in which early childhood pedagogy is framed and enacted across countries, including the majority poor countries
- Critique how particular forms of knowledge are constructed in curriculum within and across countries
- Explore policy imperatives which shape and have shaped how early childhood education is enacted across countries
- Examine how early childhood education is researched locally and globally
- Examine the theoretical informants driving pedagogy and practice, and seek to find alternative perspectives from those that dominate many Western heritage countries
- Critique assessment practices and consider a broader set of ways of measuring children's learning
- Examine concept formation from within the context of country-specific pedagogy and learning outcomes

The series will cover theoretical works, evidence-based pedagogical research, and international research studies. The series will also cover a broad range of countries, including poor majority countries. Classical areas of interest, such as play, the images of childhood, and family studies will also be examined. However the focus will be critical and international (not Western-centric).

For further volumes:
http://www.springer.com/series/7601

Bob Perry • Sue Dockett • Anne Petriwskyj
Editors

Transitions to School - International Research, Policy and Practice

 Springer

Editors
Bob Perry
School of Education
Charles Sturt University
Albury Wodonga
NSW, Australia

Sue Dockett
School of Education
Charles Sturt University
Albury Wodonga
NSW, Australia

Anne Petriwskyj
School of Early Childhood
Queensland University of Technology
Kelvin Grove, QLD, Australia

ISBN 978-94-017-7984-5   ISBN 978-94-007-7350-9 (eBook)
DOI 10.1007/978-94-007-7350-9
Springer Dordrecht Heidelberg New York London

Foreword

This book is a compilation of contributions from Australia and New Zealand; Finland, Iceland, Scotland, and Sweden in Northern Europe; the United States of America; and Hong Kong (China) in Asia. The editors and authors are well-known members of the scientific community and highly reputed researchers in the field of educational transitions, through attending national and international conferences, or on account of their important publications, which are highly cited throughout the field. This book makes a very original contribution through reports on actual research, practical projects, and programmatic work. The work is structured in the form of an introduction, a synthesis and analysis, and finally a shared position statement. Transition to formal schooling has a different significance in different countries, depending on each nation's education system with regard to allocation of children to institutions based on different ages, occupying different professional stakeholders, different philosophies depending on existing and developing curricula, and different theoretical approaches to understanding the ongoing processes of change that all participants experience. So the work addresses early childhood education researchers, teacher educators, policy makers, practitioners, and interested parents – but in the way it is constructed, it may well be an example for working together in other scientific fields.

My part is to consider what might happen if you carefully study the book. You will learn about some of the researchers and the paths through their professional lives in relation to transitions. Connected with a historical perspective, I remember an international conference Transforming Transitions held in Glasgow, Scotland, in 2007. Urie Bronfenbrenner was to deliver a keynote speech, but owing to his demise in 2005, Glenn Elder Jr. presented it instead. With this book, you learn to think not only in a life-span perspective but from the viewpoint of the life courses that are historically embedded.

Is every dynamic change in the experiences of individuals, families, groups, or communities a transition? Is there a common idea about the meaning of transitions for the subjects to define transitions? Is there anything that family transitions, educational transitions, professional transitions, and transitions in child and adult development have in common? These are questions the reader may be eager to explore.

What does a transition do to the individual and to the context in which changes and differences are offered, and what do the individual and the context do? You will encounter many challenges while you are studying this book – not necessarily as risks, but pertaining to the motivation to cope with demands instead of seeing them as a threat. There are demands on different levels.

Individual Level

The reader will have to deal with strong emotions, their own competences, consciousness, reflectiveness, attitudes, and behavior. They will have to learn to reflect more critically about their own biases and inequities. They will have to learn to theorize in terms of historical, social, cultural, and political forces and in terms of their feeling and acting under the influence of these forces as an agent, not as a passive object. One example is the belief in continuity in learning and development through continuity in context. Could discontinuity in experience be seen as a stimulus for development, and development and learning be considered as other than a continuum? There are many stimuli in the book that help to see the world of transitions with new eyes. The reader has to understand that knowledge is socially constructed and that she/he is not alone in an ivory tower. The reader will have to reflect on ethics in terms of social justice or of the UN Convention on the Rights of the Child – an ethical canon that has been co-constructed and agreed upon by most countries in the world and is held as a legal norm in these countries. But is it respected in every relevant aspect?

The book ahead of the reader is about theories and making use of theories across research, policy, and practice. Different theoretical approaches may lead the reader to interpret the same situation differently, and reading about theories may change their own beliefs and standpoints, resulting in their working in new ways. The reader should adapt to readiness for diversity. They will have to be aware of their own values and learn to discover resources instead of emphasising deficits – also within themselves.

Interactional Level

Studying this book requires the reader to see not only themselves but also others as agents in relations. This may lead to changes in relations with other researchers in different countries, from different disciplines and with stakeholders in transitions: children, parents, and professionals. New ways of reflecting and acting in respect to the participation of stakeholders will be emergent, taking into account the interest and wishes of those who are researched. New relations are to be formed with people who are not prepared to be researched or involved into such a practice, and the reader may not be prepared to interact with and find common fields of interest with

Contents

actually living. Obviously, the scientific community has a long way to go to avoid exclusion of ideas and knowledge in other lingual-cultural contexts. The reader of the book is confronted with promoting intercultural perspectives within research, policy, and practice. Objects of research connected with transitions encompass attachment, resiliency, health, development, and language acquisition in communities of speakers and related cultures. The reader must be aware that from the perspective of a particular scientific discipline, other disciplines might appear foreshortened and not recognized in their inherent changes and development. In sociology, including ethnography and psychology, you find postmodern constructivist perspectives. In different countries, you might find different traditions in scientific disciplines, as well as in policy and practice, of course. The reader of this book will find opportunities for reflecting cultures: cultures of adults or of children in a society/community. To develop transition research, policy, and practice, it is necessary to contextualize the knowledge of partners, to understand and respect different social and cultural contexts, to value individual expertise and skills, and to negotiate objectives and processes independent of hierarchies and preconceived success formulas. As readers engage with views different from their own, they will co-construct a deeper understanding than that achieved by reading only things they already know or are agreed upon.

Why do I present before you this list of demands and challenges that may strike you when reading this book? Coping with changes and new demands in life experiences in a complex way that may be structured at individual, interactional, and contextual levels is a criterion to define a transition in the developmental psychology of families. Developmental transitions involve a restructuring of one's psychological sense of self and a shift in what Colin Murray Parkes has described as one's assumptive world, which means that in life's transitions, one's world will be seen through "new eyes." Achieving a new learning, a new attitude, and a new behavior as well as reflection and consciousness of this process is considered to be a developmental step in adulthood. If the reader takes the opportunity and exercises agency to learn, takes theories in the place of attitudes, methods, policy, and practice in the place of behaviors, and agrees on a new level of reflection, she/he gains from the development of an essential motive in (professional) life activity. It is not necessary to say in light of the complex demands that I mentioned that development and transition in adulthood are co-constructions. I promise the reader a lot of well-being.

State Institute of Early Childhood Education   Wilfried Griebel
and Research, Munich, Germany

them. The reader might have to come to interact with different age-groups of children, depending on the transition being studied. If similar processes are described in similar ways but through different theoretical lenses, it will be necessary to communicate the results with colleagues. There may occur challenging discussions between paradigms like readiness of children or of institutions, or quality education for all children in all institutions. The book will help in developing ideas with others. The reader will understand that transition research means participating in a relational process. Collaborative partnerships between institutions, services, and families have to be established. Broader stakeholders' involvement must be seen within ecological or sociocultural frames with heterogeneous instead of homogeneous groups of learners and teachers. Bias-conscious encounters with all kinds of children and parents from diverse backgrounds will happen through open processes where future predictions cannot be made. In working collaboratively, the researcher, policy maker, practitioner, and interested parent will have to address visible and invisible power relations and take a standpoint. You will have to give up – maybe unwillingly – disrespectful relations and frame consciously respectful relationships instead. The reader will have to learn to think, speak, and act in line with inclusion, in strengths-based ways. They will have to learn to listen to the voices of children, families, communities – in their languages. There is a demand to make oneself evident when things are not self-evident: like school, learning, child, family, transition. The reader will have to learn networking as a part of professionalism and learn to theorise in relativities.

Contextual Level

This book will confront you with the need to deal with a wider range of contexts and a wider understanding of contexts in international and interdisciplinary work. Let us take the question of diversity again in connection with different languages and cultures and a critical reflection on what has been achieved. The references listed in this international book are generally in English; only a few cited works are in the original language of those authors who do not come from English-speaking countries. These, such as Bronfenbrenner, van Gennep, or Vygotsky, shows that if they were not written in English, everybody has to rely on available translations into English – which means a selection from the body of available knowledge and thinking. An EU-Comenius project "Transition and Multilingualism" with partners from five European countries – not included in this book but an exemplification – made evident that exchange between scientists in a language that was not their mother tongue but in sociolects from other disciplines required intensive efforts in communicating. This difficulty encountered in the working process helped participants to understand better children and families who enter a school system that uses a language which is not their own. According to a guideline of the European Commission, and recognizing a growing migration worldwide, all children in Europe should speak at least three languages, including their family language in whatever context they are

Contributors

Marge Arnup is an early childhood educator with broad experience involving children, families, educators, and policy makers in Victoria, Australia. Working for the Department of Education and Early Childhood Development during 2002–2010, Marge developed and implemented innovative programs supporting literacy and transition to school. These programs built family and community capacity and were inclusive of all children, particularly those with a disability, Indigenous children, and children in Out-of-Home-Care. Practical resources and strong early childhood and school educator networks were an outcome of these programs. Marge lives in rural Victoria with her husband, a professional snake-catcher, keeping life interesting.

Margaret Cotman is a teacher of Year 1 and 2 students at Lucknow School in Havelock North, Hawke's Bay, New Zealand. Prior to this, she taught at Botany Downs School in Auckland, New Zealand, for six years. Margaret's professional interests include strategies for successful transitions to school and the use of information technology to enhance student learning and participation. She has recently moved to the Hawke's Bay with her fiancé and is enjoying exploring the local trails on her bicycle.

Sue Dockett is Professor of Early Childhood Education, School of Education, and the Research Institute for Professional Practice, Learning and Education (RIPPLE), Charles Sturt University, Albury Wodonga, Australia. Much of her research agenda is focused on educational transitions, particularly transitions to school, and the expectations, experiences, and perceptions of all involved. Her research also encompasses children's play and participatory rights-based research with children.

Aline-Wendy Dunlop is Emeritus Professor at the School of Education, Faculty of Humanities and Social Sciences, University of Strathclyde, Glasgow, Scotland. With the luxury of time, Aline-Wendy has chosen to focus her current research, conference, networking, and writing interests on educational transitions across the life span, autism, family engagement in education, the very youngest children, practitioner beliefs and practices, and arts-related childhood experiences. Deeply involved with her family whose ages range from 7 months to 95 years old, her new work-life balance allows for family time, travel, and the much loved hobbies of pottery, the arts, walking, films, and reading widely.

Jóhanna Einarsdóttir is a Professor of Early Childhood Education at the School of Education, University of Iceland. She is currently the Director of the Center for Research in Early Childhood Education at the University of Iceland. Her professional interests include continuity and transition in children's learning, children's well-being and learning in preschool, and research with children. Recently, she has been conducting research on children's views on their preschool education, and transition and continuity in early childhood education.

Anders Garpelin is Professor of Education/Special Needs Education and the principal scientific officer of Educational Sciences at Mälardalen University, Västerås, Sweden. His research concerns the meaning of educational transitions, also from a life perspective, for children/young people, with their diverse abilities and experiences. His current research deals with transitions young children encounter between three school forms, preschool, the preschool class, and school, with a special focus on learning and participation. Anders and his wife Merja live in a family where different cultural perspectives meet daily. The mother tongues Finnish, Hungarian, and Swedish are present almost daily with their children and grandchildren.

Bronwyn Glass is head teacher at Botany Downs Kindergarten in Howick, Auckland, New Zealand. She is a practicing teacher. Her research passions include possibility thinking, inclusive practice, building community, transitional actions, and how information technologies engage children and their families and build connections with the community. Bronwyn lives with her husband on a small rural holding with a range of animals including a rabbit that lives with the chickens.

Wendy Goff is a Lecturer at Monash University's Gippsland Campus and a doctoral student at Charles Sturt University, Albury Wodonga, Australia. She is currently researching on how working in partnership can support children's mathematical learning as they make the transition from preschool to primary school. Wendy shares her life with her beautiful children Lisa, Bradley, Joshua, and Jacob, her cat Rose, and her dog called Kevin.

Elizabeth Graue is a Professor in the Department of Curriculum and Instruction and the Director of Graduate Training at the Wisconsin Center for Education Research at the University of Wisconsin–Madison. A former kindergarten teacher, she received her Ph.D. in Research and Evaluation Methodology from the University of Colorado, Boulder. Her research interests include kindergarten policy and practice (particularly as they relate to readiness issues), home-school relations, research methodology, and classroom practice. She is currently engaged in an NSF-funded professional development program for pre-K teachers focused on developmentally and culturally relevant pre-K mathematics.

Linda J. Harrison is Professor of Early Childhood Education within the School of Teacher Education and the Research Institute for Professional Practice, Learning and Education (RIPPLE), Charles Sturt University, Bathurst, Australia. Her research and professional work focus on young children's experiences of education and care from infancy through to the primary school. She has investigated multiple dimensions of quality in early years settings and the ways that provisions and practices in childcare, preschool, and school influence children's health, learning, and well-being. Linda is a principal investigator on the Sydney Family Development Project, the Child Care Choices and Investigating Quality studies, the Sound Effects Study of young children with communication impairment, and THRIVE – a mental health intervention program for family day care. She is a founding member of the Research Consortium that is responsible for the design of the Longitudinal Study of Australian Children.

Shabnam Hinton is the Transition to School Program Coordinator at Big Fat Smile, a not-for-profit, community-owned organisation that has been supporting children and their families for 30 years in the Illawarra area of NSW, Australia. Shabnam is a trained primary educator and has worked in both early childhood and primary age services. Shabnam is passionate about the importance of early childhood development, early intervention, creativity, and giving children the best possible start to school and in turn their life. Shabnam has experienced the excitement and challenges of transition to school with her own three children.

Kathryn Hopps is a doctoral candidate at the School of Education and the Research Institute for Professional Practice, Learning and Education (RIPPLE), Charles Sturt University, Albury Wodonga, Australia. Her doctoral work focuses on intersetting communication between preschool and school educators at the time of children's transition to school. She has previously worked as an early childhood educator in a diverse range of school and prior-to-school settings.

Cathy Kaplun is a researcher working at the Centre for Health Equity Training Research and Evaluation (CHETRE), University of NSW (Faculty of Medicine), Liverpool, Australia. Cathy has recently completed her Ph.D. at Charles Sturt University, Albury Wodonga, Australia, which focused on the transition to school experiences of families and children living in a disadvantaged community. At present, Cathy is exploring the educational experiences of Aboriginal families and children as they transition to school. These families have been involved in a longitudinal project, which commenced in 2005, describing the health and development of Aboriginal babies and children (0–5 years) living in an urban area. Cathy lives in Sydney with her husband, four children, their puppy, two mischievous rabbits, and a recently acquired and rather laid-back axolotl.

Tracey Kirk-Downey is the Children & Family Services Coordinator at Wollongong City Council, Australia. Tracey is an early childhood professional who started her career as a teaching director in long day care. She is passionate about the early years of children's development and child-friendly cities initiatives – giving children a voice in their community and helping children have the best start to their school life as possible. Tracey's family includes a husband and two wonderful daughters who keep her busy and feeling loved.

Mei Seung Lam is Assistant Professor in the Early Childhood Department at the Hong Kong Institute of Education, Hong Kong. Mei Seung's current research interests include children's and parents' perspectives and experiences of transition to preschool and school, coping and identity, transition practices, parental choice of school, parental involvement, and tensions in researching with children in a Chinese context.

Amy MacDonald is a Lecturer in Early Childhood Studies within the School of Education and the Research Institute for Professional Practice, Learning and Education (RIPPLE), Charles Sturt University, Albury Wodonga, Australia. Her research interests are around the mathematics experiences and education of infants, toddlers, preschoolers, and children in the early years of primary school, with a particular focus on transitions in mathematics education. Amy is working on a number of numeracy-focused research projects utilizing data from the Longitudinal Study of Australian Children and is also involved in developing a program to support young children's numeracy development prior to school. She is also working on the Pedagogies of Educational Transitions (POET) global alliance project, with researchers from Australia, Iceland, Scotland, Sweden, and New Zealand. Amy lives in Wodonga with her husband Cody, their two dogs Burrito and Diego, their three cats Millie, Tilly, and Oscar, and their thirteen fish who are all called "Fishy."

Noella Mackenzie is a Senior Lecturer in Literacy Studies at the School of Education and the Research Institute for Professional Practice, Learning and Education (RIPPLE), Charles Sturt University, Albury Wodonga, Australia. Her current research is focused on writing acquisition and the relationship between success with early writing and ongoing literacy development. Noella's research projects involve the examination of the relationship between drawing and learning to write, the teaching and learning of writing in preschool, and the transition experience for early writers. She enjoys a rich life which centers on her family and friends. Her grandchildren are a particular source of enjoyment and challenge.

Kay Margetts is Associate Professor in Early Childhood Studies at the Melbourne Graduate School of Education, University of Melbourne, Victoria, Australia. Her research has a particular focus on issues related to children's transition, adjustment, and progress in school, including the influence of prior-to-school experiences, and considers the perspectives of educators, parents, and children. Kay regularly provides professional development to schools and early childhood providers, locally and internationally.

Elizabeth Murray is a Lecturer in the School of Teacher Education at Charles Sturt University, Dubbo, Australia. Her research interests include examining children's social and emotional adjustment to kindergarten, transition to and readiness for formal schooling, child stress and anxiety, children's coping, and quality teaching and learning environments. She is interested in both qualitative and quantitative methodologies and, in particular, working with children to examine issues of concern for them as they make the transition to formal schooling. Elizabeth has recently undertaken analyses using data from the Longitudinal Study of Australian Children to examine academic and social trajectories for young children starting school, and is currently analyzing young children's drawings to examine their perspective of the teacher-child relationship across the first year of school.

Bob Perry is Professor of Education at the School of Education and the Research Institute for Professional Practice, Learning and Education (RIPPLE), Charles Sturt University, Albury Wodonga, Australia. Bob's current research interests include powerful mathematics ideas in preschool and the first years of school, ethical tensions in researching with children, student decision making around staying on at high school, starting school within families with complex support needs, preschool education in remote Indigenous communities, transition to school for Indigenous families, and building community capacity. Bob shares his life with his partner, Sue Dockett, and their son, Will, both of whom ensure that he keeps his feet firmly on the ground.

Sally Peters is Associate Professor and Associate Director of the Early Years Research Centre at the University of Waikato. Sally has a background in early childhood education and a particular interest in children's learning and thinking. She has been researching in the area of transitions through a number of projects, currently working in partnership with teachers and colleagues to explore the experiences of children and their families as the children move from early childhood education to school and to consider ways of supporting their learning over time.

Anne Petriwskyj is Adjunct Associate Professor, School of Early Childhood Education, Queensland University of Technology, Brisbane, Australia. Her current research interests are inclusive pedagogies in early childhood, transition to school of children with diverse abilities and backgrounds, inquiry-based science and technology in early childhood, and effective professional preparation of early childhood educators. Anne's background in teaching in rural, remote, and Indigenous communities together with her science interest frames a connectedness to land that extends to organic food growing.

June Reineke earned her B.S. from the University of Wisconsin–Steven's Point, her M.S. from WSU, and is currently working on her Ph.D. in Curriculum and Instruction at the University of Wisconsin–Madison. Her area of expertise is early childhood education and policy. June has served on the state early childhood professional development subcommittee and the professional development advisory committee for childcare resource and referral. She is also on the leadership team for the Winona early childhood initiative.

Susanne Rogers is currently a Ph.D. candidate at the School of Education and the Research Institute for Professional Practice, Learning and Education (RIPPLE), Charles Sturt University, Albury Wodonga, Australia. Her research interest lies in the transition to school of children and their families. This interest has developed over decades of working as an early years educator in schools, a project manager, and recently as a coach in a literacy improvement project.

Tuija Turunen works as a Senior Lecturer in Primary School Teacher Education in the University of Lapland, Finland. She also has a position as an Adjunct Senior Lecturer within the Research Institute for Professional Practice, Learning and Education (RIPPLE), Charles Sturt University, Albury Wodonga, Australia. Tuija has two major foci in the field of transition to school research: curriculum for education commencing a year prior to compulsory schooling in Finland (Finnish preschool education) and adults' memories about starting school.

Chapter 1
Theorising Transition: Shifts and Tensions

Sue Dockett, Anne Petriwskyj, and Bob Perry

1.1 Introduction

Worldwide recognition of the significance of the early childhood years for later development and wellbeing and the importance of investing in high-quality early childhood education (Organisation for Economic Cooperation and Development (OECD) 2006) has promoted a great deal of interest in transition to school research, policy and practice. Recognition of the importance of a positive start to school acknowledges not only social and educational advantages but also the potential impact of these outcomes on disrupting cycles of social and economic disadvantage and in promoting resilience among young people (Fabian and Dunlop 2007; Smart et al. 2008).

In recent years, international attention has been drawn to the transition to school through comparative studies such as the OECD Starting Strong reports (2001, 2006). Indeed, Starting Strong II (OECD 2006, p. 1) recognised both the opportunities and challenges associated with the transition to school and urged that

> attention should be given to transition challenges faced by young children as they enter school … Facilitating transitions for children is a policy challenge in all systems. Transitions for children are generally a stimulus to growth and development, but if too abrupt and handled without care, they carry – particularly for young children – the risk of regression and failure.

The growing international focus on transition to school reflects a shift from attention at the local level to recognition that transition forms part of national and international education agendas. International comparisons, such as *Programme*

S. Dockett (✉) • B. Perry
School of Education, Charles Sturt University, Albury Wodonga, Australia
e-mail: sdockett@csu.edu.au

A. Petriwskyj
School of Early Childhood, Queensland University of Technology,
Brisbane, Australia

B. Perry et al. (eds.), *Transitions to School - International Research, Policy and Practice*,
International perspectives on early childhood education and development 9,
DOI 10.1007/978-94-007-7350-9_1, © Springer Science+Business Media Dordrecht 2014

for International Student Assessment (PISA) (OECD 2010) and *Trends in International Maths and Science Study* (TIMMS) (Mullis et al. 2012), compare children's performance well beyond the start of school but have the potential to influence what occurs within that transition, particularly around areas of curriculum and pedagogy. In several countries, such as Australia and the United States of America, state-by-state comparisons of standardised tests also drive educational agendas. These comparisons influence many educational debates, including those about curriculum continuity from prior-to-school to school settings, standards and expectations as children start school and the implementation of pedagogies of transition. In these countries, as well as in several others, it is not uncommon to hear regular media and research discussions about the age at which children should start school and the potential implications of this for their performance on later standardised assessments. Discussions of results and potential explanations for these often turn to the age of the children involved and the years of school education they have experienced at the time of the assessments (Peters 2010). As a consequence, interest in the transition to school extends well beyond the early childhood years.

1.2 Defining Transition to School

The term 'transition to school' is understood and applied in many ways in different contexts. Some approaches incorporate school readiness and adjustment, defining transition to school as:

> …children moving into and adjusting to new learning environments, families learning to work within a sociocultural system (i.e. education) and schools making provisions for admitting new children into the system. (UNICEF 2012, p. 8)

Broader definitions move beyond this focus on readiness and adjustment emphasising transition as a set of processes as individuals move from one (in this case, educational) context to another or change their role in educational communities (Dockett and Perry 2007; Fabian 2007; Vogler et al. 2008). These definitions focus on changes in identity and agency as individuals, and those around them engage in different educational contexts and adopt different roles. Within these definitions, processes of transition are regarded as both individual and social experiences, actively constructed as individuals participate in social and cultural processes that, by their very nature, are communal events (Rogoff 2003).

Other definitions of transition emphasise the intensified demands for children (Fthenakis 1998) as well as families (Griebel and Niesel 2009). Some researchers suggest that these increased demands present almost overwhelming challenges for some children (Hirst et al. 2011), while others focus on the importance of providing support and acknowledging children's strengths as they navigate these challenges and develop an enhanced sense of their own competence (Fabian and Dunlop 2007; Page 2000).

Throughout the world, debates continue about the role of adjustment, adaptation, continuity and readiness in the transition to school, the timing of transition and the teacher and/or school practices that support transition (Broström and Wagner 2003; Dockett and Perry 2013, in press; Dunlop and Fabian 2007; Petriwskyj et al. 2005; Ramey and Ramey 1999; Vrinioti et al. 2010; Yeboah 2002). While there is no universally accepted definition of transition, there is acceptance that transition is a multifaceted phenomenon (Petriwskyj et al. 2005), involving a range of interactions and processes over time, experienced in different ways by different people in different contexts. In very general terms, the outcome of a positive transition is a sense of belonging in the new setting (Dockett and Perry 2004; Fabian 2007). The ways in which this outcome may be achieved vary according to the theoretical perspective/s adopted.

1.3 Shifts in Theorising Transition to School

For many of the contributors to this book, Bronfenbrenner's bioecological theory marks a common starting point for theorising transition (see MacDonald et al. Chap. 16). However, different emphases and different connections with other theoretical perspectives lead to considerable variation in the implementation of research using this one theory. Critical perspectives also feature in the work of several contributors to this book, as does focus on rites of passage and border crossing. These variations in theoretical perspective frame three sections of this text. Such variation serves to remind us of the complexity of transition, in terms of those involved, their perspectives, the contexts in which they are located, the institutions involved and the ways that people position themselves and are positioned by others.

However, it also raises a number of questions about the role of theory in transitions research. For example, what makes a sufficient theory? Is it possible to engage with part of a theory? What is gained, and what is lost, by an eclectic approach to theorising transition? How can theories be adapted and refined without losing coherence?

Theories do not exist in isolation. They reflect particular ways of being and knowing and exist in historical time. We should not be surprised that different contexts, cultures and communities give rise to different ways of looking at things and accord importance to different elements and factors. In reflecting on the role of theory in her research, Einarsdóttir (Chap. 2) comments

> Theory helps me to see what is visible in a new light, notice novel things, and reveal new understandings. I also use it to help me understand the reality that I am investigating and explain what I see, why I see it, and what it means.

We invite readers to engage with theories and theorising transition as they explore the chapters of this book. We commence discussion of theoretical positions by considering the recent shift from a reliance on Bronfenbrenner's ecological theory in efforts to understand the transition to school. While Bronfenbrenner's early conceptualisations have been influential, later refinements of his theory, as well as a range of different theoretical positions, inform current research.

Bronfenbrenner (1979, p. xiii) noted that ecological transitions occur as an individual's 'position in the ecological environment is altered as the result of a change in role, setting, or both'. Bronfenbrenner's systems model of nested concentric circles, locating the child at the centre, is familiar to many educators and researchers. It promotes focus on the many and varied contexts in which people exist and interactions at the intersections of these contexts. Bioecological theory, which reflects Bronfenbrenner's later work (Bronfenbrenner and Morris 2006), retained this focus on context and people but placed increased emphasis on the importance of processes and time. From this emerged the Process-Person-Context-Time (PPCT) model (Bronfenbrenner and Morris 2006). Key elements of this model are proximal processes – defined as increasingly complex reciprocal interactions between an individual and the environment; the individual characteristics of each person, including their experiences, resources, temperament and motivation as well as their agency; the context, or systems including those in which individuals interact (microsystems), overlapping contexts (mesosystems), that influence their actions even though they are not direct participants in these contexts (exosystem), and the broader societal and cultural context (macrosystem); and time, which incorporates both what occurs during a specific activity or event, interactions that occur consistently as well as the chronosystem, that is, the specific historical context in which people and processes are located (Bronfenbrenner and Morris 2006). Life course theory (Elder 1996) pays particular attention to the chronosystem, arguing that people who inhabit different time periods can experience the same event in different ways. In relation to starting school, focus on the chronosystem could help explain differences in the experiences of parents and children and of children in different social, political and economic contexts.

The PPCT model provides a great deal of flexibility in researching transition to school. When applied in full, it prompts attention to the relationships and interactions associated with starting school, the characteristics and resources each individual (be they a child, family member or educator) brings with them to the transition, recognition of the various systems or contexts in which children and families are located as well as attention to specific events, patterns of interactions and historical context. It provides potential to explore issues of continuity and change, in terms of the individuals, the nature of experiences and interactions they have, the people with whom they interact and the contexts in which they are located. It also recognises that social and cultural contexts are dynamic, affected by processes of continuity and change. These elements are noted in the Ecological and Dynamic Model of Transition, developed by Rimm-Kaufman and Pianta (2000), which emphasised:

> ...the transition to school in terms of developmental processes that take place within the transition ecology. It is a system of interactions and transactions among persons, settings, and institutions that are oriented to support progress of children...rather than understanding a child's transition solely in terms of the child's skills, or the influences on those skills at any given time, this perspective emphasizes the organization of assets within a social ecology, how this organization emerges and how it supports (or hinders) child competence over time. (Pianta 2010, p. 35)

While recognising the possibilities afforded by bioecological approaches, limitations are also outlined. For example, Petriwskyj (Chap. 15) argues that these do not account sufficiently for the diversity of children's lives or inform children's longer-term trajectories. Similar criticisms are outlined by Vogler et al. (2008, p. 25), who note that 'while the identification of multiple interacting systems is conceptually elegant, there is a risk of objectifying boundaries and assuming internal sub-system coherence'. In other words, we should expect blurring of boundaries and not expect that microsystems, such as the family or school, operate in similar ways for all children. A further criticism of bioecological theory is that locating the child at the centre does not necessarily reflect the priorities of the systems and contexts, or the social constructs and power relations, in which they are located (Corsaro et al. 2002; Vogler et al. 2008). That is, not all microsystems prioritise the individual child.

Many of the contributors to this book refer to the importance of bioecological theory in their work, either as a guiding theoretical framework or as a trigger for further conceptualisation of transition. For example, Dunlop (Chap. 3) outlines her adoption of bioecological theory, noting how it offers an umbrella that can accommodate related theoretical frameworks, such as life course theory (Elder 1996), which outlines the principles of historical time, timing in lives, linked lives and human agency. Life course theory and bioecological theory can be complementary in their focus on historical time (chronosystem) and agency. Both theories accord significance to the active role of individuals as they influence, and are influenced by, the contexts in which they live. They also identify potential for change as different systems or contexts, and those located within them, interact. The combination of interactions, change and time sets up a dynamic model in which the transition to school can be explored by focusing on the overlapping or intersecting contexts of children's experience. From this, it is expected that each experience of the transition will be different; not only would it be expected that children's perspectives would be different from those of adults, but also each child's experience of their ecology would be expected to be different. This is evident in Turunen's (Chap. 11) exploration of transition to school as part of life history, where memories of starting school are described as potential turning points in each individual's life course.

One area highlighted by the combination of bioecological and life course theories is the ways in which contextual, or environmental, factors have different effects on those who experience them (Elder 1974). This is one pathway to the exploration of risk and protective factors, the identification of resilience and vulnerability, which are explored by Harrison (Chap. 5), as well as concepts of adjustment and transition (Margetts Chap. 6). It is also part of the underlying argument for the focus on high-quality early childhood education for all children, contending that this has 'the potential of supporting young children and their caregivers in coping with adversities and improving their prospects of successful school transitions' (Vogler et al. 2008, p. 28).

Some contributors incorporate a base of bioecological theory, complemented or expanded by other theoretical frameworks and conceptualisations. Peters (Chap. 8) describes the ways in which bioecological and sociocultural theories underpin her approach to transitions research; and Einarsdóttir (Chap. 2), Murray (Chap. 4),

Harrison (Chap. 5), Margetts (Chap. 6), Mackenzie (Chap. 7), Graue and Reineke (Chap. 12), Perry (Chap. 13) and Dockett (Chap. 14) all incorporate elements of bioecological theory in their explorations of transition.

Murray (Chap. 4) combines a strong focus on bioecological theory with a commitment to incorporating the perspectives of children in her research, on the basis that a successful transition to school relies not only on personal characteristics but also on interpersonal (relationship) and institutional factors. Mackenzie (Chap. 7) applies a similar model as children make the transition to becoming school students, specifically in the area of writing.

Harrison (Chap. 5) locates her research in bioecological theory, focusing particularly on proximal processes and connections between the intrapersonal (e.g. temperament) and interpersonal (e.g. attachment) worlds of the school student. She combines this with a transactional model of children development (Sameroff 2009), which holds that such development occurs as a result of continuous dynamic interactions between children and their environments. Relationships are central to this model, as is the power of relationships to effect change to, and for, individuals. The model also proposes that individual characteristics predispose children to be affected differentially by their environments. Hence, it is possible to consider both risk and protective factors that can be associated with transition to school.

Individual child characteristics are also addressed by Margetts (Chap. 6), in her discussion of transition and adjustment. In her investigations of children's capacity to adapt to the new school context, Margetts highlights the importance of children's changing sense of identity and belonging as well as their adaptive behaviour within the school setting.

In drawing on sociocultural theory, Lam (Chap. 10) and Peters (Chap. 8) incorporate the importance of social context and social interactions that is a feature of Vygotskian (1978) theory. From this perspective, interactions that occur within historical, cultural and institutional contexts shape children's development and their view of the world. At the same time, children are viewed as active agents who learn to use cultural tools to master actions that are valued within that particular culture (Wertsch 1991). When applied to the study of transition to school, sociocultural theory prompts a focus on the ways in which children's social interactions provide a basis for new ways of engaging in different contexts, where the 'process of changing participation in sociocultural activities of their communities' (Rogoff 2003, p. 52) is paramount. This translates into consideration of how children, families and educators change as a result of participating in activities and events that are significant in the context of school (such as orientation visits) but also exploring the ways in which those activities and events change over time as a result of that participation.

Children's participation in different contexts is a critical element of sociocultural theory, used by Corsaro et al. (2002) to frame transition as a process of interactions between people and involvement in activities that results in children's changed participation in sociocultural activities. These researchers regard transitions as 'always collectively produced and shared with significant others' (Corsaro et al. 2002, p. 325) and argue strongly against models of transition that focus primarily on the individual or a set of individual variables.

In its focus on children's developing mastery of culturally valued actions, sociocultural theory posits an important role for adults and peers. To this end, Rogoff (2003) describes processes of guided participation, as more knowledgeable others guide children's participation in culturally valued activities. Similarly, Lave and Wenger (1991) describe a process of legitimate peripheral participation, where those new to a community move towards becoming members of that community by engaging in peripheral activities that help them become aware of the ways in which the community is organised and operates. Experts, or more experienced others, play important roles in guiding the participation of newcomers. While it is not only adults who are regarded as more experienced, there is a clear role for adults in cultural reproduction. Intergenerational influences are also important, with parents, grandparents and other significant adults reflecting different visions of school and what it means to make the transition to school. Their perspectives shape the transition to school experiences of children and families (Turunen Chap. 11). Family habitus (Bourdieu 1997) is influenced by family history and the stories told within the family about school and education. These contribute to dispositions that support and guide particular practices within families.

The historical, social, cultural and political contexts, in which transition to school is, and has been located, are the focus of the critical constructionism that underpins Graue and Reineke's (Chap. 12) investigation of the ways in which transition and readiness have been constructed in the United States. This theoretical orientation emphasises the sociocultural construction of knowledge (Vygotsky 1978) and incorporates critical theory through a focus on the construction of cultural myths and expectations (Habermas 1972). In arguing that the ways in which people think about and enact transition and readiness are located within specific social and cultural contexts and have historical legacies, Graue and Reineke align notions of time (bioecological theory) and sociocultural theory with critical theory, arguing for the contextualisation of knowledge, promoting the importance of critical reflection on what is known, how it is known, and to whom it is known.

Critical and post-structuralist theories underpin Petriwskyj's (Chap. 15) approach to the study of transition to school as she draws attention to inequalities related to power and the exercise of power. Post-structuralist theories examine the political nature of knowledge and the role of language in the politics of knowledge:

> Poststructuralists believe that individuals may tell several – possibly competing – stories about themselves (identities) and about societies. The politics of our time and place influence which stories …are told, when and by whom, which is why some stories are heard more often and given greater status than others … identifying the sources … that are silenced or marginalised and then sharing them is a political act. (MacNaughton 2005, p. 4)

Critical theory also examines connections between knowledge and power, exploring the social and historical contexts of knowledge and the ways in which some ideas direct our understandings and explanations of phenomena. In particular, critical theory questions inequities in access to power and resources. Critical and post-structuralist perspectives direct attention towards ensuring the educational participation of marginalised or ignored groups (including children with disabilities, refugees, children in geographically isolated locations, gifted children), together with the implementation of more socially inclusive policies and practices. Transition to school approaches framed by these perspectives are directed towards listening to the perspectives of all involved in transition (children, families, educators and communities) and promoting their active engagement in decision-making around the transition.

Listening to the perspectives of children has been a hallmark of Einarsdóttir's research. In Chap. 2, she describes how her theoretical stance draws on postmodernism, arguing that knowledge is socially constructed and, because of its contextual nature, can be contradictory (Albon 2011). Moving away from accepted truths, Einarsdóttir questions assumptions about children and childhood. Her work positions children as competent and capable, able to share their perspectives and with rights to be heard.

Critical reflection characterises the approaches adopted by Perry (Chap. 13) and Dockett (Chap. 14) as each questions how power is exercised or operates in the construction of transition to school. Both chapters reflect on dominant ideologies and argue for the importance of critical knowledge in promoting social justice (Perry Chap. 13) and unsettling expectations about who is expected to experience a successful, or problematic, transition to school (Dockett Chap. 14). These chapters argue that issues of power are central to interactions and expectations and 'examine the social and political factors that produce dominant educational knowledge and practices, and … ask whose interests they serve' (MacNaughton 2005, p. 9). Critical reflection is a central plank of critical pedagogy and of approaches to social justice. It provides a basis for identifying inequality and injustice in approaches to transition to school as well as a platform for promoting change. Critical pedagogy encourages educators to engage in a 'language of possibility' (Giroux 2005, p. 68) and so to

> develop knowledge/power relations in which multiple narratives and social practices are constructed around a politics and pedagogy of difference that offers students the opportunity to read the world differently, resist the abuse of power and privilege and construct alternative democratic communities.

Studies of the transition to school recognise that schools, schooling and education are largely institutionalised. Bourdieu's (1992) description of rites of institution addresses the significance of the rituals associated with education and the function they serve to separate those belonging to the institution of school from those who do not.

Garpelin (Chap. 9) and Lam (Chap. 10) also invoke the notion of rites as they describe the transition to school as a rite of passage. To do so, they draw upon van Gennep's (1960) description of rituals associated with life transitions as rites of passage, marking significant transitions to positions of new social status across the life course. Rites of passage acknowledge the departure from one phase of life and arrival in another phase. Three phases contribute to thinking about rites of passage: preliminal rites (rites of separation, as people detach from the existing group), liminal (or threshold rites, where people are in-between states, having left one group or status, but not yet become part of another) and postliminal rites (where people become incorporated into the new group, assuming the new status and identity that goes with being a member of this group).

In considering the transition to school, it is possible to conceptualise the move from preschool to school as a process of moving from one group and status (preschooler) to another (school student). Both Garpelin and Lam emphasise the potential ambiguity for children and their families, as they encounter the liminal phase, where they are betwixt and between (Turner 1969), in this case, neither a preschooler nor school student. At this time, it is possible to describe children and their families as entering a borderland (Peters Chap. 8) as they seek to cross the border into school. Writing about individuals as they seek to cross cultural and national borders, Anzaldúa (1987, p. 3) described a borderland as a 'vague and undetermined place', full of tensions as boundaries overlap and as contexts intersect. It is possible to consider children who have left one context (preschool) but not yet entered another (school) as traversing borderlands, those spaces that surround borders. Giroux (2005, p. 2) argues that

> thinking in terms of borders allows one to critically engage the struggle over those territories, spaces, and contact zones where power operates to either expand or to shrink the distance and connectedness among individuals, groups, and places.

Conceptualising transition to school in terms of border crossing facilitates discussion about the border itself (e.g. When do children start school? Is it at the time of orientation or transition or when they have their official first day of school? Do all agree on when children start school, or when they should start school?) and the borderlands surrounding it (What happens for children between preschool and school? Is there a crossover period where school and preschool intermingle?) Such an approach also opens the space for some critical reflections around the transition to school, asking questions such as the following: Whose territory is involved in the transition to school? Who owns this space? Who is responsible for ensuring safe passage? What level of border patrol is involved? Do borders exist to keep people in or to keep people out? What credentials are required to cross borders? Who decides?

1.4   Tensions Around Transition

Across the chapters of this book, researchers involved in theorising and researching transition refer to a number of tensions. These, in turn, raise questions and provoke critical reflection. In noting the following tensions, we share some of the questions that have accompanied our discussions and invite readers to consider their own responses and theoretical positions.

1.4.1   Who Is at the Centre of Transitions Research?

Bioecological theory situates the child at the centre, focusing attention on the contexts in which the child is located and the intersections of these contexts. Yet this is also a criticism of the theory, as we are reminded that not all contexts in which

blurred? What are the strengths and weakness of such a position? Is an effective transition more likely to be one where children, families, educators and communities mark and recognise the changes that occur? How can we promote both continuity and change at times of transition? What evidence should we seek regarding the success or otherwise of particular strategies for transition? Should this evidence differ depending on the cultural context? Who should decide? While there is no suggestion that we should all agree on what makes an effective transition, it is evident that multiple strategies and multiple lenses are needed in the study of transitions in order to promote different readings and perceptions of the same situation.

1.4.6   Is There a Preferred Theoretical Model for Transition and Transitions Research?

While many of the chapter authors in this book utilise bioecological theory, there are many alternative theoretical paradigms that have been used to investigate transition to school. Critical examination of policies, practices and research evidence through alternate theoretical lenses can illuminate the shortcomings as well as the contributions of various approaches (Scott-Little et al. 2006). In adopting any model of transition, it is important to consider what is invisible or assumed within the model. All models have gaps and silences, and all contain, hide and subsume assumptions. In adopting any model, it is important to consider what is masked as well as what is highlighted. Is there value in the more eclectic theoretical positioning outlined by several researchers in this book (such as Peters Chap. 8; Dunlop Chap. 3), provided the underlying perspectives are identified?

1.4.7   Should We Focus on Transition or Readiness?

The process of naming our research and research focus is important. The terms readiness and transition are often used interchangeably, yet can be interpreted to mean quite different things. Readiness, for example, is often used to refer to characteristics of individual children or populations yet can also be used in relation to families, schools and communities. The term transition is often applied to collections of practices or programs but can also be used to refer to processes of relationship building. Are readiness and transition interrelated, and if so, what are the connections (Dockett and Perry 2013, in press)? Are they indeed complementary, as suggested by Graue and Reineke (Chap. 12)? Do their differing theoretical frames mean that should be considered separately? How do they reflect the historical time in which they are located? What is gained, and what is lost, by conceptualising our research as either readiness or transitions research or both?

1.4.8 One Transition or Many?

It is possible to focus on the transition experiences of individuals and of collective groups or cohorts. Each brings strengths and challenges. Exploring individual experiences of transition recognises diversity of experiences and acknowledges that each individual experiences their ecology in different ways. However, there are limitations in the extent to which such experiences can be generalised. Investigating collective experiences of transition has the potential to homogenise groups and mask diversity. How do we recognise starting school as a time of transition for individuals as well as an institutionalised transition?

When investigating transition, it is also possible to focus on the experiences of one group – children, families, educators, communities – and to exclude others. Do we recognise that the transition to school is a transition for all of these groups? How does our transitions research recognise both unity and diversity? Does it address one transition, or many?

There is the potential for many tensions around the research base of transition to school. These reflect the many different and varied theoretical frames that are used to study transition as well as the different theoretical lenses that are applied to the analysis and application of research outcomes.

1.5 Theory, Policy and Practice

The shifts and tensions that are evident in transitions research are also reflected in policy and practice. Although there has been an assumption that research informs policy and practice, this assumption is contested (Nutley et al. 2007). New insights in practice or new policy demands to meet changing social circumstances may also prompt research and consideration of theoretical frameworks consistent with the changing environment (Ohi 2008).

Just as theories do not exist in isolation, 'research does not speak for itself, nor does it have definitive implications for particular problems of practice or policy. Research users must always interpret the meaning of research and its implications' (Tseng 2012, p. 7). Translating theory and research involves an iterative process of engagement and knowledge exchange between researchers, policymakers and practitioners (Davies et al. 2008). Critical to these processes is recognition that practitioners and policymakers are experts in their fields, with a great deal to contribute to the identification of research questions and their resolution. Knowledge that derives from practice and from policy is key to interrogating and changing practice (Rickinson et al. 2011).

Each research chapter highlights the implications of theoretical frames or particular research evidence to policy and practice. Three chapters in this book (Kirk-Downey Chap. 17; Glass and Cotman Chap. 18; Arnup Chap. 19) explore connections between theory, policy and practice in more depth. Each chapter reports an innovative approach to the practices associated with transition to school, developed in a specific context and reflective of the characteristics of that context. Each of the approaches reflects a strong theoretical base. Glass and Cotman (Chap. 18) highlight the importance of inclusive approaches to transition and, within this, the importance of developing relationships between and among children and teachers. Their innovative use of Skype to build relationships across the school and preschool contexts and to maintain these over time reflects many elements of bioecological theory. The accompanying critical reflection on the processes and practices involved enables readers to recognise the support that was generated through the project as well as some of the ongoing challenges faced when seeking to build connections across microsystems.

Arnup (Chap. 19) and Kirk-Downey (Chap. 17) both describe the development of networks in two different geographical contexts of Australia. Each network acknowledges a range of stakeholders in the processes of transition and works to establish and maintain connections across various contexts. Both networks developed as part of broader policy imperatives related to state government initiatives which aimed to enhance positive educational outcomes for young children. They also rely on bioecological theory, recognising the importance of using a range of processes and strategies to engage with a range of people, in different contexts, over time. Both networks have been operating for some years and have adopted different guises, and those involved, and the contexts in which they operate, have changed.

All three of Chaps. 17, 18 and 19 demonstrate the ways in which practitioners have built opportunities to exchange knowledge and develop relationships to promote approaches to transition to school that make sense in their communities. While each of the strategies developed draws upon a theoretical base, and engages with researchers and research, they are driven by practitioners with commitment to promoting a positive start to school for all involved in the transition.

These approaches to transition have been influenced by research and have also influenced research. For example, some of the questions and issues raised within the Wollongong Transition to School Network have promoted specific research exploring children's perspectives of transition (Perry and Dockett 2011). At the same time, they have also had an impact on policy and policy development in their local contexts.

The final chapter of this book (Dockett and Perry Chap. 20) describes the development of a policy document, *Transition to School: Position Statement*. This statement was generated from a synthesis of a wide range of transitions research, policy and practice presented and discussed at a conference held in 2010. The collaborative involvement of policymakers, practitioners and researchers in the development of the position statement offered the opportunity to generate a common language around issues related to transition, consider ways in which research could influence policy and practice and create pathways such that issues of transitions policy and practice could generate new approaches to research.

1.6   Future Directions

The chapters in this book are also located in an historical time. They reflect both where we have been in transitions research and where we are now – our past and our present. They help us position current perspectives on transition to school as a shared responsibility between many stakeholders rather than focusing only on notions of individual children's readiness. Where notions of readiness are invoked, they include reference to 'ready schools', 'ready families' and 'ready communities' as well as 'ready' children. Reference to individual children's readiness also considers issues of adjustment, again focusing not only on children but the contexts in which children engage.

In many instances, investigations of transition to school are situated in strengths-based perspectives rather than in discourses of deficit. Strengths-based perspectives recognise that all involved in transition to school are experts about their own experiences and have a number of strengths, as well as possible challenges, on which to draw as they navigate the transition. Underpinning strengths-based approaches is the expectation that, with appropriate support and assistance, individuals and groups are capable of achieving positive change (Saleeby 1997).

The importance of supportive contexts is highlighted in current research. In addition to recognising the influence of home, prior-to-school, school and community contexts, chapters of this book explore the substantial contribution of networks to the development and implementation of approaches to transition as well as research networks that provoke and support a range of investigations of transition and policy networks that both drive and respond to research and practice.

Clearly, much is known about transition to school. The collaborative development of the *Transition to School: Position Statement* as researchers, practitioners and policymakers shared their perceptions, experiences and expectations has identified some emerging directions for transitions research. These include the following:

- Greater exploration of the role and contribution of policy to the study of transition to school
- Investigation of the ways in which the practices of transition influence, and are influenced by, policy and research
- Understanding the impact of curricula on transition, as children, their families and educators navigate different approaches to curricula and different expectations about curriculum outcomes
- Identification of the intersection of pedagogies in transition to school
- Continued attention to the significance of relationships with transition experiences
- Incorporation of the voices of all stakeholders in transition, particularly the perspectives of children
- Recognition of the role of partnerships at times of educational transition and exploration of effective partnerships
- Exploration of the short- and longer-term impacts of educational transitions
- Positioning of participants in transition as strong and competent

The principles described as the basis for an effective transition to school in the position statement aim to reconceptualise transition in terms of expectations, aspirations, opportunities and entitlements. The authors represented in this book believe that this opens up new spaces with which to engage in research, policy and practice around transition to school.

References

Albon, D. (2011). Postmodern and post-structuralist perspectives on early childhood education. In L. Miller & L. Pound (Eds.), *Theories and approaches to learning in the early years* (pp. 38–52). Los Angeles/London: Sage.

Ames, L. B. (1986). Ready or not. *American Educator: The Professional Journal of the American Federation of Teachers, 10*(2), 30–33. 48.

Anzaldúa, G. (1987). *Borderlands/La Frontera: The new mestiza*. San Francisco: Aunt Lute Books.

Bourdieu, P. (1992). The logic of practice (trans: Nice, R.). Cambridge: Polity Press.

Bourdieu, P. (1997). The forms of capital. In A. H. Halsey, H. Lauder, P. Brown, & A. S. Wells (Eds.), *Education, culture, economy and society* (pp. 46–58). Oxford: Oxford University Press.

Bronfenbrenner, U. (1979). *The ecology of human development: Experiments in nature and design.* Cambridge, MA: Harvard University Press.

Bronfenbrenner, U., & Morris, P. A. (2006). The bioecological model of human development. In W. Damon & R. M. Lerner (Eds.), *Handbook of child psychology, Vol. 1: Theoretical models of human development* (6th ed., pp. 793–828). New York: Wiley.

Broström, S., & Wagner, J. T. (Eds.). (2003). *Early childhood education in five Nordic countries: Perspectives on the transition from preschool to school.* Århus: Systime Academic.

Corsaro, W. A., Molinari, L., & Rosier, K. B. (2002). Zena and Carlotta: Transition narratives and early education in the United States and Italy. *Human Development, 45*(5), 323–349.

Davies, H., Nutley, S., & Walter, I. (2008). Why 'knowledge transfer' is misconceived for applied social research. *Journal of Health Services, Research and Policy, 13*(3), 188–190.

Dockett, S., & Perry, B. (2004). What makes a successful transition to school? Views of Australian parents and teachers. *International Journal of Early Years Education, 12*(3), 217–230.

Dockett, S., & Perry, B. (2007). *Transitions to school: Perceptions, expectations, experiences.* Sydney: University of NSW Press.

Dockett, S., & Perry, B. (2013, in press). Trends and tensions: Australian and international research about starting school. *International Journal of Early Years Education.*

Dunlop, A.-W., & Fabian, H. (2007). *Informing transitions in the early years: Research, policy and practice.* Maidenhead: Open University Press/McGraw-Hill.

Elder, G. H., Jr. (1974). *Children of the great depression.* Chicago: University of Chicago Press.

Elder, G. H., Jr. (1996). Human lives in changing societies: Life course and developmental insights. In R. B. Cairns, G. H. Elder Jr., & E. J. Costello (Eds.), *Developmental science* (pp. 31–62). New York: Cambridge University Press.

Fabian, H. (2007). Informing transitions. In A.-W. Dunlop & H. Fabian (Eds.), *Informing transitions in the early years* (pp. 3–17). Maidenhead: Open University Press.

Fabian, H., & Dunlop, A.-W. (2007). *Outcomes of good practice in transition processes for children entering primary school.* Working Paper 42. Bernard van Leer Foundation: The Hague.

Fegan, M., & Bowes, J. (2009). Isolation in rural, remote and urban communities. In J. Bowes & R. Grace (Eds.), *Children, families and communities: Contexts and consequences* (3rd ed., pp. 129–147). Melbourne: Oxford.

Fthenakis, W. E. (1998). Family transitions and quality in early childhood education. *European Early Childhood Education Research Journal, 6*(1), 5–17.

Giroux, H. A. (2005). *Border crossings* (2nd ed.). New York: Routledge.

Graue, M. E., Kroeger, J., & Brown, C. (2003). The gift of time: Enactments of developmental thought in early childhood practice. *Early Childhood Research and Practice, 5*(1). http://ecrp.uiuc.edu/v5n1/graue.html. Accessed 14 Dec 2012.

Griebel, W., & Niesel, R. (2009). A developmental psychology perspective in Germany: Co-construction of transitions between family and education systems by the child, parents and pedagogues. *Early Years, 29*(1), 59–68.

Habermas, J. (1972). *Knowledge and human interests* (2nd ed.), (trans: Shapiro J. J.). London: Heinemann.

Hirst, M., Jervis, N., Visagie, K., Sojo, V., & Cavanagh, S. (2011). *Transition to primary school: A review of the literature.* Canberra: Commonwealth of Australia.

Lave, J., & Wenger, E. (1991). *Situated learning: Legitimate peripheral participation.* Cambridge: Cambridge University Press.

MacNaughton, G. (2005). *Doing Foucault in early childhood studies.* Milton Park: Routledge.

Mullis, I. V. S., Martin, M. O., Foy, P., & Aurora, A. (2012). *TIMSS 2011 International results in mathematics.* Chestnut Hill: TIMSS & PIRLS International Study Center, Boston College. http://timss.bc.edu/timss2011/international-results-mathematics.html. Accessed 13 Jan 2013.

Munford, R., & Sanders, J. (Eds.). (2003). *Making a difference in families: Research that creates change.* Sydney: Allen & Unwin.

Nutley, S., Walter, I., & Davies, H. (2007). *Using evidence: How research can inform public services.* Bristol: Policy Press.

Ohi, S. (2008). The teacher's role in the research-praxis nexus. *Australian Journal of Education, 52*(1), 95–108.

Organisation for Economic Cooperation and Development. (2001). *Starting strong: Early childhood education and care.* Paris: OECD.

Organisation for Economic Cooperation and Development. (2006). *Starting strong II: Early childhood education and care.* Paris: OECD.

Organisation for Economic Cooperation and Development. (2010). *PISA 2009 Results: Learning trends: Changes in student performance since 2000* (Vol. V). PISA. OECD Publishing. http://www.oecd.org/pisa/pisaproducts/48852742.pdf Accessed 8 Dec 2012.

Page, J. M. (2000). *Reframing the early childhood curriculum: Educational imperatives for the future.* London: Routledge/Falmer.

Perry, B., & Dockett, S. (2011). 'How 'bout we have a celebration?' Advice from children on starting school. *European Early Childhood Education Research Journal, 19*(3), 375–388.

Peters, S. (2010). *Literature review: Transition from early childhood education to school.* Ministry of Education, New Zealand. www.educationcounts.govt.nz/publications. Accessed 24 July 2012.

Petriwskyj, A., Thorpe, K., & Tayler, C. (2005). Trends in construction of transition to school in three western regions, 1990–2004. *International Journal of Early Years Education, 13*(1), 55–69.

Pianta, R. C. (2010). Going to school in the United States: The shifting ecology of transition. In S. L. Kagan & K. Tarrant (Eds.), *Transitions for young children* (pp. 33–44). Baltimore: Paul H. Brookes.

Ramey, C. T., & Ramey, S. L. (1999). Beginning school for children at risk. In R. C. Pianta & M. J. Cox (Eds.), *The transition to Kindergarten* (pp. 217–251). Baltimore: Paul Brookes.

Rickinson, M., Sebba, J., & Edwards, A. (2011). *Improving research through user engagement.* London: Routledge.

Rimm-Kaufman, S. E., & Pianta, R. C. (2000). An ecological perspective on children's transition to kindergarten: A theoretical framework to guide empirical research. *Journal of Applied Developmental Psychology, 21*(5), 491–511.

Rogoff, B. (2003). *The cultural nature of human development.* Oxford: Oxford University Press.

Saleeby, D. (Ed.). (1997). *Common purpose: Strengthening families and neighbourhoods to rebuild America.* New York: Anchor.

Sameroff, A. J. (Ed.). (2009). *The transactional model of development: How children and contexts shape each other.* Washington, DC: American Psychological Association.

Scott-Little, C., Kagan, S., & Frelow, V. (2006). Conceptualisation of readiness and the content of early learning standards: The intersection of policy and research? *Early Childhood Research Quarterly, 21*, 153–173.

Smart, D., Sanson, A., Baxter, B., Edwards, B., & Hayes, A. (2008). *Home-to-school transitions for financially disadvantaged children: Summary report.* Sydney: The Smith Family and Australian Institute of Family Studies. http://www.thesmithfamily.com.au/site/page.cfm?u=105. Accessed 13 Mar 2010.

Tseng, V. (2012). The uses of research in policy and practice. *Social Policy Report, 26*(2), 1–16.

Turner, V. W. (1969). *The ritual process: Structure and anti-structure.* London: Routledge and Kegan Paul.

United Nations Children's Fund (UNICEF). (2012). *School readiness: A conceptual framework.* http://www.unicef.org/education/files/Chil2Child_ConceptualFramework_FINAL%281%29.pdf. Accessed 23 Jan 2013.

van Gennep, A. (1960). *The rites of passage.* (trans: Minika, B. V. & G. L. Caffee). London: Routledge and Kegan Paul.

Vogler, P., Crivello, G., & Woodhead, M. (2008). *Early childhood transitions research: A review of concepts, theory and practice.* The Hague: Bernard van Leer Foundation.

Vrinioti, K., Einarsdóttir, J., & Broström, S. (2010). Transitions from preschool to primary school (pp. 16–20). In H. Müller (Ed.) *Transition from pre-school to school: Emphasising literacy. Comments and reflection by researchers from eight European countries.* Cologne: EU-Agency, Regional Government of Cologne/Germany.

Vygotsky, L. S. (1978). *Mind in society.* Cambridge: Harvard University Press.

Wertsch, J. V. (1991). *Voices of the mind: A sociocultural approach to mediated action.* London: Harvester Wheatsheaf.

Yeboah, D. A. (2002). Enhancing transition from early childhood phase to primary education: Evidence from the research literature. *Early Years, 11*(1), 51–68.

Part I
Building on Bioecological Perspectives

Chapter 2
Readings of Media Accounts of Transition to School in Iceland

Jóhanna Einarsdóttir

2.1 Introduction

2.1.1 The Role of Theory in Educational Research

Most researchers see theory as an important aspect of educational research. Theory has been described as a map or a lens, framing and shaping what the researcher sees and examines. It is an instrument that helps to describe and explain the phenomenon being studied and allows researchers to think differently and see familiar phenomena in new and interesting ways (Ball 1995; Graue and Walsh 1998; Mertz and Anfara 2006).

There is a common belief that theory is a necessary tool and that research cannot be conducted without the conscious or unconscious use of theory. Mertz and Anfara (2006) argue that theoretical frameworks (a) help to focus a study, (b) reveal and conceal meaning and understanding, (c) situate the research in a scholarly conversation, and (d) reveal its strengths and weaknesses. They claim it is 'impossible to observe and describe what happens in natural settings without some theory that guides the researcher in what is relevant to observe and what name to attach to what is happening' (p. 195). Alford (1998) argues that every research study seeks to answer both theoretical and empirical questions. The theoretical questions include Why did something happen? What explains this? Why did these events occur? and What do they mean? Empirical questions include questions such as What happened? What is going on here? and What are the patterns here?

Others have pointed out limitations of the use of theory. Thomas challenges the use of theory in educational inquiry and argues that educators' weight on theory leads qualitative inquiry into 'sterile terrain' (Thomas 2002, p. 419). Others have

J. Einarsdóttir (✉)
University of Iceland, Reykjavik, Iceland
e-mail: joein@hi.is

B. Perry et al. (eds.), *Transitions to School - International Research, Policy and Practice*,
International perspectives on early childhood education and development 9,
DOI 10.1007/978-94-007-7350-9_2, © Springer Science+Business Media Dordrecht 2014

emphasized that just as theory can allow us to see familiar phenomena in novel ways, it can also function like a set of blinkers, restricting what we see and how we see it (Graue and Walsh 1998; Mertz and Anfara 2006). When one starts a research project with a specific theoretical perspective to guide the study, there is a danger that confirmation of the theory will become the main issue and topics and themes that do not fit the theory will be omitted. Trowler (2010) elaborates on how theory is misused in research, when researchers hold on to one theoretical perspective, using it no matter what. Theory then becomes a confirmation of belief rather than a tool for exploration and for thinking otherwise. He also reasons that educational researchers have a tendency to refer to a small number of well-known widely used theories for no good reason and use ill-defined concepts made to fit the argument (Ball 1995; Trowler 2010).

2.1.2   Different Readings of Data

The nature of qualitative research is such that, for most studies, a large amount of data is gathered that then need to be written up and made sense of. Qualitative research does not seek to show one truth nor one reality. As a researcher, what I see and how I read and make meaning from the data depends on my implicit or explicit theories. Rhedding-Jones (2005) states that what the researcher chooses to do with her research data will depend on her theories. Several good examples have been presented where researchers have chosen to use different theoretical lenses to shed light on and understand pedagogical practices and beliefs (Danby 1996; Lankshear and Knobel 2005; Lenz Taguchi 2006).

Danby (1996) studied young children's play and interactions and applied two contrasting readings of one play episode. The first reading is based on traditional early childhood practices and theories which reflect psychological and child development components, supporting the active nature of learning and the importance of children developing independence and good self-esteem. The second reading uses an alternative perspective that challenges the notions of the dominant discourse of the child-centered pedagogy, a reading that represents children as persons of gender and power constructing gendered social membership. Danby argues that the second reading provided a new lens to examine classroom interactions, where issues of gender, control, and power were made visible.

Lenz-Taguchi (2006) conducted a study with preschool teachers where they worked with children on spatial knowledge and orientation within their everyday surroundings. The children were asked to draw maps that the teachers and the researcher analyzed in four different ways: through a developmental psychological lens, through a constructivist lens, through a social constructivist perspective, and through a semiotic perspective. The purposes of taking the teachers through the process of reading the maps through different lenses were to (a) make visible their current beliefs and understandings (what they viewed as natural and taken for granted); (b) incorporate different readings with the help of other theories, thereby making visible the absences in the taken-for-granted reading; (c) consciously problematize taken-for-granted reading; (d) resist the understandings that dominate and are, therefore, most available; (e) use difference as a productive force; and (f) make conscious choices for practice driven by new understandings. The findings show that different readings of the children's maps gave a different perspective, a different truth, and by going through the process, the preschool teachers became increasingly aware of the children's perspectives and of their own taken-for-granted ideas about children, childhood, and familiar pedagogical practices.

2.2 Using Theory to Research Media Representations of Starting School

The mass media is an influential factor in children's lives today and is a part of their social environment. The media reflects cultural ideas, norms, and dominant discourses in society and in that way maintains dominant views. At the same time, the media plays a significant role in shaping peoples' beliefs and attitudes (McLuhan 2002). The aim of the study was to explore how the mass media covers the important period in children's lives when they make the transition from preschool to primary school, and what views of children the Icelandic media presents.

2.2.1 Theoretical Perspectives

The theoretical underpinnings of the study are postmodern perspectives on children, childhood, and education. Knowledge is seen as socially constructed and contingent on culture, time, and space. Thus, there is no absolute knowledge, no absolute reality waiting out there to be discovered. A universal understanding of children and childhood is questioned as well as the idea of the normal child. Children are not seen as a homogenous group of people with the same needs, interests, and competences. An emphasis is put on complexity, irregularity, diversity, and individual differences (Albon 2011; Dahlberg et al. 1999; Elkind 1997). Childhood is viewed as an important period in its own right, and children are seen as strong and competent citizens with their own views and perspectives, competencies to speak for themselves, and the right to be heard. Therefore, it is important to seek their perspectives and recognize their points of view as separate from those of their parents (Christensen and James 2000; Corsaro 1997; Dockett et al. 2009; Einarsdóttir 2007; James et al. 1998).

The research was also based on the belief that children's lives cannot be separated from their social environment. Children are part of their environment and are influenced by it, and they also influence their environment. Thus, children and the environment influence each other. With this in mind, the ecological theory of Bronfenbrenner was employed. Bronfenbrenner (Bronfenbrenner 1977;

Bronfenbrenner and Morris 1998) emphasized looking at the individual in a holistic context. He saw the child as being at the centre of an interconnected set of contexts or microsystems. He defined microsystem as the context closest to the child, that is, the home, the neighborhood, the preschool, and the primary school. The mesosystem involves interaction between these systems. Relation and interaction between the microsystems are seen as influential in successful transition to school (Fabian and Dunlop 2002; Rimm-Kaufman and Pianta 2000). A great deal of research indicates that a successful transition from preschool to primary school is dependent on the cooperation between individuals in these systems (Dockett and Perry 2007). Peers and social relationships with peers are important during this period. Children who start school with their friends from preschool or know someone in school have more positive attitudes toward school and adjust better than children who do not have these relationships. Parents are important supporters for their children during the transition period, and they create a link between the preschool, the home, and the primary school. Continuity in children's education has been stressed (Organisation for Economic Cooperation and Development 2001, 2006). To create continuity, the teachers of the two school levels need to cooperate, and the primary school should endeavor to build on the experience and knowledge that the children bring from home and from preschool.

The research questions that guided the study were as follows:

- How is starting school and the transition from preschool to primary school presented in the mass media?
- Whose images and voices on transitioning to school are heard in the media?

2.2.2   Method

Data were gathered for 5 weeks, 3 weeks before school started and 2 weeks after school started. Everything in the media that mentioned starting primary school or was aimed toward children starting school was gathered, including news coverage, discussions, and texts. The following sources were scrutinized: television news and news-related programs on two of the major television channels, radio news and news-related programs on the radio, three major national newspapers, and magazines and local papers. The radio and television data was transcribed into written text. After reading and rereading, the material was coded and categorized according to the research questions.

Discourse analysis was employed to systematically categorize and analyze the text. The purpose of discourse analysis is not to provide definite answers but to expand one's horizons, to reveal what is going on behind the scenes and see what determines action (Gill 2005). To shed light on the data, different theories of children were reviewed. Conflicting views of children and opposites were put forward (Lowe 2004; Mills 2000; Myhre 2001). First, the intrinsically kind child, originating from Rousseau, is at one end of the spectrum and on the other end is the evil child in need of improvement. Second, there is John Locke's child, born as a tabula rasa or blank sheet of paper and moulded by the environment, an idea which stands in opposition to developmental theories that regard development as innate and believe there are stable stages of development that all children go through. Third, there is the view of children as innocent, vulnerable, and in need of protection, and fourth, there is a view of children as strong and competent with their own rights.

Ecological models of transition emphasising continuity of children's experiences and support and cooperation of peers, parents, and teachers were also used as a basis of analysis. The child in educational transitions occupies three worlds or microsystems: their home world, the preschool world, and the school world (Dunlop and Fabian 2002). Emphasis was placed on examining how the roles of the individuals in these systems were presented, during transitions.

2.2.3 Findings: Discussions

The collected data show that the media focuses on and builds up expectations for primary school with a wealth of advertisements and articles with information and advice for parents. When reading through the data with the lens of the ecological theory of Bronfenbrenner, it becomes obvious that, of the individuals in the microsystems surrounding the child, parents were seen as most important. They were looked upon as key supporters of their children during the transition to school, and the journalists and advertisers appealed to them. There were discussions about children's anxieties and worries about starting primary school because of increasing demands and discussions about how parents could prepare their children. Practical advice was given concerning, for example, homework, nutrition, and sleeping habits, choosing the right clothes, shoes, writing utilities, and schoolbags (Fig. 2.1). The traffic was also discussed extensively, and emphasis was placed on parents walking to school with their children and teaching them the easiest walking route instead of driving them (Fig. 2.2). Further, it was emphasized that parents should train their children to be self-reliant and follow instructions, because that is what would be beneficial for them when they started school. Publishing companies appealed to parents and advertised books to prepare children for reading and mathematics instruction. One advertisement said "Give your child a head-start" and pointed out that the books stimulated children aged 3–5 and prepared them for starting school.

The media coverage seldom mentioned children's connections with siblings or friends. Other children are an important part of children's social context, and interactions and relationships with other children are core dimensions of children's well-being (Kernan et al. 2011). Research has shown that children identify friends as a key element in the transition to school, that is, starting with children from the same preschool, forming friendships with new school mates, and knowing someone older in the school (Dockett and Perry 2007). The media coverage gave little attention to support from other children. The only time that came up was when children were interviewed. One

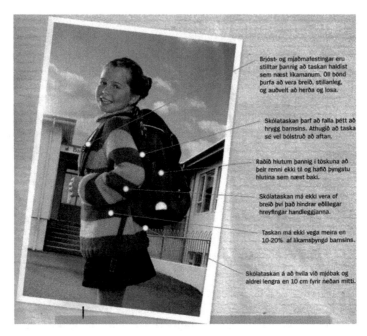

Fig. 2.1 Advertisement for school bags (With kind permission of Jónson og Lemac'ks 2009)

Fig. 2.2 Children and traffic (With kind permission of Morgunblaðið 2008)

girl said, for instance, "I have a big cousin who is ten now and she knows her way around the whole school … She helps me sometimes if boys are teasing me."

No emphasis was placed on continuity in children's education, and the transition between the two school levels did not seem important in the media coverage. The media seldom mentioned children's prior experience in preschool, and often it sounded like the children were leaving their parents for the first time, although most Icelandic children attend preschool at least 7 h a day from the age of 2 (Statistics Iceland 2011). Although preschool has been by law the first educational level for almost two decades, preschools were rarely mentioned. Only once was the view of preschool teachers sought, stating that children are also learning in preschool and that language stimulation is important as a preparation for primary school.

When the data are read with the perspective in mind that childhood is socially constructed, dependent on culture, time, and space, and there are different views of children and childhood, then diverse views of children can be noted. Often different views were evident in the same article, which is to be expected: persons can have more than one view of children, either implicit or explicit. The most commonly identified view of children was seeing them as innocent and in need of protection. This view was, for example, noted in photos, in advice given to parents, and in discussions about the danger of traffic. This is consistent with the view of children as vulnerable with the right to adult's protection, guidance, and support, which is one of the two main emphases in the *Convention on the Rights of the Child* (United Nations 1989). There the emphasis is placed on the safety of children and their rights to protection and guidance of adults. The other viewpoint that characterizes the convention is the emphasis on children's competencies, their rights to express their opinions, make decisions, and be active participants in society. This latter view featured less in the media. A preschool teacher who was interviewed, however, mentioned the challenging activities the children were able to manage in preschool. Although children are the people that starting school centres on, they were seldom asked for their opinions and solutions. During the data-gathering period, only four articles were based on interviews with children about starting school.

Developmental theories that build on the view that children develop according to predetermined stages were evident in the data. Journalists and psychologists who wrote articles about starting school and preparation for school talked about children's developmental stages and what children were ready to do at this age. One newspaper heading was "You should make demands on children according to their developmental stage." The view of children as bad and in need of improvement, and the necessity to punish children, was not prominent in the data. Only in one article where a mother of a child who had been bullied was interviewed was it discussed that children who bullied other children should be punished. Rousseau's view of the child as good and innocent was on the other hand particularly notable, especially in pictures in the media. Pictures of children often accompanied articles in newspapers and on television (Fig. 2.3). With few exceptions, these were pictures of healthy, happy children with fair skin and blond hair. These findings can be interpreted that the media see children as a decoration; they cannot contribute much, but they are innocent and cute (Einarsdóttir 2009).

Fig. 2.3 Pictures of happy school children were part of the media's coverage (With kind permission of Reykjavíkurborg 2008)

2.2.4   Other Readings of the Same Data

In this study, the data gathered from the Icelandic mass media was read through the lens of postmodern views of children and childhood and the ecological perspective of Bronfenbrenner. The study was guided by the following questions: "How is starting school and the transition from preschool to primary school presented in the mass media?" and "Whose images and voices on transitioning to school are heard in the media?" It would also have been an option to ask different questions and read the data through other theoretical lenses and in that way shed light on other issues. Postcolonialist thinking and poststructuralism (Albon 2011; Cannella and Viruru 2004) would, for instance, have steered the focus toward the concepts of power and truth. Questions like Who holds the power? Is the multicultural society presented in the media? How are boys and girls presented? Whose images are salient? and What is missing? would have been asked. If the lens of developmental psychology would have been selected, other questions and other readings of data would have been made. The focus would have been on the child in the process of becoming an adult, on what is normal and natural in young children's behavior, and how this could be measured. Indicators and screening of children's readiness for school would be of interest. The questions asked would, for instance, be What do children need to be ready for school? When are children ready for school? What can parents do to prepare children for school?

2.3   Final Words

Theories are an important part of educational research. I use theory as a tool to develop research questions and to shed light on the generated data. Theory helps me see what is visible in a new light, notice novel things, and reveal new understandings. I also use it to help me understand the reality that I am investigating and explain what I see, why I see it, and what it means. However, I usually do not explicitly start a study with a specific theory; rather, I let the data help me decide which theory to use. I find that determining the theory beforehand could become restricting and could limit what I see and how I analyze and interpret what I see. On the other hand, I am well aware that my implicit theories and beliefs about children, childhood, and education influence my decisions about what to study, the design of the study, what I see, and how I interpret it. In that way, theory is also a foundation for the study design.

This chapter gives an example of how theories are used in one study on media representations on transitions from preschool to primary school. The theories that were utilized shaped the research questions and thus the lens through which the data were analysed and interpreted. However, I am aware that any situation can be interpreted in different ways. Thus, the same data can also be examined through other theoretical perspectives, and then other issues would be in the forefront. That way a more comprehensive picture of media representation of transition to school could be received.

References

Albon, D. (2011). Postmodern and post-structuralist perspectives on early childhood education. In L. Miller & L. Pound (Eds.), *Theories and approaches to learning in the early years* (pp. 38–52). Los Angeles/London: Sage.

Alford, R. R. (1998). *The craft of inquiry*. New York: Oxford University Press.

Ball, S. J. (1995). Intellectuals or technicians? The urgent role of theory in educational studies. *British Journal of Educational Studies, 43*(3), 255–271.

Bronfenbrenner, U. (1977). Toward an experimental ecology of human development. *American Psychologist, 32*(7), 513–531.

Bronfenbrenner, U., & Morris, P. A. (1998). The ecology of developmental processes. In W. Damon & R. M. Lerner (Eds.), *Handbook of child psychology: Theoretical models of human development* (pp. 993–1029). New York: Wiley.

Cannella, G. S., & Viruru, R. (2004). *Childhood and postcolonization: Power, education, and contemporary practice*. New York/London: Routledge/Falmer.

Christensen, P. M., & James, A. (2000). Researching children and childhood: Cultures of communication. In P. Christensen & A. James (Eds.), *Research with children: Perspectives and practices* (pp. 1–8). New York: Falmer Press.

Corsaro, W. A. (1997). *The sociology of childhood*. Thousand Oaks: Pine Forge Press.

Dahlberg, G., Moss, P., & Pence, A. R. (1999). *Beyond quality in early childhood education and care: Postmodern perspectives*. London: Falmer Press.

Danby, S. (1996). Constituting social membership: Two readings of talk in an early childhood classroom. *Language and Education, 10*(2 & 3), 151–170.

Dockett, S., & Perry, B. (2007). *Transitions to school: Perceptions, expectations, experiences*. Sydney: UNSW Press.

Dockett, S., Einarsdóttir, J., & Perry, B. (2009). Researching with children: Ethical issues. *Journal of Early Childhood Research, 7*(3), 283–298.

Dunlop, A.-W., & Fabian, H. (2002). Conclusion: Debating, transitions, continuity and progression in the early years. In H. Fabian & A.-W. Dunlop (Eds.), *Transitions in the early years: Debating continuity and progression for children in early education* (pp. 146–154). London: Routledge/Falmer.

Einarsdóttir, J. (2007). Research with children: Methodological and ethical challenges. *European Early Childhood Education Research Journal, 15*(2), 197–211.

Einarsdóttir, J. (2009). *"Frábær skólaföt á hressa krakka!"Rannsókn á umfjöllun fjölmiðla um börn við upphaf grunnskólagöngu" [Great school clothes for lively children! "Study on media discussion about children starting primary school]*. Netla – Veftímarit um uppeldi og menntun. http://netla.khi.is/greinar/ritrynt.asp. Accessed 9 July 2012.

Elkind, D. (1997). The death of child nature: Education in the postmodern world. *Phi Delta Kappan, 79*(3), 241–245.

Fabian, H., & Dunlop, A.-W. (2002). *Transitions in the early years: Debating continuity and progression for children in early education*. London: Routledge/Falmer.

Gill, R. (2005). Discourse analysis. In M. W. Bauer & G. Gaskell (Eds.), *Qualitative researching with text, image and sound* (pp. 172–190). London: Sage.

Graue, E. M., & Walsh, D. J. (1998). *Studying children in context: Theories, methods and ethics*. Thousand Oaks: Sage.

James, A., Jenks, C., & Prout, A. (1998). *Theorizing childhood*. Cambridge: Polity Press.

Kernan, M., Singer, E., & Swinnen, R. (2011). Introduction. In M. Kernan & E. Singer (Eds.), *Peer relationships in early childhood education and care* (pp. 1–14). New York: Routledge.

Lankshear, C., & Knobel, M. (2005). *A handbook for teacher research: From design to implementation* (2nd ed.). Maidenhead: Open University Press.

Lenz Taguchi, H. (2006). Reconceptualizing early childhood education: Challenging taken-for-granted ideas. In J. Einarsdóttir & J. Wagner (Eds.), *Nordic childhoods and early education: Philosophy, research, policy, and practice in Denmark, Finland, Iceland, Norway, and Sweden* (pp. 257–288). Connecticut: Information Age.

Lowe, A. R. (2004). Childhood through the ages. In T. Maynard & N. Thomas (Eds.), *An introduction to early childhood studies* (pp. 65–74). Thousand Oaks: Sage.

McLuhan, M. (2002). The medium is the message. In K. Askew & R. W. Richard (Eds.), *The anthropology of media* (pp. 18–27). Oxford: Blackwell.

Mertz, N. T., & Anfara, V. A. (2006). Conclusion: Coming full circle. In V. A. Anfara & N. T. Mertz (Eds.), *Theoretical frameworks in qualitative research* (pp. 189–196). Thousand Oaks: Sage.

Mills, R. (2000). Perspectives of childhood. In J. Mills & R. Mills (Eds.), *Childhood studies: A reader in perspectives of childhood* (pp. 7–38). New York: Routledge.

Myhre, R. (2001). *Stefnur og straumar í uppeldissögu* (trans: Bjarni Bjarnason.). Reykjavík: Rannsóknarstofnun Kennaraháskóla Íslands.

Organisation for Economic Cooperation and Development (OECD). (2001). *Starting strong: Early education and care*. Paris: OECD.

Organisation for Economic Cooperation and Development (OECD). (2006). *Starting strong II: Early childhood education and care*. Paris: OECD.

Rhedding-Jones, J. (2005). *What is research?* Oslo: Universitetsforlaget.

Rimm-Kaufman, S. E., & Pianta, R. C. (2000). An ecological perspective on the transition to kindergarten: A theoretical framework to guide empirical research. *Journal of Applied Developmental Psychology, 21*(5), 491–511.

Statistics Iceland. (2011). http://www.hagstofa.is/Hagtolur/Mannfjoldi. Accessed 11 June 2011.

Thomas, G. (2002). Theory's Spell – on qualitative inquiry and educational research. *British Educational Research Journal, 28*(3), 419–434.

Trowler, P. (2010). *Wicked issues in situating theory in close up research. Higher education close up*. http://www.lancaster.ac.uk/staff/trowler/Wicked%20Issues%20-%20Trowler.pdf. Accessed 28 Aug 2011.

United Nations. (1989). *Convention on the rights of the child*. http://www2.ohchr.org/english/law/crc.htm. Accessed 3 July 2011.

Chapter 3
Thinking About Transitions: One Framework or Many? Populating the Theoretical Model Over Time

Aline-Wendy Dunlop

3.1 Introduction

The way in which we treat the most vulnerable is the mark of a civilised society (Socrates). During my training as a primary school teacher, I developed a particular interest in working with the 'infant' children – aged 5–8 years old – and took up the specialist Scottish Froebel year end on to my initial training in order to be registered to teach children from the age of two and a half onwards. This course steeped young teachers in the philosophy, psychology and creative practices of early childhood and developed a great trust in the competence, companionship, capabilities, cultures, creativity, contributions and drive to communication that even the youngest children bring to life and learning. It influenced my approaches and responses over my 23 years of early years work with children from 0 to 8 and their parents and communities. Formative from the start, this background led to a strong observational way of working in which research and researching was daily practice and in turn was carried forward into my work as a lecturer and researcher in higher education.

This early experience set the values for a career: values which underpin my work and continue to develop over time. Currently, I would express those values by placing importance on belief in the innate capacity of children; striking a respectful balance in adult-child interactions; evidence to inform day-to-day teaching; the effect not just of educational culture but primarily of home culture; the recognition that theory provides us with the tools to do a good job; awareness of the curiosity, motivation and drive of nearly all children to find out, experience and learn so driving their development forward; the central importance of children's interests and curiosities in that process and the importance of continually questioning how to capture the interest of children who are less able, for a variety of reasons, to focus and delve deep into exciting and interesting discoveries; and the very important adult skill of

A.-W. Dunlop (✉)
University of Strathclyde, Glasgow, Scotland
e-mail: a.w.a.dunlop@strath.ac.uk

B. Perry et al. (eds.), *Transitions to School - International Research, Policy and Practice*,
International perspectives on early childhood education and development 9,
DOI 10.1007/978-94-007-7350-9_3, © Springer Science+Business Media Dordrecht 2014

what I have called 'following ahead' of children. Emerging alongside each of these concepts is the value of paying attention to transitions in that they too can be a tool. It is with these values in mind that I approach the task of writing this chapter about my theoretical framework for researching transition to school and some of my key results.

3.2 Implications of Theoretical Foundations: Theory Informing Research

This chapter reflects the emergence of new influences and forms of theorising about transitions over time, largely led by the author's longitudinal study of transitions (Dunlop 2010a) which has followed a single cohort of children through 14 years of schooling (1997–2010) from early childhood to school leaving in one local authority area in Scotland.

In a recently completed investigation of the match between theoretical models and methods used in transitions research in relation to the types and purposes of the particular transitions studies, I sought to answer the question Is there a best fit transitions' methodology? and concluded that a mixed methodology is needed for the effective study of educational transitions over time (Dunlop 2009). By extension I find now that I want to assert not one single frame, but to consider the variety of the theoretical lenses that have informed my own transitions study over time. Alongside this, because literature reviews also provide important backdrops to studies, I want to acknowledge the groupings of transitions studies that emerge from the literature and reveal some principal thrusts in the field of transitions research.

Studies which address school readiness, school preparation, adaptation to school, adjustment to school and the learning of school culture lead to models which focus on the strengths and difficulties of the child or young person who is in transition from one setting to another (for a discussion of readiness, see Dockett and Perry 2009). These studies may be viewed as intrapersonal in nature, with the success and effectiveness of transition resting on the individual competence (or perceived competence) of the child or young person, whose individual development forms the boundaries for successful or less than successful transition. Included here are studies that address psychological aspects of transition, such as identity, self-esteem and competence. On the other hand, there is a set of studies which focus on context and the capacity of systems to adapt and change in order to accommodate the transitioning child or young person, by embracing ideas of difference in learning environments, teacher adaptation, curriculum adjustment and attuning relationships. These studies could be classified as context without development in that they tend to consider links between policy and practices, standards and benchmarks. Further, a different set of studies focus on development in context: these studies could be classified as interpersonal and sociocultural in nature combining context with development and emphasising the interrelatedness of the two (Fig. 3.1).

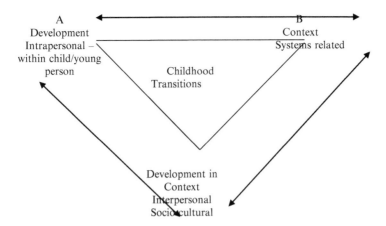

Fig. 3.1 Models of transitions study (Dunlop 2009)

Many writings open with reflections on theory, some critically review the workability of theory to inform transitions, and others take clear positions on single informing pieces of work which provide a major influence, for example, Fabian's (2002) early work drawing on van Gennep (1960); Griebel and Niesel's (2002) early attention to Cowan and Cowan's (1992) work on family transitions; and Dunlop (2002), Kienig (2002), Peters (2002) and others making use of Bronfenbrenner's ecological systems theory (Bronfenbrenner 1989). Some take particular approaches such as the present author's concept of 'transitions capital' and 'transitions ease' or particular ideas such as resilience and emotional well-being; cognitive challenge; development; and school readiness, school adjustment and co-construction of transitions: all ways of thinking about children and the environment that fix the major influences on educational and other transitions.

Further there is something in the writing about transitions that assumes transition to be an issue, and here it is necessary to challenge the status quo – to ask if transitions are an important part of life, if transitions should be promoted and if transitions are a good thing, as opposed to the rhetoric of transitions as a problem. A philosophy of transitions may then be needed: what would make for a sufficient theory of transitions? Would philosophical argument have to assert that a good theory of transitions would explain all features of transitions, would propose an underlying mechanism and would produce a testable hypothesis?

3.3 Setting the Context for Transition to School Research in Scotland: Change Over Time

As I look back over 40 years of teaching – half in schools, the second half in universities – it is increasingly clear to me that my own work on transitions must in some way be rooted in earlier experiences of both childhood and working as a teacher of young children in preschool, primary and special educational settings. As an army child, my father's work took us through 14 places to live and 11 schools – transitions were a way of life – continuity was family and home wherever that happened to be. We built a resilience and a looking forward to change, adept at finding out I did not form friendships until a few days in to each new school as the system rarely placed us in the appropriate class upon arrival.

As a teacher I worked in a variety of early childhood settings at a time that children 'transferred' to school, and though there was a good awareness on entry to preschool of the need to settle children in, this was less evident upon entry to primary school – what in contemporary Scotland is now called a 'soft start'. As a nursery school head teacher in the late 1980s/early 1990s, I collaborated with colleagues in neighbouring schools to work with our local primaries towards a more graduated approach to school entry. Relationship building was at the heart of what we did then – promoting the capabilities of the school entrants and sharing the experiences they had had in preschool: pushing all the time from bottom up.

In Scotland during the years I have studied transitions, there have been major policy shifts that inevitably have influenced children's early schooling. In 1993 when I began to research, there was little focus on transitions but new writings on the need to reflect on the early childhood experience were emerging (Scottish Consultative Council on the Curriculum 1993). During the years from 1988 to 1996, each Scottish Local Authority administrative area considered developing a local early childhood curriculum – 8 of the 12 regions did so. This drove forward a national intent to match the emerging primary school curriculum documentation with the production of a draft curriculum for the preschool year. This draft curriculum was put out for consultation (Dunlop and Hughes 1997) and was the basis for several further iterations of a curriculum framework for early childhood (Scottish Consultative Council on the Curriculum 1999). In 2000 the new Scottish Parliament was opened and although previously always a Scottish devolved responsibility, education earned a new focus, curriculum was reviewed, and a Curriculum for Excellence 3–18 (Scottish Executive 2004a, b) was proposed. It was accompanied by Birth (and then Prebirth) to Three (Scottish Executive 2005; Scottish Government 2010), by Building the Curriculum 2 – Active Learning in the Early Years 3–6 (Scottish Government 2007) and by the Early Years Framework (Scottish Government 2008). Each of these curriculum and strategy frameworks has promoted that attention be given to transitions and indeed provided paper-based vehicles for changes in classroom practices as leverage for improving transitions.

3.4 Theoretical Foundations: Weaving the Web

Giroux (in Palmer 2001a) demands reflection on the nature and influence of curriculum, saying 'the curriculum is a "cultural script" whose messages should be susceptible to critique' (p. 282). He also proposes that 'radical pedagogy needs a vision, one that celebrates not what is but what could be, that looks beyond the immediate to the future and links struggle to a new set of human possibilities' (Giroux 1983, p. 242). The ethics of early childhood practice – questioning practices that perpetuate inequalities; language not for a single version of education or a single grand narrative, but to embrace several scripts; and several versions of curricula and of education, as particular cultures promoted in curriculum may be controlling and may create power inequalities. Dewey (1959) too gives messages about democracy, culture and society, curriculum, the exhilarating notion of experience and the compulsion embedded in genuine educational experience. Piaget's constructivism (1950); Donaldson's making human sense (1992); Vygotsky's (1978) culture as the product of social life and human social activity; Trevarthen's (2002) ideas about companionship; key points from Bruner (1996) about culture and first-hand learning; Rogoff's (2003) learning in the culture and Rogoff et al.'s (2003) work on intent participation; Lave and Wenger's (1991) influences upon situated learning; Corsaro and Molinari's (2000) views on early childhood experiences as priming events; Eisner's (in Palmer 2001b) concepts of knowing; Bourdieu's (1990) emphasis on rites of institutions; and Bernstein's (1996) work on language, symbolic control, identity and persistent patterns of disadvantage each contributes to a theoretical web that draws together the key ideas identified to influence the development of my work over time and my understanding of early childhood itself. Such a web (Table 3.1) is at first glance eclectic, but more so it makes demands on the research process to take multiple perspectives and to develop appropriate tools that take account of the complexity of transitions.

Each of the chosen theorists tells something about capacities, agency, imagination, creativity and, by invoking culture, about the scripts that educational systems create. The learning challenge of different phases of education in early childhood lies in disjunctions of culture, human sense making and the place of process- or subject-based pedagogies in curriculum scripts. We need to place children at the centre of our thinking, and this may mean embracing broader concepts of education than readiness or schoolification. In education, children and adults can jointly create meaning (Dunlop 2010b) and groups of children can work together to understand motivating and sometimes self-motivated tasks and their own learning – telling each other about what they have learned links the individual to the collective mind – so that children are aware of knowledge and that knowledge can be said in words.

The theoretical models used in transitions research are selected for their relevance to the particular concepts of transition held by and being developed in each researcher. The way in which the researcher's thinking about transitions develops creates frames and tools to explain their developing understanding and the relevance of theory to the ways in which they support research in any given transition process. The field of study and its purpose – whether family transitions, educational transitions, professional transitions, or personal transitions – will also determine the particular models and frames used for research.

Table 3.1 Weaving the web – theories that have both informed and grown out of the author's longitudinal research

Time point	Education	Psychology	Sociology and anthropology	History	Emerging
Preschool year 1996–1997	Pianta and Kraft-Sayre (2003) (successful transitions) Ladd (1990) (going to school with friends) Nutbrown (1994) (threads of thinking) Laevers (1994) (well-being)	(Piaget/Donaldson (1992) actions vs. human sense) Bruner (1996) (narratives of experience) Vygotsky (1978) (play, cultural tools) Rogoff (2003) (social constructivism)	Corsaro and Molinari (2000) (priming events) Gee (1999) (discourse) Wells (1985) (meaning making)	Froebel MacMillan Isaacs	Parental participation Power of environments Situated learning Child as expert Children's agency Continuities Curriculum as a tool
School entry 1997–1998	Clay (2000) (literacy) Ginsburg and Seo (1999) (maths and play) Freire (1970) (critical pedagogy; starting points)	Bronfenbrenner (1989) (ecological systems) Rogoff (2003) (intent participation) Lave and Wenger (1991) (situated learning) Smilansky (1990) (complex play)	van Gennep (1960) (rites of passage) Bourdieu (1990) (rites of institution)	–	Teacher collaboration Joint creation of meaning (academic/social participation/control) Family contexts Discontinuities Learning making human sense The importance of the sociocultural
Middle primary 1999–2000	Edwards and Warin (1999) (school perceptions of parents)	Claxton (2005) (learning power) Carr (2001) (dispositions) Benard (1995) (resilience) Kelly's theory of personal constructs (see Palmer 2001a)	Giddens (1984), Qvortrup et al. (1994), and James and James (2008) (agency) Bourdieu (1990) (field, habitus)	–	Identity; sense of self; dispositions, leading to 'transitions ease' (Dunlop 2010a) Narratives of learning

Upper primary/ secondary 2003/2004– 2004/2005	Galton et al. (2000) (post-transition dip)	Frydenberg and Lewis (1993) (personal experience of change)	Campbell-Clark (2000) (border theory)	Robert Owen	Importance of collaboration Learning and coping trajectories Parents as the significant reference point
Mid-secondary 2006–2007	Leat and Higgins (2002) (powerful pedagogies)	Bronfenbrenner (1989) (bioecological systems) Elder (1998) (life course theory)	Bourdieu (1990) (social and human capital)		Coresearchers Concept of transitions capital (Dunlop 2007) Parental values Stages of parenthood
Secondary leaving (2008) June 2010	Dewey (1959) (democracy, culture and society, the exhilarating notion of experience, the compulsion embedded in genuine educational experience)	Eisner (see Palmer 2001b) (children come into the world mindless) Trevarthen (2002) (learning in companionship)	Bernstein (1996) (persistent patterns of disadvantage) Giroux (1988) (curriculum as a cultural script)	Adam Smith (Scottish Enlightenment)	Looking back/forward over time – following ahead (Dunlop 2010a) Complexity – changes of relationships, space, time, contexts for learning, and demands of learning itself, combine at times of transition Complex capital

3.5   Researching Transitions

The backdrop of longitudinal study of transitions challenges the notion of a single successful transition setting the individual up for later 'transitions ease', by considering how transitions differ, the many other factors that may have an impact on the educational journey and the growing understanding that transitions exist throughout life. As a consequence of exploring transitions over an extended period, both in practice and as a main research focus, I find there is a continuous return to theoretical frames as part of reading, research design and analysis. At different points in time, different influences have been more or less strongly felt and used.

In Table 3.1 – Weaving the web – I try to show the influences of different disciplines, theories and writers matched to the phases of my Longitudinal Study of Educational Transitions (Dunlop 2010a). The sample for this study is a cohort of 150 children of whom 28 were focal children. Sources at the first phase of the study included observation, interviews, questionnaire, assessment measures, video data allowing analysis of classroom discourse, a range of documentation and school audits. Overall six time points were considered in order to understand which variables might be significant over time: early years nursery, early years primary, primary Year 3, primary Year 7, secondary Year 2 and school leaving at secondary Year 6.

The transitions models identified through the literature in Table 3.1 are also reflected in my longitudinal study, which can be divided in terms of measures used into individual data, systems data and interactive data, as shown below in Table 3.2.

At later phases of the study (Dunlop 2005a, c, 2007, 2009), use was made of the local authority's standardised testing, Laevers' (1994) Involvement Scales, and the 79-item, 18-factor Frydenberg and Lewis (1993) Adolescent Coping Scale designed to measure the frequency of usage of a variety of coping strategies typically used by adolescents, diary accounts and discussions. Throughout, the perspectives of children, parents and educators were sought – examples are the descriptions of self, primary school attended, secondary school, the programme of prior-to-entry visiting, some of the things people told transitioners about school, accounts of feelings and sentence completion activities. Throughout this research process, I have asked to what extent do the children (and young people) have a sense of agency.

Other projects such as policy development (Dunlop 2005d), a government-steered project into young children's behaviour (Dunlop et al. 2008), a participative study of ten families over 5 years of their children's young lives (Dunlop and Grogan 2004) and a pilot study of parental thinking and experience at the time of their children's transition to school (Dunlop 2005b) have also contributed to my current perspectives on transitions as a field of enquiry.

Certain transitions are educational markers: the entry to the first out of home setting, joining an early childhood group setting, starting school, moving to a new level of the school or into the next school, moving out of one school to another and eventually leaving school behind. What theorising can travel with a group on this journey and how do methods of study change, evolve and have an impact on the process of theorising?

Table 3.2 Longitudinal study data matched to models of transitions study

Data related to transitions models		
Individual data – developmental, intrapersonal and	Interactive data – interpersonal and sociocultural	Systems data – contextual
Child measures	Classroom discourse	Child friendly, rights-based policy discourse
Physical well-being and motor development	Adult-child interactions	
Social and emotional development	Interaction of developmental and contextual variables	Institutional and structural factors
	Dynamic sites for change	Standards and benchmarks
Approaches to learning	Pedagogies of transition	Documentation
Language development	Parental participation	Curriculum
Cognition and general knowledge	Transforming transitions	Pedagogical differences
Various adult measures, including parental values, individually oriented change, concepts of progress		Concepts of progression
		Issues around pastoral care
		Family structures
		Wider influences

The early childhood studies conducted by the author make a direct link between theorising and practices. Theoretical influences provide context for transitions research studies, but both research and the scholarly activity of theorising can inform practices by providing influential tools (Dunlop 2009).

3.6 Practical Implications of Theoretical Foundations: Theories as Practice Tools

Applications to practise provide powerful arenas for the interrogation of thinking about transitions and the tailoring of ideas according to their value to practice. For example, understandings of children's peripheral and intent participation (Rogoff et al. 2003) and the importance of scaffolding learning (Vygotsky 1978) and of teacher knowledge of complex play (Smilansky 1990) contribute to environments in which early educators arguably become more aware of the impact of their practices. Emerging from the range of theoretical perspectives shown in Table 3.1 Weaving the web (showing the main phases of the author's longitudinal study) is a set of ideas that inform action in practice and intend to encourage practitioners to take advantage of transitions as a time for dynamic change.

Experience over time and context leads the author to a recognition of the importance of continuing to refine such theorising in order to address differences that arise for children at times of transition when transitions themselves are normative. Why is it that for some children and young people transitions are developmentally provoking whilst temporarily stressful; for others, transitions are tolerable and facilitate adaptive coping; and, for a number, the apparently same transitions are toxic. The National Scientific Council on the Developing Child (2005) proposed such a conceptually guided taxonomy of human bio-development which is reminiscent of Bronfenbrenner's arrival at a bioecological model of development that emerged from his earlier ecological model. It is to Bronfenbrenner's work that I now turn to answer the question One framework or many?

3.7 Theoretical Framework or Frameworks?

While this chapter has introduced many different lenses on transitions, I wonder whether there may be a single framework that offers to house each of these perspectives and take account of the interrelatedness of systems, contexts and individual development. I am drawn to Bronfenbrenner and Ceci's (1994; Bronfenbrenner 2005) bioecological interpretation of ecological systems theory, as alongside Bronfenbrenner's earlier work, it offers us a model of development in context over time that emphasises, through the dual analysis of material, the interrelatedness, human agency and capacity to act that sits well with study of educational transitions and accords with my expressed values. In using the background of Bronfenbrenner's ecological systems theory, I have compared and considered the interaction of systems that affect children's lives, and upon which they may have an influence: for example, the interaction of elements across home and preschool or between preschool and school. Dual analysis of material has also provided a helpful guide for comparing the experiences of the older/younger groups of children in classes, or the different roles and contributions of educationally active/inactive parents, or compliant/reflective teachers. I find too that Bronfenbrenner's theorising is in accord with my belief systems or values, principally the agency of all involved in education and whether experiences offered to children in the different stages of education are developing or developmentally instigating. These interactions of interrelated data allow the development of empirical hypotheses with evidential support. The question that emerges is whether this dynamic theoretical model is sufficient to inform the study of transitions over time and is also valid and reliable.

The polarisations visible through dual analysis of material also work well in terms of Kelly's theory of personal constructs (see Maher 1969) and how individual personal constructs change and interact in different situations. Elder's (1998) work augments that of Bronfenbrenner by endorsing the importance of historical time to show that we are not just products but producers – that the timing of transitions in lives ensures that 'the developmental impact of a succession of life transitions or events is contingent on when they occur in a person's life' (p. 3) and therefore, in my view, can disrupt the timing and duration of normative transitions. Elder's (1998) life course theory embraces a concept of linked lives: 'lives are lived interdependently and social and historical influences are expressed through this network of shared relationship' (p. 4) in which, through their own agency, 'individuals construct their own life course through choices and actions they take within the opportunities and constraints of history and social circumstances' (p. 4). Whilst Kelly allows 'how it is in the moment', Bronfenbrenner offers us chronology in his ecological systems theory and Elder maps this out in terms of timing in a way that has informed both the design and interpretation of my longitudinal study of transitions.

For me the ecological systems theory works. It focuses on the child at the centre of the theoretical model; it acknowledges that a child affects and is affected by the settings in which time is spent; it recognises the importance of family, settings and community; it allows for the immediacy of interaction and interrelation between subjects and conditions; it encourages dual analysis of interlocking systems; used as a base framework, it can incorporate development over considerable time that is the hallmark of longitudinal study by allowing an umbrella for related theoretical frameworks generated through theorising to be incorporated in the exosystem; and it encourages research as part of the wider influences or macrosystem. The whole process is incorporated in change over time implied by Bronfenbrenner's addition of a chronological system – shown here as enveloping the rest of the model (Fig. 3.2).

These elements of Bronfenbrenner's theory embrace all the purposes of my various transitions studies but also allow scope, through the researcher asserting agency, for the possibility of the theory being used as a home for other forms of theorising and theoretical frameworks. Thus, I have made use over time of works in psychology, education, sociology, anthropology, overall historical time and through linking lived lives (Table 3.1). From this wider interpretation of systems theory in research and practice, there emerges a range of elements in early childhood transitions, and these promote new ways of looking at transitions that carry across my short-life projects and into my longitudinal study. Transitions research is thus developmentally instigating, has led to the incorporation of a range of theorising and has resulted in a study over time that now includes some of the original subjects as architects of, and researchers in, the final stage of my longitudinal work. I would argue that transitions are in themselves transforming: current work shows the degree of agency and capacity to act witnessed in transitions research participants as they become transitions researchers themselves (Dunlop 2010a).

3.8 Policy Implications of Theoretical Foundations, Research and Practices

Transitions can be seen as a way of life. In educational reform it can be seen that curriculum is frequently used as a tool for change – worldwide new iterations of curriculum are asserting values and principles that apply no matter the age of the child involved in curriculum. Differentiation of school experiences for our youngest children through prior-to-school and early school experiences is essential – governments often make this recognition by writing it down as policy – Scotland provides clear examples here: a shift from curriculum 5–14 to a curriculum 3–18,

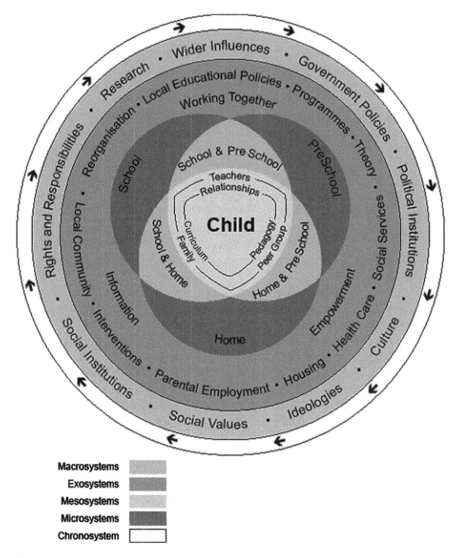

Fig. 3.2 Transition as an ecological system (© Dunlop)

a national Early Years Framework to determine a ten-year strategy for transforma-
tional change for children prebirth to 8 years old and their families, and greater
recognition that quick fixes cannot work. However, transitions remain – across the
day and over time.

Our Ten Families Study (Dunlop and Grogan 2004) showed the importance of
voice supported by collaboration in local policy development if parental quality of
life, quality of interactions, self-worth and self-esteem are to shift sufficiently to
ensure children's well-being and learning, as well as their ability to cope with and

learn from new settings and experiences. Policy and practice both need to take account of such findings as follows:

- Each child's transition is unique.
- A child's move to school is also a major transition, in particular, for mothers.
- Parental disposition and parental definition of appropriate roles to play at transition are important.
- Transitions are not always easy.

My longitudinal work has provided firm evidence of the following:

- Recognition that systems are different
- Interrogation of those differences
- Need for approaches which will support young people to cope with change
- Role of educators, parents and young people as agents in creating new, less disparate, systems
- Extent to which, if young people are having to make major adjustments, the suitability of educational approaches at times of major transition should be reconsidered

3.9 Positioning and Provocations: Challenges and Issues

One theoretical framework for transition can, if it is sufficiently interactive, embrace a range of perspectives drawn from relevant disciplines such as psychology, education and sociology. We need to interrogate these different dimensions of transition. Transition to school is normative; it happens for most children; as we have seen, the majority navigate this process successfully; but there are those who are not building resilience to change, do not have much in the way of transitions capital and for whom multiple transitions may gather together to have an impact on identity, well-being and learning.

While results from the earlier phases of this longitudinal study include a focus on the importance of parental participation, teacher collaboration, children's agency and playful learning, by also taking a focus on the dynamic times of change that transitions represent in young children's lives, classroom discourse, well-being and involvement, the central importance of relationships, the influences of classroom and out of school environments, and the need to contest and critique transitions combine in the possibility of creating '[a] more humane present and more promising future for all young children and their families' (Shonkoff 2010, p. 366).

This indicates a need to develop our capacity not only to theorise transitions alongside a repertoire of methods but also to develop a philosophy of educational transitions.

My list for future directions therefore includes unpicking curriculum for early childhood as a cultural script; considering the place of children who find themselves at the margins of family and society; safeguarding children through transitions by equipping them to build transitions capital and therefore transitions ease; engaging with parenting processes and participation in their child's transitions; and building on understandings of transitions, to challenge policy makers in their design of educational systems, curriculum and social supports for children and families and to embrace the differential impact of transitions by asking why this is still so.

References

Benard, B. (1995). *Fostering resilience in children*. Champaign Urbana: ERIC Clearinghouse on Elementary and Early Childhood Education. EDO-PS-95-9.

Bernstein, B. (1996). *Pedagogy, symbolic control and identity: Theory, research, critique*. London: Taylor and Francis.

Bourdieu, P. (1990). Rites of institution. In P. Collier (Trans.), *Language and symbolic power* (pp. 117–127). Cambridge: Polity Press and Harvard University Press.

Bronfenbrenner, U. (1989). Ecological systems theory. In R. Vasta (Ed.), *Six theories of child development: Revised formulations and current issues* (pp. 187–249). London/Bristol: Jessica Kingsley.

Bronfenbrenner, U. (2005). *Making human beings human: Bioecological perspectives on human development*. Thousand Oaks: Sage.

Bronfenbrenner, U., & Ceci, S. J. (1994). Nature-nurture reconceptualized in developmental perspective: A bioecological model. *Psychological Review, 101*(4), 568–586.

Bruner, J. (1996). *The culture of education*. Cambridge, MA: Harvard University Press.

Campbell Clarke, S. (2000). Work/family border theory: A new theory of work/family balance. *Human Relations, 53*(6), 747–770.

Carr, M. (2001). *Assessment in early childhood settings: Learning stories*. London: Paul Chapman.

Claxton, G. (2005). *Building learning power: Helping young people become better learners*. Bristol: TLO.

Clay, M. M. (2000). *Concepts about print*. London: Heinemann.

Corsaro, W. A., & Molinari, L. (2000). Priming events and Italian children's transition from preschool to elementary school: Representations and action. *Social Psychology Quarterly, 63*(1), 16–33.

Cowan, C. P., & Cowan, P. A. (1992). *When partners become parents: The big life change for couples*. New York: Basic Books.

Dewey, J. (1959). The child and the curriculum. In M. S. Dworkin (Ed.), *Dewey on education* (pp. 33–90). New York: Teachers College Press.

Dockett, S., & Perry, B. (2009). Readiness for school: A relational construct. *Australasian Journal of Early Childhood, 34*(1), 20–26.

Donaldson, M. (1992). *Human minds: An exploration*. London: Allen Lane/Penguin Books.

Dunlop, A.-W. (2002). Conclusions. In H. Fabian & A.-W. Dunlop (Eds.), *Transitions in the early years* (pp. 146–154). London: Routledge/Falmer.

Dunlop, A.-W. (2005a, November). *Don't give yourselves a reputation: Accessing the views of secondary school entrants*. Paper presented at Scottish Educational Research Association annual conference, Perth, Scotland.

Dunlop, A.-W. (2005b, August). *"I'd like to be a fly on the wall" How does children's transition to school affect parents?* Paper presented at Identity, Belonging, Participation, EECERA 15th Annual Conference, Dublin.

Dunlop, A.-W. (2005c). *Transitions continuation study: The transition to secondary school of a preschool/primary transitions cohort*. Unpublished Report.

Dunlop, A.-W. (2005d). *Research reports – Literature review of early educational transitions: Report of a study into liaison, continuity and progression from nursery to primary education*. Unpublished Draft Guidelines for Stirling Council.

Dunlop, A.-W. (2007, April). *Transforming transitions*. Keynote Lecture. Transforming Transitions International Conference, Glasgow.

Dunlop, A-W. (2009, November). *Transition methodologies: Choices and chances*. Paper presented at the Scottish Educational Research Association (SERA).

Dunlop, A.-W. (2010a) *Longitudinal study of educational transitions over time. Design for final phase of the study* (unpublished).

Dunlop, A.-W. (2010b, September) *The balance of child and teacher voice in the transition to school as understood through analysis of classroom discourse*. Paper presented at the European Early Childhood Education Research Association Conference, Birmingham.

Dunlop, A.-W., Lee, P., Fee, J., Hughes, A., Grieve, A., & Marwick, A. (2008). What practices can be identified by staff and parents as successful in relation to supporting transitions from nursery/pre-school to primary school? In A.-W. Dunlop et al. (Eds.), *Positive behaviour in the early years: Perceptions of staff, service providers and parents in managing and promoting positive behaviour in early years and early primary settings*. Edinburgh: The Scottish Government. www.scotland.gov.uk/Resource/Doc/238273/0065412.pdf. Accessed 10 June 2012.

Dunlop, A.-W., & Grogan, D. (2004). *Knightsridge project for under fives and their families: Project report*. Glasgow: West Lothian Council and University of Strathclyde.

Dunlop, A.-W., & Hughes, A. A. (Eds.). (1997). *Pre-school curriculum: Policy, practice and proposals*. Glasgow: University of Strathclyde.

Edwards, A., & Warin, J. (1999). Parental involvement in raising the achievement of primary school pupils: Why bother? *Oxford Review of Education, 25*(3), 325–341.

Elder, G. H., Jr. (1998). The life course as developmental. *Child Development, 69*(1), 1–12.

Fabian, H. (2002). *Children starting school: A guide to successful transitions and transfers for teachers and assistants*. London: David Fulton.

Freire, P. (1970). *Pedagogy of the oppressed*. London: Penguin.

Frydenberg, E., & Lewis, R. (1993). *The adolescent coping scale*. Melbourne: Australian Council for Educational Research.

Galton, M., Morrison, I., & Pell, T. (2000). Transfer and transition in English schools: Reviewing the evidence. *International Journal of Educational Research, 33*(4), 341–363.

Gee, J. P. (1999). *An introduction to discourse analysis*. London: Routledge.

Giddens, A. (1984). *The constitution of society. Outline of the theory of structuration*. Cambridge: Polity.

Ginsburg, H. P., & Seo, K. H. (1999). The mathematics in children's thinking. *Mathematical Thinking and Learning, 1*(2), 113–129.

Giroux, H. (1983). *Theory and resistance in education: A pedagogy for the opposition*. London: Heinemann.

Giroux, H. (1988). *Teachers as transformative intellectuals: Towards a critical pedagogy of learning*. Granby: Bergin & Garvey.

Griebel, W., & Niesel, R. (2002). Co-constructing transition into kindergarten and school by children, parents and teachers. In H. Fabian & A.-W. Dunlop (Eds.), *Transitions in the early years* (pp. 64–75). London: Routledge Falmer.

James, A., & James, A. (2008). *Key concepts in childhood studies*. London: Sage.

Kienig, A. (2002). The importance of social adjustment for future success. In H. Fabian & A.-W. Dunlop (Eds.), *Transitions in the early years* (pp. 23–37). London: Routledge Falmer.

Ladd, G. W. (1990). Having friends, keeping friends, making friends, and being liked by peers in the classroom: Predictors of children's early school adjustment? *Child Development, 61*(4), 1081–1100.

Laevers, F. (1994). *Leuven involvement scale for young children (LIS-YC)*. Leuven: EXE Project.

Lave, J., & Wenger, E. (1991). *Situated learning: Legitimate peripheral participation*. Cambridge: Cambridge University Press.

Leat, D., & Higgins, S. (2002). The role of powerful pedagogical strategies in curriculum development. *The Curriculum Journal, 13*(1), 71–85.

Maher, B. (Ed.). (1969). *Clinical psychology and personality: The selected papers of George Kelly*. New York: Wiley.

National Scientific Council on the Developing Child. (2005). *Excessive stress disrupts the architecture of the developing brain (Working Paper No 3.)*. http://www.developingchild.net/reports.shtml. Accessed 11 May 2012.

Nutbrown, C. (1994). *Threads of thinking*. London: Sage.

Palmer, J. (Ed.). (2001a). *Fifty modern thinkers on education. From Piaget to the present*. London: Routledge.

Palmer, J. A. (2001b). Elliot Eisner. In J. A. Palmer (Ed.), *Fifty modern thinkers on education. From Piaget to the present* (pp. 247–251). London: Routledge.

Peters, S. (2002). Teachers' perspectives of transitions. In H. Fabian & A.-W. Dunlop (Eds.), *Transitions in early years* (pp. 87–97). London: Routledge Falmer.

Piaget, J. (1950). *The psychology of intelligence*. New York: Routledge.

Pianta, R. C., & Kraft-Sayre, M. (2003). *Successful kindergarten transition*. Baltimore: Paul H. Brookes.

Qvortrup, J., Bardy, M., Sgritta, G., & Wintersberger, H. (Eds.). (1994). *Childhood matters: Social theory, practice and politics*. Aldershot: Avebury.

Rogoff, B. (2003). *The cultural nature of human development*. Oxford: Oxford University Press.

Rogoff, B., Paradise, R., Arauz, R. M., Correa-Chavez, M., & Angelillo, C. (2003). Firsthand learning through intent participation. *Annual Review of Psychology, 54*, 175–203.

Scottish Consultative Council on the Curriculum (SCCC). (1993). *Reflections on curriculum issues*. Dundee: SCCC.

Scottish Consultative Council on the Curriculum (SCCC). (1999). *The curriculum framework for children 3–5*. Dundee: SCCC.

Scottish Executive. (2004a). *A curriculum for excellence* (Ministerial response). Edinburgh: Scottish Executive.

Scottish Executive. (2004b). *Curriculum for excellence 3-18*. Edinburgh: Scottish Executive.

Scottish Executive. (2005). *Birth to three: Supporting our youngest children*. Dundee: Learning and Teaching Scotland.

Scottish Government. (2007). *Building the curriculum 2: Active learning in the early years 3-6*. Edinburgh: The Scottish Government.

Scottish Government. (2008). *The early years framework*. Edinburgh: The Scottish Government.

Scottish Government. (2010). *Birth to three, supporting our youngest children*. Glasgow: Learning and Teaching Scotland.

Shonkoff, J. P. (2010). Building a new biodevelopmental framework to guide the future of early childhood policy. *Child Development, 81*(1), 357–367.

Smilansky, S. (1990). Sociodramatic play: Its relevance to behaviour and achievement in school. In E. Klugman & S. Smilansky (Eds.), *Children's play and learning perspectives and policy implications* (pp. 18–42). New York: Teacher's College Press.

Trevarthen, C. (2002). Learning in companionship. *Education in the North: The Journal of Scottish Education, 10*, 16–25.

van Gennep, A. (1960). *The rites of passage*. London: Routledge/Kegan Paul.

Vygotsky, L. S. (1978). *Mind in society*. Cambridge, MA: Harvard.

Wells, G. (1985). *The meaning makers: Children learning language and using language to learn*. Portsmouth: Heinemann.

Chapter 4
Multiple Influences on Children's Transition to School

Elizabeth Murray

4.1 Introduction

When children start school, they are predisposed to being a certain way and interacting with others in a certain way, and this impacts upon their experiences and interactions. It also has important implications for transitions theory and practice, particularly related to understanding the importance of relationships. Relationships play a crucial role in transitions. Relationships with significant others underpin children's feelings about school, personal success in school and the support networks available for children. There is some literature dedicated to seeing shared social spaces as places for academic learning and child development (e.g. Leander et al. 2010). Seeing social spaces as contexts for perspectives and relationships is also important when attempting to understand transition processes. In considering children's perspectives of starting school, we need to acknowledge that these perspectives are part of shared social spaces between children, their peers and their teachers and other adults. Children co-construct their transition experiences (Dunlop 2003) and are not passive participants in relationships; they make an active contribution to relationships and to social spaces, based on their personal characteristics, prior relationship experience and their ways of knowing and doing. It is this dynamic nature of relationships in context which is represented by Bronfenbrenner's ecological systems theory.

E. Murray (✉)
Charles Sturt University, Dubbo, Australia
e-mail: emurray@csu.edu.au

B. Perry et al. (eds.), *Transitions to School - International Research, Policy and Practice*,
International perspectives on early childhood education and development 9,
DOI 10.1007/978-94-007-7350-9_4, © Springer Science+Business Media Dordrecht 2014

4.2 Theoretical Perspectives

Adopting an ecological perspective not only illustrates that children are placed at the centre of the transition process but also takes into account the active role they play in their learning and development and the variety of environmental factors which impact on the processes of transitioning and adjusting to school, including school transition or orientation activities, the school and classroom setting and the differences between prior-to-school settings and school settings. An ecological perspective refers to the bidirectional interactions between children and their environment and how those interactions are experienced (Bronfenbrenner and Morris 1998). This perspective is based on Bronfenbrenner's (1979) original ecological systems work which set out to explain the way development occurs in context and the 'dynamic, interactive relationships' among contexts (Bronfenbrenner and Morris 1998, p. 994). The environment in which a person lives and interacts is a key feature of the context of development and, again, something that changes over time. The multifaceted layers of context which influence children's learning and development need to be considered over time, with both individuals and contexts (e.g. social policy, opinions, cultural changes) changing over time.

Bowes and Hayes (2000) note the addition of the 'chronosystem' by Bronfenbrenner, which represents the change over time in individuals and the contexts which influence individual developmental outcomes. In 1995, Bronfenbrenner proposed the Process-Person-Context-Time (PPCT) model and explained how an individual's developmental life course is 'embedded in and powerfully shaped by conditions and events occurring during the historical period through which the person lives' (1995, p. 641). While the dimension of time is important when thinking about the influence a positive adjustment to school has on children's later outcomes, giving consideration to time also encourages us to think about transition as a process, which begins long before children start school, and continues past the first day, first week or first term. Transitioning is something which requires personal growth in the social, emotional and physical spaces of a new environment and, as with all developmental changes, requires constant theorising and reflection by practitioners, researchers and policy makers.

Placing children at the centre of the process of transition acknowledges the important influence they have on interactions and experiences. However, we need to be cautious that this 'location' does not isolate children. It seems important to ask ourselves: Does this placement allow children's relationships with others to be as important as what the children themselves bring to experiences/events during the transition process? What are the social and emotional spaces in which children interact and participate during transition? What connections do children have to these spaces and what can they contribute to social spaces in particular?

Success in transition is evidenced by positive social, emotional and academic outcomes for children, both in kindergarten and later schooling. Research has shown that the internal processes and characteristics children bring to their transitions play a major role in their success in adjusting to school (Rosier and McDonald 2011).

The proximal processes or 'enduring forms of interaction in the immediate environment' (Bronfenbrenner 1994) include relationships children have with others (such as parents and educators), and the quality of these interactions can make a significant contribution to the success of transitions. The 'internal' characteristics of the child (such as their temperament) can influence the quality of their relationships with others. This is an idea theorised by Bronfenbrenner when exploring infant-mother interactions. Bronfenbrenner (1995) examined how children's characteristics influence the quality of maternal care, with consequential effects on developmental outcomes. He also stated that 'the pattern of these relationships varies systematically as a function of the quality of the environment in which the family lives' (1995, p. 625).

4.3 Implications for Practice and Research

There are significant theoretical, methodological and practical implications associated with adopting an ecological perspective of children's transition to school. Viewing the child as an active agent (Dunlop 2003) in their transition and situating children at the centre of the transition process means understanding the unique contribution each child brings to the process. It also means understanding that children are individuals who operate within a number of contexts, not independent from external factors. Lam and Pollard (2006) explain that transition is a shift from one identity to another. This idea is promoted by Ecclestone (2009), who explains the change in agency children experience as they progress through the education system. This notion of agency or ownership over emotional, social and behavioural processes is critical in enabling children to feel empowered during this time of immense change. A central tenet of ecological perspectives is that the success of children's transition to school is dependent not only on personal factors but also on interpersonal and institutional factors.

Personal or structural factors are those factors within the child, which are immediate to the child's learning and development and which directly and indirectly influence a successful transition. These include gender, which is known to influence children's learning outcomes in early schooling (Hindman et al. 2010); temperament styles and behaviour, which have been shown to affect the way children react to and cope with new and stressful situations at school (Nelson et al. 1999; Rimm-Kaufman et al. 2005); and experience, including whether or not they have attended preschool or day care or have familiar peers when they enter school, which can affect how children cope socially once they get to kindergarten (Ladd 1990; Ladd and Price 1987; Rimm-Kaufman and Pianta 2005). In addition, child characteristics of race, mental age and language ability are included as these have been found to influence how children adjust to the academic demands of school (Birch and Ladd 1996; Carlton and Winsler 1999). Recent research examining the predictive influence of these personal or structural factors on academic and social-emotional outcomes for children (Murray 2008) has shown that at the end of the first year of school, children's academic adjustment to school relies heavily on child characteristics of age, gender and language ability, as well as their self-directedness in the classroom. Children's social-emotional adjustment at the end of the year was predicted by their feelings about school and their relationship with the teacher. Other factors of temperament, social support from peers and teachers and the quality of the classroom environment also influenced how well children adjusted socially and formed relationships with teachers over the first year of school.

Interpersonal factors are those which are based on key relationships pertinent to transition. The quality of teacher-child relationships (Baker 2006; Birch and Ladd 1997; Hamre and Pianta 2001; Howes et al. 2000) and peer relationships (Birch and Ladd 1997; Dockett and Perry 2001; Ladd et al. 1999) has significant influence on children's stress levels and ability to cope with new social and academic demands in the formal school environment. Positive relationships between parents and teachers, and between students/children and teachers in prior-to-school settings and first year of school settings, are also integral to the ease of the transition process (Dockett and Perry 2006).

Institutional factors include the physical spaces of the school and classroom as contexts for learning and development. The process of transition requires a shift from one context or 'space' to another. Many aspects of children's transition and adjustment to school occur within the contexts of the school and classroom, and adjustment is influenced by the characteristics of these environments. The classroom context incorporates two main factors: the quality of the learning environment (including the quality of instruction and the classroom management) and the social and emotional climate. The quality of the learning environment refers to how teaching and learning occurs in classrooms, as opposed to what teachers are teaching and what children are learning. Findings from the Effective Provision of Pre-school Education (EPPE) study (Siraj-Blatchford et al. 2002) suggest that the most effective early childhood settings draw on both teacher-directed and child-initiated learning activities and are responsive to children's learning and development. Classroom quality in primary schools has been shown to influence peer relationships and student behaviour (Rimm-Kaufman et al. 2005), as well as teacher-child relationships (Pianta et al. 2002). In addition, Burts et al. (1990) found that children in higher-quality classrooms exhibited less stress-related behaviours or anxiety, which would affect their adjustment to school.

The degree to which the classroom is emotionally supportive, as well as academically and socially supportive, also falls within the context of school. Reiterating the ecological notion of transition and illustrating the connectedness between aspects of interpersonal relationships and institutional factors, peer and teacher relationships are affected by the degree of support within a classroom context (Donohue et al. 2003; Hamre and Pianta 2005). Adjusting to the classroom and school context is a major challenge for many children during the transition to school. The context of the school and classroom is often culturally and socially very different from the home or prior-to-school environment (Pianta and Kraft-Sayre 2003). This is the place where many of children's peer and other social interactions and learning take place, not only in the first year of formal schooling but also for many years to come.

4.4 Challenges and Issues

Including children in research as active contributors to knowledge about their experiences, feelings, relationships and coping strategies is an important methodological and practical implication of placing children at the centre of the transition process. Viewing children as integral participants in research of direct concern to them can enhance rigour and authenticity in the measurement of transition processes and the bidirectional influences on children during this time.

There is a growing consensus in the early childhood field that research needs to include children's perspectives on their experiences of starting and adjusting to school (Dockett and Perry 2003; Einarsdóttir 2003; Griebel and Niesel 2000). To this end, an increasing number of studies have included children's perspectives or feelings about school and the teacher and their perceptions of peer acceptance and self-competence (Dockett and Perry 2003, 2005; Ladd and Coleman 1997; Lapp-Payne 2005; Valeski and Stipek 2001).

To date, two broad types of measures have been used to assess children's constructs relating to school transition and adjustment. The first group tends to measure 'global' constructs such as general school and teacher liking (Birch and Ladd 1997). School liking and school avoidance have been studied by researchers both in Australia (Harrison 2004) and internationally (Ladd and Price 1987). Some researchers have referred to school liking as school sentiment (Ladd et al. 2000), and others have referred to children's feelings about school as dispositions (Dockett and Perry 2001). Australian researchers (Dockett and Perry 2001; Harrison 2004; Harrison et al. 2007) have also found that asking young children about their experiences at school and the degree to which they like school and like their teacher elicits reliable information. Ladd et al. (2000, p. 255) have reported that the degree to which children like school 'may be an important determinant of their classroom participation, which in turn may impact their achievement'; therefore, measuring school sentiment in a global sense can be beneficial for research and practice.

The second group of 'measurements' addresses specific aspects of children's perceptions of particular elements of school during the transition process (Dockett and Perry 2003; Harrison et al. 2007; Valeski and Stipek 2001). It also examines ways in which these may be evident in different social and cultural contexts and the implications these have for these children. While Dockett and Perry (2005, p. 4) acknowledge that 'children have long been "objects of inquiry"' and recognise the importance of obtaining direct reports from children regarding their experiences of starting school, the challenge for researchers is to develop methodologies for undertaking authentic research, conducted over time, which contextualises children's perspectives and which truly allows children to have a voice.

The *Pictorial Measure of School Stress and Wellbeing* (PMSSW) (Harrison and Murray under review; Murray 2008; Murray and Harrison 2005) was designed to add to the small number of existing approaches that involve young children as primary participants in reporting on issues that are directly related to them. The aim was to measure school-related stress and well-being associated with children's initial transition to school and subsequent process of adjustment by assessing children's perceptions of personal, interpersonal and institutional school situations across the first year of school. The instrument contextualises children's perspectives and uses qualitative methods to encourage children to express how they feel about typical situations at school, say whether or not they would share their feelings with their teacher and describe the strategies they would draw on to cope in these situations. Children's responses to the PMSSW are interpreted qualitatively using an inductive approach and coded quantitatively, which provides rich data as well as the opportunity to use quantitative methods of analysis to explore intercorrelation patterns, predictive relationships and changes in children's feelings and responses over time.

The PMSSW was used in a study of 105 children, their parents and 16 teachers, with data collection at the beginning and end of the children's first year of schooling. Semi-structured interviews were conducted with children and the PMSSW was administered (along with other measures of academic ability and school liking). The PMSSW presents nine illustrations of everyday school situations, which relate to personal, interpersonal and institutional aspects of school and that are familiar to children, but which may provoke feelings of stress and challenge (such as waving goodbye to their parent in the morning, lining up outside the classroom and speaking in front of the class). Children were asked five questions for each of the nine scenarios: (1) How does the child in the picture feel? (2) Why do they feel (the child's word)? (3) Do you think they would want the teacher to know they are feeling (the child's word)? (4) Why/why not? (5) What do you think will happen next? Coding categories were developed for children's responses to the five questions, which illustrated the personal, interpersonal and institutional reasons for children's feelings, reasons for sharing their feelings with the teacher and coping strategies for these nine scenarios.

One of the purposes in using the PMSSW was to assess change in children's perceptions across the first year of school transition period. Comparisons between children's responses to the PMSSW scenarios at the beginning and end of the first year of school showed that individual children's feelings about school scenarios did not change significantly over time. If children felt positive when they started school, they were likely to report positive feelings at the end of the first year. However, changes were apparent in the reasons children gave for feeling happy or sad about school. Personal reasons (those which indicated children liked school and enjoyed the things they did at school) decreased significantly over time, while interpersonal reasons (indicating a close connection with their teacher, parent or peer) and institutional reasons (indicating an early awareness of the school rules and routines) increased significantly over time. This illustrates the impact institutional aspects of school have on children's reasoning and decision-making processes and reflects research by Dockett and Perry (2001) which also identified kindergarten children's awareness of the school rules and the need to learn the rules to function at school. Children were more focused on themselves at the beginning of the year and reported intrinsic motivators for feelings and their relationship with the teacher. In contrast, at the end of the year, children were more focused on how they should follow the school rules and whether or not they were meeting the teacher's expectations. However, the opposite was found for children's coping strategies. Although children's coping strategies changed over the school year, compared to responses at the beginning of the year, children used significantly more personal and interpersonal coping strategies and significantly fewer institutional strategies at the end of the year. At the beginning of the year, children's strategies for coping with challenging school situations indicated a reliance on the rules and routines of the formal school environment, whereas at the end of the year, children seemed to rely more on themselves and explained using more intrinsically motivated strategies.

The degree of change varied to some extent by the particular challenge presented in the PMSSW. Scenarios relating to perceived peer relationships (e.g. watching/joining in with other children play in the sandpit) and personal confidence and independence (e.g. going to the bathroom by yourself) elicited the most negative responses from children both at the beginning and at end of the year. Other scenarios, which related to becoming familiar with school rules and routines, elicited more positive responses over time, for example, lining up outside the classroom and sitting on the floor listening to the teacher. Children's reasons for their feelings suggested that as they became more confident with the institutional processes of the school environment, they felt more positive about these types of situations. However, the same could not be said for interpersonal scenarios, with results indicating that as children became more familiar with peers and peer interaction over the school year, they also became more dependent on peer acceptance and less confident approaching peers.

Overall children's social and emotional adjustment to the personal, interpersonal and institutional demands of the first year of school, as measured by the PMSSW, showed a number of differences between the beginning and end of the year indicating the change in children's perspectives on school and ways of coping over the year. These differences may be attributed to growth in children's confidence, self-awareness, social awareness, peer and teacher relationships and an understanding of the routines and expectations of the teacher and school context.

4.5 Future Directions and Policy Implications

Future directions for transitions research should draw on an ecological approach to understand the process of transition. They should enable children to be situated at the centre of the process and acknowledge the multiple and bidirectional influences for children during this time. It is important to continue to include children as active contributors to research and active agents for change. A number of specific directions for future research are discussed below.

4.5.1 Authentic, Longitudinal Research Which Involves Children as Active Participants and Active Agents for Change

Authentic research is that which 'gives power and voice to child research participants and which provides insights into their subjective world' (Grover 2004). Exploring the transition experiences for children in large-scale, authentic, longitudinal research projects, which include children as active and reliable contributors of knowledge (Dockett and Perry 2007a), is a necessary 'next step' in transition research. Examining the process of transition and adjustment to school across the first year (not just at one point in the year) and continuing to follow children's progress throughout schooling means that researchers and practitioners can understand what works at the start of school for children's longer-term social, emotional and academic outcomes. While national, longitudinal studies such as the *Longitudinal Study of Australian Children* (Harrison et al. 2009) have included information about children's first year of school, in-depth analyses of the transition process have not been undertaken on a large scale, and this has implications for the precedence we can give to findings about children's adjustment to school and long-term school trajectories. While there are methodological challenges surrounding children's inclusion in research (Einarsdóttir 2007), the benefits far outweigh these challenges. It will be important for future research to examine not only children's initial transition to school but also the factors inherent in a positive transition and children's subsequent adjustment to school over the first few years.

4.5.2 Personal Aspects of Transition

Further examination is needed to identify the personal qualities within the child which act as protective factors against negative transition experiences. Research has shown that factors within the child such as gender, age, level of vocabulary and temperament (Harrison et al. 2009; Hindman et al. 2010) are the most significant predictors of children's academic, social and emotional adjustment to school. Therefore, it will be important to examine further the impact that interpersonal and institutional factors have on these personal factors and the relationship between the personal, interpersonal and institutional predictors of a positive transition. The use of innovative methods to gather children's views, which combine qualitative and quantitative methods and which provide a rich picture of the transition process, is an important step forward for transition research. Engaging children, educators and families in ways which are mutually beneficial and which offer holistic insights into children's experiences will allow researchers to make important connections between microsystem, mesosystem and macrosystem influences and in turn allow educators and policy makers to better plan for transition. Examples of methodologies which have engaged children effectively include the PMSSW (Harrison and

Murray under review; Murray 2008; Murray and Harrison 2005), the Feelings About School scale (Valeski and Stipek 2001) and Dockett and Perry's (2003) research which collected children's drawings, photographs and journals.

The findings from Murray and Harrison's research that show children's feelings about school did not change significantly over the school year but their reasons for positive or negative feelings did are important to note. First impressions seem to matter for children. This is not necessarily surprising, but it certainly has implications for what educators do to orient children to the formal school environment prior to the start of school, to encourage the development of strong, positive and supportive relationships between children and significant others and to enable strong context familiarity. It seems that as children become more experienced in the school and classroom context, their connections with people and understanding of events become more astute and so do their coping strategies.

4.5.3 Interpersonal Aspects of Transition

Further investigation of the quality of the interpersonal aspects of school and the dyadic relations inherent throughout transition is also required by researchers, to better understand what parents and educators can do to promote successful transition experiences. The importance of positive and supportive teacher-child, child-peer, teacher-teacher and teacher-parent interactions during the transition to school and children's subsequent adjustment to school is widely acknowledged (Baker 2006; Hamre and Pianta 2001). Future transitions research needs to examine the interpersonal aspects of the transition process, from different stakeholder perspectives at the same time (Dockett and Perry 2003) and longitudinally, to gather a holistic picture of the experiences of children, teachers and parents during this time and determine the type of "united front" required to support children. While it is necessary to understand the quality of interpersonal aspects of transition, it is equally crucial for this understanding to bring about change and influence everyday interactions in the classroom and wider school environment.

4.5.4 Institutional Aspects of Transition

Institutional aspects of the transition process often present major discontinuities for young children (Dockett and Perry 2007b). Therefore, investigating the quality of the classroom environment and the supportiveness of teaching approaches, will provide important insights into the most effective teaching and learning environments and strategies in the first year of school. Ensuring research provides teachers with useful guidance about what does and does not make a difference to children's positive feelings about school, and positive learning outcomes is another important step in making research meaningful for all stakeholders.

Examining the proximal processes of transition experiences for children should address how children engage in different contexts at different times and in different ways. Research tells us that "good" or better still "excellent" teaching environments and teachers make a difference to children's educational engagement and outcomes (NSW Department of Education and Training 2003; Siraj-Blatchford et al. 2002), but unpacking the notions of good teaching remains a challenge in the early years of school.

4.6   Concluding Remarks

The challenge for both research and practice is to adopt a past, present and future approach to understanding and evaluating transition. In order to make a significant contribution to practice, ways of knowing and ways of doing, research needs to address three main questions:

1. What do children bring with them to school and what previous experiences help or hinder the transition process and children's subsequent adjustment to school?
2. What are the current processes in place to support children's transition?
3. How will the past and present influence children's social, emotional and academic abilities in their future schooling?

The first question draws on the past and aims to provide guidance about the significance of children's background knowledge and prior experiences to their current circumstances. It encourages us to address the personal aspects of transition and think about children's emotional adaptation to the formal school environment. The second question examines what is happening at the present time, what are the current external processes which are enacted to help children transition to school and how do children interact with these processes and feel about and cope with these processes. The third question aims to provide some direction for longitudinal research and to support the notion of longitudinal research which is not only authentic and collaborative but which uses mixed-design approaches to methodology. We must continue to question the ways we include children in research, so that we are not only accessing their perspectives in authentic and ethical ways to inform future theory and practice but also empowering their voice, their identity and their sense of agency while navigating the transition.

References

Baker, J. A. (2006). Contributions of teacher-child relationships to positive school adjustment during elementary school. *Journal of School Psychology, 44*(3), 211–229.
Birch, S. H., & Ladd, G. W. (1996). Interpersonal relationships in the school environment and children's early school adjustment: The role of teachers and peers. In J. Juvonen &

K. R. Wentzel (Eds.), *Social motivation: Understanding children's school adjustment* (pp. 199–225). New York: Cambridge University Press.

Birch, S. H., & Ladd, G. W. (1997). The teacher-child relationship and children's early school adjustment. *Journal of School Psychology, 35*(1), 61–79.

Bowes, J. M., & Hayes, A. (Eds.). (2000). *Children, families and communities: Contexts and consequences*. Melbourne: Oxford University Press.

Bronfenbrenner, U. (1979). *The ecology of human development*. Cambridge, MA: Harvard University Press.

Bronfenbrenner, U. (1994). Ecological models of human development. In *International encyclopaedia of education* (Vol. 3, 2nd ed.). Oxford: Elsevier. http://www.psy.cmu.edu/~siegler/35bronfebrenner94.pdf. Accessed 3 July 2012.

Bronfenbrenner, U. (1995). Developmental ecology through space and time: A future perspective. In P. Moen, G. H. Elder, & K. Luscher (Eds.), *Examining lives in context: Perspectives on the ecology of human development* (pp. 619–647). Washington, DC: American Psychological Association.

Bronfenbrenner, U., & Morris, P. (1998). The ecology of developmental processes. In W. Damon (Series Ed.) & R. M. Lerner (Vol. Ed.), *Handbook of child psychology: Vol. 1. Theoretical models of human development* (5th ed., pp. 993–1028). New York: Wiley.

Burts, D. C., Hart, C. H., Charlesworth, R., & Kirk, L. (1990). A comparison of frequencies of stress behaviours observed in kindergarten children in classrooms with developmentally appropriate versus developmentally inappropriate instructional practices. *Early Childhood Research Quarterly, 5*(3), 407–423.

Carlton, M. P., & Winsler, A. (1999). School readiness: The need for a paradigm shift. *School Psychology Review, 28*(3), 338–352.

Dockett, S., & Perry, B. (2001). Starting school: Effective transitions. *Early Childhood Research and Practice, 3*(2). http://ecrp.uiuc.edu/v3n2/dockett.html. Accessed 2 May 2012.

Dockett, S., & Perry, B. (2003). Children's views and children's voices in starting school. *Australian Journal of Early Childhood, 28*(1), 12–17.

Dockett, S., & Perry, B. (2005). 'You need to know how to play safe': Children's experiences of starting school. *Contemporary Issues in Early Childhood, 6*(1), 4–18.

Dockett, S., & Perry, B. (2006). *Starting school: A guide for educators*. Sydney: Pademelon Press.

Dockett, S., & Perry, B. (2007a). Trusting children's accounts in research. *Journal of Early Childhood Research, 5*(1), 47–63.

Dockett, S., & Perry, B. (2007b). Children's transition to school: Changing expectations. In A.-W. Dunlop & H. Fabian (Eds.), *Informing transitions in the early years*. Maidenhead: Open University Press.

Donohue, K. M., Perry, K. E., & Weinstein, R. S. (2003). Teacher's classroom practices and children's rejection by their peers. *Journal of Applied Developmental Psychology, 24*(1), 91–118.

Dunlop, A.-W. (2003). Bridging early educational transitions in learning through children's agency. In A.-W. Dunlop & H. Fabian (Eds.), *Transitions* (European early childhood education research journal themed monograph series, Vol. 1, pp. 67–86).

Ecclestone, K. (2009). Lost and found in transition: The educational implications of 'identity', 'agency', and 'structure'. In J. Field, J. Gallacher, & R. Ingram (Eds.), *Researching transitions in lifelong learning* (pp. 9–27). London: Routledge.

Einarsdóttir, J. (2003). When the bell rings we have to go inside: Preschool children's views on the primary school. In A.-W. Dunlop & H. Fabian (Eds.), *Transitions* (European early childhood education research journal themed monograph series, Vol. 1, pp. 35–49).

Einarsdóttir, J. (2007). Children's voices on the transition from preschool to primary school. In A.-W. Dunlop & H. Fabian (Eds.), *Informing transitions in the early years* (pp. 74–91). Berkshire: Open University Press.

Griebel, W., & Niesel, R. (2000, August-September). *The children's voice in the complex transition into kindergarten and school*. Paper presented at the 10th European conference on quality in early childhood education, London.

Grover, S. (2004). Why won't they listen to us? On giving power and voice to children participating in social research. *Childhood, 11*(1), 81–93. doi:10.1177/0907568204040186.

Hamre, B. K., & Pianta, R. C. (2001). Early teacher-child relationships and the trajectory of children's school outcomes through eighth grade. *Child Development, 72*, 625–638.

Hamre, B. K., & Pianta, R. C. (2005). Can instructional and emotional support in the first-grade classroom make a difference for children at risk of school failure? *Child Development, 76*(5), 949–967.

Harrison, L. J. (2004). *Do children's perceptions of themselves, their teachers, and school accord with their teacher's ratings of their adjustment to school?* Paper presented at the Australian Association for Research in Education National Conference, Melbourne. http://www.aare.edu.au/04pap/har04829.pdf. Accessed 15 Nov 2005.

Harrison, L. J., Clarke, L., & Ungerer, J. A. (2007). Children's drawings provide a new perspective on teacher-child relationship quality and school adjustment. *Early Childhood Research Quarterly, 22*(1), 55–71.

Harrison, L. J., & Murray, E. (under review). Assessing young children's perceptions of the day-to-day challenges of the first year of school using a pictorial measure. *Journal of Early Childhood Research.*

Harrison, L. J., Ungerer, J. A., Smith, G. J., Zubrick, S. R., & Wise, S. with Press, F., Waniganayake, M., and the LSAC Research Consortium. (2009). *Child care and early education in Australia. The longitudinal study of Australian children. Wave 1 thematic paper.* Social Policy Research Paper No. 40.

Hindman, A. H., Skibbe, L. E., Miller, A., & Zimmerman, M. (2010). Ecological contexts and early learning: Contributions of child, family, and classroom factors during Head Start, to literacy and mathematics growth through first grade. *Early Childhood Research Quarterly, 25*(2), 235–250.

Howes, C., Phillipson, L. C., & Peisner-Feinberg, E. (2000). The consistency of perceived teacher-child relationships between preschool and kindergarten. *Journal of School Psychology, 38*(2), 113–132.

Ladd, G. W. (1990). Having friends, keeping friends, making friends, and being liked by peers in the classroom: Predictors of children's early school adjustment? *Child Development, 61*(4), 1081–1100.

Ladd, G. W., Birch, S. H., & Buhs, E. S. (1999). Children's social and scholastic lives in kindergarten: Related spheres of influence? *Child Development, 70*(6), 1373–1400.

Ladd, G. W., Buhs, E. S., & Seid, M. (2000). Children's initial sentiments about kindergarten: Is school liking and antecedent of early classroom participation and achievement? *Merrill-Palmer Quarterly, 46*(2), 255–279.

Ladd, G. W., & Coleman, C. C. (1997). Children's classroom peer relationships and early school attitudes: Concurrent and longitudinal associations. *Early Education and Development, 8*(1), 51–66.

Ladd, G. W., & Price, J. M. (1987). Predicting children's social and school adjustment following the transition from preschool to kindergarten. *Child Development, 58*(5), 1168–1189.

Lam, M. S., & Pollard, A. (2006). A conceptual framework for understanding children as agents in the transition from home to kindergarten. *Early Years, 26*(2), 123–141.

Lapp-Payne, A. (2005, April). *Developing and testing the "Feelings about my school and teachers instrument".* Poster presented at the Biennial meeting of the Society for Research in Child Development, Atlanta.

Leander, K. M., Phillips, N. C., & Headrick Taylor, K. (2010). The changing social spaces of learning: Mapping new mobilities. *Review of Research in Education, 34*(1), 329–394. doi:10.3102/0091732X09358129.

Murray, E. (2008). *Children's perspectives on the first year of school: Adjusting to the personal, interpersonal and institutional aspects of school.* Unpublished dissertation, Charles Sturt University, Bathurst.

Murray, E., & Harrison, L. J. (2005). Children's perspectives on their first year of school: Introducing a new Pictorial Measure of School Stress. *European Early Childhood Education Research Journal, 13*(1), 111–127.

Nelson, B., Martin, R. P., Hodge, S., Havill, V., & Kamphaus, R. (1999). Modeling the prediction of elementary school adjustment from preschool temperament. *Personality and Individual Differences, 26*(4), 687–700.

New South Wales Department of Education and Training. (2003). *Quality teaching in NSW public schools: Continuing the discussion about classroom practice.* Sydney: NSW Department of Education and Training, Professional Support and Curriculum Directorate.

Pianta, R. C., & Kraft-Sayre, M. (2003). *Successful kindergarten transition: Your guide to connecting children, families, and schools.* Baltimore: Paul H. Brookes.

Pianta, R. C., La Paro, K. M., Payne, C., Cox, M. J., & Bradley, R. (2002). The relation of kindergarten classroom environment to teacher, family, and school characteristics and child outcomes. *Elementary School Journal, 102*(3), 225–238.

Rimm-Kaufman, S. E., La Paro, K. M., Downer, J. T., & Pianta, R. C. (2005). The contribution of classroom setting and quality of instruction to children's behaviour in the kindergarten classroom. *Elementary School Journal, 105*(4), 377–394.

Rimm-Kaufman, S. E., & Pianta, R. C. (2005). Family-school communication in preschool and kindergarten in the context of a relationship-enhancing intervention. *Early Education and Development, 16*(3), 287–316.

Rosier, K., & McDonald, M. (2011). *Promoting positive education and care transitions for children.* Melbourne: Australian Institute of Family Studies, Commonwealth of Australia. http://www.aifs.gov.au/cafca/pubs/sheets/rs/rs5.pdf. Accessed 3 Aug 2012.

Siraj-Blatchford, I., Sylva, K., Muttock, S., Gilden, R., & Bell, D. (2002). *Researching effective pedagogy in the early years (Research report RR356).* Institute of Education, University of London.

Valeski, T. N., & Stipek, D. J. (2001). Young children's feelings about school. *Child Development, 72*(4), 1198–1213.

Chapter 5
Intrapersonal and Interpersonal Influences on School Transition

Linda J. Harrison

5.1 Introduction

My research began with a focus on very young children's experience of child care and, subsequently, their transition year in kindergarten, the first year of formal schooling. For the most part, my research has been enacted through the design and analysis of large-scale longitudinal research studies, including the *Sydney Family Development Project* (Harrison et al. 2007), *Child Care Choices* (Bowes et al. 2009) and the *Longitudinal Study of Australian Children* (Harrison et al. 2009; Sanson et al. 2002). New directions in my research include the application of person-centred approaches to the analysis of data as a means of understanding school transition processes in the interpersonal domain. I am also interested in recent theorising in the field of human development (e.g. Belsky and Pluess 2009) and what this brings to the study of intrapersonal and interpersonal influences on transition.

5.2 Theoretical Perspectives

5.2.1 Bioecological Models of Transition

Bronfenbrenner (1979, 2005a) describes the context of development as an ecological system that directly or indirectly influences the person and development in context as an interactive process among the person, his or her proximal and distal contexts and time. The bioecological model posits direct and indirect systems, of which the "microsystem"—described as reciprocal interaction between the

L.J. Harrison (✉)
Charles Sturt University, Bathurst, Australia
e-mail: lharrison@csu.edu.au

B. Perry et al. (eds.), *Transitions to School - International Research, Policy and Practice*,
International perspectives on early childhood education and development 9,
DOI 10.1007/978-94-007-7350-9_5, © Springer Science+Business Media Dordrecht 2014

child and his or her immediate environment—is the most direct. According to Bronfenbrenner (2005b, p. 6), interactions at the level of microsystems (proximal processes) are 'the primary engines of development'. While acknowledging that both direct and indirect influences are relevant to a full understanding of children's transitions, I am primarily interested in these proximal processes and the connections between the intrapersonal and interpersonal worlds of the school student.

Proximal processes are highlighted, for example, in Birch and Ladd's (1996) early model of school adjustment, which illustrates the interplay between child characteristics (psychological, organismic, behavioural) and interpersonal relationships—their type (school and nonschool) and contribution (emotionally supportive or stressful)—in explaining children's perceptions (e.g. school liking), affect (e.g. anxiety), involvement (e.g. engagement, school avoidance) and performance (e.g. achievement). Birch and Ladd's (1996) model has informed the selection of measures in my studies of children's development across prior-to-school and school transitions. For example, I have included child characteristics of temperament as a psychological factor, gender and communication impairment as organismic factors and externalising and internalising behaviours as behavioural factors. I have also included child–parent attachment and student-teacher relationships as nonschool and school types of interpersonal factors and considered the emotionally supportive or stressful effects of attachment security and student-teacher closeness and conflict.

My research has examined contemporaneous links among child characteristics, interpersonal relationships and adjustment components of transition processes, an approach described by Rimm-Kaufman and Pianta (2000, p. 498) as the Indirect Effects Model in which 'child characteristics interact with contexts through a transactional process – the child is affected by his or her context and the context, to some degree, is affected by the characteristics of the child'. This model also examines links between contexts (e.g. home and school) but is limited by a focus on one point in time. Longitudinal studies, on the other hand, are able to examine these processes over time, through what Rimm-Kaufman and Pianta (2000, p. 499) refer to as the Dynamic Effects Model, or the Ecological and Dynamic Model of Transition. This model proposes that 'child characteristics and contexts interact through a transactional process' which over time forms 'patterns and relationships that can be described not only as influences on children's development, but also as outcomes in their own right'. My research has examined longitudinal patterns by investigating trajectories in interpersonal relationships between the student and teacher from prior-to-school and school transition into the primary school years. Relationship trajectories are both a contributor to children's learning and wellbeing and an outcome of interpersonal and intrapersonal processes. Longitudinal research conducted in the United States (Hamre and Pianta 2001; Howes et al. 2000) and Australia (Bowes et al. 2009; Harrison and Ungerer 2006) has reported continuities in the characteristics of teacher-student relationships from children's preschool and child care through to the end of primary school. Further to this, longitudinal analyses have identified patterns of stable, increasing and declining conflict and closeness in teacher-student relationships that differentially affect academic achievement (Harrison et al. 2012; Spilt et al. 2012).

5.2.2 Transactional/Dual-Risk Models

Sameroff's (1983, 1995) transactional model of child development proposes that individual vulnerabilities, which may be genetic, psychological or organismic, predispose children to be more adversely affected by environmental stressors. This model of dual or cumulative risk underpins many early intervention/compensatory programmes in early childhood, which aim to provide intensive, high-quality education and parent support for disadvantaged or "at risk" children. The expectation, and evidence, is that appropriate preventative intervention, through improving competence and promoting protective factors in the family (Greenberg 2006) or at school (Hamre and Pianta 2005), can tip the balance towards school success rather than failure. My work aligns with this approach to the extent that I am interested in the layering of risk (or protectiveness) that may occur during school transition via the interaction of child intrapersonal characteristics, such as temperament, and interpersonal relationships, particularly child–parent and teacher-student. Both domains, intrapersonal and interpersonal, have been shown to influence children's experiences during the transition and adaptation to school, but for the most part, they have been investigated separately.

5.2.2.1 Interpersonal Relationships

Attachment theory proposes that children's earliest relationships are formed through the day-to-day interactions that infants have with their parents, siblings, close relatives and regular child care providers. These relationships provide the child with the emotional security and confidence they need to venture into novel territory, to explore the world of objects and to engage socially with others. Three components of dyadic attachment relationships—emotion regulation, secure base behaviour and affective sharing—are thought to lay the foundation for individual development of self-regulation, self-awareness, self-reliance, autonomy and cognitive growth (Sroufe 1996). All three are important abilities for children's transition to the early years of school. Additionally, attachment theory posits that these early relationships provide a blueprint for the formation of future close relationships, including student-teacher relationships in kindergarten (Howes et al. 2000; Pianta et al. 1997). A significant international body of research has shown that insecurity, conflict and relational negativity in teacher-student relationships are associated with difficulties in school adjustment (Ahnert et al. 2006; Hamre and Pianta 2005; Harrison et al. 2007). In contrast, close teacher-child relationships can have a protective function during the stress of transition (Thyssen 2000).

5.2.2.2 Intrapersonal Qualities

Temperament is defined broadly as 'constitutionally based differences in behavioural style that are visible from the child's earliest years' (Sanson et al. 2004, p. 143). Temperament is demonstrated through three broad domains: reactivity/negative emotionality (irritability, negative mood, high-intensity negative reactions), self-regulation (persistence, non-distractibility, self-soothing) and approach-withdrawal/inhibition-sociability. Of these, attention regulation, particularly persistence, is most strongly associated with enhanced school functioning (Sanson et al. 2004). However, reactivity/negative emotionality has also been linked to poorer outcomes for school performance, social behaviour and externalising/internalising problems in 3rd grade (Nelson et al. 1999) and for literacy and numeracy in kindergarten (Coplan et al. 1999). Only a small number of studies have examined the influences of temperament on children's response to transition. Ahnert et al. (2004) studied changes in diurnal cortisol patterns, fussing/crying and child-mother attachment security during toddlers' transition to centre-based child care in relation to child sex and temperament and the time mothers spent with their child before separation. They found that differences in transition experiences were not affected by temperament. Results for similar psychobiological studies using cortisol as a biomarker for children's experience of stress over the period of school transition have been mixed. Findings indicate a universal stress response: 'all children showed a healthy increase in cortisol levels' (Turner-Cobb et al. 2008, p. 387), which was evident 'on all school days compared to nonschool days' across the first term of school (Russ et al. 2012, p. 470). Russ and colleagues explain this finding as follows: 'in line with a repeated preparatory/reactive stress response, perhaps serving to equip the child for coping with the continual demands inherent in the school/peer environment' (p. 470). For the children with greater temperament vulnerability, school transition was associated with higher cortisol response at school (Turner-Cobb et al. 2008) and an extended period of elevated cortisol into the evening (Russ et al. 2012), suggesting that transition was a more challenging experience for these children.

5.2.3 Diathesis-Stress Theory and Differential Susceptibility Theory

Temperament is, at least in part, genetically/biologically determined, and for this reason some research into the potential risks associated with difficult temperament has draw on diathesis-stress theory, which posits that children who have a genetic predisposition to vulnerability (diathesis) and are exposed to difficult environments (stress) are at risk for poorer outcomes. Diathesis-stress theory can be likened to Sameroff's transactional, cumulative risk model. For example, Blair (2002, p. 120) has shown that temperamentally difficult, 'emotionally reactive children in unsupportive environments are likely at a high risk for ... poor school readiness'. The focus of diathesis-stress theory on vulnerability and compensation, some argue, limits understandings of children's experiences to the negative effects of intrapersonal or interpersonal adversity, at the expense of possible positive effects (Belsky and Pluess 2009). Differential susceptibility theory, in contrast, distinguishes between 'vulnerability', which is inherently linked to adversity and risk, and 'heightened susceptibility' which can be linked to positive and negative influences (Belsky et al. 2007, p. 301). Differential susceptibility theory proposes that 'some children … will be more susceptible than others to both the adverse and beneficial effects of, respectively, unsupportive and supportive contextual conditions' (Belsky and Pluess 2009, p. 886). Further, it suggests that vulnerable individuals 'most adversely affected by many kinds of stressors may be the very same ones who reap the most benefit from environmental support and enrichment, including the absence of adversity' (p. 886). A differential susceptibility model of development suggests not just dual risk but dual gain, demonstrated by 'a crossover interaction' between the moderator (heightened susceptibility) and 'the negative and positive aspects of the environment' (p. 888). For example, Kochanska et al. (2007) reported that toddlers with more difficult temperaments (high on fearfulness) were more affected by both negative (power assertion) and positive (supportive) parenting practices than their temperamentally less difficult peers.

Whilst there is a growing body of research conducted in the home, or with parents, that supports the differential susceptibility thesis (Belsky et al. 2007; Belsky and Pluess 2009), fewer studies have examined evidence for this theory in out-of-home environments. Those that have focus in the main on child care settings, where quality of care is conceptualised as either a negative (low-quality) or a positive (high-quality) influence. These studies have shown mixed support for a differential susceptibility explanation. For example, Volling and Feagans (1995) found that children's nonsocial play activity was predicted by quality of child care in highly fearful children, but not low-fear children. Similarly, Pluess and Belsky (2009) showed that teacher-rated behaviour problems in kindergarten were higher when the quality of child care attended was lower, and lower when quality was higher, for children with difficult temperaments, but not for children with easy temperaments. De Schipper et al. (2004), in an examination of behaviour problems in day care in relation to difficult temperament and the experience of multiple child care arrangements, found that attending several parallel care arrangements interfered with children's adaptation to day-care settings for children who showed more irritable distress, but not for children with low levels of irritable distress. However, the interaction between temperament difficulty and multiple care was only evident for child internalising problems, not for externalising or general wellbeing in day care. A further study, designed to test the links between temperamental irritability and caregivers' sensitive interaction in day care as a predictor of child-carer attachment, found no support for the expectation of differential susceptibility (de Schipper et al. 2008).

A comparative analysis of the effectiveness of diathesis-stress versus differential susceptibility models has been applied to an examination of the long-term outcomes of high- and low-quality child care for children with and without difficult temperament (Belsky and Pluess 2012). Using adolescents' self-ratings of externalising problems as the outcome measure, results showed that problems were highest for the children with more difficult temperaments who had received low-quality child care in the years prior to starting school; however, there was no evidence that these children had received greater benefit from attending higher-quality care. Belsky and Pluess (2012) conclude that these 'results prove more consistent with a diathesis-stress model of environmental action than a differential-susceptibility-related one' (p. 2).

Taking the work of Belsky and Pluess (2009, 2012) and others into account, there is clear evidence that some children are temperamentally more susceptible than others to the negative influence of poor-quality environments and some evidence that they may also be more susceptible to positive influences. Children's school transition will not only be differentially affected by individual temperament but also by the developmental history each child brings to their transition. Australian research has shown that temperament characteristics contribute to children's interpersonal experiences in prior-to-school (Bowes et al. 2009) and school settings (Murray 2008). Children with more difficult temperaments as toddlers were rated by their preschool teachers as being less prosocial with peers and having a less close relationship with the teacher (Bowes et al. 2009). At school age, children rated by their parents as being more temperamentally difficult were less likely to share their feelings with the teacher and more likely to experience conflict in the teacher-student relationship (Murray 2008).

5.3   Implications for Practice and Research

5.3.1   Research Design

Researching within the theoretical frameworks of bioecological, transactional, diathesis-stress and differential susceptibility models begins with the assumption that individual development is a two-way process that occurs within and is influenced by the wider environments of home, child care, early education, school and community. The implication is that research designs must take account of these contexts by including appropriate measures of family circumstances, including levels of stress or support; children's prior-to-school child care or preschool experience, including levels of quality; and current features of the school classroom, including teacher-student relationships. All of these are likely to have direct or indirect influence on children's experience of school transition and, when included in large-scale studies (sample size > 100) using statistical analysis techniques for modelling complex interactions amongst influencing factors, are able to explain children's different outcomes and developmental pathways through school. *The Child Care Choices* (CCC) study, for example, which collected data on a sample of over 400 children annually for a period of 7 years, assessed the combined effects of 38 distinct variables, including longitudinal indicators of social-emotional characteristics and cognitive abilities, child care experience and carer-child relationship closeness and conflict, as predictors of children's learning, behaviour and attitudes in the year before starting school and at the end of the first year of school (Bowes et al. 2009). A similar approach has been taken in the *Longitudinal Study of Australian Children* (LSAC) (Harrison et al. 2009), which is following 5,000 babies and 5,000 4–5-year-old children over a period of 16 years. Data collection includes biennial assessments of family functioning and parenting, children's education and child care experiences and outcomes for child health, learning and socio-emotional development. As well as including a broad range of domains, the CCC and LSAC studies also tap different perspectives, by including children as well as parents and teachers as respondents. From age 5 to age 6, children were asked to report how they felt about school, their teachers and peers. The large-scale, longitudinal nature of these and other such studies makes it possible for researchers to examine different pathways of development, prior to, during and after children's school transition. For example, by analysing teachers' ratings of relationship closeness and conflict with the LSAC study children at ages 4–5, 6–7 and 8–9 years, Harrison et al. (2012) were able to identify normative/adaptive and less adaptive trajectories over time. A pattern of teacher-child interpersonal difficulty, characterised by either consistently high levels of conflict or increasing levels, was found to predict poorer literacy and numeracy achievement at age 10–11 compared to the normative pattern of consistently low teacher-student conflict. The theoretical frameworks discussed in this chapter also rely on the inclusion of indicators of individual characteristics, measuring the intrapersonal domain. Diathesis-stress and differential susceptibility models need to include a marker of vulnerability or heightened susceptibility, such as a difficult or negative temperament, described by high reactivity, irritability or fearfulness. In studying differential responses to school transition, it is important therefore to include a measure that captures difficult temperament. Studies have drawn on parent-reported child temperament, observations of childhood inhibition and child self-report questionnaires, as well as parent self-reports of their own temperament as a genetic marker for intrapersonal disorders such as social phobia.

5.3.2   Practice: What Works for Whom?

Recent theorising asserts that 'differential susceptibility is a new way to address the perennial issue of what works for whom' (van IJzendoorn and Bakermans-Kranenburg 2012, p. 773). Research with children in prior-to-school settings has shown that more fearful children are more susceptible to caregiver stress than less fearful children: specifically, child wellbeing in child care was lower when caregivers were more stressed and higher when caregivers were less stressed, but only for the temperamentally susceptible children (Groeneveld et al. 2012). Children with a relatively easy temperament were less affected by caregiver stress. Extrapolating these findings to school transition suggests that children who are more temperamentally reactive, fearful or socially anxious will benefit the most from low stress, supportive classrooms and suffer the most from high-stress classrooms. Teachers, parents and schools need to appreciate that classroom climate and teachers' interpersonal availability are particularly important for children with a difficult temperament.

Classroom research has yet to be carried out to investigate the interaction between temperament characteristics and features of the classroom environment on children's transition to school. The challenge is to frame such research within a model that effectively sets out and assesses the processes that might be expected from differential susceptibility or diathesis-stress theory.

5.4 Challenges and Issues

5.4.1 Measurement: Types, Sources and Timing of Data Collection

Large-scale studies tend to cover a wide range of constructs but are often restricted in the depth and breadth of what can be measured. *The Longitudinal Study of Australian Children*, for example, relies primarily on questionnaire-type measures with "closed" response options. Observation and other in-depth sources of data collection are not possible for such a large and dispersed sample. The logistics of this national study also require that each wave of data collection extends for most of a year. This has meant, for example, that families could have been asked to report on their child's first experiences of school many months after starting school. For this reason, LSAC tends to include general measures of school adjustment and achievement, rather than specific measures that tap time-definite events.

Longitudinal studies of children's development are able to gather information on temperament characteristics in infancy or at an early age. Parents are acknowledged as the best source of information on child temperament (Sanson et al. 2004). However, there is some evidence that mothers' ratings of the child's behavioural characteristics tend to reflect not only the child's unique temperament but also their own intrapersonal qualities. For example, Pesonen et al. (2008) found that maternal mental health was moderately correlated with ratings of infant temperament and that these maternal and infant characteristics together predicted child temperamental negativity, extraversion and effortful control 5 years later. This and other longitudinal studies raise questions about the continuity or stability of child temperament over time, as well as the environmental influences that contribute to changes in temperament. A challenge for the researcher, therefore, is when to measure temperament and how best to model it in longitudinal analyses. The potential for overlap in measures assessed concurrently is an issue, especially as the "lines" between temperament characteristics and the social behaviours that are of interest in studies of school transition (e.g. feelings/attitudes towards peers and adults, parent–child relations, adjustment) 'are often blurred' (Sanson et al. 2004, p. 145). Alternately, whilst longitudinal studies can test the predictive validity of early indicators of temperament, such an approach ignores the 'changes (that) might be stimulated by changes in the child's environment' (Sanson et al. 2004, p. 160), as when the child enters a new kindergarten class at school transition.

Interpersonal relationships pose another measurement challenge in large-scale, longitudinal research. While studies of children's transition to child care have a history of using observational measures of child-teacher interaction and relationships (e.g. Ahnert et al. 2004; de Schipper et al. 2008; Howes et al. 2000; Pianta et al. 1997), studies of school transition/adjustment have tended to rely on teachers as the primary source of data on student-teacher relationships (e.g. Bowes et al. 2009; Hamre and Pianta 2001; Howes et al. 2000). In the few studies that have included children's perspectives on relationship quality, for example, via child-teacher drawings (Harrison et al. 2007) or rating scales assessing children's feelings about the teacher (Valeski and Stipek 2001), teacher support (Mantzicopoulos and Neuharth-Pritchett 2003) or teacher acceptance (Harrison et al. 2007), results show relatively weak ($r < .30$) correlations with teachers' ratings. There is clearly some overlap between children's and teachers' perspectives on the interpersonal dynamics of teacher-student interactions in the classroom but also some differences. It is important, therefore, that researchers include student-generated data as well as teacher reports when assessing student-teacher relationships or the supportiveness of the classroom environment.

5.4.2 Analysis Techniques: Variable-Centred Dimensions Versus Person-Centred Prototypes

Approaches to data analysis in large-scale research studies of school transition or school adjustment have tended to employ regression analyses which rely on correlational associations between variable-centred dimensions, both as predictors and as outcomes. These dimensions are typically measured on a linear scale from higher to lower, for example, of ratings of introversion problems or teacher-student relationship closeness, or scores on a test of receptive vocabulary. In contrast, person-centred studies employ cluster analysis, latent class analysis or other techniques to generate relatively homogeneous subgroups, or prototypes, of people who have similar profiles on a selected set of variables or repeated measures of a single variable. In my own research, person-centred techniques have identified different longitudinal patterns of student-teacher relationships and shown that patterns of increasing conflict with teachers from age 4–5 to age 8–9 predicted poorer academic achievement (Harrison et al. 2012). In other work, studying children's school transition year, cluster analysis was used to combine three dimensions of student-teacher relationship (closeness, conflict and dependency) to identify four distinct relationship profiles. Two of these, typified by low closeness and either conflict or independence, were associated with poorer learning and social skills at school (Harrison 2012). In the application of research to practice, it may be that such typologies or prototypes are more meaningful for teachers, who are able to "recognise" similar patterns in their classrooms.

5.5   Future Directions

5.5.1   International Policy Directions in School Transition

Recent research in Australia, the United States, Canada and the United Kingdom (Bowes et al. 2009; Bradbury et al. 2011; Claessens 2009; Duncan et al. 2007) points to a growing recognition of the importance of the early years by governments and public policy makers. The political focus on ensuring that children enter school "ready to learn" is translated in large-scale international studies into a search for the prior-to-school and school entry predictors that differentiate children's subsequent achievement at school. In essence, this approach aims to identify pathways in children's learning and development from preschool to school and through their primary school years. For example, Duncan et al. (2007) identified key dimensions of children's school entry "readiness to learn" as general cognitive ability (e.g. oral language), basic skills in mathematics and literacy (e.g. number/letter recognition), attention-related skills (e.g. task persistence, self-regulation, impulsivity) and socio-emotional skills and behaviours (e.g. internalising and externalising behaviours). These were tested for their predictive significance on academic achievement in primary school in six different longitudinal studies from three countries. After accounting for child, family and contextual influences, the results showed a general pattern of 'relatively strong prediction from school-entry reading and math skills, moderate predictive power for attention skills, and few to no statistically significant coefficients on socio-emotional behaviors' (Duncan et al. 2007, p. 1437). Similar results were also identified by Claessens (2009) in her analysis of three waves (from age 4–5 to 8–9 years) of the LSAC dataset: school achievement in early and middle primary school was predicted by children's cognitive skills, academic skills (particularly early numeracy) and hyperactivity/inattention at age 4–5 years. The results from these and other similar studies have provided the "evidence" for policies focusing on improving school readiness, particularly for disadvantaged or "at risk" children, through government-funded prekindergarten or preschool programmes (reviewed in Harrison et al. 2011). The assumption that a "school ready" child, with competencies in early reading and numeracy, will succeed at school positions the child as in some way 'responsible for their own success or failure' (Dockett and Perry 2004, p. 172) and fails to account for the complexities of school transition.

5.5.2   Continuities in School Transition

The Child Care Choices study examined children's academic competencies and approaches to learning in early childhood education and care (ECEC) settings in the year before starting school and again in the first year of school. The set of predictors included child and family characteristics, as well as features of children's ECEC experience. At both time points, children's abilities in literacy and numeracy were predicted by numeracy skills and behavioural difficulties in their ECEC settings at age 3–4. Children with higher ratings on aggressive social interaction had lower scores for academic ability (Bowes et al. 2009). Socio-emotional adjustment, in ECEC and at school, including prosocial behaviour, socio-emotional difficulties, teacher-child relationship and child-reported feelings about school, was also predicted by children's earlier behavioural difficulties as well as by relationships with caregivers. In this study, not only were early signs of intrapersonal and interpersonal difficulties continuous with later difficulties at school transition, but early problem behaviour was a predictor of academic progress across the 2-year transition from prior-to-school ECEC to school. These findings echo earlier reports from a national survey of kindergarten teachers in the United States whose predominant concern in regard to the essentials of being ready to start school was about 'regulatory aspects of children's behavior' (reviewed in Blair 2002, p. 112). Self-regulation ability aligns with temperamental qualities of persistence, non-distractibility and being able to cope when faced with difficult social situations. These qualities are also connected with and supported by more positive relationships with teachers. Interpersonal connection between children and their adult carers/teachers was also found to have continuity from children's earliest experience of child care through to the first year of school (Bowes et al. 2009). Attending to the intrapersonal and interpersonal in children's earliest, and all subsequent, experiences of education and care, including at school, is therefore an essential requirement for a positive and effective school transition.

References

Ahnert, L., Gunnar, M. R., Lamb, M. E., & Barthel, M. (2004). Transition to child care: Associations with infant-mother attachment, infant negative emotion, and cortisol elevations. *Child Development, 75*(3), 639–650.

Ahnert, L., Pinquart, M., & Lamb, M. E. (2006). Security of children's relationships with non-parental caregivers: A meta-analysis. *Child Development, 77*(3), 664–679.

Belsky, J., Bakkermans-Kranenburg, M. J., & Van IJzendoorn, M. H. (2007). For better and for worse: Differential susceptibility to environmental influences. *Current Directions in Psychological Science, 16*(6), 300–304.

Belsky, J., & Pluess, M. (2009). Beyond diathesis stress: Differential susceptibility to environmental influences. *Psychological Bulletin, 135*(6), 885–908.

Belsky, J., & Pluess, M. (2012). Differential susceptibility to long-term effects of quality of child care on externalizing behaviour in adolescence. *International Journal of Behavioral Development, 36*(1), 2–10.

Birch, S. H., & Ladd, G. (1996). Interpersonal relationships in the school environment and children's early school adjustment: The role of teachers and peers. In J. Juvonen & K. R. Wentzel (Eds.), *Social motivation. Understanding children's school adjustment* (pp. 199–225). Cambridge, UK: Cambridge University Press.

Blair, C. (2002). School readiness. Integrating cognition and emotion in a neurobiological conceptualisation of children's functioning at school entry. *American Psychologist, 57*(2), 111–127.

Bowes, J., Harrison, L. J., Sweller, N., Taylor, A., & Neilsen-Hewitt, C. (2009). *From child care to school. Influences on children's adjustment and achievement in the year before school and the first year of school. Findings from the Child Care Choices Longitudinal Extension Study.* NSW Department of Community Services. http://www.community.nsw.gov.au/docswr/_assets/main/documents/research_childcare_school.pdf. Accessed 1 Aug 2012.

Bradbury, B., Corak, M., Waldfogal, J., & Washbrook, E. (2011). *Inequality during the early years: Child outcomes and readiness to learn in Australia, Canada, United Kingdom, and United States.* IZA Discussion Paper No. 6120. Social Science Research Network. http://ssrn.com/abstract=1965137. Accessed 15 July 2012.

Bronfenbrenner, U. (1979). *The ecology of human development.* Cambridge, MA: Harvard University Press.

Bronfenbrenner, U. (2005a). Ecological systems theory. In U. Bronfenbrenner (Ed.), *Making human beings human: Bioecological perspectives on human development* (pp. 106–173). Thousand Oaks: Sage.

Bronfenbrenner, U. (2005b). The bioecological theory of human development. In U. Bronfenbrenner (Ed.), *Making human beings human. Bioecological perspectives on human development* (pp. 3–15). Thousand Oaks: Sage.

Claessens, A. (2009, December). *School readiness and achievement in middle childhood.* Paper presented at the 2nd Growing Up in Australia: Longitudinal Study of Australian Children (LSAC) Research Conference, Melbourne.

Coplan, R. J., Barber, A. M., & Gagne-Seguin, D. G. (1999). The role of child temperament as a predictor of early literacy and numeracy skills in preschoolers. *Early Childhood Research Quarterly, 14*(4), 537–553.

de Schipper, C., Tavecchio, L. W. C., & van IJzendoorn, M. H. (2008). Children's attachment relationships with day care caregivers: Associations with positive caregiving and child's temperament. *Social Development, 17*(3), 454–470.

de Schipper, C., Tavecchio, L. W. C., van IJzendoorn, M. H., & van Zeijl, J. (2004). Goodness-of-fit in centre day care: Relations of temperament, stability and quality of care with the child's adjustment. *Early Childhood Research Quarterly, 19*(2), 257–272.

Dockett, S., & Perry, B. (2004). Starting school. Perspectives of Australian children, parents and educators. *Journal of Early Childhood Research, 2*(2), 171–189.

Duncan, G. J., Dowsett, C. J., Claessens, A., Magnuson, K., Huston, A. C., Klebanov, P., Pagani, L., Feinstein, L., Engel, M., Brooks-Gunn, J., Sexton, H., Duckworth, K., & Jape, C. (2007). School readiness and later achievement. *Developmental Psychology, 43*(6), 1428–1446.

Greenberg, M. T. (2006). Promoting resilience in children and youth. Preventative interventions and their interface with neuroscience. *Annals of the New York Academy of Sciences, 1094*(1), 139–150.

Groeneveld, M. G., Vermeer, H. J., van IJzendoorn, M. H., & Linting, M. (2012). Stress, cortisol and well-being of caregivers and children in home-based child care: A case for differential susceptibility. *Child Care, Health and Development, 38*(2), 251–260.

Hamre, B. K., & Pianta, R. C. (2001). Early teacher-child relationships and the trajectory of children's school outcomes through eighth grade. *Child Development, 72*(2), 625–638.

Hamre, B. K., & Pianta, R. C. (2005). Can instructional and emotional support in the first-grade classroom make a difference for children at risk of school failure? *Child Development, 76*(5), 949–967.

Harrison, L. J. (2012, April). *Teacher-student relationship profiles in Australian children.* Paper presented in the symposium, Teacher-child relationships from an attachment perspective. International Conference on Interpersonal Relationships in Education, Vancouver.

Harrison, L. J., & Ungerer, J. A. (2006, July). *Child and teacher perspectives on their relationship with each other: Concurrent and longitudinal relations.* Paper presented in the symposium, Gender differences in child-teacher relations and school adjustment, Biennial meetings of the International Society for the Study of Behavioral Development, Melbourne.

Harrison, L., Clarke, L., & Ungerer, J. (2007). Children's drawings provide a new perspective on linkages between teacher-child relationship quality and school adjustment. *Early Childhood Research Quarterly, 22*(1), 55–71.

Harrison, L. J., Ungerer, J. A., Smith, G. J., Zubrick, S. R., & Wise, S., with Press, F., Waniganayake, M. and the LSAC Research Consortium. (2009). *Child care and early education in Australia. The Longitudinal Study of Australian Children. Social Policy Research Paper No. 40.* Canberra: Australian Government Department of Families, Housing, Community Services and Indigenous Affairs.   http://www.fahcsia.gov.au/sites/default/files/documents/05_2012/sprp_40.pdf. Accessed 14 May 2012.

Harrison, L., Sumsion, J., Press, F., Wong, S., Fordham, L., & Goodfellow, J. (2011). *A shared early childhood development research agenda: Key research gaps 2010–2015.* Research report commissioned by the Australian Research Alliance for Children and Youth for the Australian Government Department of Education, Employment and Workplace Relations. http://www.deewr.gov.au/Earlychildhood/Resources/Documents/ASharedECDResearchAgenda.pdf. Accessed 12 July 2012.

Harrison, L. J., Spilt, J. L., & Walker, S. (2012, July). *Trajectories of teacher-student relationships to age 8 years and achievement in literacy and numeracy in a nationally representative study of Australian 4–5 year olds.* Paper presented in Symposium 80: Stability and change in teacher-student relationships at school transition and through the elementary school years. Biennial meetings of the International Society for the Study of Behavioral Development, Edmonton.

Howes, C., Phillipsen, L. C., & Peisner-Feinberg, E. (2000). The consistency of perceived teacher-child relationships between preschool and kindergarten. *Journal of School Psychology, 38*(2), 113–132.

Kochanska, G., Aksan, N., & Joy, M. E. (2007). Children's fearfulness as a moderator of parenting in early socialization. *Developmental Psychology, 43*(1), 222–237.

Mantzicopoulos, P., & Neuharth-Pritchett, S. (2003). Development and validation of a measure to assess Head Start children's appraisals of teacher support. *Journal of School Psychology, 41*(6), 431–451.

Murray, E. (2008). *Children's perspectives on the first year of school: Adjusting to the personal, interpersonal and institutional aspects of school.* Unpublished dissertation. Charles Sturt University.

Nelson, B., Martin, R. P., Hodge, S., Havill, V., & Kamphaus, R. (1999). Modeling the prediction of elementary school adjustment from preschool temperament. *Personality and Individual Differences, 26*(4), 687–700.

Pesonen, A.-K., Räikkönen, K., Heinonen, K., Komsi, N., Järvenpää, A.-L., & Strandberg, T. (2008). A transactional model of temperamental development: Evidence of a relationship between child temperament and maternal stress over five years. *Social Development, 17*(2), 326–340.

Pianta, R. C., Nimetz, S. L., & Bennet, E. (1997). Mother-child relationships, teacher-child relationships, and school outcomes in preschool and kindergarten. *Early Childhood Research Quarterly, 12*(3), 263–280.

Pluess, M., & Belsky, J. (2009). Differential susceptibility to parenting and quality child care. *Developmental Psychology, 46*(2), 379–390.

Rimm-Kaufman, S. E., & Pianta, R. C. (2000). An ecological perspective on the transition to kindergarten: A theoretical framework to guide empirical research. *Journal of Applied Developmental Psychology, 21*, 491–511.

Russ, S. J., Herbert, J., Cooper, P., Gunnar, M. R., Goodyer, I., Croudace, T., & Murray, L. (2012). Cortisol levels in response to starting school in children at increased risk for school phobia. *Psychoneuroendocrinology, 37*(4), 462–474.

Sameroff, A. J. (1983). Developmental systems: Contexts and evolution. In P. Mussen (Ed.), *Handbook of child psychology* (Vol. 1, pp. 237–294). New York: Wiley.

Sameroff, A. J. (1995). General systems theories and psychopathology. In D. Cicchetti & D. Cohen (Eds.), *Developmental psychopathology* (Vol. 1, pp. 659–695). New York: Wiley.

Sanson, A., Nicholson, J., Ungerer, J., Zubrick, S., Wilson, K., Ainley, J., Berthelson, D., Bittman, M., Broom, D., Harrison, L. J., Rodgers, B., Sawyer, M., Silburn, S., Strazdins, L., Vimpani, G., & Wake, M. (2002). *Introducing the longitudinal study of Australian children. LSAC Discussion Paper No. 1.* Melbourne: Australian Institute of Family Studies. http://www.growingupinaustralia.gov.au/pubs/discussion/dp1/discussionpaper1.pdf. Accessed 12 June 2012.

Sanson, A., Hemphill, S. A., & Smart, D. (2004). Connections between temperament and social development: A review. *Social Development, 13*(1), 142–170.

Spilt, J. L., Hughes, J. N., Wu, J.-Y., & Kwok, O.-M. (2012). Dynamics of teacher-student relationships: Stability and change across elementary school and the influence on children's academic success. *Child Development, 83*(4), 1180–1195.

Sroufe, L. A. (1996). *Emotional development: The organization of emotional life in the early years*. Cambridge, UK: Cambridge University Press.

Thyssen, S. (2000). The child's start in day care centre. *Early Child Development and Care, 161*(1), 33–46.

Turner-Cobb, J. M., Rixon, L., & Jessop, D. S. (2008). A prospective study of diurnal cortisol responses to the social experience of school transition in four-year-old children: Anticipation, exposure, and adaptation. *Developmental Psychobiology, 50*(4), 377–389.

Valeski, T. N., & Stipek, D. J. (2001). Young children's feelings about school. *Child Development, 72*(4), 1198–1213.

van IJzendoorn, M. H., & Bakermans-Kranenburg, M. J. (2012). Differential susceptibility experiments: Going beyond correlational evidence: Comment on beyond mental health, differential susceptibility articles. *Developmental Psychology, 48*(3), 769–774.

Volling, B. L., & Feagans, L. V. (1995). Infant day care and children's social competence. *Infant Behavior and Development, 18*, 177–188.

Chapter 6
Transition and Adjustment to School

Kay Margetts

6.1 Introduction

6.1.1 Transition

Transition and adjustment are closely intertwined. Transition is viewed as the process of moving into a new setting, in this instance the school (Fabian 2007). Rather than being an event occurring over a few days or weeks, current views of transition to school see this as a lengthy process occurring weeks and frequently months prior to, and after, school commencement. Fabian notes that it is not necessarily a linear process but rather a series of complex and diverse interactions. These interactions typically include transition programmes—a series of activities and events designed and implemented prior to and in the early weeks of schooling to support understanding and familiarity of children and families with the new school and the school with the children and families. The activities usually involve visits to schools for children and families, visits between schools and early childhood services for children and educators, and the formal and informal sharing of information (Margetts 2007a). This reflects the contemporary view of children's transition to school being the shared responsibility of families, children, schools and communities (Petriwskyj 2010). It has been suggested that transition is not complete until the child and family have achieved a sense of well-being or comfort and 'oneness' with the new setting (Laevers et al. 1997), and this is recognised by educators (Educational Transitions and Change (ETC) Research Group 2011).

This 'oneness' or belonging is a key indicator of a successful transition. The greater the changes that need to be negotiated, the more difficult it can be for children and

K. Margetts (✉)
The University of Melbourne, Melbourne, Australia
e-mail: k.margetts@unimelb.edu.au

B. Perry et al. (eds.), *Transitions to School - International Research, Policy and Practice*,
International perspectives on early childhood education and development 9,
DOI 10.1007/978-94-007-7350-9_6, © Springer Science+Business Media Dordrecht 2014

families to manage the increasing demands of the new environment and to make a successful transition and adjustment in the early years of school (Margetts 2007b).

6.1.2 Adjustment

Oneness is associated with a child's sense of identity and belonging—the extent to which they feel valued and supported and connected with others and the new setting—as they encounter the inevitable challenges of a new environment, people, routines, rules and expectations. This capacity to adapt to and contribute to the new school setting is evidence of children's resilience and well-being (Compas 2006; Dunlop and Fabian 2002), characterised by children feeling secure, relaxed and comfortable (rather than anxious, lonely, confused or upset) and having positive attitudes and feelings about school and learning (Astbury 2009; Broström 2003; Chaplin et al. 2009). Feeling competent and capable is closely linked to children's ongoing learning and well-being and their sense of identity or self-concept (Jindal-Snape and Miller 2008; Richards and Steele 2007). Having a strong sense of identity appears to support children's ability to persevere and to protect them from experiencing stress during transitions and other potentially stressful situations (Merry 2002). Identity can also be supported through a shared collective vulnerability: as newcomers, children starting school are not alone. Regardless of different abilities and experiences, they are in the same position as the other children starting school (Garpelin 2004).

There has been strong support for adjustment to be measured in terms of social and emotional/behavioural adjustments in a variety of domains, and including academic competence (Gresham et al. 2010). Gresham and Elliott (1987) suggested that the constructs of adjustment involve social skills and adaptive behaviour in combination. Social skills contribute to adjustment and represent behaviours which, in specific situations, predict important social outcomes for children, including interpersonal behaviour, self-related behaviour, academic-related skills, assertion, peer acceptance and communication skills. Adaptive behaviour is viewed as the effectiveness and degree to which an individual meets social or cultural standards related to personal independence and social responsibility. These behaviours include independence, physical development, self-direction, personal responsibility and functional academic skills.

Measures of adjustment in terms of social skills have included constructs or domains related to peer relationships (Klein and Ballantine 1988; Ladd et al. 1997); the degree of discomfort and avoidance children express relative to peers (Ladd and Price 1987); social competence (Ladd and Price 1987; Moore et al. 1988); the forming of relationships with adults in the school (Klein and Ballantine 1988); dependency (Barth and Parke 1993); independence (Harrison and Ungerer 2000); loneliness and social dissatisfaction, school liking and avoidance (Ladd et al. 1997; Reynolds et al. 1992); and anxiety (Spence 1998).

The social behaviours that contribute to children's adjustment to school include interactional skills, problem-solving skills, self-reliance and determination and knowing about 'not knowing' and what to do about it (Fabian 2000). Cooperative play behaviours, nondisruptive group entry strategies and skilled verbal communication are also important (Maxwell and Eller 1994).

Behavioural domains of adjustment include describing difficulties in terms of internalising and externalising behaviours (NICHD Early Child Care Research Network 1996, 2001), anxiety behaviours in class (Ladd and Price 1987), adaptability (Moore et al. 1988), accepting and conforming to the demands of classroom routine and organisation (Renwick 1984), and restlessness, fidgeting and poor concentration (Rydell 1989). Being responsible for one's own behaviour, responding appropriately to conflict and controlling one's feelings such as not hitting or hurting others or not verbally abusing others are behaviours that contribute to children's adjustment and are closely associated with emotional understanding and regulation (Margetts 2004).

As well as evidence of achievement in mathematics and literacy (Broström 2010; Hansen 2010), academic domains of adjustment include classroom involvement (Ladd et al. 1997), work habits, task orientation, metacognitive skills, intelligent behaviour and independence (Harrison and Ungerer 2000). Other domains of adjustment have included children's attitudes to the first year of schooling (Barth and Parke 1993; Ladd and Price 1987) and children's behaviours at home (Barth and Parke 1993; Margetts 1997).

6.2 Importance of Transition and Adjustment

Adjustment depends partly on past experiences and on children possessing the skills and knowledge to respond to the demands of the new setting (Margetts 2009). Transition and adjustment may impact on '…how children view themselves, how others value them, their sense of wellbeing and their ability to learn' (Dunlop 2000 cited in Margetts 2007b, p. 108).

Children are at risk of not adjusting easily to school when there is a mismatch between the skills, attitudes and knowledge they bring to school and the expectations of the school itself (Lombardi 1992). Children may therefore experience personal incompatibilities and dislocations as they commence the first year of schooling (Bronfenbrenner 1986; Erikson 1963). For example, children who start school neurodevelopmentally and behaviourally immature, with poor self-regulation and attention difficulties, often have lower academic performance than their peers. Difficulties in coping with learning and academic demands can then generate anger, frustration and despair and lead to behaviour problems (Prior 1996). Associations have been reported between high levels of hyperactivity and impulsive behaviour as children commenced school and lower levels of academic performance 3 years later (Merrell and Tymms 2001) and between low levels of cooperation, self-control and assertion and reading and writing as children commenced school, with these relationships persisting into Grade 2 and Grade 6 (McClelland and Morrison 2003).

How well children adjust to school also has long-term implications. Successful transition and adjustment into formal schooling have been associated with long-term social and educational benefits (Alexander et al. 2001; Wildenger et al. 2008). The ability of children to meet the academic and other demands of school is supported by social and emotional competence (Fabian and Dunlop 2002). However, social, behavioural or academic difficulties in the first year of school predict similar outcomes 6 years (Margetts 2009) and 8 years later (Hamre and Pianta 2001). Risk factors in the early years of schooling are reported to increase children's vulnerability for difficulties in the next 10–12 years and may persist into later life (Cowan et al. 1994; Taylor 1998).

6.2.1 Assessing Adjustment

In practice, adjustment has typically been assessed through the use of rating scales or rankings completed by teachers and/or parents or peers. These instruments have been found to be useful for identifying specific behaviours and for validating and assessing social acceptance or rejection (Gresham et al. 2010). Sattler (1988) suggested that the use of checklists and rating scales based on prolonged contact with the child may capture rare and significant issues that could be missed in the direct observational method. Furthermore, it has been noted that checklists and rating scales are easily administered and time economical and cover a wide range of behaviours (Merrell 1989).

The involvement of teachers and parents in identifying and describing children's behaviour has been strongly supported. While essentially subjective, ratings by teachers and parents provide meaningful judgements of children's behaviour in the naturalist settings of school and home (Gresham et al. 2010). Teachers spend considerable time with children of similar age and different levels of functioning, and this contributes to their ability to identify and describe standards for academic and social behaviour (Teltsch and Breznitz 1988).

More recently the value of multiple perspectives—that of teachers, children and their families—has been advocated in evaluating and providing a comprehensive picture of children's adjustment. These perspectives can provide rich, cross-situational information, and any disparities can present opportunities for interpretative challenges and further investigation. The use of qualitative tools including questionnaires, sociometric measures, naturalistic observations, behaviour logs or journals and interviews with children, family, school and community members helps to construct more explanatory, personalised and culturally relevant perspectives of transition to school and provides a rich addition to quantitative sources.

The quality of parents' relationships with school staff and the level of parent involvement in their child's education may also be a valid indicator of a positive transition outcome that can serve to sustain and support the child through transition points over time (Bohan-Baker and Little 2004; Rimm-Kaufman et al. 2000).

6.2.2   Influences on Adjustment

The outcomes of transition are mediated by a complexity of factors. The variability in children's development and early school success is influenced by a number of interdependent factors including biological and developmental characteristics and social and cultural factors (Bronfenbrenner 1986; Broström 2000; Crnic and Lamberty 1994). The settings or contexts in which children actively participate strongly influence their development (Bronfenbrenner and Morris 2006).

The bioecological model of child development (Bronfenbrenner 1979, 1986; Bronfenbrenner and Morris 1998, 2006) views the contexts or environments of development as a series of concentric structures. The innermost structures, or microsystem, include the child's actual experiences within the home, family, childcare and wider community. The next structures, the exosystem, include indirect influences on children's development such as parental employment, socioeconomic status and government policies and practices. More broadly, the components of the macrosystem influence children's development through the subculture or dominant beliefs and ideologies of the society in which the child lives. Furthermore, children's development is strongly influenced by the relationships between the settings or contexts—the mesosystem—in which the child actively participates, such as factors limiting the choice of childcare or opportunities for comprehensive transition to school programmes (Bronfenbrenner 1979, 1986). Interactions and collaborative relationships between family, school, preschool and community are important and should be acknowledged and strengthened during the transition to school. The fifth structure is the chronosystem—the cumulative history associated with the timing and duration of events and changes in the lives of children and families (Bronfenbrenner 1986). While starting school is a normative event, that is, it is relatively predictable as is the age at which it occurs, transition and adjustment are culturally and contextually determined and can change over time (Wesley and Buysse 2003). For example, Australia, the United States and some other countries have experienced a change in the focus of children's adjustment to school from age and cognitive skills to a focus on characteristics and qualities within the child such as their social and emotional skills, their cultural context and the transition processes that support these (Mashburn and Pianta 2006). Just as the practices around transition can change, the chronosystem also recognises that the context and practices associated with children's transition to school have the potential to support changes in children's ongoing trajectories.

It can be argued that children's transition and adjustment to school are strongly influenced by how children, families, schools and communities interact and support each other. Thus, investigations of social contexts from a bioecological or interactional approach provide understandings of children's development and background and the opportunity to identify both positive and negative outcomes for children's adjustment to school. The identification of these factors should provoke the development of supportive, preventative or intervention strategies.

Consequently, studies of the effects and outcomes of transition to schooling must consider the shared influences of the child and their prior experiences as well as the influences of family, school and community contexts. These include child, gender, birth order, child's level of functioning, temperament, friendships, attachment relationships, self-awareness, self-esteem, prior-to-school childcare, family demographics and structure, parental attitudes and values, family cohesion, parent–child relationships and teacher-child relationships and classroom and school organisational factors, including transition support.

6.3 Implications for Research

In reflecting this bioecological or interactional approach to school transition and adjustment, my research has investigated interactions among and between a range of child and family characteristics, demographic influences, school practices and experiences. Although not addressed in this paper in detail, qualitative projects have involved the use of interviews and drawing with children, surveys and interviews with teachers to identify and describe key issues for them in children's transition and adjustment to school. For example, in a study that sought the views of children in the first and second years of school about starting school (Margetts 2008), children referred to their own feelings of being worried or nervous and suggested that children starting school needed to know they might feel like this. Analyses revealed a 'strong relationship between what children believed new children needed to know … and (their) suggestions about what schools could do to help new entrant children' (Margetts 2008, p. 15). Thus, schools should build on this ability of young children to provide authentic advice for dealing with issues that affect new entrant children and developing relevant transition to school programmes.

In quantitative research (Margetts 1997, 2000, 2004, 2009), the Social Skills Rating System (SSRS) (Elementary Level) (Gresham and Elliott 1990) has been employed to measure children's school adjustment. The SSRS provides norm-referenced behaviour rating scales for the domains of social skills, behavioural responses and academic competence (Gresham and Elliott 1987). The social skills domain (items 1–30) involves the subscales of cooperation (including follows directions, moves easily between activities, uses free time appropriately, ignores distractions), assertion (including initiates interactions, makes friends easily, joins ongoing activities, invites others to join in) and self-control (including controls temper, copes with frustration, compromises in conflict). The problem behaviour domain includes the subscales of externalising behaviour (gets angry easily, fights with others), internalising behaviour (appears lonely, acts sad or depressed, has low self-esteem, shows anxiety about being with a group of children) and hyperactivity (does not listen to what others are saying, disturbs ongoing activities, fidgets and moves excessively, is easily distracted). Academic competence is one small domain including reading competence, mathematics competence, motivation and parent encouragement to succeed.

Class teachers have completed the SSRS (Elementary Level) for each child during or after the ninth week of schooling. This timing is consistent with the literature and reflects psychometric views about the duration of the transition/adjustment period following school commencement (Ladd and Price 1987; Pianta and Steinberg 1992). Longitudinal studies have involved completion of the SSRS at different year levels of children's schooling (Margetts 2009).

Descriptive analyses have been used to describe demographic characteristics and background variables of children and their families, including participation in different transition to school activities, and correlation analyses and stepwise regression analyses have been employed to determine the relationships and contributions of transition activities and other background factors to children's adjustment (Margetts 2007a).

6.4 Challenges and Issues: Implications for Policy and Practice

Important findings from my research suggest that the participation of children and their families in comprehensive transition programmes is associated with children's early school adjustment, including higher levels of social skills and academic competence (Margetts 1997, 2003). It is important that transition programmes are developed in collaboration with key stakeholders including the children themselves to enable an appropriate degree of continuity between prior-to-school and school experiences, relationships and learning and social expectations (Margetts 1997). However, not all schools make these opportunities available.

Results have shown that children's adjustment to school was stronger for girls, children from homes where English was spoken or children whose fathers were in full-time employment. Girls were more cooperative than boys, and girls and children from higher socioeconomic families (represented by father employed full-time) had higher levels of self-control and summed social skills and lower levels of externalising and hyperactive behaviours. Higher socioeconomic status/father in full-time employment contributed significantly to higher academic competence. Children who spoke English at home had higher levels of cooperation and academic competence than those who did not speak English at home in the first year of school although this effect dissipated by the end of Grade 1. It may be that the background experiences of children afford some protection against the stresses and challenges of starting school. Children also had significantly higher levels of social skills and academic competence and less problem behaviours when they commenced school with a familiar playmate in the same class. Significantly studies have also reported that children had higher levels of social skills and academic competence and lower levels of problem behaviours if they attended preschool for

1 or 2 years prior to commencing schools. However, deficits in these domains were noted for children who attended childcare for 30 or more hours per week (Margetts 1997, 2000, 2004, 2009).

Benefits in terms of self-control and summed social skills and academic competence were also related to the participation of children and their families in high numbers of transition activities. Many opportunities to become familiar with the new school may act to ameliorate the negative effects of being a boy, not speaking English at home, and low socioeconomic status/father unemployment on children's adjustment to school, but not for children with problem behaviours.

The importance of adopting a bioecological perspective of transition is particularly pertinent when determining whether or not a child has made a successful transition to school. Since the conceptualisation of transition is in itself contextually and historically bound and experienced in different ways, it must be acknowledged that while teachers and parents may share some expectations relating to children's transition to school, they also have some very different ideas and expectations about what makes for a successful transition and adjustment to school. Teachers need to confront their own expectations and judgements and the extent to which they marginalise or stereotype children and families particularly in relation to socioeconomic status, ethnicity and culture (Rimm-Kaufman et al. 2000). Thus, when evaluating what constitutes a successful transition, it makes sense to obtain information in this regard from multiple perspectives—those of teachers, children and their families. The quality of the parent's relationship with the school staff and parental involvement in their child's education may also be a valid indicator of a positive transition outcome that can serve to sustain and support the child through transition points over time (Bohan-Baker and Little 2004).

In supporting children's adjustment to school, it is important that schools review the extent to which they provide flexible and relevant transition experiences with many opportunities for children and families to become familiar with the new school prior to commencement, and the extent to which they identify and support children "at risk" of poor transition and adjustment. Strategies that are inclusive of parents and carers who may have different backgrounds to the majority of the community or have fewer resources to be able to participate are essential.

Questions need to be asked about why particular cohorts are, or are not, participating in different activities and what activities are most effective for different groups. It is important to avoid deficit-focused normative comparisons of children, and rather than viewing differences as deficits, a strength-based approach should be adopted. In this way more equitable relationships can be developed that respect all people involved, build on the personal and cultural resources with children and families and promote shared decision-making (Davis et al. 2007; Petriwskyj 2010). This can be facilitated when there is collaboration between school, children, parents and community members in developing transition programmes relevant to the needs of particular groups of the school community (Margetts 2003). For example, given that fewer children/families with parents in full-time employment participated in visits to schools, including orientation visits, questions are raised about the timing of these visits and reasons for non-attendance by this group—evening or weekend visits may facilitate higher participation. Further questions should consider the extent to which single parent families and families of children with a disability are included.

Schools should be encouraged to provide additional or targeted opportunities for children who are at risk of adjustment difficulties: boys, those from low socioeconomic backgrounds or those who speak only languages other than English at home. This may mean that schools focus on the importance of relationships (Dockett and Perry 2001) and become more culturally sensitive (Clancy et al. 2001). Pairing children with familiar playmates or with children from similar cultural backgrounds or providing opportunities for friendships to develop before school commences may support a smooth adjustment to school. Teacher interactions are also important. As noted by Skinner et al. (1998), children from poor or ethnic minority groups benefit when teachers are compassionate and build on children's strengths, have high expectations of all students and support individual behaviour, learning and development. The acquisition and development of skills and behaviours related to self-regulation and behavioural control seem to have significant benefit for children's progress through school, and it is important that educators are aware of these and support their development.

Further research is needed to identify factors that influence the participation of children and families in transition programmes, as well as strategies, both prior to and following the commencement of school, that best support children's adjustment.

The challenge is to build on the research in practice to maximise the advantages and prevent or minimise the potentially detrimental risks for children starting school. In particular, there is a need to support the acquisition and development of skills and behaviours related to resilience, self-regulation and behavioural control, for it seems that these have the greatest power to benefit children's progress through school, even for those children deemed most at risk.

The research on children's transition to schooling suggests that the entire context of the child's ability to adjust to the demands of this new situation must be considered. A broad range of factors including the child's personal characteristics, family influences and the broader social mechanisms supporting the family and child should be considered to provide insight into factors that support children at this time or predispose them to risk of poor adjustment. This information will then permit parents, teachers and policymakers to be more informed about the type of support needed by different children prior to, and during, the transition to schooling. In so doing, let us not focus on mindless conformity but rather on creating the conditions that empower all children to have a sense of belonging and to be "in control".

References

Alexander, K., Entwisle, D., & Kabbani, N. (2001). The dropout process in life course perspective: Early risk factors at home and school. *Teachers College Record, 103*(5), 760–822.

Astbury, B. (2009). *Evaluation of transition: A positive start to school pilots.* The University of Melbourne, Centre for Program Evaluation.

Barth, J., & Parke, R. (1993). Parent–child relationship influences in children's transition to school. *Merrill-Palmer Quarterly, 39*(2), 173–195.

Bohan-Baker, M., & Little, P. M. (2004). The transition to kindergarten: A review of current research and promising practices to involve families. Cambridge, MA: Harvard Family Research Project, Harvard Graduate School of Education, Harvard University. http://www.gse. harvard.edu/hfrp/content/projects/fine/resources/research/bohan.pdf. Accessed 13 July 2012.

Bronfenbrenner, U. (1979). *The ecology of human development*. Cambridge, MA: Harvard University Press.

Bronfenbrenner, U. (1986). Ecology of the family as a context for human development: Research perspectives. *Developmental Psychology, 22*(6), 723–733.

Bronfenbrenner, U., & Morris, P. A. (1998). The ecology of developmental processes. In W. Damon & R. M. Lerner (Eds.), *Handbook of child psychology, Vol. 1: Theoretical models of human development* (5th ed., pp. 993–1023). New York: Wiley.

Bronfenbrenner, U., & Morris, P. A. (2006). The bioecological model of human development. In W. Damon & R. M. Lerner (Eds.), *Handbook of child psychology, Vol. 1: Theoretical models of human development* (6th ed., pp. 793–828). New York: Wiley.

Broström, S. (2000, September). *Communication and continuity in the transition from kindergarten to school in Denmark*. Paper related to poster symposium on "transition" at the EECERA 10th European Conference on Quality in Early Childhood Education, University of London.

Broström, S. (2003). Objects and media in frame play. In L.-E Berg, A. Nelson, & K. Svensson. (Eds.), *Toys in educational and socio-cultural contexts. Toy research in the late twentieth century, Part 1*. Selection of papers presented at the International Toy Research Conference, Halmstad University, Halmstad, Sweden.

Broström, S. (2010). Fiction, drawing and play in a Vygotskian perspective. In J. Hayden, & A. Tuna (Eds.), *Moving forward together: Early childhood programs as the doorway to social cohesion. An east–west perspective*. An ISSA publication: Cambridge: Scholars Publishing.

Chaplin, T. M., Gillham, J. E., & Seligman, E. P. (2009). Gender, anxiety and depressive symptoms: A longitudinal study of early adolescents. *The Journal of Early Adolescence, 29*(2), 307–327.

Clancy, S., Simpson, L., & Howard, P. (2001). Mutual trust and respect. In S. Dockett & B. Perry (Eds.), *Beginning school together: Sharing strengths* (pp. 56–61). Canberra: Australian Early Childhood Association.

Compas, B. E. (2006). Psychobiological processes of stress and coping: Implications for resilience in children and adolescents – Comments on the papers of Romeo and McEwen and Fisher et al. *Annuals New York Academy of Science, 1094*, 226–234.

Cowan, P., Cowan, C., Shulz, M., & Henning, G. (1994). Prebirth to preschool family factors in children's adaptation to kindergarten. In R. Parke & S. Kellart (Eds.), *Exploring family relationships with other social contexts* (pp. 75–114). Hillsdale: Lawrence Erlbaum Associates.

Crnic, K., & Lamberty, G. (1994). Reconsidering school readiness: Conceptual and applied perspectives. *Early Education and Development, 5*(2), Retrieved from http://readyweb.crc.uiic. edu/library/1994/crcnic1.html.

Davis, K., Gunn, A., Purdue, K., & Smith, K. (2007). Forging ahead: Moving towards inclusive and anti-discriminatory education. In L. Keesing-Styles & H. Hedges (Eds.), *Theorising early childhood practice: Emerging dialogues* (pp. 99–117). Sydney: Pademelon.

Dockett, S., & Perry, B. (2001). Starting school: Effective transitions. *Early Childhood Research & Practice, 3*(2), 1–18.

Dunlop, A.-W., & Fabian, H. (2002). Conclusions: Debating transitions, continuity and progression in the early years. In A.-W. Dunlop & H. Fabian (Eds.), *Transitions in the early years: Debating continuity and progression for children in early education*. London: Routledge/Falmer.

Educational Transitions and Change [ETC] Research Group. (2011). *Transition to school: Position statement*. Albury-Wodonga: Research Institute for Professional Practice, Learning and Education, Charles Sturt University.

Erikson, E. (1963). *Childhood and society*. New York: Norton.

Fabian, H. (2000, August). *Empowering children for transitions.* Paper presented at the EECERA 10th European Conference on Quality in Early Childhood Education, London.

Fabian, H. (2007). Informing transitions. In A.-W. Dunlop & H. Fabian (Eds.), *Informing transition in the early years: Research, policy and practice* (pp. 3–20). Maidenhead: Open University Press.

Fabian, H., & Dunlop, A. (2002, March). *Inter-conneXions.* Paper presented as a parallel session at the 'Progress with Purpose' Conference, Edinburgh. http://extranet.edfac.unimelb.edu.au/LED/tec/pdf/Interconnexions.pdf. Accessed 7 Apr 2010.

Garpelin, A. (2004). Accepted or rejected in school. *European Educational Research Journal, 3*(4), 729–742.

Gresham, F., & Elliott, S. (1987). The relationship between adaptive behavior and social skills: Issues in definition and assessment. *Journal of Special Education, 21*(9), 167–181.

Gresham, F. M., & Elliott, S. N. (1990). *Social skills rating system manual.* Circle Pines: American Guidance Service.

Gresham, F., Elliott, S., Cook, C., Vance, M., & Kettler, R. (2010). Cross-informant agreement for ratings for social skill and problem behavior ratings: An investigation of the Social Skills Improvement System—Rating Scales. *Psychological Assessment, 22*(1), 157–166.

Hamre, B., & Pianta, R. (2001). Early teacher-child relationships and the trajectory of children's school outcomes through eighth grade. *Child Development, 72*(2), 625–638.

Hansen, O. H. (2010, August). *Early language and thought.* Paper presented at the 26th OMEP World Congress, Göteborg, Sweden.

Harrison, L., & Ungerer, J. (2000, May). *Children and child care: A longitudinal study of the relationships between developmental outcomes and use of nonparental care from birth to six.* Paper prepared for the Department of Family and Community Services, Panel Data and Policy Conference, Canberra.

Jindal-Snape, D., & Miller, D. J. (2008). A challenge of living? Understanding the psycho-social process of the child during primary-secondary transition through resilience and self-esteem theories. *Education Psychology Review, 20*(3), 217–236.

Klein, H. A., & Ballantine, J. H. (1988). The relationship of temperament to adjustment in British Infant Schools. *The Journal of Social Psychology, 128*(5), 585–595.

Ladd, G. W., & Price, J. M. (1987). Predicting children's social and school adjustment following the transition from preschool to kindergarten. *Child Development, 58*(5), 1168–1189.

Ladd, G., Kochenderfer, B., & Coleman, C. (1997). Classroom peer acceptance, friendship, and victimization: Distinct relational systems that contribute uniquely to children's school adjustment? *Child Development, 68*(6), 1181–1197.

Laevers, F., Vandenbussche, E., Kog M., & Depondt, L. (1997). *A process-oriented child monitoring system for young children.* Katholieke Universiteit Leuven: Centre for Experiential Education.

Lombardi, J. (1992). *Beyond transition: Ensuring continuity in early childhood services.* (Report No. EDO-PS-92-3). Washington, DC: Office of Educational Research and Improvement. (ERIC Document Reproduction Service No. ED 345867).

Margetts, K. (1997). Factors impacting on children's adjustment to the first year of primary school. *Research Information for Teachers, 2,* 1–4.

Margetts, K. (2000). Indicators of children's adjustment to the first year of schooling. *Journal for Australian Research in Early Childhood Education, 7*(1), 20–30.

Margetts, K. (2003). Does adjustment at preschool predict adjustment in the first year of schooling? *Journal of Australian Research in Early Childhood Education, 10*(2), 13–25.

Margetts, K. (2004). Identifying and supporting behaviours associated with co-operation, assertion and self-control in young children starting school. *European Early Childhood Education Research Journal, 12*(2), 75–86.

Margetts, K. (2007a). Preparing children for school – benefits and privileges. *Australian Journal of Early Childhood, 32*(2), 43–50.

Margetts, K. (2007b). Understanding and supporting children: Shaping transition practices. In A.-W. Dunlop & H. Fabian (Eds.), *Informing transition in the early years: Research, policy and practice* (pp. 107–119). Maidenhead: Open University Press.

Margetts, K. (2008, September). *Transition to school. What children think about how it works and how it is going to be different things.* Paper presented at the 18th EECERA Conference, Stavanger, Norway.

Margetts, K. (2009). Early transition and adjustment and children's adjustment after six years of schooling. *Journal of European Early Childhood Education Research, 17*(3), 309–324.

Mashburn, A. J., & Pianta, R. C. (2006). Social relationships and school readiness. *Early Education and Development, 17*(1), 151–176.

Maxwell, K., & Eller, C. (1994). Children's transition to kindergarten. *Young Children, 49*(6), 56–63.

McClelland, M. M., & Morrison, F. J. (2003). The emergence of learning-related social skills in preschool children. *Early Childhood Research Quarterly, 18*(2), 206–224.

Merrell, K. W. (1989). Concurrent relationships between two behavioural rating scales for teachers: An examination of self control, social competence, and school behavioural adjustment. *Psychology in Schools, 26*(3), 267–271.

Merrell, C., & Tymms, P. (2001). Inattention, hyperactivity and impulsiveness: Their impact on academic achievement and progress. *British Journal of Educational Psychology, 71*(1), 43–56.

Merry, R. (2002). The construction of different identities within an early childhood centre: A case study. In A.-W. Dunlop & H. Fabian (Eds.), *Informing transition in the early years: Research, policy and practice* (pp. 45–60). Maidenhead: Open University Press.

Moore, B., Snow, C., & Poteat, G. (1988). Effects of variant types of child care experiences on the adaptive behaviour of kindergarten children. *American Journal of Orthopsychiatry, 58*(2), 297–303.

National Institute of Child Health and Human Development [NICHD] Early Child Care Research Network. (1996). Child care and the family – An opportunity to study development in context. *Family Matters, 44*(Winter), 33–35.

National Institute of Child Health and Human Development [NICHD] Early Child Care Research Network. (2001, April). *Further explanations of the detected effects of quality of early child care on socioemotional adjustment.* Paper presented at the Society for Research in Child Development Annual Conference. Minneapolis.

Petriwskyj, A. (2010). Diversity and inclusion in the early years. *International Journal of Inclusive Education, 14*(2), 195–212.

Pianta, R., & Steinberg, M. (1992). Teacher–child relationships and the process of adjusting to school. *New Directions for Child Development, 57*, 61–80.

Prior, M. (1996, September). *Learning and behavioural difficulties: Implications for intervention.* Free Public Lecture, The University of Melbourne.

Renwick, M. (1984). *To school at five: The transition from home or pre-school to school.* Wellington: NZCER.

Reynolds, A., Weissberg, R., & Kasprow, W. (1992). Prediction of early social and academic adjustment of children from the inner city. *American Journal of Community Psychology, 20*(5), 599–624.

Richards, M. M., & Steele, R. G. (2007). Children's self-reported coping strategies: The role of defensiveness and repressive adaptation. *Anxiety, Stress and Coping, 20*(2), 209–222.

Rimm-Kaufman, S. E., Pianta, R. C., & Cox, M. J. (2000). Teachers' judgements of problems in the transition to kindergarten. *Early Childhood Research Quarterly, 15*(2), 147–166.

Rydell, A. M. (1989). School adjustment, school performance and peer relations among first-graders in a Swedish suburban area. *Scandinavian Journal of Psychology, 30*(4), 284–295.

Sattler, J. (1988). *Assessment of children* (3rd ed.). San Diego: Jerome M. Sattler.

Skinner, D., Bryant, D., Coffman, J., & Campbell, F. (1998). Creating risk and promise: Children's and teachers' co-constructions in the cultural world of kindergarten. *The Elementary School Journal, 98*(4), 297–310.

Spence, S. H. (1998). A measure of anxiety symptoms among children. *Behaviour Research and Therapy, 36*(5), 545–566.

Taylor, J. (1998). *Life at six: Life chances and beginning school.* Fitzroy: Brotherhood of St. Laurence.

Teltsch, T., & Breznitz, Z. (1988). The effect of school entrance age on academic achievement and social-emotional adjustment of children. *Journal of Genetic Psychology, 149*(4), 471–483.

Wesley, P. W., & Buysse, V. (2003). Making meaning of school readiness in schools and communities. *Early Childhood Research Quarterly, 18*(3), 351–375.

Wildenger, L. K., McIntyre, L. L., Fiese, B. H., & Eckert, T. L. (2008). Children's daily routines during kindergarten transition. *Early Childhood Education Journal, 36*(1), 69–74.

Chapter 7
Transitions and Emergent Writers

Noella Mackenzie

7.1   Introduction

Writing is understood to be a creative or conventional means of making meaning, composing and recording messages in ways that can be read. The writing transition to be discussed here is the transition from sign creation to sign use. Children's drawings are an example of sign creation, while standard or non-standard uses of conventional print are examples of sign use. Most children transition from sign creation to sign use in the period of time that includes the year before they start school and the first year of school. This transition is potentially complicated by five areas of possible mismatch between what happens in preschool classrooms and schools in regard to standards, curricula, assessment processes (Kagan et al. 2006 teachers' beliefs about children's print literacy development (Lynch 2009) and differing approaches to writing pedagogy in the two settings. I will consider how the preschool, including the proximal processes or forms of interaction evident within this environment, supports emergent writers; consider how that may be different to the more formal school environment; and examine some of the possible issues for emergent writers as they transition from one environment to the other. While the home environment is recognised as the most influential and ongoing environment (Davis-Kean 2005; Farver et al. 2006; Foster et al. 2005; Hattie 2009; Neuman et al. 2008), it is not the focus of the study discussed here.

N. Mackenzie (✉)
Charles Sturt University, Albury Wodonga, Australia
e-mail: nmackenzie@csu.edu.au

B. Perry et al. (eds.), *Transitions to School - International Research, Policy and Practice*,   89
International perspectives on early childhood education and development 9,
DOI 10.1007/978-94-007-7350-9_7, © Springer Science+Business Media Dordrecht 2014

7.2   Context

The study informing this chapter is part of an ongoing programme of research, which began in 2007, and focuses on emergent writing and the teaching/learning processes that support this journey. In 2010, the research included an investigation of children's writing during the last 6 months of preschool. Data were gathered from early childhood educators in schools, preschools and long day care facilities and children, over the course of the study. Twenty-three early childhood educators working in preschools or the preschool room in long day care facilities provided the data informing this chapter.

Many Australian children participate in a preschool programme before they start school. Preschools and most long day care facilities offer preschool programmes for children who are 3 years of age or older, but have not yet started school. In Australia, teachers with a Bachelor of Education (Early Childhood) may teach in a preschool, long day care facility or a primary school. The Australian Government Department of Education, Employment and Workplace Relations (DEEWR) (2009) reforms are seeking to ensure that early childhood graduates with 4 years of training operate all preschool programmes. It is therefore becoming increasingly more common for preschool teachers to have Early Childhood qualifications at a graduate level. Throughout this chapter, I use the term preschool teacher when referring to those early childhood educators who work in preschools or run the preschool programme in a long day care facility. The first year of formal schooling in Australia has a number of different names including Kindergarten (NSW, ACT), Preparatory (Victoria, Queensland) and Reception (South Australia). Throughout this chapter, I use the term kindergarten, to refer to the first year of school and kindergarten teacher to refer to the teachers who are teaching children in the first year of formal schooling.

7.3   Theoretical Perspectives

Bronfenbrenner (1994) is credited with the development of an ecological model of human development, which considers human development within the context of a number of interacting environments. At least three external environments affect the literacy learning of most young Australian children between the ages of three and six. These environments are the home, the child's prior-to-school setting and the school he or she attends. Each of these environments includes the relevant persons, objects, symbols and opportunities to engage in learning. From an ecological perspective, learning takes place because of interactions between children and other children, children and adults, adults and other adults (e.g. teachers and parents), children and objects, and children and symbols within an environment. According to Bronfenbrenner and Morris (1998), 'human development evolves through processes of progressively more complex reciprocal interaction between an active, evolving biopsychological human organism and the persons, objects, and symbols in its immediate external environment' (p. 996). 'Proximal processes' or 'forms of interaction in the immediate environment' (Bronfenbrenner and Morris 1998, p. 996) are therefore the primary engines for development. The interactions that promote learning may be further understood by reference to the work of Lev Vygotsky (1997). According to Vygotsky, development cannot be separated from its social context, children construct knowledge, and language plays a central role in mental development (Bodrova and Leong 2007). What adults or peers point out to a learner influences the knowledge that the learner constructs. The adult's ideas 'mediate what and how the child will learn; they act as a filter in a sense, determining which ideas' (Bodrova and Leong 2007, p. 9) the child will learn.

7.3.1 Becoming a Writer

Writing is about meaning making or composing. It is one of the methods used by humans to record and communicate ideas, feelings, personal reflections, stories, discoveries, history, facts, laws, etc. Writing is complex and entails the interaction of cognitive and physical factors involving the hand, eye and both sides of the brain. Writing has both graphic and linguistic dimensions (Haas Dyson 1985), differing from speech, signing and reading because it leaves visible traces (Tolchinsky 2006). According to Byrnes and Wasik (2009), writing skills rival reading skills in their importance to being successful in school and in life.

Dyson (2001) suggests that 'the act of composing - the deliberate manipulation of meaning – occurs first in more directly representative media, among them gesture, play and drawing', as children create messages using 'multiple symbolic media' (p. 129). An important developmental transition takes place as children realise that speech can be recorded and the marks in books or on the computer mean something (Tolchinsky 2006; Vygotsky 1997). They notice that others around them are making marks on paper, texting on the phone, typing on a keyboard or reading and start to make their own marks on paper, walls or the ground, the computer, tablet or phone. They begin the process by experimenting with drawing and scribble. Scribbles gradually become 'writing like' with linearity, appropriate directionality, individual 'letter like' symbols and non-phonetic strings of letters. Over time, children learn the conventional forms of writing used in their society (Chan et al. 2008). While some theorists argue for a linear progression of writing stages (Ferreiro and Teberosky 1982; Kamii et al. 2001), others suggest that meaning making at this early stage involves multiple forms of media, and children demonstrate considerable variability in their methods of engaging with the writing process (Clay 1975; Kenner 2000; Tolchinsky 2006). Drawing is one of the early forms of meaning making, which may be described as sign creation.

Learning to write is, therefore, a transitional process whereby children move from producing their own creative forms to learning to produce messages using the conventional sign system of their cultural context. Parents, siblings, peers and teachers act as mediators between child and text, assisting the 'young learner's gradual

Fig. 7.1 A recipe for
broccoli soup by Charlie,
aged 4½

transition from assisted to unassisted performance' (Steward 1995, p. 13) although
the environment and resources within the environment also play a role. Up to age
three, writing and drawing are indistinguishable, nonrepresentational graphic products (sign creation), although between the ages of 3 and 4, action plans for writing
and drawing differ, even if the end products look similar (Tolchinsky 2006).

Tolchinsky (2006), argues that 'by the age of four, children's writing already
appears as a linearly arranged string of distinctive marks separated by regular spac-
ing' (p. 87) and children create letter shapes based upon those provided in their
environment. Children's own names constitute the first meaningful and consistently
written text (Tolchinsky 2006), and they use the letters from their names as a reposi-
tory of conventional letter shapes (Drouin and Harmon 2009; Welsch et al. 2003).
If left to their own devices, there is an important period of overlay, when children
produce texts, which incorporate a mix of sign creation (drawing) and elements
of the sign system they are beginning to learn (Mackenzie 2011). For example, in
Fig. 7.1, Charlie (aged 4½) has written a recipe for broccoli soup and shows that he
understands the need for letters and words in his recipe. In Fig. 7.2, he has drawn an
underwater scene, with little use of letters/words. The two works were both created
at home, two days apart. While Charlie was yet to have received any formalised
instruction in writing, he showed his understanding of the difference between drawing
and writing and had a clear purpose for each.

Fig. 7.2 Underwater sea
creatures by Charlie, aged 4½

7.4   Implications for Practice and Research

Early childhood literacy is regarded as 'the single best investment for enabling children to develop skills that will likely benefit them for a lifetime' (Dickinson and Neuman 2006, p. 1). Opportunities for literacy learning come from children's engagement with people, objects and symbols within the environments in which they participate. The process of becoming literate, however, is complex and takes time. A literate person is defined by Wing Jan (2009) as someone who has the 'skills and knowledge to create, locate, analyse, comprehend and use a variety of written, visual, aural and multi-modal texts for a range of purposes, audiences and contexts' (p. 3). An unhappy or traumatic transition into school literacy may lead to frustration, avoidance and an ongoing negative attitude towards school literacy. In contrast, successful early engagement with school literacy often leads to future success and a positive attitude towards school and literacy. Explanations of success or failure to engage with school literacy often refer to children's intelligence (Rowe 1994), background or socioeconomic status (Bradley and Corwyn 2002; D'Angiulli et al. 2004). While intelligence, background and socioeconomic circumstances provide part of the story, it can also be enlightening to examine what is happening in and across the various learning environments in which children are engaged.

Learning to write is an important part of becoming literate, playing a key role in later reading and literacy skills (National Early Literacy Panel (NELP) 2008). If adults working with children in the various learning environments have consistent or complimentary approaches to supporting children as they transition from their own forms of meaning making (sign creation) to conventional forms of meaning making (sign use), children are more likely to feel able to successfully engage with the writing process in all its forms. This requires adults in prior-to-school learning environments to be cognisant and supportive of the ways early writing is approached at school, particularly in kindergarten. Likewise, kindergarten teachers should understand, value and build on the approaches to early writing used in prior-to-school settings. In other words, the more the proximal processes or forms of interaction evident within each environment are supportive of one another, or at least not contradictory, the more likely it is that a child will transition from sign creation to sign use without disruption.

7.5   Learning Environments: Preschool and School

While it is acknowledged that the home and childcare settings are equally important literacy learning environments, the two environments being discussed here are those of the preschool (or preschool room in long day care facilities) and the first year of formal schooling (kindergarten). In Australia, children must be enrolled in school by the age of six, unless parents register with the relevant state or territory education authority to home school their children (Board of Studies, NSW 2011). Some children start school in New South Wales (NSW), Australia, as young as 4 years and 6 months, while others may not begin until they are 5 years and 6 months or older. This age range is a result of the policy which requires children to turn five by July of the year they begin school, a policy of one intake per year (at the commencement of the school year) and a voluntary trend towards delayed entry for some children from higher-income families (Datar 2006). Given the delayed entry to school for some children, this means that preschool teachers may be catering for children from 3 to 6 years of age. This also suggests that children between the ages of 4 ½ and 6 years of age could be attending preschool or school.

Preschools in Australia tend to place an emphasis on care, a healthy environment, play, and child-centred methods, while schools emphasise subjects, knowledge, skills, lessons and student assessments although both are seen as educational institutions (Margetts 2002). These differences have also been noted in New Zealand (Peters 2000), the United Kingdom (Cassidy 2005; Kwon 2002; Stephen and Cope 2003) and Iceland (Einarsdóttir 2006). Emergent writing is fostered within preschool environments through learning opportunities which are 'open-ended, allowing the learner to surprise the teacher and expand any aspect of his or her existing knowledge' (Clay 2001, p. 12). According to the *Early Years Framework for Australia* (EYLF) (DEEWR 2009, p. 38), literacy is the 'capacity, confidence and disposition to use language in all its forms'. The EYLF suggests that literacy incorporates music, movement, dance, storytelling, visual arts, media and drama, as well as talking, listening, viewing, reading and writing. Children are expected to become effective communicators who can:

- Interact verbally and non-verbally with others for a range of purposes
- Engage with a range of texts and gain meaning from these texts
- Express ideas and make meaning using a range of media
- Begin to understand how symbols and pattern systems work
- Use information and communication technologies to access information investigate ideas and represent their thinking (DEEWR 2009, p. 39)

The processes of emergent literacy or emergent writing are not specifically discussed within the EYLF, and interpretation of the above points is left to each preschool teacher. Learning is defined as 'a natural process of exploration that children engage in from birth as they expand their intellectual, physical, social, emotional and creative capacities' (DEEWR 2009, p. 46). Intentional, deliberate, purposeful and thoughtful teaching is also described in the EYLF (DEEWR 2009, p.15). Early childhood educators are required to 'promote learning' but they are also required to 'teach children skills and techniques that will enhance their capacity for self-expression and communication' (DEEWR 2009, p. 42).

From the very start, the emphasis in schools is on teaching for learning, in contrast to the preschool approach of learning through play (Margetts 2002). In schools, the approach is more structured and planned; children have limited influence over what they get to do and teachers work from a programme that follows a required syllabus or curriculum. Clay (1991) argues that the school also 'represents external evaluation; opportunities for success and failure; the setting for peer group formation and social evaluation; and the initiation of a set of experiences which in adulthood may lead to advancement of economic status' (p. 55). There is also a shift in language, as children become students, as seen in the following excerpt from the K-6 English Syllabus:

> Students produce simple texts that demonstrate an awareness of the basic grammar and punctuation needed. Students know and use letters and sounds of the alphabet to attempt to spell known words and use most lower and upper case letters appropriately to construct sentences. Students explore the use of computer technology to construct texts. (Board of Studies, NSW 2007, p. 12)

While preschool teachers gather data through observation and detailed anecdotal records, school systems have a range of assessment tools they use, beginning at school entry. For example, in NSW all kindergarten children are administered the *Best Start Assessment* (NSW Department of Education and Training 2010), when they enter school. The information gathered about children's current literacy and numeracy knowledge and understandings is designed to assist teachers to plan teaching and learning programmes aimed at building on the literacy and numeracy knowledge children have when they begin school.

There is more verbal instruction in schools than there is in preschools along with a more formal focus on literacy, numeracy and the need to use pencils and small equipment. Margetts (2002) suggests that schools provide 'a cognitive curricula approach including restrictions on the use of time which emphasise the work/play distinction, confining gross motor activities to physical education lessons and playtime, less art and tactile experiences, and less opportunity for imaginative play' (p. 105) than preschools. In school classrooms, literacy instruction is often divided into a number of strands, which are taught discretely: reading, writing, listening and speaking spelling, handwriting, grammar, phonics and phonemic awareness. Literacy instruction may also include viewing, representing and the organised use of technologies that support literacy. In many NSW kindergarten classrooms, the teacher applies the 'Language, Learning and Literacy' (L3) kinder-garten classroom intervention, which identifies explicit instruction in reading and writing (NSW Department of Education and Training 2012). These approaches seem likely to continue as the new Australian Curriculum organises English into three strands: Language, Literature and Literacy (Australian Curriculum Assessment and Reporting Authority (ACARA) 2012) with the literacy strand including reading, writing, listening, speaking, vocabulary development, spelling, handwriting and phonics. In the current era, there is also a sense of urgency in many kindergarten classrooms, as teachers deal with pressures of accountability (Genishi and Dyson 2009), and a contemporary push down of the curriculum (Elkind 2003; Genishi and Dyson 2009) designed to raise standards in literacy (Stephenson and Parsons 2007).

7.6   The Study

The study informing this discussion took place in late 2010 and involved 23 pre-school teachers. The participants were all female. Fifteen participants had a Bachelor of Education or a Bachelor of Teaching with a specialisation in Early Childhood Education. The remaining eight participants had either a Diploma of Teaching or Diploma of Children's Services. Two of the participants did not have Early Childhood qualifications. Experience working in prior-to-school settings ranged from 1 to 30 years, with an average of 11 years. Seven participants had experience teaching in schools as well as in prior-to-school settings. Twelve participants were working in community preschools, three in preschools attached to schools and the remaining eight worked in the preschool room in long day care facilities. All partici-pants identified themselves as preschool teachers. Teachers in preschools attached to schools had significant contact with the teachers in the school, attending staff meetings, sharing resources, visiting classrooms etc. None of the preschool teachers working in long day care facilities had close relationships with the schools that their children would attend. The preschool teachers in community preschools had varied contact with the schools their children would attend.

Open-ended interviews, which took between 30 and 105 min, were conducted at venues and times chosen by the participants. The interviews were recorded, tran-scribed and returned to the participants for comment. This provided participants with the opportunity to remove or clarify any comments made throughout the inter-view. A number of participants returned their transcript having added information or clarified original responses. Data were also gathered from the children although those data are not discussed in this chapter.

The participants discussed how they were starting to work with the EYLF (DEEWR 2009), but none mentioned the expectation of 'intentional, deliberate, purposeful and thoughtful forms of teaching' (DEEWR 2009, p. 38) when asked to share their approaches to supporting emergent writing. This is consistent with the earlier findings of David et al. (2001). Instead, processes for supporting children's exploration of writing at preschool included the following:

- The provision of a variety of writing implements (as part of a writing centre, literacy corner or to support role play activities)
- Modelling drawing and painting
- Encouraging children to draw their experiences
- Modelling words and letters (in particular writing children's names on their art works)
- Teaching children how to write their names, if and only if a child indicated to the preschool teacher that they wished to learn to do this for themselves
- Making cards to celebrate occasions (e.g. Mother's Day)
- Acting as scribe for children

The study findings suggest that preschool teachers see their role as providing opportunities for children to explore writing through play, but not to proactively seek or initiate opportunities to interact with them in ways that might assist them to move along the writing continuum.

> Within our creative play area we set up an office or a restaurant or something like that . . . we've always got heaps and heaps of the old blank pads or old forms . . . (Study participant)

This is consistent with the findings of Cassidy (2005): 'Children are encouraged to initiate their own learning activities and to explore and develop their intellectual, physical, emotional, social, moral and communication skills with play as the medium for development' (p. 144). However, this seems counter to Vygotsky's notion of how adults (or peers) support children's learning and contrary to Steward's (1995) notion of how a more experienced other (parent, sibling, peer or teacher) acts as a mediator assisting 'young learner's gradual transition from assisted to unassisted performance' (p. 13). Only two participants indicated that they ever took a 'teaching' approach with older children who showed a particular interest in learning more about letters and words. They were quick to explain that this only happened on rare occasions. There were no expectations that children would have achieved any specific writing benchmarks or standards before leaving preschool, although being able to write their own name was desirable. The following participant's description of the writing journey children take in the year before they start school is representative of the comments made by most participants.

> It will start off and it will be just your little scribbled jottings and then you'll notice that they're writing letters, strings of letters and then towards the end of the year they'll be writing words. . . (Study participant)

It would appear that the preschool environment is a place for children to explore writing, if they wish, when they wish and how they wish.

7.7   Challenges and Issues

An emergent writer is destined to find that the supports and challenges within the school environment are quite different to that of the preschool. The discontinuities experienced as children move from one environment to another may be stressful, and although Einarsdóttir (2006) suggests that most children adapt quickly to the social demands of school, an unsuccessful transition into school literacy may lead to 'frustration, avoidance and an ongoing negative attitude towards school literacy' (Mackenzie et al. 2011, p. 284). Moyles (2007) argues that the vital element in all transitions is the 'teachers', practitioners' and parents' skills in understanding how the change affects the individual child' (p. xvi). The adults involved should, according to Moyles (2007), be on the same wavelength in order to support the transition, as new 'curriculum expectations ... build on ... children's previous learning experiences and understanding' (p. xvii). For this to occur, preschool teachers need a thorough knowledge of what is expected of emergent writers when they begin school. Likewise, kindergarten teachers need to understand how writing has been approached and supported in the preschool, and wherever possible, parents should have knowledge of what is expected of their young writers in both contexts. The sharing of knowledge between the three contexts would help to support emergent writers as they transition from preschool to school. However, while preschool teachers generally maintain regular and detailed observational records of children's cognitive, affective and behavioural progress, 'this rich information is rarely passed-on or effectively communicated to staff in the primary schools' (Thomson et al. 2005, p. 196). Kindergarten teachers have little, if any, contact with preschool teachers and minimal opportunities to discuss children with parents at the time of enrolment in school. This can create major challenges and issues for children.

When asked about the transition from preschool to school, participants often replied that this was something that schools organised through parents and rarely involved them. They were not aware of what happened in the "transition programmes" but they knew that they had children attending a variety of different transition programmes leading up to Christmas. Participants from preschools attached to schools had significant contact with teachers in the school. They attended staff meetings, shared resources and the children visited classrooms quite regularly. Despite this contact, they had very different attitudes and approaches to early writing. None of the preschool teachers working in long day care facilities had close relationships with the schools that their children would attend. Preschool teachers in community preschools had varied contact with the schools as illustrated by the following comment.

> We talk with X School a lot and they listen to us about things like children's strengths and needs and who would they best be grouped with or not grouped with . . . Y School has not been open to that sort of communication. (Study participant)

According to a number of participants, most conversations between preschool teachers and kindergarten teachers are conducted by telephone. They claimed that it was rare for kindergarten teachers to visit their preschools, but if they did, it was usually only to find out if there were any children with physical, learning or behavioural problems.

> They don't really want to know about the kids . . . it's just if X has fine motor difficulties or other problems . . . now I suppose that's maybe the time factor or something but it's a bit disheartening for us because the preschools would love to have them [Kindergarten teachers] come in . . . to see the kids here. (Study participant)

In a few cases, the preschool and local school did have a positive connection, sometimes facilitated by the close proximity of the local school and/or the interest of individual staff. Where this did happen there seemed to be a very positive two-way communication although this had not lead to a common understanding or complimentary approach to emergent writing.

> The kindergarten teachers come here and they actually become familiar with the children, they do a little activity with the children here and read a story . . . and then in term 4 we go to the school and take the children into the classroom and they meet the teachers and the parents are able to come along . . . (Study participant)

According to a number of participants, it is impossible to work closely with all of the schools that their children feed into. One preschool had children transitioning to 12 different schools, making coordination with kindergarten teachers unworkable.

> We find it hard because we feed so many schools, we visit X School, because it is the closest but we couldn't go to all the potential schools. (Study participant)

None of the participants could talk confidently or knowledgeably about how the schools in their area approached literacy instruction. Most referred back to what they thought happened based upon their training or the experiences of their own children. Discussions with participants about transition to school focused on social issues, although when pressed to discuss transition issues related to literacy, most said they wanted their children to know how to recognise and write their names on entry to kindergarten. The following comment is representative of those made by participants when they were invited to discuss what they thought schools expected from them in regard to emergent literacy:

> It is quite tricky; we get different feedback from different schools. Some schools don't want us to do too much because they're worried that we might do it in the wrong way or a different way to the school. (Study participant)

Other preschool teachers talked about running their preschool sessions a little more school like leading up to Christmas (Australian school years run from February to December), although only two had actually been into a school classroom in recent times to see what was happening in the first year of school. The school-like approach tended to revolve around the reading of picture books to the whole group, completion of worksheets focused on phonics or the use of commercial phonics programmes. It is evident from the data that the participants involved in this study were uncertain of approaches to early literacy instruction in schools.

7.8   Future Directions

Each year, thousands of children move from a preschool environment to a school environment and most start school with anticipation, excitement and expectation. Their challenge is to successfully transition from 'one set of rules, understandings and expectations to quite a different set' (Elkind 2003, p. 43). Such a big step should be scaffolded to ensure that children make the shift safely. The writing transition is only one of the many transitions taking place as children move from preschool to school. However, given the important role of writing in a child's literacy learning future, it is arguably worth consideration. Children, by the very nature of their ages, individual interests, the environments they are part of and the opportunities they have experienced, will be at different stages on the writing continuum when they start preschool and then again when they begin school. It seems likely that in Australia there will be children in their final year of preschool, who may want to explore the conventions and structures of text in ways that go beyond self-exploration. Likewise, there may be children in kindergarten who need time and opportunity to explore writing in a more play-based approach. To cater for this overlap requires a greater understanding of the writing transition from both sides of the school gate.

Preschools do not need to become kindergarten classrooms. Nor do kindergarten classrooms need to mirror preschools. Shared understandings of what it means to be literate and how children become literate, some shared approaches to emergent writing and some shared knowledge of the learning journeys of children prior to school would support the writing transition. By bringing together, the teachers from the two external environments that interact as a child begins school, and creating some congruency between the proximal processes within each, continuities may be created and shifts may be supported, which would sustain the emergent writer. Given that preschool teachers and kindergarten teachers have similar, if not the same, qualifications, it should not be difficult for these two groups of professionals to share an understanding of how to support children as they make this important transition from sign creation to sign use.

References

Australian Curriculum Assessment and Reporting Authority (ACARA). (2012). *Australian Curriculum* (Version 3.0). http://www.australiancurriculum.edu.au/ Accessed 16 Oct 2012.

Board of Studies, NSW. (2007). *English K-6 syllabus*. Sydney: Board of Studies.

Board of Studies, NSW. (2011). *Home education in NSW information package*. Sydney: Board of Studies. http://www.boardofstudies.nsw.edu.au/parents/pdf_doc/home-edu-info-pack-11.pdf Accessed 18 Oct 2012.

Bodrova, E., & Leong, D. J. (2007). *Tools of the mind: The Vygotskian approach to early childhood education* (2nd ed.). Upper Saddle River: Pearson.

Bradley, R. H., & Corwyn, R. F. (2002). Socioeconomic status and child development. *Annual Review of Psychology, 53*(1), 371.

Bronfenbrenner, U. (1994). *Ecological models of human development* (2nd ed., Vol. 3). Oxford: Elsevier.

Bronfenbrenner, U., & Morris, P. A. (1998). The ecology of developmental processes. In W. Damon & R. N. Lerner (Eds.), *Handbook of child psychology: Theoretical models of human development* (5th ed., Vol. 1, pp. 993–1029). New York: Wiley.

Byrnes, J. P., & Wasik, B. A. (2009). *Language and literacy development: What educators need to know*. New York: The Guilford Press.

Cassidy, M. (2005). 'They do it anyway': A study of Primary 1 teachers' perceptions of children's transition into primary education. *Early Years, 25*(2), 143–153.

Chan, L., Cheng, Z. J., & Chan, L. F. (2008). Chinese preschool children's literacy development: from emergent to conventional writing. *Early Years, 28*(2), 135–148.

Clay, M. M. (1975). *What did I write? Beginning writing behaviour*. Auckland: Heinemann.

Clay, M. M. (1991). *Becoming literate: The construction of inner control*. Auckland: Heinemann.

Clay, M. M. (2001). *Change over time in children's literacy development*. Portsmouth: Heinemann.

D'Angiulli, A., Siegal, L. S., & Hertzman, C. (2004). Schooling, socioeconomic context and literacy development. *Educational Psychology, 24*(6), 867–883.

Datar, A. (2006). Does delaying kindergarten entrance give children a head start? *Economics of Education Review, 25*(1), 43–62.

David, T., Goouch, K., & Jago, M. (2001). Cultural constructions of childhood and early literacy. *Reading, 35*(2), 47–53.

Davis-Kean, P. E. (2005). The influence of parent education and family income on child achievement: The indirect role of parental expectations and the home environment. *Journal of Family Psychology, 19*(2), 294–304.

Department of Education Employment and Workplace Relations (DEEWR). (2009). *Belonging, being and becoming: The early years learning framework for Australia*. Canberra: Department of Education Employment and Workplace Relations (DEEWR).

Dickinson, D. K., & Neuman, S. B. (Eds.). (2006). *Handbook of early literacy research* (Vol. 2). New York: Guildford.

Drouin, M., & Harmon, J. (2009). Name writing and letter knowledge in preschoolers: Incongruities in skills and the usefulness of name writing as a developmental indicator. *Early Childhood Research Quarterly, 24*(3), 263–270.

Dyson, A. H. (2001). Writing and children's symbolic repertoires: Development unhinged. In S. B. Neuman & D. K. Dickinson (Eds.), *Handbook of early literacy research* (Vol. 1, pp. 126–141). New York: The Guilford Press.

Einarsdóttir, J. (2006). From pre-school to primary school: When different contexts meet. *Scandinavian Journal of Educational Research, 50*(2), 165–184.

Elkind, D. (2003). The first grade challenge: Transition stress. *Childcare Information Exchange* (November/December), 42–43.

Farver, J. A. M., Xu, Y., Eppe, S., & Lonigan, C. J. (2006). Home environments and young Latino children's school readiness. *Early Childhood Research Quarterly, 21*(2), 196–212.

Ferreiro, E., & Teberosky, A. (1982). *Literacy before schooling*. Exeter: Heinemann Educational Books.

Foster, M. A., Lambert, R., Abbott-Shim, M., McCarty, F., & Franze, S. (2005). A model of home learning environment and social risk factors in relation to children's emergent literacy and social outcomes. *Early Childhood Research Quarterly, 20*(1), 13–36.

Genishi, C., & Dyson, A. H. (2009). *Children, language and literacy: Diverse learners in diverse times*. New York/London: Teachers College Press.

Haas Dyson, A. (1985). Individual differences in emerging writing. In M. Farr (Ed.), *Advances in writing research* (Vol. 1, pp. 59–126). Norwood: Ablex Publishers.

Hattie, J. (2009). *Visible learning: A synthesis of over 800 meta-analyses relating to achievement*. Abingdon: Routledge.

Kagan, S. L., Carrol, J., Comer, J. P., & Catherine, S.-L. (2006). A missing link in early childhood transitions. *Young Children, 61*(5), 26–30.

Kamii, C., Long, R., & Manning, M. (2001). Kindergarteners' development toward "invented" spelling and a glottographic theory. *Linguistics & Education, 12*(2), 195–210.

Kenner, C. (2000). Symbols make text: A social semiotic analysis of writing in a multilingual nursery. *Written Language & Literacy, 3*(2), 235–266.

Kwon, Y.-I. (2002). Changing curriculum for early childhood education in England. *Early Childhood Research & Practice, 4*(2). http://ecrp.uiuc.edu/v4n2/kwon.html Accessed 5 Oct 2012.

Lynch, J. (2009). Preschool teachers' beliefs about children's print literacy development. *Early Years, 29*(2), 191–203.

Mackenzie, N. M. (2011). From drawing to writing: What happens when you shift teaching priorities in the first six months of school? *Australian Journal of Language & Literacy, 34*(3), 322–340.

Mackenzie, N. M., Hemmings, B., & Kay, R. (2011). How does teaching experience affect attitudes towards literacy learning and teaching in the early years? *Issues in Educational Research, 21*(3), 281–293.

Margetts, K. (2002). Transition to school – Complexity and diversity. *European Early Childhood Education Research Journal, 10*(2), 103–114.

Moyles, J. (2007). Foreword. In A.-W. Dunlop & H. Fabian (Eds.), *Informing transitions in the early years: Research, policy and practice* (pp. xv–xvii). Maidenhead: Open University Press.

National Early Literacy Panel (NELP). (2008). *Developing early literacy: Report of the national early literacy panel.* Washington, DC: National Association for the Education of Young Children.

Neuman, S. B., Koh, S., & Dwyer, J. (2008). CHELLO: The child/home environmental language and literacy observation. *Early Childhood Research Quarterly, 23*, 159–172.

NSW Department of Education and Training. (2010). *Best start.* http://www.curriculumsupport. education.nsw.gov.au/beststart/index.htm Accessed 1 Aug 2010.

NSW Department of Education and Training. (2012). *Language, learning and literacy (L3).* http:// www.curriculumsupport.education.nsw.gov.au/beststart/lll/index.htm Accessed 12 Oct 2012.

Peters, S. (2000, August). *Multiple perspectives on continuity in early learning and the transition to school.* Paper presented at the "Complexity, diversity and multiple perspectives in early childhood" Tenth European Early Childhood Education Research Association Conference, London.

Rowe, D. C. (1994). *The limits of family influence.* New York: The Guilford Press.

Stephen, C., & Cope, P. (2003). An inclusive perspective on transition to primary school. *European Educational Research Journal, 2*(2), 262–276.

Stephenson, M., & Parsons, M. (2007). Expectations: Effects of curriculum change as viewed by children, parents and practitioners. In A.-W. Dunlop & H. Fabian (Eds.), *Informing transitions in the early years: Research, policy and practice* (pp. 137–148). Maidenhead: Open University Press.

Steward, E. (1995). *Beginning writers in the zone of proximal development.* Hillsdale: Lawrence Erlbaum Associates.

Thomson, S., Rowe, K., Underwood, C., & Peck, R. (2005). *Numeracy in the early years: Project Good Start (Final Report).* Canberra: Department of Education Science and Training. http:// www.acer.edu.au/documents/GOODSTART_FinalReport.pdf. Accessed 10 Oct 2012.

Tolchinsky, L. (2006). The emergence of writing. In C. A. MacArthur, S. Graham, & J. Fitzgerald (Eds.), *Handbook of writing research* (pp. 83–95). New York: The Guilford Press.

Vygotsky, L. S. (1997). *The collected works of L. S. Vygotsky* (Vol. 4). (R. W. Rieber & A. S. Carton, Trans.). New York: Plenum Press

Welsch, J. G., Sullivan, A., & Justice, L. M. (2003). That's my letter!: What preschoolers' name writing representations tell us about emergent literacy knowledge. *Journal of Literacy Research, 35*(2), 757–776.

Wing Jan, L. (2009). *Write ways: Modelling writing forms* (3rd ed.). South Melbourne: Oxford.

Part II
Borderlands, Life Course and Rites of Passage

Chapter 8
Chasms, Bridges and Borderlands: A Transitions Research 'Across the Border' from Early Childhood Education to School in New Zealand

Sally Peters

8.1 Introduction

Theories are set within particular ways of seeing the world. 'Different discourses produce different kinds of explanations – they even draw our attention to different kinds of problems' (Claibourne and Drewery 2009, p. 23). When considering theoretical approaches, it is important to see theory as a resource for understanding (Claibourne and Drewery 2009), rather than a justification for universal claims. The theories themselves are often shaped and changed as their authors refine their ideas.

Like a number of other transitions researchers, I have been drawn to ecological and sociocultural theoretical approaches to provide a framework for understanding transitions. These approaches acknowledge the complexity inherent in understanding the multiple transactional factors that influence each child's learning and transition experiences and the diversity that exists within groups as well as between groups of children.

8.2 Theoretical Perspectives

Bronfenbrenner's ecological model, which forms the basis of my theoretical foundation, was developed and refined over time. Later iterations (e.g. Bronfenbrenner and Morris 1997) offer a dynamic structure, at the core of which is the notion that developmental pathways vary as a result of proximal processes, the interaction of individual and environment over time. The power of such processes to influence development

S. Peters (✉)
University of Waikato, Hamilton, New Zealand
e-mail: speters@waikato.ac.nz

B. Perry et al. (eds.), *Transitions to School - International Research, Policy and Practice*,   105
International perspectives on early childhood education and development 9,
DOI 10.1007/978-94-007-7350-9_8, © Springer Science+Business Media Dordrecht 2014

varies as a function of the characteristics of the person, the immediate and more remote environments and the time periods in which the transactions take place.

Key features of the person in this model are the individual's dispositions, resources (e.g. ability, experience) and demand characteristics (that invite or discourage reactions from the social environment). These interact with features of the environment that inhibit, permit or invite engagement (Bronfenbrenner and Morris 1997). Environmental features of the immediate microsystem include interactions with people (who also have the individual characteristics described above), as well as with objects and symbols. This idea resonates with the approach to learning in the early childhood and school curriculum documents in New Zealand. The early childhood curriculum recognises that 'children learn through positive and reciprocal relationships with people, places, and things' (Ministry of Education 1996, p. 14). Similarly, the school curriculum notes the role in children's learning of interactions with 'people, places, ideas, and things' (Ministry of Education 2007, p. 12).

When applied to transitions research, Bronfenbrenner's ecological model draws attention to the patterns of activities, roles and relationships experienced in a given setting (microsystem) and the ways in which a child's positioning in the ecological environment is altered during a transition, as a result of entry into a new microsystem (Bronfenbrenner 1979). There can be a paradoxical sense of stepping up to the next level of the education system but also a step down in terms of status (Hallinan and Hallinan 1992, cited in Jindal-Snape and Miller 2010) as the early childhood 'expert' is positioned as a novice at school. In this process, 'the star of the crèche' can sometimes be transformed into 'a new entrant with problem behaviour' (Norris 1999). Understanding how these positions are shaped by the interactions within a particular setting, rather than due solely to an individual's characteristics, can add valuable explanatory insights. Almost any child is at risk of making a poor or less successful transition if their individual characteristics are incompatible with features of the environment they encounter. This understanding provides a focus for action as adjustments can be made to the contexts and strategies implemented to support more positive experiences (Peters 2010).

If development is thought of as a process of 'people's changing participation in the sociocultural activities of their communities' (Rogoff 2003, p. 52), the idea that transition to school may require a transformation of participation within the new learning community offers another lens on the process. Although Rogoff draws our attention to participation, rather than the internalisation of knowledge, Vygotsky's theory offers some perspectives on providing support or scaffolding in this process. He noted that '…a variety of internal development processes… are able to operate only when the child is interacting with people in his [sic] environment and in cooperation with his peers' (Vygotsky 1978, p. 90). Once these processes are internalised, they become part of the child's independent developmental achievement. The distance between what can be achieved independently, and the level of potential development as determined through problem solving under adult guidance or in collaboration with more capable peers, is described as the 'zone of proximal development' (Vygotsky 1978, p. 86).

Later Bruner (1985) proposed that the person offering support provides

a vicarious form of consciousness until such a time as the learner is able to master his [sic] own consciousness and control.... The tutor in effect performs the critical function of "scaffolding" the learning task to make it possible for the child, in Vygotsky's words, to internalize external knowledge and convert it into a tool for conscious control. (pp. 24–25)

With regard to transition, it is not only adults but older siblings and peers who can support the child within the zone of proximal development. In New Zealand, this approach is consistent with the Māori practice of tuakana/teina where an older child assists a younger one in his/her learning (Royal-Tangaere 1997). However, not all assistance in becoming a member in a new setting involves deliberate scaffolding. Some of the strategies children might use are observation, eavesdropping and imitation. Similar to anyone learning in an unfamiliar cultural setting, children may stay near trusted guides: watching what they do and getting involved where possible (Rogoff 2003). This view also supports the notion of allowing time for legitimate peripheral participation as newcomers move towards full participation in the sociocultural practices of a community (Lave and Wenger 1991). This may be particularly important in countries like New Zealand where enrolment practices mean that children often join an established class and may be faced with a range of potentially bewildering experiences such as sports events or school concerts, when they first arrive. The challenge however is to decide when and how to assist some children to move towards fuller participation.

Returning to the experience of transitioning from one microsystem to another, each with its activities, roles and relationships (Bronfenbrenner 1979), there is a potential link to the notion of 'rites of passage' which Van Gennep used to describe the various forms of ritual by which an individual comes to occupy a new position in a social structure (cited in Piddington 1957). Fabian (1998) applied this idea to school entry, looking at the preliminal rites (rites of separation), liminal rites (rites of transition) and postliminal rites (rites of incorporation) that form this process. Turner (1968, cited in James and Prout 1997, p. 247) noted in the liminal zone, demanding feats of endurance may be required from those being initiated, which implies that transition is an opportunity for change and some challenges could be expected. In earlier research (Peters 2004) it appeared that children who valued the new role of school pupil (perhaps because it provided status or opportunities they wanted, such as a child who was now able to join her older sister's gym class) were more likely to accept and navigate some challenges compared to children who did not seem to value the new role. While not articulated by the children as a rite of passage, the willingness to endure some initiation challenges to gain a new status means that it could be viewed as such.

External factors at other levels of the environment (meso-, exo- and macrosystems) also contribute to each individual's cycle of experience (Bronfenbrenner, 1979, 1986). The mesosystem comprises the interrelationships between the microsystems. Events in one microsystem can affect what happens in another (Bronfenbrenner 1986), so that experiences at school can impact on experiences at home and vice versa. The mesosystem also considers the connections between the microsystems, (e.g. a child's friends from early childhood settings may be present when the child starts school; siblings may be part of the current microsystems at both home and school). Respectful relationships and communication between settings are also important. For example, Pianta (2004) proposed that 'the quality of the parents' relationships with teachers, with school staff, and with the child's schooling' may be a key indicator of how successful a transition to school has been (p. 6). The mesosystem therefore provides another site to consider in relation to transitions.

These central levels of the ecological framework link to other theoretical approaches. One useful example is Bourdieu's (1997) notion of cultural capital and habitus. Brooker (2002) drew on Bourdieu's work to consider primary habitus, resulting from learning to be a child (in the microsystem of the family), and secondary habitus, learning to be a pupil (in the new microsystem at school). She described a continuum of advantage for children whose social and cultural capital was evident to their teachers and who experienced continuity between home and school. For others, learning to be a pupil meant learning to be someone quite different from their primary habitus. Thomson (2002) made a similar point in her proposal that we can picture children coming to school with 'virtual school bags' filled with knowledge, experiences and dispositions. In some contexts, schools only draw on the contents of selected bags, 'those whose resources match those required in the game of education' (Thomson and Hall 2008, p. 89). If this practice continues, the gap grows between the children whose 'virtual school bags' are opened and welcomed, when compared with those whose existing knowledge and dispositions are ignored (Thomson 2002). The idea of different habitus (as opposed to assuming all children from a similar background also have similar 'ways of being' and experiences) helps to explain findings such as those documented by Ledger (2000, p. 7), where children from wealthy, well-educated families, from the dominant culture (who one would assume had what Bourdieu (1997) described as both social and cultural capital), had transitions that were 'fraught with difficulties'. In these cases, their habitus, or the contents of their 'virtual backpacks', may not have been identified or valued.

The exosystem refers to settings that do not involve the developing person but affect, or are affected by, what happens in the microsystem (e.g. the parents' workplace, decision-making groups such as the school management or Board of Trustee groups). For example, parents who have tight working schedules may feel pressured in the mornings and find it difficult to take time to settle a new child at school; management groups can decide to support teachers at the beginning school level by reducing their out of classroom school duties (such as supervising road crossings or breaks) to increase their availability to children and families.

The macrosystem refers to the overriding beliefs, values, ideology, practices and so on that exist within a culture (Bronfenbrenner 1986). Theories and beliefs at the macrosystem level help to shape curriculum and pedagogy in each sector and inform people's thoughts about transition. They also include policies that determine the nature and number of educational transitions that children make and the age at which these typically happen.

Bronfenbrenner (1992) added the element of time to his model, noting that the environment is not a fixed entity. This is helpful, not only for thinking about the length of a transition process and changes in the child, family and school over time but also changes in the historical context and the dominant discourses that shape how education, children, families, etc., are viewed. Developmental processes are not only shaped by these changes, they also produce these changes in society (Bronfenbrenner and Morris 1997).

8.3   Implications for Practice and Research

My own research has been underpinned by a strong social justice perspective, which seeks to address some of the inequities in the practices and definitions described by Skinner et al. (1998):

> there are classroom practices and constructions that, even in the first weeks of school, begin moving some children into the track of school failure. That a child can be on a trajectory for school failure by the age of 5 has led us to examine closely how various meanings and practices, which are historically and culturally constructed, work to define both kindergarten teachers and children and place them in certain relationships vis-a-vis one another. (p. 307)

Although Furedi (2002) suggests that adults in the twenty-first century have been socialised to pathologise challenging events in ways that are unhelpful to children's development, the idea of 'rites of passage' indicates some challenges could be anticipated as part of attaining a new role. Simply to ignore difficulties that are beyond the children's abilities to negotiate for themselves raises important equity issues and therefore leads to research and practice implications.

The complexity inherent in understanding transitions through ecological and sociocultural lenses raises a number of challenges for researching transitions. Research is necessarily bounded by time, place and culture (Holliday 2002; Miles and Huberman 1994), and the data that are gathered and analysed form only a small segment of the much wider mélange of social life (Holliday 2002). In addition, the data that are gathered will be influenced by the preoccupations and agendas of the participants, including the researcher (Holliday 2002). The implications of this include the necessity to keep the bigger picture in mind while focusing on the segment(s) that are being researched and to acknowledge the preoccupations that drive particular studies. In New Zealand, kaupapa Māori research approaches (Bishop 1996, 1997) help to make these agendas visible to participants as well as researchers.

My early research on 'border crossing' (Peters 2004) involved an interpretive approach and explored detailed case studies over time, as children moved through their last months in early childhood education into the first year at school. Follow up interviews continued until the children were aged eight. The study provided insights into the complex interweaving of characteristics of individual children and their immediate and more remote environments, providing some understanding of the ways in which different patterns of experiences developed. Nevertheless, even with rich detail and thick description, only part of the picture was captured.

This early research was conducted when there was, in many settings in New Zealand, something of a chasm between prior-to-school early childhood education (ECE) and school in terms of curriculum, pedagogy, image of a learner, role of the family and so on. Hence, the children's journey to becoming a school pupil involved crossing a cultural as well as a physical border. Giroux's (1992) discussion of cultural borders could be appropriated to consider this experience and Mullholland and Wallace's (2000) analogy of 'border crossing' applied to children and their families as they made the transition journey to school. This connected with the theoretical ideas about supporting children through scaffolding and other ways to gain confidence in the new setting. It challenged the practice of focusing on the increased independence of the five-year-old and instead highlighted the value of fostering relationships with peers and keeping families informed. For example, at the time of the study, school visits were to be made by the child alone, and parents were discouraged from parent helping in the classroom until the child was 'settled'. Children were discouraged from playing with siblings at lunchtimes because 'brothers and sisters can be a bit protective'. The benefits of peer tutoring were acknowledged, but generally only within same-age groups. Over time, in many schools, all of these practices have changed in favour of a more sociocultural approach to learning.

The temporal dimension of the ecological approach acknowledges the changes to the expectations and events in the wider society (Bronfenbrenner and Morris 1997). Since my first transition study, described above (Peters 2004), a review of the school curriculum in New Zealand has drawn on national and international perspectives regarding what might be seen as valuable learning in the twenty-first century. This led to a new approach to learning, within which key competencies (such as relating to others and participating and contributing) were central. The resulting changes mean that the key competencies in the school curriculum (Ministry of Education 2007) now align with the strands of the early childhood curriculum Te Whāriki (Ministry of Education 1996). The school curriculum also includes explicit statements about supporting the transition from early childhood education to school, including building on and making connections with early childhood learning and experiences (see Ministry of Education 2007, pp. 41–42). In addition, the aspirations for children underpinning Te Whāriki (Ministry of Education 1996) sit comfortably with the vision for learners at school (Ministry of Education 2007).

These curriculum changes, and the research opportunities that eventuated, sharpened my focus on children's learning journeys, a key thread within their complex transition journeys. The curriculum changes provided a potential bridge to support many aspects of border crossing between early childhood education and school. However, through two collaborative research projects which explored the key competencies at school and their potential links with the early childhood curriculum's focus on dispositions (Carr and Peters 2005; Carr et al. 2008), it became clear that these theoretical links would only make a difference to children's learning in practice if teachers on both sides worked to create a bridge and turned this potential into reality. The strength of the bridge will depend on the connections made (Peters 2008, 2009).

Research with Mangere Bridge Kindergarten in their Centre of Innovation study (Hartley et al. 2010, 2012) explored ways of building these bridges and enhancing 'border crossing'. This involved creating and enhancing relationships between transition partners (including teachers in both sectors) through mutually interesting tasks and a range of strategies for fostering familiarisation and a sense of belonging at school for children and families. Learning connections, through key competencies and literacies, were also explored. The community negotiation of this transition was firmly located within a sociocultural approach.

Focusing on learning raises another key issue. Whilst we can theorise that enhancing transitions will support children's learning, given the complexity of the interacting variables, there are challenges in developing research models that can demonstrate the difference that has been made or that can determine if transitions have been successful or effective. In 2010, I undertook a literature review for the New Zealand Ministry of Education (Peters 2010), which addressed some of these points. The Ministry was interested in broad questions regarding what successful transitions might look like and the role that characteristics of children, families and settings might play in how well children transition from early childhood education to school. Whilst these might appear to be straightforward questions on the surface, many issues arise, including whose voices are sought, the time frame under consideration and the ways in which success is conceptualised.

The complexity of individual experiences, and the multiple factors that influence each child's learning, mean that rather than definitive indicators of successful and/ or unsuccessful transitions, the review identified themes in the recent New Zealand and related overseas literature regarding ways in which success might be viewed. Key issues for consideration related to the following:

- Belonging, well-being and feeling 'suitable' at school
- Recognition and acknowledgement of culture
- Respectful, reciprocal relationships
- Engagement in learning
- Learning dispositions and identity as a learner
- Positive teacher expectations
- Building on funds of knowledge from early childhood education and home (Peters 2010)

Some of these features are not directly observable in children, although they may be inferred. They also draw attention for both policy and practice to the ecological system rather than the individual alone. For example, a focus on belonging, involvement and well-being 'places the onus for the outcomes for children on the adults, making a judgment about the context, rather than the child. It gives immediate feedback about the effect of the educators' approach and the environment they establish' (Laevers 1999 cited in Goldspink et al. 2008, p. 3). Rather than locating the 'problem' within the individual, it recognises the complexity of influences and offers a number of sites for action within the ecological system.

All of these ideas have led to a current project, which is exploring children's learning journeys from early childhood into school.

8.4   Challenges and Issues

Some of the challenges and issues that the ecological and sociocultural foundations of my work provoke have been alluded to above, with regard to the complexity of the issues involved in both understanding and researching transitions. Within these concerns there is a key question regarding whose voices are heard (and not heard) in the process. Many researchers have worked hard to gain a variety of perspectives, including those of the children themselves, and families with complex support needs (Dockett et al. 2011). However, in my review of New Zealand research (Peters 2010), many voices were absent, in particular from the groups for whom the Ministry of Education was most interested in enhancing transitions. These include children and families who identify as Māori or Pasifika, those who have English as an additional language, draw from low socioeconomic backgrounds or have children with special educational needs. It is important that policies and strategies draw on insights from the groups concerned and also acknowledge the diversity within these groups.

8.5   Future Directions

Beliefs and practices at the macrosystem level have changed enormously over the 17 years that I have been involved in transitions research. At the same time, the body of research literature has grown exponentially. There are a range of theories and research findings that can provide insights, each drawing from particular world-views. The competing discourses that surround transitions add to the complexity and may coexist and even do battle 'inside our own heads' (Stainton-Rogers 1989, cited in Jenks 2005, p. 68). I find myself wanting to both deconstruct the discourses and the ways our understandings are framed and also to navigate through the complexity to understand more about the experiences of those involved and assist in developing approaches that address inequities and support children, families and teachers engaged in transitions in ways that have ongoing benefits for children's learning.

In New Zealand we have reached the point where much has been achieved in relation to transition practices and policies, and many schools and early childhood settings are working hard to enhance the transition to school for children and their families. However, we are short of research evidence that indicates what makes both an immediate, and lasting, difference to children's overall experience, and within this, to their learning. In addition, there are many voices that are missing from the research literature, often from the groups for whom educational transitions may be most challenging.

My current work with Vanessa Paki involves working with teachers to explore ways of enhancing children's learning journeys from early childhood education into school and to explore the impact of transition practices upon learning over time. Although the work focuses on transitions for all children, a key thread is to work towards developing understandings of the perceptions of Māori children and their families. Improving transitions to school for Māori children is a key goal in Ka Hikitia Managing for Success: The Māori Education Strategy 2008–2012 (Ministry of Education 2008), and yet Māori voices are noticeably absent from the transitions research literature. We are fortunate to be working in a number of settings, one of which has up to 97 % Māori children attending.

The second broad theme in this study focuses on curriculum links to support learning. In this aim we have considered the possibility that rather than a bridge across a chasm, through shared understandings, we might develop a 'borderland' or shared space of understanding between early childhood education and school (Britt and Sumsion 2003). Borderlands can be thought of as 'those spaces that exist around borders' and which do 'not have a sharp divide line where one leaves one way of making sense for another' (Clandinin and Rosiek 2007, p. 59). We are investigating the alignment between the New Zealand ECE and school curricula in practice and the ways in which shared understandings might develop. A number of strategies are facilitating this process. One has been 'a day in the life of...' observations where a teacher observes in the other sector and then discusses with the teacher from the observed setting what has been noticed, to gain a more informed understanding of the things that have been seen. Teachers from both of the schools involved commented especially on how useful that had been:

They [our teaching team] feel the most valuable time has been to visit [ECE setting] to build a picture and understanding of their programme, and in turn develop trust with their team. (Primary School 1)

During the last few months it has been encouraging to see the growing contacts between [ECE setting] and [Primary school 2]. Visits by staff have provided a closer understanding of the learning journeys undertaken by children. This building of relational trust is so important in helping develop future understandings. (Primary School 2)

The curriculum analysis and looking for connections led in some cases to an enhanced understanding for teachers of their own sector's document:

We realised that aspects of shared understanding, language, meaning, pedagogies and philosophies (for all) are important in supporting a child through transitions.
  We had opportunities to explore these throughout the first year of the project - Exploring the key competencies, shared visits [including 'A day in the life...'] and dialogue with teachers at [Primary School 2].

Linking the two curriculums took us on a journey, which surprisingly led us back to looking at Te Whāriki with fresh eyes. We realised that supporting successful transitions did not necessarily require us 'moving up' to a new curriculum, but fully embracing our own. There were benefits when using both as a lens to position the child and filter their learning - however, it is the curriculum 'in action' and 'in context' that ultimately makes meaning. (ECE teacher researcher)

Finally, while a number of recent New Zealand projects have developed strategies for supporting children's transition to school, none of these have looked at the impact on children's learning in the longer term. The research literature is clear about the negative implications for children's learning of poor transitions, but it is important that robust evidence is provided of the longer-term impact of strategies designed to support transitions. In addressing this aspect we are cognisant of the fact that children's learning journeys are shaped by a complex interaction of different factors. Nevertheless, developing frameworks for evaluation of the work being undertaken is key if these approaches are to meet their aims. Review is essential as potentially useful strategies may be 'too late, too impersonal, and too cursory to have much of an effect' (Pianta 2004, p. 6). In addition, practices have to be renegotiated over time, through staff changes and new dilemmas (Hartley et al. 2012).

We have struggled with the challenges regarding ways to analyse success and effectiveness and are working with the communities involved in order to discover what success looks like from the point of view of the participants and ways in which they feel this can be achieved. Addressing the concerns and interests of the participants means that the research has the potential to support the self-determination of their aspirations (Bishop 1996, 1997; Bishop and Glynn 1999). The ways in which these views align with, or inform, aspirations at the policy (macro) level can then be considered.

The current project is providing a range of new insights, but I hope to build on this in the future to look at a wider range of transition experiences, including for children who have not attended early childhood education. Developing shared meanings with groups whose voices have not been well represented in transitions research will assist in one of my other areas of interest, which is to deconstruct the discourses that shape our understandings. I feel that it is timely to pay more overt attention to the competing discourses around transitions and transitions research as this field intersects with so many other areas of human development and education. This larger project would involve international research connections to examine current knowledge of transitions and explore ways of moving forward in this field to provide new insights into transitions in the twenty-first century. There is a place for new analysis of the theories and agendas that drive transitions research and consideration of social justice within the competing theoretical and political agendas.

References

Bishop, R. (1996). *Collaborative research stories: Whakawhanaungatanga*. Palmerston North: Dunmore Press.
Bishop, R. (1997). Māori peoples concerns about research into their lives. *History of Education Review, 26*(1), 25–41.
Bishop, R., & Glynn, T. (1999). *Culture counts. Changing power relation in education*. Palmerston North: Dunmore Press.
Bourdieu, P. (1997). The forms of capital. In A. H. Halsey, H. Lauder, P. Brown, & A. S. Wells (Eds.), *Education, culture, economy and society* (pp. 45–58). Oxford: Oxford University Press.
Britt, C., & Sumsion, J. (2003). Within the borderlands: Beginning early childhood teachers in primary schools. *Contemporary Issues in Early Childhood, 4*(2), 115–136.
Bronfenbrenner, U. (1979). *The ecology of human development*. Cambridge, MA: Harvard University Press.
Bronfenbrenner, U. (1986). Ecology of the family as a context for human development: Research perspectives. *Developmental Psychology, 22*(6), 723–742.

Bronfenbrenner, U. (1992). Ecological systems theory. In R. Vasta (Ed.), *Six theories of child development* (pp. 187–250). London: Jessica Kingsley.

Bronfenbrenner, U., & Morris, P. A. (1997). The ecology of developmental processes. In W. Damon & R. M. Lerner (Eds.), *Handbook of child psychology* (Theoretical models of human development 5th ed., Vol. 1, pp. 993–1029). New York: John Wiley.

Brooker, L. (2002). *Starting school: Young children's learning cultures.* Buckingham: Open University Press.

Bruner, J. (1985). Vygotsky: A historical and conceptual perspective. In J. V. Wertsch (Ed.), *Culture, communication and cognition: Vygotskian perspectives* (pp. 21–34). Cambridge, UK: Cambridge University Press.

Carr, M., & Peters, S. (2005). *Te Whāriki and links to the NZ Curriculum Research Projects.* Hamilton: University of Waikato.

Carr, M., Peters, S., Davis, K., Bartlett, C., Bashford, N., Berry, P., … Wilson-Tukaki, A. (2008). *Key learning competencies across place and time. Kimihia te ara tōtika, hei oranga mō to aō.* Wellington, New Zealand: Teaching and Learning Research Initiative. http://www.tlri.org.nz/ece-sector/. Accessed 2 Apr 2010.

Claibourne, L., & Drewery, W. (2009). *Human development: Family, place and culture.* Sydney: McGraw Hill.

Clandinin, J., & Rosiek, J. (2007). Mapping a landscape of narrative inquiry. Borderland spaces and tensions. In J. Clandinin (Ed.), *Handbook of narrative inquiry* (pp. 35–75). London: Sage.

Dockett, S., Perry, B., Kearney, E., Hampshire, A., Mason, J., & Schmied, V. (2011). *Facilitating children's transition to school from families with complex support needs.* Albury: Research Institute for Professional Practice, Learning and Education, Charles Sturt University.

Fabian, H. (1998). *Induction to school and transition through Key Stage One: Practice and perceptions.* Unpublished PhD thesis, Coventry University.

Furedi, F. (2002). *Culture of fear: Risk taking and the culture of low expectation* (Rev. ed.). London: Continuum.

Giroux, H. (1992). *Border crossings: Cultural workers and the politics of education.* New York: Routledge.

Goldspink, G., Winter, P., & Foster, M. (2008, September 10–12). *Student engagement and quality pedagogy.* Paper presented at the European Conference on Educational Research, Göteborg.

Hartley, C., Rogers, P., Smith, J., Peters, S., & Carr, M. (2010). Building relationships between early childhood and school: Mutually interesting projects. In A. Meade (Ed.), *Dispersing waves. Innovation in early childhood education* (pp. 19–26). Wellington: NZCER Press.

Hartley, C., Rogers, P., Smith, J., Peters, S., & Carr, M. (2012). *Across the border: A community negotiates the transition from early childhood to primary school.* Wellington: NZCER Press.

Holliday, A. (2002). *Doing and writing qualitative research.* London: Sage.

James, A., & Prout, A. (1997). Re-presenting childhood: Time and transition in the study of childhood. In A. James & A. Prout (Eds.), *Constructing and reconstructing childhood: Contemporary issues in the sociological study of childhood* (2nd ed., pp. 230–250). London: Falmer Press.

Jenks, C. (2005). Zeitgeist research on childhood. In P. Christensen & A. James (Eds.), *Research with children: Perspectives and practices* (pp. 62–76). London: Falmer Press.

Jindal-Snape, D., & Miller, D. J. (2010). Understanding transitions through self-esteem and resilience. In D. Jindal-Snape (Ed.), *Educational transitions: Moving stories from around the world* (pp. 11–32). New York: Routledge.

Lave, J., & Wenger, E. (1991). *Situated learning: Legitimate peripheral participation.* Cambridge, UK: Cambridge University Press.

Ledger, E. (2000). *Children's perspectives of their everyday lives with a focus on the transition from early childhood centre to school.* Unpublished PhD thesis, University of Otago, Dunedin.

Miles, M. B., & Huberman, A. M. (1994). *Qualitative data analysis* (2nd ed.). London: Sage.

Ministry of Education. (1996). *Te whāriki. He whāriki mātauranga mō ngā mokopuna o Aotearoa: Early childhood curriculum.* Wellington: Learning Media.

Ministry of Education. (2007). *The New Zealand curriculum: The English-medium teaching and learning in years 1–13*. Wellington: Learning Media.

Ministry of Education. (2008). *Ka Hikitia – Managing for success: The Māori education strategy 2008–2012*. www.educationcounts.govt.nz. Accessed 16 Mar 2009.

Mullholland, J., & Wallace, J. (2000, April). *Restorying and the legitimation of research texts*. Paper presented at the annual meeting of the National Association of Research in Science Teaching, New Orleans.

Norris, J. A. (1999). *Transforming masculinities: Boys making the transition from early childhood education to school*. Unpublished MA thesis, Victoria University of Wellington, Wellington.

Peters, S. (2004). *"Crossing the border": An interpretive study of children making the transition to school*. Unpublished PhD thesis. The University of Waikato, Hamilton.

Peters, S. (2008, September). *Learning dispositions to key competencies: Navigating learning journeys across the border from early childhood education to school*. International symposium on Images of Transition at the European Early Childhood Education Research Association 18th annual conference, Stavanger University, Norway.

Peters, S. (2009). Responsive, reciprocal relationships: The heart of the Te Whāriki curriculum. In J. Moyles (Ed.), *Learning together in the early years: Relational pedagogy* (pp. 24–35). London: Routledge.

Peters, S. (2010). Literature review: Transition from early childhood education to school. Report commissioned by the Ministry of Education. Wellington: Ministry of Education. http://www.educationcounts.govt.nz/publications/ece/78823. Accessed 3 May 2012.

Pianta, R. (2004). Transitioning to school: Policy, practice, and reality. *The Evaluation Exchange, X*(2), 5–6.

Piddington, R. (1957). *An introduction to social anthropology*. Edinburgh: Oliver & Boyd.

Rogoff, B. (2003). *The cultural nature of human development*. Oxford: Oxford University Press.

Royal-Tangaere, A. (1997). Māori human development learning theory. In P. Te Whaiti, M. McCarthy, & A. Durie (Eds.), *Mai i rangiatea. Māori wellbeing and development* (pp. 85–109). Auckland: Auckland University Press with Bridget Williams Books.

Skinner, D., Bryant, D., Coffman, J., & Campbell, F. (1998). Creating risk and promise: Children's and teachers' co-constructions in the cultural world of kindergarten. *The Elementary School Journal, 98*(4), 297–310.

Thomson, P. (2002). *Schooling the rustbelt kids: Making the difference in changing times*. Sydney: Allen & Unwin.

Thomson, P., & Hall, C. (2008). Opportunities missed and/or thwarted? 'Funds of knowledge' meet the English national curriculum. *Curriculum Journal, 19*(2), 87–103. doi:10.1080/09585170802079488.

Vygotsky, L. S. (1978). Interaction between learning and development. In M. Cole, V. John-Steiner, S. Scribner, & E. Souberman (Eds.), *Mind in society* (pp. 79–91). Cambridge, MA: Harvard University Press.

Chapter 9
Transition to School: A Rite of Passage in Life

Anders Garpelin

9.1 Introduction

Sweden has a comprehensive school system with 9 years of compulsory school (for children aged 7–16 years), called "grundskola". This compares with primary and lower secondary school in other countries. Often, the first 5 or 6 years of schooling are in a smaller school with class teachers, while the remaining 3 or 4 years are in a larger school with subject teachers. In Sweden the day-care institutions/kindergarten for children aged 1–5 years are called "preschools", with their own national curriculum. Another early childhood institution is the preschool class (children aged 6 years). Although the preschool class is not compulsory, it is attended by almost everyone in the age group. Most preschool classes are located with the lower level of the compulsory school and are regulated by the same curriculum as the compulsory school but with no specified goals for the children to attain.

In Sweden today, there is a concern that children are not achieving as well as they used to, as evidenced by the comparative assessment analysis of country-based data, PISA and TIMSS. In Sweden, questions have been asked about whether the limited results might be due to the fact that Swedish children begin school at 7, while most countries start school at 6. Such questions also raise challenges for the field of transitions in early childhood education.

Transitions in educational systems are organised in different ways around the world, but in each case, children pass through a number of marked transitions, organised on the basis of age group, stages or types of schools (European Commission 2009; Marlow-Ferguson 2001).

This chapter reports research conducted within the research group TIES, Transitions In Educational Settings. The group has its base at Mälardalen University in Västerås, Sweden (www.mdh.se). The TIES researchers all have experience as

A. Garpelin (✉)
Mälardalen University, Västerås, Sweden
e-mail: anders.garpelin@mdh.se

B. Perry et al. (eds.), *Transitions to School - International Research, Policy and Practice*, 117
International perspectives on early childhood education and development 9,
DOI 10.1007/978-94-007-7350-9_9, © Springer Science+Business Media Dordrecht 2014

preschool teachers, schoolteachers and/or special needs educators. During the last two decades, with an interpretive research approach, the group has developed its understanding of issues linked to educational transitions encountered by children and young people. All studies have a focus on what education means from a child and/or teacher perspective. Recently, the focus has been on transitions within preschool (children aged 1–5 years) and between preschool, preschool class and school. TIES aims to explore the nature, impact, diversity, governmental and generational investment in early childhood transitions, with a view to enhancing the daily and cumulative experience of education and its lifelong impact.

TIES has studied transitions in the educational system of Sweden, focusing especially on a perspective of what they mean for children and young people (Garpelin 1997, 2003, 2004b; Garpelin et al. 2008; Garpelin and Sandberg 2010; Hellberg 2007; Sandberg 2012). The group has made connections between educational transitions and the concept of rites of passage (van Gennep 1960). In this chapter, theoretical foundations for these studies are considered along with how these have influenced our research. Finally, some implications and dilemmas arising from the research are discussed.

9.2 Theoretical Perspectives

9.2.1 Rites of Passage

The anthropologist van Gennep (1960) introduced the concept "les rites de passage" for ceremonies, which have the form of rituals and occur with regularity.

> The life of an individual in any society is a series of passages from one age to another and from one occupation to another … there are ceremonies whose essential purpose is to enable the individual to pass from one defined position to another which is equally well defined … we encounter a wide degree of general similarity among ceremonies of birth, childhood, social puberty, betrothal, marriage, pregnancy, fatherhood, initiation into religious societies, and funerals. In this respect, man's life resembles nature, from which neither the individual nor the society stands independent … a periodicity which has repercussions on human life, with stages and transitions, movements forward, and periods of relative inactivity. (van Gennep 1960, pp. 2–3)

Other anthropologists have also reported on rites of passage (Bateson 1958; Mead 1939), and the concept has been used in other contexts, often with reference to psychoanalytic theory (Bettelheim 1954; Erikson 1982; Freud 1953; Grimes 2000; Holm and Bowker 1994; Kreinath et al. 2004), as well as in educational research (Fabian 2007; Lam and Pollard 2006).

For van Gennep (1960), culturally bounded ceremonies were linked to different life crises in relation to transitions between different stages in the life of individuals. He identified how the act of passing through a door into a house or from one room to another had a certain meaning in many cultures. The act was given a symbolic significance with respect to transitions from one stage to another.

Van Gennep introduced the metaphor of crossing the threshold of a door: the moment when you are neither in the room you are leaving nor in the new room to help explain such transitions. He applied the Latin word for threshold: "limen" to form the concepts he used to describe the rites of passage process. He divided the process into three phases: "preliminal" for the separation phase, "liminal" for the transition phase and "postliminal" for the incorporation phase.

In the transition process, the individual is in a well-known room (status/position/stage) and then is guided by significant others (those in power) onto the threshold (into the passage), where the individual, for a short moment, neither exists in the well-known room the individual has just left (the former status/position/stage) nor has entered the new room where the individual has never been before (the new status/position/stage). Rather, the individual is being, without belonging, to any room (being without any status/position/stage). Finally, the individual passes into the new room (status/position/stage). Van Gennep saw how the transition, wherein the individual passes from one status to another, was made more obvious, in most countries, by culturally bound ceremonies: rites of passage.

Turner (1969) specifically focused on human relations during the middle phase of rites of passage: the liminal phase. Turner characterised being a part of a movement or a collective, with shared experiences, as experiencing a sense of "communitas". Later, Turner (1982) introduced the concept of "liminoid" for the situation when someone is going through a liminal phase with others, sharing the same experiences and feelings as they are. This moment of shared experience might be characterised as a moment when circumstances previously regarded to be of great importance are set aside. This experience might have such an impact that the surrounding world does not appear to be itself anymore. Old truths and beliefs might be abandoned.

9.2.2   An Interpretive Approach and a Relational Perspective

To deepen the understanding of transitions from the perspective of those involved, we have applied an interpretive approach in our research (Denzin 1997; Garpelin 1997; Mehan 1992) with its roots in hermeneutics and phenomenology (Dilthey 1976; Giorgi 1985; Ödman 2007; Ricoeur 1981; Turner and Bruner 1986). The main focus is on getting a deeper understanding of the meaning those involved give the phenomena studied. It is about understanding the experiences of individuals by interpreting the expressions they make, explicitly or implicitly, since it is impossible to capture the actual experience of an individual (Dilthey 1976).

A relational interpretation perspective formulated by Garpelin (1997, 2004a, 2011) emanates from the work of Asplund (1987), Erikson (1959), Goffman (1959, 1961, 1963, 1967), Laing (1969), Mead (1934) and Schutz (1967). This perspective can be summed up as follows:

Even if we experience the world around us individually, human beings still take an existing shared reality for granted. The reality exists prior to the individual, but each and every one of us is bound to interpret and give a meaning to it. Forming a meaning can be regarded as an ongoing process where we influence and are influenced by each other. Communicating with others means taking each other's roles in interplay where we gradually learn more and more about ourselves. Taking the role of the other gives us an opportunity to look at ourselves from the other person's perspective. Following the process of role-taking, mind and self are social products formed in interaction with others, where mutually shared significant symbols indicate an important condition for the interpretation of each other's actions. As individuals we act out of two perspectives of ourselves, a social one, starting from position, role and group membership and a personal one, taking the point from our view of ourselves, independent of how the environment differs. We try to protect our own integrity by affecting the inner life of people around us. We act in social situations, determined to force our personal projects, something that is due to individual background, common sense knowledge, present actions and other things in the context. We act intentionally, considering the past, the present and the future. The way we have managed challenges/crises earlier in our life will affect the way of dealing with similar ones later on. Common experiences not only facilitate the conditions for interpreting the role-taking of the other. Such knowledge can also affect one's way of taking others' roles, not unreservedly but with preconception. A group is characterised by mutual opinions of all members, opinions of the relations that exist within the group. Every group has its own common events to refer to at regular intervals. When a group interacts with other groups, acting as a team, presenting how they define a situation, everyone, including the audience, is aware of the potential existence of a "front region" everyone can be a part of and a "back region" open for team members only (Garpelin 1997, 2004a, 2011).

Van Gennep (1960) identified a gap between socially and individually defined identity. Indeed, he saw "status" as a position coming from society and "identity" as an internal process of becoming. Society has a crucial role in leading the individual through transition. In this way, the individual might be helped to understand him/herself better. This can be compared with Mead's (1934) theory on self and the role of the generalised other. If society offers nothing but undefined transitions for children and young people, this might have an influence on their capability to understand and master the crises of their lives (Erikson 1959, 1982), and this might cause difficulties in the development of a sense of coherence in life (Antonovsky 1987).

9.3   Rites of Passage and Transitions in Preschool and School

9.3.1   School Transitions as Rites of Passage

In Swedish society, traditional rites of passage, such as baptism (christening) and confirmation have lost their significance. In a longitudinal study over 10 years, Garpelin (1997, 2003) has shown how young people in Sweden experience the transition to the senior level of compulsory schooling (at the age of 12/13) as a critical incident, from both a pupil as well as a life perspective. This was a transition from the world of children to the world of adolescents, organised and sanctioned by the world of grownups: the society. The concepts of van Gennep (1960) and Turner (1982) were applied to understand the transition in three phases: *Separation* from the previous world, in our case, leaving the world of school children; *Transition*, on the threshold, before entering the new world, the summer between the two school worlds; and *Incorporation* into the new world, entering the world of school adolescents.

After the split from the world of schoolchildren, the young people in this study spent a whole summer preparing for their future life among school adolescents. Being in a liminoid position had a significant impact on their life situation. During this time they were occupied by thoughts about the new world. Others too were in the same position. Knowing that they were not alone, they were all aware of the fact that they would be the newcomers at the new school. With significant others, they went through what they could experience entering the new school, expecting to share a collective vulnerability such as meeting older pupils in the rest rooms. They had heard many frightening stories about how newcomers were bullied by those in upper classes. Also in the new school class, there would be much at stake, with fears to experience individual vulnerability. Would they be accepted or rejected in the new school class? Could they trust their best friend when they together met the new acquaintances? Would their best friend desert them for some new more interesting classmate? The question of choosing a desk mate might turn into a problem for one's self-confidence. Other big issues included who to go with, how to act and what to wear on the first school day in August. Some also felt a fear that they would not master the new subjects, stand the pressure from the new teachers or make the change of books in the locker during break in time for the next class. During this time, they were in the position of being on the threshold between the two worlds, that of children and that of adolescents.

Entering the new school and meeting the older school students resulted in the feeling of shared collective vulnerability. Soon this phase was over. But, for some, the incorporation phase meant experiencing individual vulnerability, victimisation and bullying which could last for years (Garpelin 2003, 2004a).

9.3.2   Transitions Within Preschool

The data collected in the transition to secondary school study (Garpelin 1997, 2003) indicated that transitions between other educational levels, including between preschool and compulsory school, might also be interpreted as rites of passage.

In a research overview about transitions in early childhood (Ekström et al. 2008), the TIES research group learned how studies of transitions from home to preschool, but above all, transitions from preschool to school, dominated. Studies of transitions within preschool institutions, such as between units with different age-groupings, were rare. These findings are reinforced in other literature (Dunlop and Fabian 2006; Stephen 2006; Vogler et al. 2008).

A new study (Garpelin and Kallberg 2008; Garpelin et al. 2010) was conducted at two preschools (Ship and Butterfly) to obtain a deeper understanding of the meanings transitions within preschool might have for children, their parents and preschool teachers.

The children at the Ship preschool experienced three transitions between age groups, while those at Butterfly had only one transition between age groups. Two different approaches were identified.

In the Ship, the transitions were regarded as natural rites through which everyone in the age group passed at the same time. A point of departure was the fact that the children differed with regard to their development and experience – and the emphasis was on how the pedagogical environment was prepared to offer opportunities to challenge, stimulate and recognise all children. The receiving unit in the preschool was emptied of children who in turn went on to the next unit.

The teachers made the transition together with the children, taking with them their common culture, including norms and socio-emotional atmosphere. The children brought their personal belongings with them. They moved on a special day – having "a moving-in party", emphasising the fact that the children were taking over the new unit. The children's group was regarded as a resource in the transition and the encounter with the new environment.

The idea was that the transition brings the individual to a new pedagogical environment so that they can be challenged and inspired and to which they can respond. All pedagogical work was permeated by the individuals striving to feel secure and relying on their self-esteem. The aim was that they would be curious about the new environment. The transitions were meant to be clear, natural and obvious to all involved.

In the Butterfly preschool, there was a stress on the importance that external factors such as economy and politics have on transitions. Maturity played a central role in forming an opinion of whether the child was "mature" enough to adjust himself/herself to the new pedagogical environment and the conditions that prevailed in the new unit.

The idea was that the individual should manage the transition to the new situation. For the children involved, the transition to the unit for older children was mostly about adjusting to a new environment, new older children and new teachers within existing culture, attitudes, rules and norms. It was also a question of being able to feel confident in the new unit.

The teachers viewed the transition as "a necessary evil" with which they had to deal. Consequently, they strived to make transitions at a time when the individual child was mature enough. The pedagogical idea was that transitions should be as smooth, unnoticed and adjusted as possible – as if the child was "floating over" to the new unit.

The analysis revealed two approaches, one in favour of transitions as rites of passage and the other trying to make them as unnoticed as possible. In the latter case, there is less stress on the social definition of identity (van Gennep 1960). The two approaches also offer different conditions with reference to individual and collective vulnerability (Garpelin 2003, 2004a). In the Ship preschool, the transition is mostly connected to a collective experience, which might assist in the prevention of victimisation and bullying (Corsaro et al. 2003).

9.4 Spending One Year on a Bridge Between Preschool and School

This chapter began by asking why Swedish children are not achieving as well as they used to, as evidenced by PISA and TIMSS. Perhaps the limited results are because Swedish children begin school at 7, while most countries have a school start at 6. There are many other possible reasons for this phenomenon. In this chapter, the emphasis is on what happens in Swedish children's transitions between the preschool, the preschool class and the school.

9.4.1 The Lesson of Failure in Primary School

In a recent evaluation study undertaken by TIES (Garpelin et al. 2009), the crucial question was why some children, despite the massive resources invested, did not obtain the goals of the national curriculum in grade 3. Class teachers and special needs educators were interviewed. In addition, a parallel case study was made on the transition between the preschool class and the first year in school (Garpelin and Sandberg 2010; Sandberg 2012).

These studies raised some challenges. Firstly, does the preschool class have a role as a "bridge" between the worlds of the preschool and the school? The results of the studies indicated that the aim to make the transition as "smooth" as possible contributed to an uncertainty for everyone: children as well as teachers. Secondly, the Matthew effect (Stanovich 2000), through which children with advantage before the transition gained more than the less advantaged, was observed as the gap between able and slower learners increased over time. Thirdly, there was a lack of a holistic perspective, with the class teachers seeing any problems being due to the individual child and not to the learning environment.

9.4.2 Transitions Between Preschool and School and the Role of the Preschool Class

Several studies have documented how transition to school impacts on children's well-being and learning opportunities (Bulkeley and Fabian 2006; Dockett and Perry 2005). Fabian and Dunlop (2006) and Garpelin (2003) stress how transition to school can be one of the most important events in the life of a child, both from a perspective of here and now and from a longer-term perspective.

The preschool class was introduced in Sweden in 1998 to facilitate the transition between preschool and school (Skolverket 2008). Children in many other countries start school at 6 years of age and play, and creativity are common characteristics of the pedagogy in their first year (Broström and Wagner 2003; Dockett and Perry 2005; O'Kane and Hayes 2006).

Einarsdóttir (2006) studied how teachers in Iceland work in preschool, compared with first years of school. She found that in preschool the priority was on nurturing, play and freedom, while it was on subjects, lessons and guidance in school. When the Icelandic preschool class became a part of the compulsory school, the way of working in the preschool class tended to become similar to that of the school.

Children begin school at 6 years of age in Norway, but unlike Iceland, the first year of school is characterised by a mixture of both free play and formalised literacy work (Eriksen Hagtvet 2003), drawing on both preschool and school traditions.

Some Swedish studies (Peréz Prieto et al. 2003; Skolverket 2001) conclude that there are strong signs of school approaches being introduced into preschool classes. Our own study (Garpelin et al. 2009), on the other hand, indicated that the teachers working in the preschool classes often defended their way of working against what was regarded as a school tradition.

9.5   Borderlands, Bridges and Rites of Passage: Understanding Children's Learning Journeys from Preschool into School

The new TIES research project (Garpelin 2011), funded by the Swedish Research Council, is designed to deepen our understanding about the transitions and the educational practices that children meet during the years from preschool and the preschool class into the first year of school. Of particular importance is what these transitions mean for children with different abilities and experiences. The project offers opportunities to scrutinise the educational settings in the preschool, the preschool class and the school and the transitions between them, especially with reference to processes of inclusion and exclusion. As well, it allows study of the impact the transitions have upon children's learning and participation over time.

An interpretive approach and a relational interpretation perspective will be applied in the study as we seek to ascertain the perspectives of teachers, parents and children. Data will be gathered in six ethnographic case studies through participant observation and interviews. Interviews and a survey will be conducted with teachers and parents will be interviewed. Finally, "learning journey interviews" will be conducted with children and their parents to understand the processes through which children pass during their early childhood educational transitions. The results will be analysed, together with those from former studies, all with the purpose of deepening our understanding of the meaning of these transitions in the life of children.

The results will also be compared with those from a similar project from New Zealand (Peters 2010). In particular, our project has adopted the concepts of bridges as supports for learning and "borderland" as a shared space of understanding. Further, we have adopted Peter's formulation of how children's learning processes during transitions from preschool to school can be understood in terms of "learning journeys" (Peters 2010).

9.6   Implications, Dilemmas and Crucial Questions

An important issue arising from our research is whether school start should be considered as a rite of passage for the collective or an invisible/smooth transition for the individual. We can identify some crucial dilemmas from our research so far:

- Should we try to protect the individual or rely on group processes as we organise transitions?
- Will the individual child cope with the demands and expectations of the transition, or should the learning environment be prepared to offer opportunities and challenge, stimulate and recognise all children, regardless of their different abilities and experiences?
- Should the pedagogical environment in preschool/preschool class be adjusted so that it resembles the first year of school or should the first year of school's pedagogical environment be adjusted to resemble that of the preschool/preschool class?
- How should the pedagogical environments in preschools/preschool classes and schools be organised so that they have their focus on the well-being of the children's here-and-now, but still offer them opportunities so that they will have the best chances to cope with the demands they will encounter as pupils in school.
- By encouraging those that are eager and potentially quick learners to develop their reading skills and, at the same time, assisting others to develop their talents on the football ground, teachers fulfil the Matthew effect (Stanovich 2000). How can we decrease the gap between able and less able learners over time, not holding back the quick learners?

"Curling parents" (Hougaard 2002) is a phenomenon discussed in the Nordic countries. These are parents who, like a curler, wipe out all roughness on the path on which their children are about to embark. If the marked transitions within and between preschool and school are reduced or even erased, it would be like creating a system of "curling schools". The Swedish preschool class has such a role, that of a bridge to smooth the transition between preschool and school.

From a child's perspective, the transition to school might be recognised as an institutionalised border between the life of a preschool child and that of a schoolchild. Passing this border could be interpreted as a rite of passage (van Gennep 1960): an initiation rite recognised by the adult world, a rite children go through together with others of the same age. After leaving preschool class behind, they experience a liminoid position (Turner 1982) on the threshold to school. As they start school, they might feel vulnerable because of contact with older school students and the new environment. But they can feel a little more secure because of a shared collective vulnerability (Garpelin 2003). As newcomers, they are not alone, and they can experience the strength of togetherness and resilience. They are in the same position as the others in their school class, regardless of their different abilities and experiences.

Our ongoing research with our colleagues from New Zealand should reveal more about the transitions between the preschool, the preschool class and the school for Swedish children. With an interpretive approach (Denzin 1997; Garpelin 1997; Mehan 1992), a relational perspective (Garpelin 1997) and the theory of rites of passage, together with our colleagues from New Zealand, we will reveal more about what the life for children in preschool, the preschool class and school means in general and what the transitions between the three institutions mean, in particular. We might also be able to contribute to knowledge about how we can lessen school failure for those not ready to meet the demands and expectations of school.

References

Antonovsky, A. (1987). *Unravelling the mystery of health. How people manage stress and stay well*. San Francisco: Jossey-Bass.
Asplund, J. (1987). *Det sociala livets elementära former* [The elementary forms of social life]. Göteborg: Korpen.
Bateson, G. (1958). *Naven. A survey of the problems suggested by composite picture of the culture of a New Guinea tribe drawn from three points of view* (2nd ed.). Stanford: Stanford University Press.
Bettelheim, B. (1954). *Symbolic wounds*. Glencoe: Free Press.
Broström, S., & Wagner, J. (Eds.). (2003). *Early childhood education in five Nordic countries*. Århus: Systime.
Bulkeley, J., & Fabian, H. (2006). Well-being and belonging during early educational transitions. *International Journal of Transitions in Childhood, 2*, 18–30.
Corsaro, W. A., Molinari, L., Gold Hadley, K., & Sugioka, H. (2003). Keeping and making friends: Italian children's transition from pre-school to elementary school. *Social Psychology Quarterly, 66*(3), 272–292.
Denzin, N. (1997). *Interpretive ethnography*. Thousand Oaks: Sage.
Dilthey, W. (1976). *Selected writings*. (Ed. H. P. Rickman translated to English). Cambridge: Cambridge University Press. (Original published 1883).
Dockett, S., & Perry, B. (2005). *"As I got to learn it got fun": Children's reflections on their first year at school*. Presented at the annual conference of the Australian Association for Research in Education, 2004. www.aare.edu.au/04pap/doc04324.pdf. Accessed 12 Nov 2007.
Dunlop, A. W., & Fabian, H. (Eds.). (2006). *Informing transitions in the early years: Research, policy and practice*. Maidenhead: McGraw-Hill/Open University Press.
Einarsdóttir, J. (2006). From pre-school to primary school: When different contexts meet. *Scandinavian Journal of Educational Research, 50*(2), 165–184.
Ekström, K., Garpelin, A., & Kallberg, P. (2008). Övergångar under förskoleåren som kritiska händelser för barnet, föräldrarna och verksamheten – en forskningsöversikt. [Transitions during the pre-school years as critical incidents for the child, the parents and the institution]. *Tidskriftförlärarutbildningochforskning, 15*(1), 45–61.
Eriksen Hagtvet, B. (2003). Skriftspråkstimulering i første klasse: faglig innhold og didaktiske angrepsmåter. [Stimulating written language in first grade: Subject content and didactical

approaches]. In K. Klette (Ed.), *Klassrommets praksisformer etter Reform* (Vol. 97). Oslo: Det utdanningsvitenskaplige fakultet. Universiteteti Oslo.

Erikson, E. H. (1959). *Identity: Youth and crises.* New York: W.W. Norton.

Erikson, E. H. (1982). *The life cycle completed: A review.* New York: W.W. Norton.

European Commission. (2009). *Key data on education in Europe 2005.* Luxembourg: Office for Official Publication. http://eacea.ec.europa.eu/education/eurydice/documents/key_data_series/105EN.pdf Accessed 25 Jan 2009.

Fabian, H. (2007). Informing transitions. In A.-W. Dunlop & H. Fabian (Eds.), *Informing transitions in the early years: Research, policy and practice* (pp. 3–17). Maidenhead: McGraw-Hill/ Open University Press.

Fabian H., & Dunlop A.-W. (2006). *Outcomes of good practice in transition processes for children entering primary school.* Paper commissioned for the EFA Global Monitoring Report 2007, Strong Foundations: Early Childhood Care and Education, Geneva.

Freud, S. (1953). *The standard edition of the complete works of Sigmund Freud. Vol. 13 (1913–1914). Totem and taboo and other works.* London: Hogarth Press.

Garpelin, A. (1997). Lektionen och livet [Lesson and life. How young people meet and form a school class]. *Uppsala Studies in Education, 70.* Uppsala: Acta Universitatis Upsaliensis.

Garpelin, A. (2003). *Ung i skolan* [Young in school]. Lund: Studentlitteratur.

Garpelin, A. (2004a). Accepted or rejected in school. *European Educational Research Journal, 3*(4), 729–742.

Garpelin, A. (2004b). Unga människors rätt till riter [Young peoples' rights for rites]. *Pedagogiskamagasinet, 2,* 61–65.

Garpelin, A. (2011). *Borderlands, bridges and rites of passage – Understanding children's learning journeys from preschool into school.* Application. Swedish Research Council, VR. Västerås: Mälardalen University.

Garpelin, A., Ekström, K., Kallberg, P., & Sandberg, G. (2008, September 10–12). *Transitions in early childhood education.* Paper presented at the ECER Meeting in Gothenburg, Sweden.

Garpelin, A., & Kallberg, P. (2008). Övergångar i förskolan som kollektiva passageriter eller smidiga transitioner. [Transitions in pre-school as collective rites of passage or smooth transitions]. *Tidskrift för lärarutbildning och forskning, 15*(1), 63–84.

Garpelin, A., & Sandberg, G. (2010, August). *School starts now! Transitions to school from a perspective of inclusive.* Paper presented at the ECER Meeting, Helsinki.

Garpelin, A., Kallberg, P., Ekström, K., & Sandberg, G. (2010). How to organize transitions between units in preschool. *International Journal of Transitions in Childhood, 4*(1), 4–11.

Garpelin, A., Sandberg, G., Andersson, S., & Hellblom-Thibblin, T. (2009). *Hur klarar skolan åtgärdsgarantin – att ge stöd åt alla barn, att kunna läsa, skriva och räkna när de lämnar årskurs 3?* [How does the school manage the guarantee for interventions – to give support to all children to learn how to read, write and count as they leave grade 3]. Working paper. Västerås: Mälardalen University.

Giorgi, A. (1985). *Phenomenology and psychological research.* Pittsburgh: Duquesne University Press.

Goffman, E. (1959). *The presentation of self in everyday life.* New York: Doubleday.

Goffman, E. (1961). *Asylums.* New York: Doubleday.

Goffman, E. (1963). *Stigma: Notes on the management of spoiled identity.* Englewood Cliffs: Prentice-Hall.

Goffman, E. (1967). *Interaction ritual: Essays on face-to-face behavior.* New York: Doubleday.

Grimes, R. (2000). *Deeply into the bone. Re-inventing rites of passage.* Berkeley: University of California Press.

Hellberg, K. (2007). *Elever på ett individuellt anpassat gymnasieprogram: Skolvardag och vändpunkter* [Pupils in an individually adapted upper secondary school programme: Their daily lives at school and their turning points]. Linköpings universitet: Institutionen för beteendevetenskap och lärande.

Holm, J., & Bowker, J. (Eds.). (1994). *Rites of passage.* London: Pinter Publishers.

Hougaard, B. (2002). *Curling-foraeldreog service-børn: debatomvortnyebørnesyn* [The curling-parents and service-children: A debate about our new view of children]. Vejle: Hougaardsforlag.

Kreinath, J., Hartung, C., & Deschner, A. (Eds.). (2004). *The dynamic of changing rituals: The transformation of religious rituals within their social and cultural context.* New York: Peter Lang.

Laing, R. (1969). *Self and others.* London: Tavistock Publications.

Lam, M. S., & Pollard, A. (2006). A conceptual framework for understanding children as agents in the transition from home to kindergarten. *Early Years: An International Journal of Research and Development, 26*(2), 123–141.

Marlow-Ferguson, R. (Ed.). (2001). *World education encyclopedia: A survey of educational systems worldwide (Volumes 1–3)* (2nd ed.). Detroit: Gale.

Mead, G. H. (1934). *Mind, self and society from a standpoint of a social behaviorist.* Chicago: University of Chicago Press.

Mead, M. (1939). *From the South Seas. Studies of adolescence and sex in primitive societies.* New York: William Morrow.

Mehan, H. (1992). Understanding inequality in schools: The contribution of interpretive studies. *Sociology of Education, 65*(4), 1–20.

O'Kane, M., & Hayes, N. (2006). The transition to school in Ireland: Views of preschool and primary school teachers. *International Journal of Transitions in Childhood, 2,* 4–17.

Ödman, P.-J. (2007). *Tolkning, förståelse, vetande: hermeneutik i teori och praktik.* [Interpretation, understanding, knowledge: Hermeneutics in theory and practice] (2.a uppl.). Stockholm: Norstedts akademiska förlag.

Peréz Prieto, H., Sahlström, F., & Melander, H. (2003). *Från förskola till skola. Berättelser från ett forskningsprojekt* [From preschool to school. Stories from a research project]. Uppsala: Department of Education, Uppsala University.

Peters, S. (2010). Shifting the lens: Re-framing the view of learners and learning during the transition from early childhood education to school in New Zealand. In D. Jindal-Snape (Ed.), *Educational transitions: Moving stories from around the world* (pp. 68–84). New York: Routledge.

Ricoeur, P. (1981). The model of the text: Meaningful action considered as a text. *P. Ricoeur: Hermeneutics and the human sciences* (J. B. Thompson, Trans.). Cambridge, UK: Cambridge University Press.

Sandberg, G. (2012). *På väg in i skolan. Om villkor för olika barns delaktighet och skriftspråkslärande* [The start of school. Conditions for participation and literacy for different children]. In *Studia Didactica Upsaliensia* (Vol. 6). Uppsala: Acta Universitatis Upsaliensis.

Schutz, A. (1967). *The phenomenology of the social world.* New York: Northwestern University Press.

Skolverket (2001). *Att bygga en ny skolform för 6-åringarna. Om integrationen förskoleklass, grundskola och fritidshem* [Building a new school form for 6-year olds. About integrating preschool class, compulsory school and leisure time centres]. Stockholm: National Agency of Education.

Skolverket. (2008). *Förskoleklass* [Preschool class]. Stockholm: National Agency of Education.

Stanovich, K. E. (2000). *Progress in understanding reading: Scientific foundations and new frontiers.* New York/London: Guilford.

Stephen, C. (2006). *Early years education: Perspectives from a review of international literature.* Edinburgh: Scottish Executive Education Department. http://www.scotland.gov.uk/Publications/Recent/06145130/0. Accessed 9 Oct 2009.

Turner, V. (1969). *The ritual process: Structure and anti-structure.* London: Routledge & Kegan Paul.

Turner, V. (1982). *From ritual to theatre.* New York: PAJ Publications.

Turner, V., & Bruner, E., Jr. (Eds.). (1986). *The anthropology of experience.* Urbana: University of Illinois Press.

van Gennep, A. (1960). *Rites of passage* (M. B. Vizedom & G. L. Caffee, Trans.). Chicago: The University of Chicago Press. (Original published in French 1908)

Vogler, P., Crivello, G., & Woodhead, M. (2008). *Early childhood transition research: A review of concepts, theory, and practice* (Working paper No. 48). The Hague: Bernard van Leer Foundation.

Chapter 10
A Sociocultural Approach to Children in the Transition from Home to Kindergarten

Mei Seung Lam

10.1   Introduction

Early childhood education refers to the provision of education and care to young children by child care centres, kindergarten-cum-child care centres, and kindergartens in Hong Kong. Child care centres provide services to children below the age of three. Kindergartens and kindergarten-cum-child care centres provide services for children from 3–6 years old. Most kindergartens operate on a half-day basis and offer three levels: nursery classes (3–4 years), lower kindergarten (4–5 years) and upper kindergarten (5–6 years). Moreover, many kindergartens run extracurricular activities such as Kumon maths, English oral, drawing, ballet and musical instrument classes for their pupils after school or on Saturday mornings, which are well received by many parents.

In 2007, a Pre-primary Education Voucher Scheme was launched in Hong Kong to provide a direct subsidy to parents who choose to send their children to non-profit kindergartens that offer a local curriculum and charge tuition within the required ranges. In addition, many parents have high aspirations for their children's education, perhaps relating to the Chinese ethos of "wishing the son to become a dragon" and the hope that preschool education gives their child a competitive edge for later schooling. Due to the different settings and functions of the early childhood sectors, Hong Kong parents in general have a perception that kindergarten is a place of learning and acquiring the 3Rs (reading, writing and arithmetic). Thus, many parents choose kindergarten for their children so that they receive early childhood education at the age of three.

The transition to kindergarten is the first educational transition for most 3-year-old children in Hong Kong. In making this transition, children cross a cultural boundary between home and kindergarten and begin to make sense of school as a

M.S. Lam (✉)
Hong Kong Institute of Education, Hong Kong, China
e-mail: mlam@ied.edu.hk

B. Perry et al. (eds.), *Transitions to School - International Research, Policy and Practice*,   129
International perspectives on early childhood education and development 9,
DOI 10.1007/978-94-007-7350-9_10, © Springer Science+Business Media Dordrecht 2014

place to learn and of themselves as pupils. Home and kindergarten are different social contexts with their own unique functions, expectations and practices. In the transition between the two, children move from a more family-controlled setting to a cultural context specifically designed for the education of children. In the process, they face many new situations, new learning experiences, new relationships and new expectations.

The transition involves a change of social context and a shift of status from child to pupil while adapting to the expectations of being a kindergartener (Fabian 2002; Lam and Pollard 2006). In Vygotsky's view, the historical, cultural and institutional context shapes children's individual development, and children are active agents in the process of adaptation. Children may feel a great deal of tension between their personal characteristics, experiences, ways of doing things and the knowledge they have obtained at home and their new experience in the classroom. They may build on their existing biographies and personal needs to devise their own creative responses or strategic actions in order to cope with the demands of the new classroom environment such as physical environment, rules and routines, relationships, play and learning activities.

This chapter aims to present a reconceptualised framework (Lam and Pollard 2006) illustrated by a case study of a 3-year-old girl (Lam 2005, 2009). The case shows the interrelationships between cultural processes at home and in kindergarten during the child's adaptation process. Finally, in light of the conceptual framework, future directions for transition research will be discussed.

10.2 Theoretical Perspectives

10.2.1 A Sociocultural Approach to Transition

The conceptual framework is developed from sociocultural theory and select literature on rites of passage and pupil career. Vygotsky's sociocultural approach makes an important contribution to the development of the conceptual framework, which perceives children as active agents in coping with various classroom situations during the transition to kindergarten within the wider context of Hong Kong society. The major elements of the framework include van Gennep's (1960) notion of rites of passage, which describes children's transition from home to kindergarten as a process of changing context and social status, including preliminal, liminal and postliminal stages, and Pollard and Filer's (1999) notion of pupil career, which explains children's preparedness for kindergarten in the preliminal stage and adaptation in the postliminal stage. It highlights the relationships between children's strategic actions and layers of cultural and institutional context, stages of transition and adaptation outcomes for understanding children as agents during the passage from home to kindergarten. The conceptual framework is depicted in Fig. 10.1.

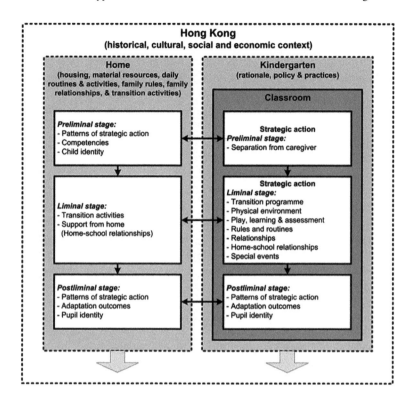

Fig. 10.1 A sociocultural approach to transition (Reconceptualised from Lam and Pollard (2006))

In the following paragraphs, the theoretical foundations – sociocultural theory, rites of passage and pupil career – of the conceptual framework and their implications will be elaborated.

10.2.1.1   Sociocultural Theory: Understanding Transition as a Mediated Process

In Vygotsky's (1978) view, historical, cultural and institutional contexts shape a person's view of the world, and consequently, a child's individual development (biography) should be understood in their situated social context. He claimed that all higher mental functions are mediated processes and that "human action, on both social and individual planes, is mediated by tools (technical tools) and signs (psychological tools)" (Wertsch 1991, p. 19). Mediated process refers to a series of transformations, including the following: (1) an operation that initially represents an external activity is reconstructed and begins to occur internally; (2) an interpersonal process is transformed into an intrapersonal one; and (3) the transformation of an interpersonal process into an intrapersonal one is the result of a long series of developmental events (Vygotsky 1978).

Wertsch (1991, 1998) extended Vygotsky's idea of mediation to develop the notion of mediated action. He explained that "action is mediated" and "cannot be separated from the milieu in which it is carried out" (Wertsch 1991, p. 18). This concept emphasises that human actions are not isolated and do not occur in a vacuum, but are mediated by cultural tools such as language, concepts, objects, routines, forms of expression and ways of doing things in a cultural context (Anning and Edwards 1999; Wertsch 1991, 1998).

Through social interaction, we learn how to use the cultural tools available to us. Consequently, the term "agent" is redefined. It is not only the individual as agent – that is, the person who is doing the acting (who does it) – but rather the agent is the "agent-acting-with-mediational-means" (how he or she does it) (Wertsch 1998, p. 24). To analyse mediated action, Wertsch specified that the agent, the mediational means, the action, the scene and the purpose should all be considered. Moreover, Wertsch characterised the relationship between the agent and meditational means in two forms: internalisation as mastery (ability) and internalisation as appropriation (willingness). Mastery refers to the ability to know how to use meditational means, whereas appropriation refers to the process of "taking something that belongs to others and making it one's own" (Wertsch 1998, p. 53). He claimed that people could have mastery without appropriation or appropriation without mastery (Wertsch 1998).

In light of sociocultural theory, children are considered as active agents (active and cultural learners) in the process of adaptation. When crossing the cultural boundary from home to kindergarten, they bring with them what they have developed and learned at home to make sense of classroom situations in order to adapt as kindergarten pupils. The classroom situations (mediational means) include physical environment, rules and routines, relationships, play and learning activities.

In response to the classroom situations, children may experience different degrees of familiarity or unfamiliarity, since they come from different families. They may suddenly find that their knowledge and established ways of responding (strategic biography) are no longer appropriate or that their experiences have not prepared them for knowing how to act in the new environment. They may be confronted with a totally different cultural model. When they face these cultural variations, they may feel culture shock. They may have different purposes that may conflict with the embedded goals of the mediational means in the classroom and so may respond in different ways in order to adapt.

As Pollard and Filer (1999) stated, "Individual children will respond to this in different ways. By drawing on their accumulated experience and biographical resources, they will act strategically in accommodating to the demands of the new situations" (p. 25). Children may master or appropriate the cultural tools, transform the tools into new forms ("spin-off", in Wertsch's words) or misuse the tools by borrowing from their prior home experience or by using the tools for a different purpose from that which the teachers intended. Children may get to know their teachers' expectations but will also test their skills and abilities to resolve the tensions and contradictions. Similarly, teachers have strategies for responding to children's strategic actions. As a result, new meanings may be created in unpredictable ways.

Children's strategic actions are the results of their interactions with the mediational means in the situated classroom. In brief, children may communicate effectively through non-verbal behaviour, altering their own social environments and the people with whom they interact.

In fact, there is tension between children and the mediational means in the classroom. This is an interactive and dynamic process of negotiation between teachers and children, as well as parents and children, from their different standpoints, concerns and interests, until they arrive at a working consensus (Pollard 1985; Pollard and Filer 1999). In other words, children may mediate (produce) and are mediated (reproduce) until they settle into the teacher's and the school's expectations, or there is mutual acceptance of each other over time. Eventually, it becomes "legitimate peripheral participation" as they move towards full participation in the community and become part of the "community of practice" (Lave and Wenger 1991). Thus, some children may experience more stress, take longer and exert more effort to adapt or create (reproduce) new ways to participate in the collective activities and become members of the classroom.

Moreover, as children commute between home and kindergarten, they have to maintain their dual identity and perform appropriately in the two settings. This does not mean that their family values are replaced once they learn the new ways and values of the kindergarten. Their family values and practices may be modified by the kindergarten or remain separate from the kindergarten classroom. Thus, the conceptual framework takes a parallel perspective (i.e. children commute between home and kindergarten every day) as well as a linear perspective (i.e. children go through the stages of transition) in the rites of passage.

In order to understand how children make sense of, interact and settle into kindergarten, it is necessary to understand their biographies at home and observe how they interpret and interact with the mediational means in the classroom and what strategic actions they employ for using these mediational means. It is also necessary to look into the wider context that influences both the home and school contexts and practices (Bruner 1996; Pollard and Filer 1996).

10.2.1.2 Rites of Passage: Understanding the Stages of Transition

The use of sociocultural theory in understanding the contextual elements (milieu) affecting children's strategic actions and adaptation during the transition to kindergarten has been elaborated above. The temporal element (stages) of the conceptual framework comes from van Gennep's notion of "rites of passage". Van Gennep's (1960) notion implies that children's transition from home to kindergarten is a process of change in context and social status. He claimed that transition is the process of habituating to the new expectations of a new social status in a new world, as distinct from the old status in the old world. He categorises rites of passage into three stages: preliminal rites (rites of separation), liminal (or threshold) rites (rites of transition) and postliminal rites (rites of incorporation). Turner (1969) focused on the intermediate phase of rites of passage as the most consequential. He introduced the concept of "liminal space". Liminal means transitional, which is "betwixt and between". It represents a period of ambiguity, a marginal and transitional stage. The liminal stage is where the core experiences of transition take place. Moreover, van Gennep (1960) found that different people move through each stage with different speed and intricacy with regard to individuals incorporating into groups.

The preliminal stage refers to children's separation from their caregivers at home (in the old world) as they move away from their parents and are positioned alone in the classroom to learn to be pupils (in the new world). The transition programme is the start of the liminal stage, in which children set out to learn to become pupils in kindergarten. The transition activities are not only a spatial (physical) passage but also a status passage; this passage is the symbolic meaning of the "legal position" that is the children's pupil status (van Gennep 1960). Children are viewed as "candidates for kindergarten" when the parents prepare them for the transition in various ways, such as talking about the kindergarten and buying new school uniforms. When children participate in transition activities such as school visits or pre-entry classes for newcomers, it is clear that they are physically in the new world – kindergarten. At this time, the expectations associated with being a pupil start to be placed on children by both parents and teachers, even though their official pupil status does not start until they enter the classroom on their first official day of school. As "candidates for kindergarten" or "kindergarten beginners", they are expected to follow the practices of the school and fulfil the expectations required of pupils. Children need to cope with the rituals of the classroom, including the daily ritual of separating from caregivers, engaging in play and learning activities, following rules and routines and establishing relationships with others. This is a transition process of learning to become a pupil and is a period of ambiguity, marginality and transformation. The children are not yet integrated into their new pupil status. The postliminal stage is the end of the process of transition. At this point, children have learned and adapted and have completed the transition to their new pupil identity during their first year in kindergarten.

The stages of transition provide an understanding of how children may go through contextual changes, progressing from the preliminal (rites of separation) to the liminal (rites of transition) and postliminal (rites of incorporation) stages. This is a process of habituation through which children may adapt to kindergarten over periods of time that differ in length and intricacy. It tells us that some children may adapt easily whereas other children may take a few days, a few weeks or even longer or require more effort to adapt to their new pupil status.

10.2.1.3 Pupil Career: Understanding Children's Readiness and Adaptation

The conceptual framework adopts Pollard and Filer's (1999) notion of "pupil career" to understand children's competencies for starting kindergarten in the preliminal stage and adaptation outcomes in the postliminal stage for transitioning to kindergarten. They provide a holistic view with respect to the goal of discerning children's preparation and adaptation – how well children are prepared for starting kindergarten and how well they incorporate themselves into the pupil status. They claim that pupil career is a social product, and they identify three components: patterns of strategic action, patterns of outcomes (learning competence and learning dispositions) and pupil identity.

Patterns of strategic action can be understood as strategic biographies that refer to children's preferred and relatively coherent repertoires of actions in response to the classroom situations. These actions may change over time due to the tension between the individual child and their teachers or peers in successive settings. To understand children's patterns of strategic action, Pollard and Filer (1999, pp. 27–28) identified four dimensions of action:

- Conformity: being compliant to the school structures and teacher expectations and integrated into mainstream classroom life; conformity to others' agenda
- Anti-conformity: refusing to conform through deviance; having an oppositional agenda
- Nonconformity: being independent with respect to formal school expectations, having own agenda
- Redefinition: negotiating, challenging and pushing the boundaries of the school norms and expectations, influencing the shared agenda

"Patterns of outcomes" include formal (academic) and informal (social) outcomes. The major type of formal outcome is school curriculum attainment (i.e. learning competence; e.g. in Hong Kong, nursery-class (3-year-old) children are expected to recognise Chinese words, the English alphabet from A to Z, numbers 1–10), whereas informal outcomes are social and status outcomes (i.e. learning dispositions and identity). Learning dispositions include self-confidence, motivation, autonomy (self-regulation) and relatedness (sense of belonging) (Bronson 2000; Brooker 2002; Carr 2001; Dowling 2010; Grolnick et al. 1999; Pollard and Filer 1999). The assumption is that in real-life situations children not only adapt to the learning context but also to the social context of the classroom. Regarding the evolving pupil identity, Pollard et al. (2000) drew attention to the learning dispositions that children adopted in coping with the learning challenges.

10.2.2   A Case Study Illustrating the Conceptual Framework

To illustrate the conceptual framework above, this section presents and analyses a 3-year-old girl's behaviours during the transition from home to kindergarten in terms of three stages: preliminal (readiness), liminal (the home-school transition itself) and postliminal (adaptation). A brief description of the home and classroom sets the context for better understanding of her behaviours.

10.2.2.1 Setting the Context: Home Context and Experiences

Yan was a 3-year-old girl from a single-child working-class family who was taken care of by her Indonesian domestic helper. The family lived in a 700 sq ft two-bedroom rented flat in a village. Her father was a foreman on a construction site and her mother was a dental assistant. They worked 6 days a week and had long working hours. They came home from work after 8 pm. Yan had free and relaxed daily routines that revolved around her. Her daily activities consisted of playing with her favourite toys – toy kitchen and dolls, watching TV or videos and listening to songs. On weekends, the whole family usually went to the supermarket and to visit grandparents.

Her mother told Yan that she was going to enter kindergarten without describing it in advance and only showed her the school uniform and schoolbag before she started kindergarten. Her parents tended towards strict discipline and the discipline method was explanation followed by firm order. They had no clear education aspirations for her, as she was their first child. They did not put academic pressure on her but wanted her to feel loved and have a happy childhood. However, after Yan started kindergarten, her mother struggled with the conflict between hoping for a happy childhood and having a good start academically that was mediated from the milieu. Her mother supported her learning at home by supervising Yan's homework and revision of words and numbers after dinner, despite being tired after a long working day. This was a shift from a relaxed and intimate parent–child interaction to a more academic-oriented parent–child interaction.

10.2.2.2 Preliminal Stage: Patterns of Strategic Actions, Competencies and Identity

Through interaction with the materials, cultural and language resources (mediational means) at home, Yan gradually developed strategic actions in response to her home situations. She persisted in playing with her favourite toys, initiated and negotiated with her caregivers while playing, and, at times, was influenced by them. She was used to free routines and asked for immediate help when she needed it. She negotiated her wants or the home rules with her mother at first and then usually conformed when her mother was firm. She was afraid of her father because her father was very strict and did not play with her. Her predominant strategic actions at home were redefinition and conformity.

Regarding her evolving sense of identity and kindergarten readiness, her mother described her as a happy child, good tempered, expressive, friendly and loving to help others. She was competent, confident and persistent in playing with her toy kitchen. She enjoyed free play, free movements and free routines. She was not ready for self-care as her domestic helper did all the self-care for her. She had a close rapport with her caregivers and could get along with her peers. She had been given little information about going to kindergarten from her parents. She had little experience with literacy, drawing and educational toys.

10.2.2.3 Setting the Context: School Context and Experiences

Yan entered a kindergarten that adopted a story approach to learning. The two class teachers incorporated stories into the curriculum or used the stories as the main strand in designing structured activities. The learning activities were grouped into whole-class learning activities and group activities. The whole-class learning activities included theme time, language time (English and Putonghua), music and structured physical play activities. Group activities included academic-related activities (e.g. prewriting exercises and teaching aids for learning 3Rs) and free play in activity centres. The whole-class learning and academic-related activities were teacher directed in order to accommodate the curriculum, and free play was child directed.

After a month, the teachers changed the rotation method of group activities from a group basis to an individual basis. This was because the teachers found that some children had a different pace of doing an activity and consequently drifted around and caused chaos while waiting for the whole group to finish. The rotation methods showed that learning was viewed as standard or collective regardless of an individual child's interest, habits and the level of persistence in activities. Children were viewed as passive in the ownership of learning. The change of rotation method also showed that the children were successfully negotiating with the teachers. The teachers' values of collective learning and classroom order, rather than the individual child's learning pace, were challenged by children's collective and consistent responses. In effect, by their behaviours, the pupils had effectively modified their teachers' strategies and hence the overall classroom environment.

The timetable was the meditational means for delivering curriculum and pedagogy. The timetable mediated what the kindergarten and teachers expected of the children in relation to how and what they learned. The daily timetable was arrival, registration and prayer, theme time, language activities, toileting, music, group activities, toileting, snack time, physical play and dismissal (Table 10.1). The daily schedule of the class seemed tightly programmed.

10.2.2.4 Liminal Stage: Strategic Actions to Classroom Situations

Yan brought with her personal characteristics, competence, knowledge about kindergarten and preferred strategic actions to cope with the situations in the kindergarten classroom. Yan's strategic actions in response to the classroom situations of (1) separation from caregivers (preliminary stage), (2) classroom environment, (3) play and learning, (4) routines and rules and (5) social relationships were as follows. The numbers indicated in the paragraphs below are for plotting the diagram of patterns of strategic actions of Yan.

- Separation from Caregivers

Yan was brought into the classroom by her domestic helper. She looked apprehensive while sitting on her assigned seat. She *refused* to separate from her

Table 10.1 Daily schedule of the class

Time	Mon	Thu	Time	Tue	Wed	Fri
8:45–9:00	Arrival and free play					
9:00–9:20	Assembly	Exercise	9:00–9:10	Registration and prayer		
9:20–9:45	Registration and theme time		9:10–9:35	Theme time		Bible
9:45–10:05	English		9:35–9:55	English		Putonghua
10:05–10:10	Toileting		9:55–10:00	Toileting		
10:10–10:30	Music		10:00–10:20	Music		
10:30–11:30	Group activities		10:20–11:20	Group activities		
11:30–11:55	Physical play		11:20–11:25	Toileting		
11:55–12:00	Toileting		11:25–11:45	Snack time		
12:00–12:25	Snack time		11:45–12:00	Story time		
12:25–12:30	Getting ready to go home and dismissal		12:00–12:05	Getting ready to go home		
			12:05–12:30	Physical play and dismissal		

domestic helper by asking her to stay with her and holding her domestic helper's hand only on the first day. Starting from the second day, Yan did not ask her domestic helper to stay with her in the classroom. Perhaps she found that physical attachment with her domestic, a familiar person, could provide her a sense of security and a starting point to understand this new place. Her earlier experience of attending all seven pre-entry classes with her domestic helper might also have assisted her make sense of this new classroom.

• Classroom Environment

The classroom was a rectangle, roughly 17 ft × 24 ft, and it was crowded to accommodate activity centres for 30 children. Yan passively reconstructed the classroom by *watching* and looking for familiar toys – toy kitchen in the home centre – for 30 min before responding on the first day (2a). As she was interested in playing with the toy kitchen in the home centre, she tried different strategies to get into the home centre. She knew that she had to get a place in order to play in the home centre (i.e. four children were allowed to play at a time and their shoes should be placed on one of the labels on the floor). She did not conform to the teachers' established rules for entering the home centre, nor did she ignore the rules. She negotiated with the teachers continuously. Her responses included moving a child's pair of shoes from a label on the floor and putting her shoes on the label; shouting at the children who were playing in the home centre "tidy up, I'm gonna play"; leaning her body into the home centre in order to play with the toy kitchen; standing close to the home centre and watching and waiting for a place; taking out the toys from the centre and playing on the table; and, while playing, using her hands to hide her face and saying, "don't let the teachers see".

In short, she *re-territorised* the spatial routines (2b) and attempted alternative ways to *tap* the rules of entering the activity centres from peripheral actions to legitimate participation (2c) so that she could operate in the classroom. Her actions ranged from passive to active and from peripheral action to legitimate action. After a series of negotiations, she followed the rules of going to the home centre.

- Play and Learning

During whole-class activities, children were required to sit in an orderly manner, being quiet and attentive in listening for collective learning as a class of 30 children. Yan *withdrew* from theme time (3a) and language time (3b). She was passive and *withdrew* from answering questions and *refused* to be called out to answer questions in front of the class (3c). She was *slow to respond* to new learning situations (3d) but she was *involved* and enjoyed music activities from the beginning (3e).

In group activities, she had two distinct approaches to academic-related activities and free play. She *avoided or withdrew* from academic-related activities (e.g. prewriting exercises and teaching aids), whereas she was eager and devoted to participation in free play (e.g. artwork and toys) regardless of the rules or time allowance.

With respect to her favourite activities – free play, during the period of rotation of activities on a group basis, she *ignored* the assigned sequence of activities and shifted to her preferred activities (3f1). If she were "discovered" by the teachers, she would *negotiate* with the teacher to continue with her preferred activity and to play longer (3f2). Most of the time, the teachers asked her to go back to her group. When the teachers changed the rotation of group activities on an individual basis, she would *ignore* teachers' request to change activities and keep on playing (3f3). Sometimes, she refused to stop playing and move on to the next activity by replying directly that she had not finished and wanted to continue (3f4).

In contrast, Yan was reluctant to complete academic-related activities that she disliked or did not fully understand. She tended to be *slow at completing* (3g1). She looked around, talked and *redefined* the prewriting exercise as drawing (3g2). When the teacher sat with her and monitored her progress, she would *smile and tell the teacher she did not know how to do it*, and sometimes she would lean on the table (3g3). Once she had managed to do the exercise, she would ask to do it on her own. When she had the autonomy to choose the activity sequence, Yan *withdrew* from prewriting activities by *putting them off* till the last and, at times, after free play (3g4). She showed reluctance to do prewriting exercises and teaching aids by *drifting around* (evasion) (3g5). She started to become concerned with evaluative feedback on her prewriting exercises by seeking verbal recognition and receiving *more stamps* as reward (negotiation) (3h).

- Routines and Rules

As indicated in the timetable, there were frequent transitions between activities in the classroom, and the transitions always went with tidy-up and lining up as a class. The transition methods were more collective moves rather than personalised to individual children. Yan i*gnored* the transition routines by keeping on playing (4a1) and *avoided* these by drifting around until the teachers "caught" her (4a2).

She successfully *negotiated* the seating arrangements in theme time (4b). The teachers compromised and allowed her to sit on a chair as she wished instead of on the floor as assigned. She managed to *help herself* in snack time (4c). She *resisted* defecation in school by crying and refused to allow adults to help her (4d).

- Social Relationships

The teachers' preferred classroom interactions focused on empathy, order, fairness and safety, and the classroom atmosphere was supportive, relaxed and secure in intellectual and social learning. Yan was gentle in dealing with peer conflicts and was socially accepted by her peers and at times bossy (5a). She had informal rapport with Miss Chan and always succeeded in negotiating her wants with Miss Chan (5b).

- Home-School Relationships

Yan's case exemplifies that a child's transition from home to kindergarten may be hindered or helped by the total home environment as well as the school environment. Yan seemed to be disadvantaged in academic learning at the start because the meditational means available at home were relatively unfavourable for preparing her for the transition to kindergarten. There were discontinuities between home activities and the classroom practice. Discontinuities in learning experiences forced her to attempt a variety of strategies to cope with the new situations in order to adapt to pupil status.

In order to support Yan's comparatively low interest and confidence in her ability to work on prewriting exercises and teaching aids, the teachers' strategies were to approach her cheerfully, encouraging her and patiently accompanying her to try the activity by holding her hand to teach her and appraising her writing by giving stamps as a reward. The teachers created a supportive, relaxed and secure atmosphere to encourage Yan to experience success in prewriting activities and using teaching aids. All their pleasant attempts were aimed at helping Yan do what she did not want to do. This demonstrated that the teachers were sensitive to Yan's needs and were helping her to meet the academic demands of the kindergarten.

Moreover, Yan's mother supported her learning by supervising Yan doing homework and revision of words and numbers after dinner, despite being tired after a long working day. With the help of her mother and the teachers, eventually, Yan mastered these activities even though she was reluctant to appropriate them. This showed the joint efforts by herself, the teachers and her mother in supporting both the transition and learning. It is important to note that though Yan's behaviours were not consciously planned, focused or verbalised as an adult might cope with, say, entering into a new job, she was nonetheless an effective agent in her own transition from home to school.

10.2.2.5   Postliminal Stage: Patterns of Strategic Actions, Adaptation Outcomes and Pupil Identity

When plotting Yan's strategic actions in response to context-specific situations in the classroom (Fig. 10.2), it appears that her strategic actions fell into the dimension

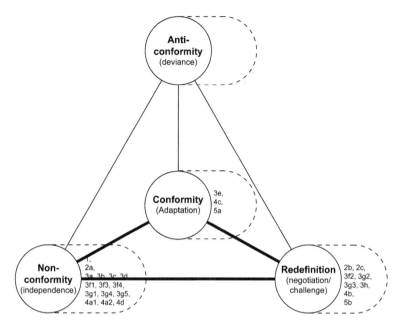

Fig. 10.2 Plotting Yan's patterns of strategic action

of nonconformity, redefinition and adaptation but mainly nonconformity. She went through an ongoing dynamic process of construction and reconstruction to regulate her responses until they were mutually accepted by herself and the teachers and thus "adapted" to the classroom. She exhibited a sequence of strategic actions in response to most of the situations in the classroom. Her preferred strategic actions were watching, being slow to respond, ignoring (non-verbal, passive construction and reconstruction), gently refusing, negotiating, operating in alternative ways (verbal, active reconstruction and negotiation) and following the practice and expectation of the class (regulation and conformity).

In sum, her negotiation strategy in class was consistent with her strategic actions at home. However, her evasion in academic-related activities might be because she was not confident in these new learning experiences. As she had limited formal learning experience at home, this might be her response to stressful new learning activities. This showed her academic learning ability had faced challenges.

Yan's strategic actions reflected her adaptation outcomes and pupil identity. Yan was described by teachers as cheerful, always in a good temper and loving to play with and help others. She showed initial anxiety but soon adapted to the separation from her domestic helper. She was involved in free play, particularly in the home centre at the start. She adapted to most of the whole-class learning activities in 2 months time, but she took a longer time to adapt to teaching aids and prewriting exercises. At the end of the year, she had made steady progress and enjoyed moderate academic achievement.

She became more confident in learning, but often needed encouragement. She favoured a low-risk approach to learning and was extrinsically motivated by the attractiveness of activities and reward. She developed a wider interest in, and was devoted to, free play. She adapted to the classroom physical environment. She showed awareness of rules, first negotiating and then conforming. She developed self-regulation and required less external regulation from the teachers. She was competent in interacting with others and was, at times, bossy. She was socially accepted by peers and developed informal rapport with Miss Chan.

Yan's case consolidates the theoretical framework in understanding how children go through the transition process and context. The duration and adaptation outcomes of children during the transition from home to kindergarten are affected by the continuity of the two settings and the support from both teachers and parents. These confirm the previous studies that continuity between settings contributes to children's successful adaptation (Anning and Edwards 1999; Brooker 2002; Cleave et al. 1982; Graue 1999).

10.3   Conclusion

10.3.1   Challenges and Issues

The conceptual framework presented above draws on sociocultural theory and the notions of rites of passage and pupil career. The sociocultural approach to transition offers a comprehensive contextual and process model for studying the transition from home to kindergarten. It assists in understanding how children experience and cope with various classroom situations as they adapt to becoming pupils in a new school. The case study showed that children are active and creative participants in their own transition, rather than passive receivers as adults often perceive them to be. When facing new and challenging situations in the new kindergarten classroom, they use their biographical resources (characteristics, abilities, accumulated experiences) to help them cope. There are interactions between children and their parents and children and their teachers in the context of the home and kindergarten. Children may assimilate or appropriate others' expectations of them as pupils into their ways of coping, and they may influence adults' practices to arrive at a working consensus.

Thus, adaptation is an interactive and dynamic process of negotiation and change between the goals and actions of an individual child and the situated contexts in which they take place. It also offers a comprehensive concept of transition – agents, contexts, process and adaptation.

Agents: Children are active and creative agents in negotiating their transition.
Contexts: The cultural practices and continuity of the transition contexts of home and kindergarten are influential to children's adaptation.

Process: Transition is a relational process and its duration is subject to the individual child and his or her situated transition contexts.

Adaptation: Children's adaptation can be assessed not only by their academic attainment but also by their development as independent learners.

10.3.2 Future Directions

The theoretical framework set out in this chapter highlights that the agent-context-process-adaptation model can be further explored, examined and modified with respect to understanding children's transitions in early-years settings, thus contributing to further research into transition in different countries. As children are the agents in their kindergarten transition, it is appropriate and necessary to conduct research with children rather than on them (Clark 2010; Clark and Moss 2001).

However, in Hong Kong, children's first-hand experiences and views about their lives are often neglected in transition research in a Chinese context. Children are perceived as too young (i.e. age of ignorance) and considered unable to articulate or speak for themselves and thus are regarded as an unreliable source of data. However, in my studies, observing children's strategic actions in response to different classroom situations has helped me understand which aspects are easier to adapt to and which aspects are more difficult. Even at the age of three, children are able to "voice" their views about going to kindergarten, their favourite activities at home and in school and their understanding of the classroom routines and teachers' requirements. This provides a user perspective on transition practices that are culturally appropriate in the Hong Kong context.

This chapter shows how awareness of children's behaviours can have important consequences in understanding their transition from home to kindergarten – consequences in particular for teachers and parents who all too often assume that because children cannot conceptualise their feelings, needs and objectives in words, they are not effective agents of change in their own lives and environment.

Finally, researching the 3-year-old children's perceptions of their lived experiences at home and in school is new in Hong Kong, as well as in other countries, and may yield a new conceptualisation of childhood that may change adults' views of what children can do.

References

Anning, A., & Edwards, A. (1999). *Promoting children's learning from birth to five: Developing the new early years professional*. Buckingham: Open University Press.

Bronson, M. (2000). *Self-regulation in early childhood: Nature and nurture*. New York: Guilford Press.

Brooker, L. (2002). *Starting school – Young children learning culture*. Buckingham: Open University Press.

Bruner, J. (1996). *The culture of education*. Cambridge, MA: Harvard University Press.

Carr, M. (2001). *Assessment in early childhood settings: Learning stories*. London: Paul Chapman.

Clark, A. (2010). Young children as protagonists and the role of participatory, visual methods in engaging multiple perspectives. *American Journal of Community Psychology, 46*(1–2), 115–123.

Clark, A., & Moss, P. (2001). *Listening to young children: The mosaic approach*. London: National Children's Bureau and Joseph Rowntree Foundation.

Cleave, S., Jowett, S., & Bate, M. (1982). *And so to school*. Windsor: Education Foundation for Education Research.

Dowling, M. (2010). *Young children's personal, social and emotional development*. London: Paul Chapman.

Fabian, H. (2002). *Children starting school: A guide to successful transitions and transfers for teachers and assistants*. London: David Fulton.

Graue, M. E. (1999). Diverse perspectives on kindergarten contexts and practices. In R. C. Pianta & M. J. Cox (Eds.), *The transition to kindergarten* (pp. 109–142). Baltimore: Paul H. Brookes.

Grolnick, W. S., Kurowski, C. O., & Gurland, S. T. (1999). Family processes and the development of children's self-regulations. *Educational Psychologist, 34*(1), 3–14.

Lam, M. S. (2005). *Transition from home to kindergarten: Case studies of young children's strategic actions*. Unpublished doctoral dissertation, University of Cambridge, UK.

Lam, M. S. (2009). Crossing the cultural boundary from home to kindergarten in Hong Kong: A case study of a child's strategic actions. *European Early Childhood Education Research Journal, 17*(1), 125–145.

Lam, M. S., & Pollard, A. (2006). A conceptual framework for understanding children as agents in the transition from home to kindergarten. *Early Years: An International Journal of Research and Development, 26*(2), 123–141.

Lave, J., & Wenger, E. (1991). *Situated learning: Legitimate peripheral participation*. Cambridge, UK: Cambridge University Press.

Pollard, A. (1985). *The social world of the primary school*. London: Holt, Rinehart and Winston.

Pollard, A., & Filer, A. (1996). *The social world of children's learning*. London: Cassell.

Pollard, A., & Filer, A. (1999). *The social world of pupil career*. London: Cassell.

Pollard, A., Triggs, P., Broadfoot, P., McNess, E., & Osborn, M. (2000). *What pupils say: Changing policy and practice in primary education*. London: Continuum.

Turner, V. W. (1969). *The ritual process: Structure and anti-structure*. London: Routledge and Kegan Paul.

van Gennep, A. (1960). *The rites of passage*. (B. V. Minika & G. L. Caffee, Trans.). London: Routledge and Kegan Paul. (Original work published 1910)

Vygotsky, L. S. (1978). *Mind in society: The development of higher psychological processes*. (M. Cole, V. John-Steiner, S. Scribner & E. Souberman, Eds. & Trans.). Cambridge, MA: Harvard University Press.

Wertsch, J. V. (1991). *Voices of the mind: A sociocultural approach to mediated action*. London: Harvester Wheatsheaf.

Wertsch, J. V. (1998). *Mind as action*. Oxford: Oxford University Press.

Chapter 11
Experienced and Recalled Transition: Starting School as Part of Life History

Tuija Turunen

11.1 Introduction

Often people can recall memories about starting school and carry them into adulthood and even to old age as part of their autobiographical narratives. This chapter brings together transition to school as part of life course (Elder 1998) and autobiographical narratives as a story of 'continuing me' (Nelson 2003). It argues that starting school is one of the key life events and might contribute to a person's identity and life trajectory. It also locates transition to school as an influential factor within the life course and facilitates the application of autobiographical narrative methodologies to early childhood transition research.

Previous research has shown that transition to school has an impact on the school years that follow (Dockett and Perry 2007). Positive transition is linked to positive school outcomes in academic achievement and social competence. A child's image of himself/herself as a learner is influenced by school experiences, and experiences of success have an impact on a child's future success at school and sense of self. This chapter contributes to the field of transition studies by opening a new view to starting school as part of an individual's life course and story of 'continuing me'. It continues the work of the previous studies on memories related to childhood (Andersson and Strander 2004; Lahelma 2002; McNicol 2007; Rosewarne et al. 2010; van Hook 2002) and concentrates on memories and autobiographical narratives of starting school that recall happenings even decades after they occurred.

Memories about starting school are part of autobiographical narratives which people construct to understand their lives as entities (Bruner 1990, 2001; Polkinghorne 1988; Webster and Mertova 2007). Autobiographical narratives are

T. Turunen (✉)
Charles Sturt University, Albury Wodonga, Australia

University of Lapland, Rovaniemi, Finland
e-mail: tuija.tuurnen@ulapland.fi

B. Perry et al. (eds.), *Transitions to School - International Research, Policy and Practice*,   145
International perspectives on early childhood education and development 9,
DOI 10.1007/978-94-007-7350-9_11, © Springer Science+Business Media Dordrecht 2014

places to establish a sense of personal history in the social world where other people have their own histories. They are one way to explain to the self why certain things happened the way they did and their significance for the present (Nelson 2003). Autobiographical narratives are complex forms of cognition in which knowledge, emotions, identity and culture intersect during the process of remembering (Conway 2004). In their stories, people make sense of their experiences and memories, themselves, the world and their relationships. This process often begins at about the same time as children start school. It contains awareness of self in the past and future and the difference between self and others' narratives. It is linked to language development and the establishment of a unique and coherent life story (Howe et al. 2003).

In this chapter, I integrate the theoretical foundations and examples from my finished and ongoing research projects with memories about starting school in Finland and Australia. In these projects, the participants were asked to tell their story about starting school in autobiographical narrative interviews. The studies so far include stories from Finland during the Second World War and the post-war reconstruction (Turunen 2012). In Australia, the stories were told by early settlement Australians, immigrant-background Australians who started school either in Australia or first overseas and then in Australia and Indigenous Australians (Turunen 2009; Turunen and Dockett 2013; Turunen et al. 2012). The extracts from the stories are used to highlight the implications of the theoretical foundations for research and practice.

11.2   Starting School as Autobiographical Knowledge

Following Conway's (2004, p. 9563) statement, 'the term autobiographical memory refers to memory for the events of our lives and also to memory for more abstract personal knowledge such as schools we attended, people we had relationships with, places we have lived, places we have worked, and so on'. Memories of special events can be vivid and detailed, whereas personal knowledge is more general.

In the following extract, the narrator first describes her personal vivid memory about the event of not understanding and knowing what to do on her first day at school and the strategy she used to cope with that situation. At the end of the extract, she moves from this personal experience to more general knowledge about English as a Second Language (ESL) programme in her school:

> So I just had this sheet in front of me and I just looked over at the girl next to me and whatever she did I would do. So I do remember writing down like ... Trying to ... Well I thought I'll just put ... So I just put 'Carolyn' on my sheet. I mean, I didn't know how to write so I just did my best. So I copied her. Basically I just copied her, whatever she did I did. That's my memory of the very first day. And obviously I kept returning to school and the school started to have an ESL program for me. (Started school in Australia 1979, immigrant heritage)

In the following extract, the knowledge about moving and the age of the baby brother represent general knowledge which is accompanied with a personal experience of the uncle's truck. This memory was told as part of a relocation story before starting school.

> But we lived at [the name of the town] till I was about two years old, I think, and then moved down [to the place she started school]. So my baby brother was just born when we … Must have been six months old when we moved down. And that's probably my earliest memory, is coming in that truck. I can vaguely remember the truck, my uncle's truck with the furniture on the back and us sort of coming down. (Started school in Australia 1956, Australian heritage)

These two examples illustrate how different kinds of memories are needed in the construction of autobiographical narrative. The personal experiences and vivid memories about them are placed in the context of general knowledge about one's life during the experience.

Autobiographical memories form a resource of autobiographical knowledge. Conway and Pleydell-Pearce (2000) have identified three areas of autobiographical knowledge: lifetime periods, general events and event-specific knowledge. Lifetime periods are distinct periods of time with identifiable beginnings and endings, such as the period of schooling. In the stories, starting school marks a new lifetime period – schooldays – as can be seen in the following extract:

> It's just really bits and pieces but as I said we lived very close to the school. I just really have very positive memories of all of the primary school years anyway. And I found most people very, very helpful and I don't remember, even though I couldn't speak English at all when I went, it didn't seem to matter. (Started school in Australia 1959, immigrant heritage)

In the following extract, the narrator tells about her whole education from Year 1 to Year 9.

> I don't remember there being a kinder class, there may have been but I know I started in first class. Yes, and so sometimes there might have been only two and three in a class. Some classes I can remember there was probably up to five of us. The classes went from either kinder or first through to intermediate, Year 9. And so yes, I was always last in the class because I never had time to do homework. I had to milk the cows to start with before I went to school and milk the cow when I went home. And was always sent to bed early because I had to ride the bike I suppose, that and all the jobs I had to do. (Started school in Australia 1939, Australian heritage)

As can be seen from these extracts, in their stories, people constructed starting school as part of a bigger lifetime period which contained primary school years, as in the first example, or even the whole schooling experience as in the second example. Previous studies have indicated that starting school is not something that happens in one day but is a longer process occurring over six months to several years, including preschool years and the first 2 or 3 years of school (Fabian 2002; Karikoski 2008; Petriwskyj et al. 2005). In autobiographical narratives, starting school is an even longer period than the previous studies have indicated.

Lifetime periods contain general events, which are more specific, but at the same time more heterogeneous. They are usually repeated events like going to school every day, having a school lunch and playtime. They can be identified from time-related words such as 'ever', 'we used to' and 'always'. In the first one of the following extracts, the word 'ever' marks a general event of not having a seat in the school bus. In the second one, the narrator identifies the general event of lunchtime by using 'used to' and 'always'.

> And I remember me starting school and I just didn't like it because I was nearly the last kid to get picked up at [place-name] and there was no seats, ever. (Started school in Australia 1993, Australian heritage)

> We used to have this great big shed with chairs in it and you could have your lunch and that. Yeah, playground was always fun. I always had a lot of friends. (Started school in Australia 1962, immigrant heritage)

Some general events contain event-specific knowledge. These are typically characterised by vivid and detailed imagery. The previous example of copying a schoolmate's name on the first day at school is a good example of event-specific knowledge. The narrator could vividly remember the details of the incident and how she managed to overcome the difficult situation. Other examples of this kind of autobiographical knowledge in the stories often contained strong emotions.

In this extract, the narrator tells about her joy of learning and success:

> At school everything was new: rules, lunch, kits and real crayons. We also moulded with plasticine and that was the first success of my school work! (Started school in Finland 1953)

In the following example, the narrator tells a vivid memory about being separated from her carer:

> I can still remember those moments after 60 years. My stepmother had taken me to the railway station and left me with a nurse. I clenched my doll in my arms and embarked onto the train. There were plenty of children in the railway carriage, some of them crying inconsolable. The destination was unknown. All the children had a cardboard nametag on their neck. (A Finnish child who was sent to Denmark during the Second World War. She started school in Denmark, 1942.)

The following memory was told in the very beginning of the interview. It was a strong memory and the narrator told that it was the reason he wanted to participate in the study:

> I remember being chased through the, it must have been at lunchtime, I got chased, now how they got, they used to call me Mount Kosciusko ... but to be chased by these people. Of course once you start running that is it. I remember most vividly, I saw a nun and I was running towards her and I was hiding behind her dress, you know the veil and everything. I see her smile, but I don't remember her face. (Started school in Australia 1954, immigrant heritage)

This kind of event-specific knowledge can become part of self-defining memories. They are the most significant memories that influence a person's emotions and behaviours and can often be referred as 'turning points' in one's life course (Conway and Pleydell-Pearce 2000; Singer and Salovey 1993). They are important to understand a person's life goals and essential conflicts and become repeated touchstones in one's autobiographical narrative (Blagov and Singer 2004; Singer and Salovey 1993).

Blagov and Singer (2004) have studied self-defining memories and define four dimensions of them: specificity, integrative meaning, content and affect. Self-defining memories are specific episodic memories which a person uses as integrative tools in the construction of his/her autobiographical narrative. They are lessons about the self, important relationships or life in general. The content of self-defining memories is associated with success in relationships or achievement, personal adjustment and levels of distress, and they arouse positive or negative feelings at the time of recall.

The following extract can be understood as a self-defining memory. Recalling this memory of bullying was still seemingly stressful for the teller, over 70 years after the event:

> I hated being different. I had plaits, bucked teeth, Chinese so I didn't have much going for me. They used to tie my plaits, the ribbons on the chair and then … And I used to get taunted at the high school. It was really … You wanted to make yourself this big [showing a tiny space with her fingers] so people didn't notice you. Anyway, I became form captain, house captain. I played in school hockey teams. So I think that it was all in my head, this inferiority complex, but it carried … I carried that right through until I was married, this inferiority complex. (Started school in Australia 1935, immigrant heritage)

In her story, this person kept coming back to her ethnic background and how it had affected her throughout her life course. In the following extract, the narrator draws inferences from his childhood experiences to how he acted later as an adult:

> [after telling about bullying] Then I decided: when I am an adult and the boss, I surely will be in the side of the underdog and will not allow anyone to bully a defenceless person! I was able to fulfil the promise when I worked as a regular in the army and later in a position of responsibility. (Started school in Finland 1943)

Self-defining memories integrated the autobiographical narratives and narrators often interpreted the meaning of them via the present and the future as we can see from the previous example. They became repeated 'touchstones' in one's autobiographical narrative (Blagov and Singer 2004). The construction and integration process can be seen in 'time travelling' during the story. The following extract is a good example:

> I didn't like reading so much and I found it really difficult. We used to have to stand up in front of class and read out and I found that really difficult. That actually went right through school. I even found that difficult in later years, until one of my teachers encouraged me to join the debating team and that really helped. And I haven't shut up since in public really. But that was a challenge and yet I could … We used to have morning talk and we used to just have to stand up and talk about what's happening and that I found really easy. (Started school in Australia 1970, Australian heritage)

The narrator first describes her anticipation to read aloud and then jumps to her later school years and from that to adulthood. When she has given an explanation, she comes back to her starting school experiences.

11.3   Starting School Within Life Course

According to Elder and Shanahan (2006), life course is a sequence of socially defined, age-graded events and roles that define the contours of biography. Individual life happens in a time and place and is linked with other people's lives (Elder 1998). Life courses consist of transitions combining a role exit and entry, of leaving a state and entering a new state (van Gennep 1960). Transitions in the life course and especially the first transitions in early childhood can affect further transitions because the advantages and disadvantages tend to accumulate (Elder 1998). Accordingly, Dunlop (2007) talks about "transitions capital" and how a child can gain this through successful transitions. With transitions capital, a person has more knowledge and skills to successfully address transitions later in his/her life.

As Elder (1998, p. 1) puts it, transitions 'are always part of social trajectories that give them distinctive meaning and form'. Starting school represents an institutionalised transition established by laws and educational policies (Elder 2004). It starts a new trajectory, school days, and influences people's identification of themselves as learners and members of school communities. In the following extract, the narrator tells about her feelings related to this new identity:

> Tomorrow it finally starts, the school. I am allowed to visit my grandma to pick some apples which are good snacks on the way to school. In the spring I had to sit in on my sister's class and now I was treated like a schoolchild. (Started school in Finland 1950)

Many transitions are age-graded and can be evaluated as a cohort status. People are located in special cohorts, and there are expectations of timing and the order of the transitions within that cohort (Elder and Shanahan 2006). Starting school is very much linked to age. It happens to nearly all children when they are 'old enough'. The age of schoolchildren thus has a socially constructed meaning in the life course; one needs to do it on time, not too early or too late (Elder and Shanahan 2006).

In the stories, the expectation of starting school at the right age was often revealed:

> I don't know, it [starting school] was just something we all did. We all had to go to school and once you turned … [right age]. My birthday is in June but I know I would have probably started pretty much at the beginning of the year. But I was probably a bit young you see, 4 ½. (Started school in Australia 1944, Australian heritage)

The failure to start school at the right age can be a difficult experience:

> Well I think it is important because it is different to most children's story of starting school where you automatically start school and there is no question whether you should or shouldn't go to school and you had a right to have an education regardless of your ability or disability. Because of my disability I had to wait until my brother was four and a half and I was six years old before the education department would allow me to go to school instead of staying at home and not getting an education. (Started school in Australia 1942, Australian heritage)

In the first of these two examples, the narrator first talks about the 'right age' of starting school and then explains that he was not quite 'old enough'. In the second example, the narrator was 'too old' when she started school. Because of her disability, she had to wait for her young brother to grow up so that he could assist her. This failure to fulfil the cohort status was a difficult experience for the narrator, and she kept coming back to it throughout the interview.

11.4   Starting School in Context

Starting school happens in time and place, just like all the other transitions during the life course. It is embedded in and shaped by the context (Elder 1998). Memories are culturally framed, and the context is used to make sense of experiences (Nelson 2003). Autobiographical narratives are the places where individual memories and sociocultural contexts meet and are linked to wider social narratives (Haynes 2006; Markowitsch and Welzer 2009).

In the stories, starting school happens within numerous sociocultural contexts. Bronfenbrenner's (1979) ecological model describes children's development as influenced by direct and indirect experiences within sociocultural contexts and describes the interaction between individuals and contexts as the driving force behind an effective transition to school. It provides a framework for considering the ways in which different contexts, processes and people interact and intersect over time. In the transition to school, the contexts of family, preschool and school intersect and are influenced by broader community, political and social contexts and the people and processes operating within these.

The macrosystem is shaped by home and school cultures and the historical time, and it influences the narratives of starting school. For example, in Finnish stories, the wartime narratives were more sombre than the post-war ones (Turunen 2012). The narratives from the years 1937 to 1943 were affected by war, and it was somehow present in all of them. In the wartime narratives, there were many sinister events, including events that were not related to war, such as accidents and sickness. Latvala (2006) has indicated that memory knowledge related to home and school shows how children perceive the unusual everyday life, for example, during wartime. Children see, hear, experience and sense the war and the threat of death and loss. The war memories of childhood are not forgotten (Latvala 2006).

Starting school in Finland between 1937 and 1957 was influenced by the Second World War, the post-war reconstruction of the country and paying war debts to the Soviet Union. These incidents influenced the sociocultural context in general and starting school in particular during those decades and can be identified in the narratives as can be seen in the following extract:

> After walking about three kilometres, the road ended with a railway and a freight train was greeting me. I was startled and panicked. I plunged for 'a shelter' behind the road and under a fir. (Started school in Finland 1943)

This extract tells about a fear of bombing. During the Second World War, Finland was heavily bombed. Because most people lived in rural areas where no bomb shelters were available, people ran to forests when they heard bombers coming. For children, a stentorian noise was frightening, because it was a sign of a danger.

Transition to school is meeting an unknown school culture for the majority of children (Broström 2007), but added to that, immigrant children encounter people from the other culture, habits that they are not familiar with and often also a language barrier. It appears that starting school is also often the first meeting with the mainstream culture without the parents. In the following extract, the narrator illustrates this:

> Then when it was my time and I was given permission to go, even in primary school, it was like I was going over a fence into another culture. Of course when I went over the fence my language changed, my behaviour changed, my food changed-because if I was having lunch at someone else's place there was stuff I didn't eat at home. (Started school in Australia 1957, immigrant heritage)

These examples of the influence of macrosystems on starting school experiences illuminate how the narrators were required to cope with demanding macro-level circumstances simultaneously with starting school.

The exosystem is the level where a child is not participating but which influences his/her life indirectly (Bronfenbrenner 1979). From a child's point of view, it is usually the adults' world. In the stories about starting school, the exosystem is noted by the child and often interpreted by the narrating adult in the stories. For example, it could be the absence of father because of the war or seeking work:

> In Block 21 [Reception and Training Centre for immigrants, in Victoria, Australia] for a few days until they were shifted to Block 15 that was the official hostel block for long term people staying as we were. Meanwhile dad ended up walking or mostly hitch-hiking all the way up to Sydney, all over the place trying to get some work. Poor old mum was left to look after the four of us. (Started school in Netherlands 1950 and in Australia 1952, immigrant heritage)

or financial challenges after the immigration:

> So things were 'pretty tight' in those days. The joy of my life was when I was given a pair of shoes, but they were school shoes —that was my Christmas present, [laughing] because that was something special, you know. Parents could not afford things in those days because we lived in poor, very poor circumstances. (Started school in Australia 1951, immigrant heritage)

The microsystems are the systems where a child is personally involved (Bronfenbrenner 1979), like home, school, friends and their homes. In stories about starting school, microsystems were often intertwined. The life of the child is an entity and school is part of it, and not always the most important part.

> I think the best thing about school and the best thing about being in New Guinea was that my mum came from a village and every weekend we would drive three hours to the village and spend the weekend at the village and then come back for school. So I just liked being there, a break, a mini-break and then coming back, it was good. (Started school in Papua New Guinea 1980, immigrant heritage Australian)

> My memory of that time was that we had a very free life, running around outside because I can remember running around with my friends, all around [the name of the town]. (Started school in Australia 1956, Australian heritage)

In the following extract, academic learning was not recalled, and that seemed to surprise the narrator:

> I remember getting chastised for playing in the school garden, by the teacher, just silly things really. But the actual schooling, subjects and such I don't remember much, just that I used to talk a lot in school. (Started school in 1949 in Germany, immigrant heritage Australian)

In the stories, some of children's microsystems were invisible for adults. They were the children's own places, which adults did not understand or have access. Often this 'secret world of childhood' was explicitly expressed:

> And if you wanted to swim above the water you held this ball, you held a ball and you could sort of manage to keep your head up above water. Well my parents would have been … Mum would have been horrified to think that I'd let my children do that but she did it. She didn't know what we were up to. But we all survived. (Started school in Australia 1950, immigrant heritage)

11.5   Future Directions and Policy Implications

According to Elder (1998), studying the life course is important in order to identify and understand the impact of various changes in children's lives. It is not always possible or expedient to have extended longitudinal studies. Studying memories is one way to use life course theory to investigate the past and interlocking trajectories in human life. Transitions, like starting school, are substantial times of change and can be represented as turning points (Elder and Shanahan 2006). Starting school is an educational marker which may influence coming school years and even the choices a person makes later in his/her life. In their stories, people construct starting school as part of their autobiographical narratives and interpret it in their life course. It becomes part of the story of 'continuing me' (Nelson 2003).

These autobiographical narratives are oral histories which mediate relationships of individual and public life and provide insights into how macro-level social, cultural, economic and political changes are experienced by individual people (Clary-Lemon 2010; Portelli 2004; Schiffrin 2003). Portelli (2004) says that oral history as a coherent narrative story does not exist in nature, but people tell pieces and episodes about their lives. Thus, the stories about starting school told during research interviews had usually never been told in that form before. They were stories about the past, interpreted and constructed in the present (Freeman 2007).

Studying memories is about studying things that happened in the past, and this makes a question of historical methodologies relevant. Historical incidents need to be taken into account, and that leads the researcher to historical resources like archives and documents. These sources are important to illuminate the context of the stories, even though the emphasis of this kind of study is to contribute understanding of starting school memories as part of a person's constructed autobiographical narrative (Ghosh 2007).

This study approach also arouses issues about 'accurate' and 'inaccurate' memories. Are the memories of starting school historically correct? The stories may not be verifiable in terms of their correspondence to the actual event as it happened at the time but are illustrative of how the past gets revisited and reshaped across one's life course. They are combinations of a person's own experiences, stories told in family and community, photos and other artefacts and the time and place of starting school and recalling it. They represent experienced and recalled constructions of an individual person's self-history, unique to him/her (Nelson 2003). Following Thelen's (1989) ideas, this brings the constructed recollections into the centre of study, rather than the accuracy of the memory.

Understanding transition to school in the autobiographical context can help educators and parents to become more aware of the impact of their own experiences and memories about starting school when working with children. There is some research evidence that shows intergenerational trends in experiences from generation to generation (Barnett and Taylor 2009; Elder 2001; Turunen and Dockett 2011). Starting school experiences and memories through generations in the same family are worthy of further study.

By understanding and reflecting on their own experiences, educators and parents can move towards empathy and understanding around a child's experiences (Rosewarne et al. 2010). This can provide the basis for positive relationships – the essence of a successful transition to school (Dockett and Perry 2007). Bronfenbrenner's ecological theory sets up some interesting scenes on starting school. Understanding the meaning and impact of the macro- and exosystems requires paying attention to the meaning of starting school for children, who nowadays live in critical situations such as financial difficulties, violence, war or natural catastrophes. Elder and Shanahan (2006) emphasise how sociocultural context and historical changes affect the life course. They define them as exogenous processes in human development. Children live in sociocultural contexts which influence their experiences and memories about starting school and will become part of their autobiographical narratives and self-understanding. In difficult situations, starting school can represent a normal and safe everyday life.

Beside the macro- and exosystems, children live their individual lives and have their own microsystems. Some of them can be invisible for adults and represent "the secret world of childhood". Home and family, friends and their homes, lessons and playtime at school are parts of children's microsystems and are all intertwined. An interesting question for further study might be what impact children's own microsystems have on transition to school.

References

Andersson, B.-E., & Strander, K. (2004). Perceptions of school and future adjustment to life: A longitudinal study between the ages of 18 and 25. *Scandinavian Journal of Educational Research, 48*(5), 459–476.

Barnett, M. A., & Taylor, L. C. (2009). Parental recollections of school experiences and current kindergarten transition practices. *Journal of Applied Developmental Psychology, 30*(2), 140–148.

Blagov, P. S., & Singer, J. A. (2004). Four dimensions of self-defining memories (specificity, meaning, content, and affect) and their relationships to self-restraint, distress, and repressive defensiveness. *Journal of Personality, 72*(3), 481–512.

Bronfenbrenner, U. (1979). *The ecology of human development: Experiments by nature and design.* Cambridge, MA: Harvard University Press.

Broström, S. (2007). Transitions in children's thinking. In A.-W. Dunlop & H. Fabian (Eds.), *Informing transitions in the early years. Research, policy and practice* (pp. 61–73). Maidenhead: Open University Press.

Bruner, J. (1990). *Acts of meaning.* Cambridge, MA: Harvard University Press.

Bruner, J. (2001). Self-making and world-making. In J. Brockmeier & D. Carbaugh (Eds.), *Narrative and identity. Studies in autobiography, self and culture* (pp. 25–43). Amsterdam: John Benjamins.

Clary-Lemon, J. (2010). We're not ethnic, we're Irish: Oral histories and the discursive construction of immigrant identity. *Discourse & Society, 21*(5), 5–25.

Conway, M. A. (2004). Memory: Autobiographical. In N. J. Smelser & P. B. Baltes (Eds.), *International encyclopedia of the social and behavioral sciences* (pp. 9563–9567). Amsterdam: Elsevier.

Conway, M. A., & Pleydell-Pearce, C. W. (2000). The construction of autobiographical memories in the self-memory system. *Psychological Review, 107*(2), 261–288.

Dockett, S., & Perry, B. (2007). *Transitions to school: Perceptions, expectations, experiences.* Sydney: University of New South Wales Press.

Dunlop, A.-W. (2007). Bridging research, policy and practice. In A.-W. Dunlop & H. Fabian (Eds.), *Informing transitions in the early years. Research, policy and practice* (pp. 151–168). Maidenhead: Open University Press.

Elder, G. H. (1998). The life course as developmental theory. *Child Development, 69*(1), 1–12.

Elder, G. H. (2001). Families, social change, and individual lives. *Marriage & Family Review, 31*(1/2), 187–202.

Elder, G. H. (2004). Life course: Sociological aspects. In N. J. Smelser & P. B. Baltes (Eds.), *International encyclopedia of the social and behavioral sciences* (pp. 8817–8821). Amsterdam: Elsevier.

Elder, G. H., & Shanahan, M. J. (2006). The life course and human development. In W. Damon & R. M. Lerner (Eds.), *Handbook of child psychology. Theoretical models of human development* (6th ed., Vol. 1, pp. 665–715). Hoboken: Wiley.

Fabian, H. (2002). Empowering children for transitions. In H. Fabian & A.-W. Dunlop (Eds.), *Transitions in the early years* (pp. 123–134). London: Routledge.

Freeman, M. (2007). Autobiographical understanding and narrative inquiry. In J. D. Clandinin (Ed.), *Handbook of narrative inquiry: Mapping a methodology* (pp. 120–145). London: Sage.

Ghosh, R. (2007). Interdisciplinarity and the 'doing' of history: A dialogue between F. R. Ankersmit and Ranjan Ghosh. *Rethinking History, 11*(2), 225–249.

Haynes, K. (2006). Linking narrative and identity construction: Using autobiography in accounting research. *Critical Perspectives on Accounting, 17*(4), 399–418.

Howe, M. L., Courage, M. L., & Edison, S. C. (2003). When autobiographical memory begins. *Developmental Review, 23*(4), 471–494.

Karikoski, H. (2008). *Lapsen koulunaloittaminen ekologisena siirtymänä. Vanhemmat informantteina lapsen siirtymisessä esiopetuksen kasvuympäristöstä perusopetuksen kasvuympäristöön* [Starting school as an ecological transition. Parents as informants in the transit of children from pre-school to school environments]: *Vol. 100. Acta Universitatis Ouluensis E.* Oulu: Oulun yliopisto.

Lahelma, E. (2002). School is for meeting friends: Secondary school as lived and remembered. *British Journal of Sociology of Education, 23*(3), 367–381.

Latvala, P. (2006). Lapsuuteeni kuuluivat sota, siirtolaiset ja sankarihautajaiset [In my childhood there were the war, evacuees and soldiers' funerals]. *Historiallinen aikakauskirja [The Historical Journal], 104*(2), 142–152.

Markowitsch, H. J., & Welzer, H. (2009). *The development of autobiographical memory*. Hove: Psychology Press.

McNicol, S. (2007). Memories of reading in the 1940s and 1950s. *New Review of Children's Literature and Librarianship, 13*(2), 101–116.

Nelson, K. (2003). Narrative and self, myth and memory: Emergence of cultural self. In R. Fivush & A. C. Hayden (Eds.), *Autobiographical memory and the construction of narrative self* (pp. 3–28). Mahwah: Lawrence Erlbaum.

Petriwskyj, A., Thorpe, K., & Tayler, C. (2005). Trends in construction of transition to school in three western regions, 1990–2004. *International Journal of Early Years Education, 13*(1), 55–69.

Polkinghorne, D. (1988). *Narrative knowing and the human sciences*. Albany: State University of New York Press.

Portelli, A. (2004). Oral history as genre. In M. Chamberlain & P. Thompson (Eds.), *Narrative and genre: Contexts and types of communication* (pp. 23–45). New Brunswick: Transaction Publishers.

Rosewarne, S., White, J. E., Hard, L., & Wright, L. (2010). Exploring transition through collective biographical memory work: Considerations for parents and teachers in early childhood education. *Australasian Journal of Early Childhood, 35*(3), 24–32.

Schiffrin, D. (2003). Linguistics and history: Oral history as discourse. In D. Tannen & J. E. Alatis (Eds.), *Linguistics, language, and the real world: Discourse and beyond* (pp. 84–113). Washington, DC: Georgetown University Press.

Singer, J. A., & Salovey, P. (1993). *The remembered self. Emotion and memory in personality.* New York: Free Press.

Thelen, D. (1989). Memory and American history. *Journal of American History, 75*(4), 1117–1129.

Turunen, T. A. (2009, August). *Memories about starting school. What is remembered after decades?* Paper presented at the European Early Childhood Education Research Association (EECERA) Conference, Strasbourg.

Turunen, T. A. (2012). Memories about starting school. What is remembered after decades? *Scandinavian Journal of Educational Research, 56*(1), 69–84.

Turunen, T. A., & Dockett, S. (2011, October). *Family members' memories about starting school.* Paper presented at the Oral History Association of Australia (OHAA) Conference, Melbourne.

Turunen, T. A., & Dockett, S. (2013). Family members' memories about starting school. An intergenerational aspect. *Australasian Journal of Early Childhood, 38*(2), 103–110.

Turunen, T. A., Dockett, S., & Perry, B. (2012, August). *When I started school... Recalled traditions of transition.* Paper presented at the European Early Childhood Education Research Association (EECERA) Conference, Oporto.

van Gennep, A. (1960). *The rites of passage*. London: Routledge.

van Hook, C. W. (2002). Preservice teachers reflect on memories from early childhood. *Journal of Early Childhood Teacher Education, 23*(2), 143–155.

Webster, L., & Mertova, P. (2007). *Using narrative inquiry as a research method*. London: Routledge.

Part III
Critical Perspectives

Chapter 12
The Relation of Research on Readiness to Research/Practice of Transitions

Elizabeth Graue and June Reineke

12.1   Introduction

It is only in the last 25 years that US researchers and policymakers have begun looking beyond the child- and skill-centered notion of readiness to include ideas about ready families, schools, and communities (Graue 2006; Kagan 1990; National Education Goals Panel (NEGP) 1998; National Governors Association (NGA) 2005). This shift has paralleled the progression of transition research, framing transition as a process that is facilitated through an ecological systems understanding of early childhood education (Pianta and Cox 1999; Rimm-Kaufman and Pianta 2000; Rous et al. 1994).

To better understand the ebb and flow of the relationship between readiness and transition in research and practice, we contrast these two constructs across several dimensions. By examining their theoretical foundations, their evolution over time, and their inherent complementarity, we will illuminate how they have shaped and are shaped by early learning initiatives in the past, present, and future. We ask that the reader recognize that our approach is parochial, representing only our experience in the United States. We are confident that our colleagues' work in other chapters will connect ours to global notions of transitions so that we are not quite so isolated in the story we tell. We will begin by providing a brief historical overview, working to define commonly used ideas in transition and readiness in the United States, exploring the theoretical foundations of our research, the challenges and resources these foundations have provided, and the future directions of our research in the area.

E. Graue (✉)
University of Wisconsin, Madison, WI, USA
e-mail: graue@education.wisc.edu

J. Reineke
Winona State University, Winona, MN, USA
e-mail: JMReineke@winona.edu

B. Perry et al. (eds.), *Transitions to School - International Research, Policy and Practice*,   159
International perspectives on early childhood education and development 9,
DOI 10.1007/978-94-007-7350-9_12, © Springer Science+Business Media Dordrecht 2014

12.2   Theoretical Foundations

Our intellectual work around transitions and readiness comes from a stance of critical constructionism. From this perspective, these constructs are not self-standing entities "out there" but are instead, products of historical, social, cultural, and political forces. Rather than counting ready children or working to find the best transition plan, we assume that readiness is socially constructed in local communities that differ in terms of their ideas about children, the role of schooling, and the nature of development (Graue 1993). As a result, one child will be ready on one side of town and not ready on the other.

The same is true of transitions – transition practices develop in response to, and reflect, local values and power relations, typically serving the needs of some but not of others. Looking closely at the interactions among people, places, and local practices shows that children experience readiness and transition practices in real time and in real life. Social constructs create material realities. Conversely, material realities create social constructs. But it does separate to some degree the constructs from the child and makes us, as capable adults, culpable for the consequences of our measures and practices. Critical constructivism is a step away from the mainstream developmentalism that has shaped so much of thought and practice in early childhood education as it examines how children, families, and educators come to think about readiness and transitions in particular social and historical contexts. It leads us to look at how these ideas have historical legacies and to look carefully at the consequences of our conceptualisations.

For example, readiness and transition did not exist until children and education were placed into a life-stage framework. That is, neither construct was conceivable until children moved from home to school. This life-altering transition has historically been wrapped around ideas about developmental maturation, environmental opportunities, or the interaction of the two. In each of the perspectives, the role of intervention is seen as a mechanism that can leverage success.

Early in US history, readiness took on a remedial tone, with interventions provided for children from impoverished environments. Often children of immigrants or children living in poverty were provided socialisation so that they could succeed not only in school but in life as well. This notion is observed in the development of the US settlement house that served an explicit transitional purpose in the nineteenth century (Bloch 1987). Through the settlement house, immigrants (parents and children) were to be socialised to American ways of life, taught hygiene and language, and given childcare for working mothers. The transition in this case was from one culture to another, from one set of norms to another. The most relevant issue was leveling the playing field for children with fewer resources at home than their more affluent peers. Readiness for these children was framed from a deficit perspective as illustrated by the sparse institutional surroundings in Fig. 12.1.

This can be contrasted to the other side of town shown in Fig. 12.2, where children attended private nursery schools offering sandboxes, dress-up clothes, and

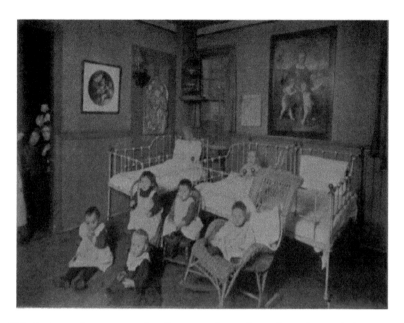

Fig. 12.1 Settlement house nursery (http://www.google.com/imgres?q=settlement+house+nursery&u m=1&hl=en&sa=N&rlz=1G1GGLQ_ENUS377&biw=1260&bih=790&tbm=isch&tbnid=bDNuvVj QJEZ_GM:&imgrefurl=http://americafrom1865.blogspot.com/2012/02/early-20th-century-struggle-for-civil.html&docid=wwyYIc3z5vlxJM&imgurl=http://www.swarthmore.edu/Library/peace/ Exhibits/janeaddams/photoshullhouse/Nursery1.jpg&w=900&h=577&ei=p6uXUMDfJ_GgyAGmzo Fo&zoom=1&iact=rc&dur=429&sig=103433073126969172997&page=1&tbnh=141&tbnw=238&st art=0&ndsp=25&ved=1t:429,r:0,s:0,i:71&tx=79&ty=39) (Originating in the Jane Addams Collection, Swarthmore)

a wide variety of freely chosen opportunities for play. Learning how to think and create were desired skills for success in the real world.

Transition and readiness for more affluent children was respectful of the resources that children had at home and was primarily a kind of bridge that facilitated the move from home to school. Rather than the institutional perspective of the settlement house, transition and readiness for these children was viewed as enrichment that occurred through interaction with the natural world.

While we could trace the discussion on developmental patterns, ages, and stages back centuries, the notion of readiness crystallised in the early twentieth century when the Child Study Movement claimed the potential to map children's passage through the early years. Through careful and systematic observation of thousands of children, scientists were able to describe patterns in development in samples of young children. The following image (Fig. 12.3) shows Arnold Gesell, a key figure in the empirical study of children in an observation room with multiple data collectors recording interactions. This practice was replicated with thousands of children to create a developmental map that was correlated with age.

Fig. 12.2 Private nursery garden (http://www.loc.gov/pictures/resource/cph.3a25266/) (Library of Congress Prints and Photographs Division Washington, DC. 20540 USA)

Fig. 12.3 Arnold Gesell in the Child Study Center (http://www.childstudycenter.yale.edu/Images/med337_101604Gesell%20Dome4.jpg) (Image courtesy of the Yale Child Study Center, Yale University School of Medicine)

Developmental mapping moved early childhood education from the realm of the romantic and mystical (Froebel, Waldorf) to a practice informed by science. This created experts who could identify what was normal and give advice about practices to support children's development. The creation of the expert gave some people authority and minimized the expertise of others. Pediatricians rose in credibility as individuals well acquainted with ages and stages, and parents deferred to them in seeking advice.

Depending on how children were conceptualised, this empirical framing might take on a maturationist flavor, arguing that development was primarily a biological process that could not be changed. When this was the framework, à la Gesell, the role of early schooling was to support the natural unfolding of children's development, keeping educational demands slightly lagging behind maturation. Biology was the mechanism that shaped readiness, assuming that the home environment provided sufficient support for learning. Transitions often focused on determining whether children had sufficient maturity to benefit from schooling.

As the impact of environmental factors on readiness drew attention from researchers, another interventionist approach gained prominence and was at the heart of the development of Head Start, a key element of the US war on poverty in the 1960s. Developed in a period of faith in the federal government to move people from poverty to prosperity, Head Start included a comprehensive approach to child development (Zigler and Valentine 1979). This was comprised of preschool for children in poverty, health and social services, and a parent involvement program that was designed to move parents to teaching positions in the program. This kind of transition paired a deficit perspective with a community empowerment approach, based on the assumption that children in poverty lacked the skills and dispositions to succeed in school, while valuing the cultural cache that parents could bring to a community preschool program. The picture below (Fig. 12.4) shows the president's wife, Lady Bird Johnson, chatting with children in a Head Start program.

Head Start's introduction as a comprehensive program aimed at transcending poverty through child and parent success triggered an influx of research that looked beyond a child- and skill-centered view of readiness to thinking about the role of transition in linking preschool and kindergarten programs. Longitudinal studies began showing the benefits of targeted early childhood programs on school and life success (Campbell et al. 2002; Ramey et al. 2000; Reynolds 2000, 2011; Schweinhart et al. 1986, 2005). Economists used this information to show the economic benefits of these programs (Grunewald and Rolnick 2003; Heckman et al. 2006; Reynolds and Temple 2008). In 1997, the US National Education Goals Panel declared that "by the year 2000 all children will start school ready to learn" (NEGP 1997). Cumulatively, from this work, the role of early childhood program quality has emerged as an organizing factor for state readiness and transition work. This has resulted in attention on the ready child being coupled with thinking about ready schools (programs) and communities.

Responsiveness to these ideas is seen in the recent introduction of the US Race to the Top Early Learning Challenge Grants designed to support the state's work of building quality early learning systems. US Secretary of Health and Human

Fig. 12.4 Lady Bird Johnson at Head Start (http://www.google.com/imgres?q=lady+bird+johnso
n+head+start&um=1&hl=en&rlz=1G1GGLQ_ENUS377&biw=1260&bih=790&tbm=isch&tbni
d=kYO2iyioBgIIoM:&imgrefurl=http://www.tumblr.com/ZI1-WxIEXFNy&docid=K4S4TSGkG
PermM&imgurl=http://25.media.tumblr.com/tumblr_m0jflkHZmZ1qjih96o1_500.jpg&w=500&
h=333&ei=-6yXUL3ZOsOYyAHv84DAAg&zoom=1&iact=rc&dur=453&sig=1034330731269
69172997&page=1&tbnh=134&tbnw=226&start=0&ndsp=23&ved=1t:429,r:1,s:0,i:71&tx=83
&ty=71) (©LBJ Library photo by Robert Knudsen)

Services, Kathleen Sebelius says, "The Race to the Top-Early Learning Challenge
takes a holistic approach to early education, promotes innovation, and focuses on
what it takes to help put young children on the path of learning, opportunity, and
success" (White House Press Office 2011). This effort is imagined to support continued construction of statewide systems of high-quality early learning and development programs by aligning and raising standards for existing early learning and
development programs; improving training, support, and articulation for the early
learning workforce; and building evaluation systems that promote effective practices and programs to help parents make informed decisions about their child's early
learning (LeMoine 2008).

A critical constructionist perspective reads these examples as historical moments
that created resources for thinking about children, their needs, and their education.
Rather than make an argument about their readiness over time or testing transition
practices for their effects in the long or short term, we are interested in how the
practices and processes related to readiness and transition came to be and how they
were taken up by parents, teachers, politicians, and even children. Each of these
moments reflected a particular set of social and cultural forces. The ability to know
patterns in development, particularly in a scientifically validated way, was made
possible because observational methods, including the development of scales and
the use of both still and action photography provided tools that supported the

documentation of development as well as the very patterns themselves. The need to close opportunity gaps, which were created when immigrants came to the United States or when poverty was an enemy to be conquered, opened the window to programs that framed readiness in terms of deficits to be filled and transitions as critical periods between contexts. The intervention was focused on changing the consequences of poverty or immigration rather than eradicating the risk itself. It is not clear yet whether the newest initiative will make any greater progress.

In the meantime, while these questions persist and early learning system work continues, a growing body of research is influencing normative readiness and transition practices (Crosnoe 2007, Dockett and Perry 2009; Graue 1992, 2006; Kagan and Tarrant 2010; Moore 2008; Pianta et al. 2007). This work is enhancing initial transition research that presented a two-dimensional model looking at the vertical (across time) and horizontal (across contexts) progress of children (Doucet and Tudge 2007; Kagan and Neuman 1998). Publicly adopted documents, definitions, and recent initiatives support a multifaceted understanding of readiness and transition. This encourages a perspective that moves from an individually child-focused event to creating larger institutionally linked agendas looking at processes occurring between contexts, stakeholders, and time.

This nested ecological systems perspective first described by Urie Bronfenbrenner (1977) has been adopted by some researchers aiming to describe how 'links among child, home, school, peer, and neighbourhood factors create a dynamic network of relationships that influence children's transition to school both directly and indirectly' (Rimm-Kaufman and Pianta 2000, p. 492). This can be understood by looking briefly at the framing of transition goals that attempt to build synchronicity between pre-K and kindergarten systems, thereby establishing ready schools.

Ready schools need to base transition on three related principles:

1. Reaching out. Schools reach out and link with families and preschools in order to establish relationships and engage in two-way communication about how to establish effective transition practices.
2. Reaching backward in time. Schools establish links particularly with families before the first day of school.
3. Reaching with appropriate intensity. Schools develop a range of practices with varying intensity (i.e., low-intensity flyers or pamphlets, high-intensity personal contacts or home visits) (Pianta et al. 1999).

The continuity espoused by this model is rooted in the chronological links created as the child moves from pre-K to kindergarten. Presently, it appears that little readiness information from the model's pre-K side is transmitted to teachers at school during the transition to kindergarten. This correlates with transition research studying ways that kindergarten reaches out to pre-K parents, which indicates that schools often share information about kindergarten with parents but seldom initiate relationships that encourage parents to share developmental information about their children (Boethel 2004; Bohan-Baker and Little 2004). This is particularly curious considering the emphasis placed on continuity in the transition research. In part, this may be due to the "reaching back" instead of "sending forward" conceptualization of transition often encouraged in transition work guides (Pianta and Kraft-Sayre 2003; Sullivan-Dudzic et al. 2010). This research has formed an institutional conceptualisation of the transition process, looking primarily through a lens focused on elementary school practices informing parents about kindergarten. Current NAEYC and Head Start program standards require transition activities prior to kindergarten entry (Head Start 2012; National Association for the Education of Young Children (NAEYC) 2006). Compliance with these standards is encouraging the pre-K community to collectively reach forward to kindergarten classrooms. This change in momentum, with activities being initiated by pre-K professionals, places greater focus on the types of relationships needed for school success rather than the informational emphasis found in the institutional conceptualisation of transition. The relationship-based framing of transition emerges from research highlighting the importance of relationships in the teaching/learning process (Harrison et al. 2006), ways that children's and parent's knowledge about school is constructed (Bohan-Baker and Little 2004; Doucet 2008), and showing types of information and relationships that prove most successful for children as they enter school (Boethel 2004; Weiss 2003). This relational framing of transition seeks to understand readiness and transition implications for children from different backgrounds (Crosnoe 2007; Magnuson et al. 2006). Researchers studying readiness and transition from sociocultural perspectives have provided insights about transitional triggers and relationships that are needed between parents, classrooms, and communities to support transitions (Arimura et al. 2011; Bohan-Baker and Little 2004; Corsaro and Molinari 2005; Doucet 2008; Doucet and Tudge 2007).

From a more distant policy perspective, a layered, ecological systems approach has emphasized intensified collaboration among education, health, and social service agencies as they attempt to understand and address community readiness and transition needs. This approach has led to increased interagency discussions as organisations identify, pool, and blend limited resources for targeted projects. Unlike previous Head Start work, which offered multiple services for children, current efforts look for ways to collaborate in their support of families with comprehensive programs under one roof. Kagan (2010) suggests that the diverse nature of this work needs a more systematic focus that can be framed by looking at structure through the lens of pedagogies, programs, and policies. These efforts, while deemed essential, must find connections to the realities of the families that they are designed to serve. This includes understanding transition through the eyes of children and adults as part of the larger effort (Laverick and Jalongo 2011). Researchers who recognize the potential for disconnect among children, provider, and policy system layers are calling attention to the need for reflexive research and systems with mechanisms that are culturally and locally responsive (Brown and Gasko 2012; Patton and Wang 2012).

In an attempt to understand the needed reciprocity between layers, a more modern ecological approach, as theorized by Bronfenbrenner (1995), is being suggested (Graue et al. 2011; Tudge et al. 2009). This more comprehensive approach – known as the Person-Process-Context-Time theory (PPCT) – provides a holistic means of understanding and building a dynamic framework for amalgamating transition and readiness work. The complementary nature of these concepts becomes apparent as readiness is viewed as a flexible construct that develops across time and contexts, and transition focuses on the relationships and processes connecting preschool years to kindergarten classrooms. This foundational reconceptualisation offers new implications for our readiness and transition research.

12.3   Implications for Practice and Research

Using this framework from a critical constructionist stance makes it challenging to give concise answers to typically asked questions about transition and readiness – or even to frame a concise question. Questions like, "At what age should children begin kindergarten?" or "How should we organize transitions to school?" elicit very unsatisfying answers like "It depends" or "There isn't." Framing questions is just as nebulous – you end up tripping over queries like, "Who is advantaged by particular transition practices?" The implications or the "so what" are not directly derived – there is something unsettling about an expert who does not profess with certainty or who professes uncertainty with certainty. It tends to undermine authority.

From this stance, readiness and transition are framed relationally – children are always ready for something or they are transitioning to something. But just as importantly, their readiness or transition is always in comparison to others – to other children, to other families, and to other classrooms. This normative component puts a kink in defining, building, or evaluating policy and practices that are responsive to the assets that children bring – how do you make sense of something whose meaning and implications are framed in absolutely relative terms?

Some of this tension may be eased by using an elongated and enmeshed view of readiness and transition that provides a natural transparency with which to look 'simultaneously forward and backward evaluating the adequacy of social, personal, economic and educational resources afforded by communities' (Graue 2006, p. 51). The PPCT framework has the potential to shift from a deficit to an asset-based way of thinking about children and their opportunity structures by focusing on how families understand, access, and use community-constructed readiness and transition mechanisms. By understanding what children and families from diverse backgrounds understand about schools and schooling, professionals have the opportunity to be responsive in their construction of systems.

Unfortunately, policymakers who want easy answers to simple questions are permanently irritated by critical constructionist analyses. The best example of this is the response to a recent grant proposal that said: "We don't need any more research that says, 'It depends!'" For those without a willingness to deal with the relational aspects of these constructs, the value of this approach is quite limited. However, when given a different lens for asking those questions, the answers and subsequent questions become influential in current readiness and transition work that is often initiated federally but enacted locally. Critical constructionism using social, historical, and cultural analyses becomes a viable approach for encouraging examination of ready schools and communities.

12.4 Challenges and Issues

We have come to this place in our research from different paths. Beth has spent more than 20 years doing research related to readiness. She has actually been trying to leave the readiness business for at least 5 years. One narrative would be that her research interests have evolved to focus on other topics. But also true is that she is tired – of feeling like Sisyphus, pushing a critical constructionist perspective up a hill, and not going anywhere; of worrying that her research is irrelevant; and of the deep dark fear that her perspective is just as arbitrary as those who have competing views. She recognizes that as a social scientist, it's not supposed to be about her – it is supposed to be about the research. But from a critical constructionist perspective, she is indistinguishable from her research, as it is, in the very same way that transition and readiness are, a relational activity. While Beth has tried to back away from this complex and very messy topic, the historical, cultural, and social forces she depends on in her research are pulling her back into the middle of this discussion during an unmatched time of intensity in early childhood education and care.

June has spent more than 20 years working as a pre-K teacher and program administrator of a campus-based early learning center enmeshed in local readiness and transition practices. As a Ph.D. candidate, her emerging research agenda is focused on the construction of local, non-urban, birth-to-grade-three early learning systems. Her years of interactions with early childhood professionals and deep relationships with children and families led her to methods that were contextually and process based. Working in real time with real people provides the opportunity for detailed understanding of complex questions that cannot be gleaned from faceless methods. Understanding the questions from the outside-in and inside-out creates challenges and opportunities for shaping emerging early childhood education systems.

But from a perspective broader than our own, the US context provides unique challenges and issues. The culture of individuality, particularly prominent in middle-class white communities, frames the issues of readiness and transition in very different ways than a more social or community perspective prevalent in communities of colour and in poverty. The culture of individuality sees parenting as concerted cultivation (Lareau 2003), with efforts by parents and educators focused on the individual child. The point of parenting is to situate your child for success, with success defined as a child who is a leader, emotionally secure, socially adept, physically robust, and academically open to learning. Readiness for many middle-class families has a competitive flavor, requiring children to be the biggest, oldest, and most mature.

In contrast, less affluent families seek to have their children in school as soon as possible, often without a résumé of enrichment activities. The parents are no less committed to their children, as they approach the task of caring for their children as a natural task, one that emerges out of the interactions of family and community.

These different perspectives on readiness set up what seem to be parallel universes, where the roles and responsibilities for early education promote different practices and different consequences. What is particularly vexing is the value placed on concerted cultivation, often seen as the "right" way to raise children and approach schooling. Further, when moving children to the top is seen as the goal of parenting, any critical constructionist critique of concerted cultivation is met with disbelief or even disdain as it conflicts with its central goal. "Do you mean I am supposed to worry about the experiences of somebody else's kid as I make decisions about my child? And that somebody else isn't willing to invest in the way that I am? Forget it!" This view of parenting as investment with both short-term and long-term dividends makes discussion of equity in readiness and transition a dead end for many families.

From a systems perspective, significant challenges exist as more emphasis is placed on the alignment and regulation of early childhood systems as part of the pre-K and K-12 networks. The affordances created by this system also provide possible constraints. The birth through five education system is the last educational system for a professional that offers curricular freedom and responsivity to children's interests and abilities in a non-prescribed environment. The daily early learning curriculum is integrated across content areas and offers choice and freedom to make friends through each activity. By creating systems that seek to align practices, we risk losing one of the most intrinsically motivated educational opportunities of one's life. The challenge that exists will be crafting a readiness and transition system with accompanying research that is beneficial to the other. This notion has implications for our future research agendas.

12.5   Future Directions

In the past, Beth has described the social processes and meanings that shaped children's, families', and school experiences related to readiness. From these descriptive accounts, she has suggested implications for enhancing transitions for children and families through more equitable school entrance practices and less normatively framed curriculum that put less mature children at risk.

She continues to view the world through a critical constructionist framework but is shifting the focus of her work. Rather than study existing practices that vary by social and cultural resources, she is currently working to build capacity for equity in local pre-K programs. She is working very pragmatically on readiness and transition issues by designing and implementing a professional development program for public pre-K teachers in Madison, WI. She has joined forces with mathematics educators to develop a program that connects best practices in early education and funds of knowledge teaching through a focus on early mathematics. Her group is working with multiple cohorts of teachers in both public elementary schools and community childcare centers to help individual teachers enhance their knowledge and skills in this area but also to develop a vibrant and well-educated community of early educators. A natural part of this program will be considering systematically, the transition practices at two points – the transition to kindergarten in which the teachers will be intimately involved as they work with 4-year-olds and a new transition which will occur as children come into the 4K (4-year-old kindergarten) program. The collaborative nature of this program, which blends the public schools with the early childhood community and the local university, provides an interesting opportunity to think about transitions.

Using a critical constructionist lens and the PPCT framework, June is researching readiness and transition issues in a midsized Midwestern community whose local school board has charged a task force with the responsibility of studying and implementing a seamless birth-to-grade-three early learning system. Working with a group of community members and professional early childhood/elementary stakeholders from the private and public sector, three areas of primary interest have been identified: curriculum and assessment, transition, and professional development. She is leading the transition subgroup charged with examining the current practices and identifying areas of interest. As part of this work, she is hosting four ongoing parent focus groups, each with membership from a diverse early childhood educational experience, Head Start, in-home childcare, center-based childcare, and family providers. Through across-time conversations, she will analyze the mechanisms accessed and used by diverse families to ready and transition their children into kindergarten. The results will be shared with the task force so that the family voices are integrated into institutional and community practices. This work models using a structure that collects family feedback shares it with the task force and in turn guides the construction of community readiness and transition practices. The reflexive work of the task force, families, and evolving community practices offers an interesting place to examine the notion of ready schools and communities.

Both of our projects are interventionist, strategically designed to enhance the capacity of early childhood educators, study processes, and explore how programs connect with local communities in meaningful ways. They also have the potential to study student/family careers longitudinally so that we can develop a better understanding of the outcomes of our projects. A key element is designing our projects from the perspective of what we are calling reciprocal funds of knowledge, working to highlight the knowledge and practices that all families bring to their children's schooling. We hope to make information and expertise flow in a two-way manner so that curriculum and school practice takes up the resources that children bring to school and so that families have access to high-status educational knowledge and relationships needed to succeed. Our projects are certainly critical in intention and constructionist in practice. We are each just beginning this work, and we are full of hope that it will provide useful knowledge locally and beyond.

We recognize that by taking up an interventionist agenda as part of our research, we run the risk of being criticized by other researchers as we teeter between research and practice. We find the risk manageable as we see an ethical responsibility for researchers and their research in this time of advancement and refinement of early childhood practices and programs. It would be unconscionable to sit passively on the side observing when we are convinced that there are structural changes that are needed to create equitable opportunities for quickly growing populations of underserved children and parents. It appears that researchers with some early childhood education experience and knowledge can use their research as a tool to build the capacity of a system for children and families.

In many ways, we feel that we have come full circle. We began our work in early childhood teaching 3–4-year-olds and working with their families to enhance their experience. On reflection, we did not come with an openness for learning about what families had to give; instead, we came as parent educators, full of supposed knowledge in our 25-year-old heads. We are now much less certain of our knowledge but much more likely to be able to capitalize on families' deep cultural knowledge and resources because we finally recognize that we have much to learn from them. Our scenic trips through early childhood classrooms, graduate school, parenting, positions in higher education, and advocacy in political arenas bring us to our current readiness and transition questions and activities. If this is not evidence of the value of critical constructionism, we are not sure what is.

References

Arimura, T. N., Corter, C., Pelletier, J., Janmohamed, Z., Patel, S., Ioannone, P., & Mir, S. (2011). Schools as integrated hubs for young children and families. In D. M. Laverick & M. R. Jalongo (Eds.), *Transitions to early care and education: International perspectives on making schools ready for young children* (pp. 189–202). New York: Springer.

Bloch, M. (1987). Becoming scientific and professional: An historical perspective on the aims and effects of early education. In T. Popkewitz (Ed.), *The formation of school subjects: The struggle for creating an American institution* (pp. 25–62). New York: Falmer Press.

Boethel, M. (2004). *Readiness: School, family and community connections.* Austin: National Center for Family & Community Connections with Schools, Southwest Educational Development Laboratory.

Bohan-Baker, M., & Little, P. M. D. (2004). *The transition to kindergarten: A review of current research and promising practices to involve families* (Harvard Family Research Project). Cambridge, MA: Harvard Graduate School of Education.

Bronfenbrenner, U. (1977). Toward an experimental ecology of human development. *American Psychologist, 32*(7), 513–531.

Bronfenbrenner, U. (1995). Developmental ecology through space and time: A future perspective. In P. Moen, G. H. Elder Jr., & K. Luscher (Eds.), *Examining lives in context: Perspectives on the ecology of human development* (pp. 619–647). Washington, DC: American Psychological Association.

Brown, C. P., & Gasko, J. W. (2012). Why should pre-k be more like elementary school? A case study of pre-k reform. *Journal of Research in Childhood Education, 26*(3), 264–290.

Campbell, F. A., Ramey, C. T., Pungello, E. P., Sparling, J., & Miller-Johnson, S. (2002). Early childhood education: Young adult outcomes from the Abecedarian Project. *Applied Developmental Science, 6*(1), 42–57.

Corsaro, W., & Molinari, L. (2005). *I Compagni: Understanding children's transition from preschool to elementary school.* New York: Teachers College Press.

Crosnoe, R. (2007). Early child care and the school readiness of children from Mexican immigrant families. *International Migration Review, 41*(1), 152–181.

Dockett, S., & Perry, B. (2009). Readiness for school: A relational construct. *Australian Journal of Early Childhood, 34*(1), 20–26.

Doucet, F. (2008). How African American parents understand their and teachers' roles in children's schooling and what this means for preparing preservice teachers. *The Journal of Early Childhood Teacher Education, 29*(2), 108–139.

Doucet, F., & Tudge, J. (2007). Co-constructing the transition to school: Reframing the novice versus expert roles of children, parents, and teachers from a cultural perspective. In R. Pianta, M. Cox, & K. Snow (Eds.), *School readiness and the transition to kindergarten in the era of accountability* (pp. 307–328). Baltimore: Brookes.

Graue, M. E. (1992). Social interpretations of readiness for kindergarten. *Early Childhood Research Quarterly, 7*(2), 225–243.

Graue, M. E. (1993). *Ready for what? Constructing meanings of readiness for kindergarten.* Albany: State University of New York Press.

Graue, M. E. (2006). The answer is readiness–Now what is the question? *Early Education & Development, 17*(1), 43–56.

Graue, M. E., Delaney, K., Karch, A., & Romero, C. (2011). *Data use as a reform strategy.* The Wisconsin Center for Educational Research. http://mpsportal.milwaukee.k12.wi.us/portal/server.pt/comm/research_and_evaluation/340/research_reports/41172. Accessed 14 Sept 2012.

Grunewald, R., & Rolnick, A. (2003). *Early childhood development: Economic development with a high public return.* Fedgazette: Federal Reserve Bank of Minneapolis. http://www.minneapolisfed.org/publications_papers/pub_display.cfm?id=3832. Accessed 12 Apr 2012.

Harrison, L., Clarke, L., & Ungerer, J. (2006). Children's drawings provide a new perspective on teacher-child relationship quality and school adjustment. *Early Childhood Research Quarterly, 22*(1), 55–71.

Head Start. (2012). *Head Start performance standards.* http://eclkc.ohs.acf.hhs.gov/hslc/standards/Head%20Start%20Requirements. Accessed 2 June 2012.

Heckman, J. J., Grunewald, R., & Reynolds, A. J. (2006). The dollars and cents of investing early: Cost-benefit analysis in early care and education. *Zero to Three, 26*(6), 10–17.

Kagan, L. S. (1990). Readiness 2000: Rethinking rhetoric and responsibility. *Phi Delta Kappan, 72*(4), 272–289.

Kagan, S. L. (2010). Seeing transition through a new prism: Pedagogical, programmatic, and policy alignment. In S. L. Kagan & K. Tarrant (Eds.), *Transitions for young children: Creating connections across early childhood systems* (pp. 3–17). Baltimore: Paul H. Brookes Publishing.

Kagan, S. L., & Neuman, M. J. (1998). Lessons from three decades of transition research. *The Elementary School Journal, 98*(4), 365–379.

Kagan, S. L., & Tarrant, K. (2010). *Transitions for young children: Creating connections across early childhood systems.* Baltimore: Paul H. Brookes Publishing.

Lareau, A. (2003). *Unequal childhoods: Class, race, and family life.* Berkeley: University of California Press.

Laverick, D. M., & Jalongo, M. R. (2011). *Transitions to early care and education: International perspectives on making schools ready for young children.* New York: Springer.

LeMoine, S. (2008). *Workforce designs: A policy blueprint for state early childhood professional development systems.* Washington, DC: National Association for the Education of Young Children.

Magnuson, K., Lahaie, C., & Waldfogel, J. (2006). Preschool and school readiness of children of immigrants. *Social Science Quarterly, 87*(5), 1241–1262.

Moore, T. (2008). Rethinking the transition to school: Linking schools and early years services. *Policy Brief: Translating early childhood research evidence to inform policy and practice (Vol. 11).* Victoria: Centre for Community Child Health. http://eclkc.ohs.acf.hhs.gov/hslc/standards/Head%20Start%20Requirements. Accessed 9 May 2012.

National Association for the Education of Young Children. (2006). *Program accreditation standards*. Washington, DC: National Association for the Education of Young Children.

National Education Goals Panel. (1997). *Special early childhood report*. Washington, DC: U.S. Government Printing Office.

National Education Goals Panel. (1998). *Ready schools*. Washington, DC: US. Government Printing Office.

National Governors Association. (2005). *Final report NGA task force on school readiness: Building the foundation for bright futures*. Washington, DC: National Governors Association.

Patton, C., & Wang, J. (2012). *Ready for success: Creating collaborative and thoughtful transitions into kindergarten*. Cambridge, MA. Harvard Family Research Project. Harvard Graduate School. http://www.hfrp.org/publications-resources/browse-our-publications/ready-for-success-creating-collaborative-and-thoughtful-transitions-into-kindergarten. Accessed 14 Sept 2012.

Pianta, R., & Cox, M. (Eds.). (1999). *The transition to kindergarten*. Baltimore: Brookes.

Pianta, R., & Kraft-Sayre, M. (2003). *Successful kindergarten transition: Your guide to connecting children, families, and schools*. Baltimore: Brookes.

Pianta, R., Rimm-Kaufman, S., & Cox, M. (1999). An ecological approach to kindergarten transition. In R. Pianta & M. Cox (Eds.), *The transition to kindergarten* (pp. 3–12). Baltimore: Brookes.

Pianta, R., Cox, M., & Snow, K. (2007). *School readiness and the transition to kindergarten in the era of accountability*. Baltimore: Brookes.

Ramey, C. T., Campbell, F. A., Burchinal, M., Skinner, M. L., Gardner, D. M., & Ramey, S. L. (2000). Persistent effects of early intervention on high-risk children and their mothers. *Applied Developmental Science, 4*(1), 2–14.

Reynolds, A. (2000). *Success in early intervention: The Chicago Child–parent Centers*. Lincoln: University of Nebraska Press.

Reynolds, A. (2011). Age 26 cost-benefit analysis of the Child Parent Center early education program. *Child Development, 82*(1), 379–404.

Reynolds, A., & Temple, J. (2008). Cost-effective early childhood development programs from preschool to third grade. *The Annual Review of Clinical Psychology, 4*, 109–139.

Rimm-Kaufman, S., & Pianta, R. C. (2000). An ecological perspective on the transition to kindergarten: A theoretical framework to guide empirical research. *Journal of Applied Developmental Psychology, 21*(5), 491–511.

Rous, B., Hemmeter, M. L., & Schuster, J. W. (1994). Sequenced transition to education in the public schools: A systems approach to transition planning. *Topics in Early Childhood Special Education, 14*(3), 374–393.

Schweinhart, L. J., Weikart, D., & Larner, M. B. (1986). Consequences of three preschool curriculum models through age 15. *Early Childhood Research Quarterly, 1*(1), 15–45.

Schweinhart, L. J., Montie, J., Xiang, Z., Barnett, W. S., Belfeld, C. R., & Nores, M. (2005). *Lifetime effects: The HighScope Perry preschool study through age 40*. Ypsilanti: HighScope Press.

Sullivan-Dudzic, L., Gearns, D., & Leavell, K. (2010). *Making a difference: 10 essential steps to building a preK-3 system*. Thousand Oaks: Corwin.

Tudge, J. R. H., Mokrova, I., Hatfield, B., & Karnik, R. (2009). Uses and misuses of Bronfenbrenner's bioecological theory of human development. *Journal of Family Theory and Review, 1*(4), 198–210.

Weiss, H. (2003). From the director's desk. *The Evaluation Exchange. IX*(3), 1. http://www.hfrp.org/evaluation/the-evaluation-exchange/current-issue-scaling-impact/from-the-director-s-desk. Accessed 14 Sept 2012.

White House Press Office. (2011). *Awards help build statewide systems of high quality early education programs*. http://www.whitehouse.gov/the-press-office/2011/12/16/we-cant-wait-nine-states-awarded-race-top-early-learning-challenge-grant. Accessed 10 May 2012.

Zigler, E., & Valentine, J. (1979). *Project Head Start: A legacy of the war on poverty*. New York: The Free Press.

Chapter 13
Social Justice Dimensions of Starting School

Bob Perry

13.1 Introduction

At a recent professional development evening with local early childhood educators, I asked the question What do you understand by "social justice" in early childhood? Most of the educators remained silent in response to this question, even though this was the advertised topic for discussion. No doubt, they were concerned that they would not provide the right answer or guess the answer that was in the professor's head. However, some did respond and mentioned matters such as equal opportunities, equal outcomes, equity, cultural diversity, language diversity, poverty, reacting to stereotypes, patience and respect. The participants continued to discuss social justice largely in terms of the respect that needed to be shown to individuals, particularly children and families, with whom they interacted. It was generally agreed that such respect was most likely to arise from the building of positive relationships with people. These two elements – respect and relationships – are evident in broader discussions of social justice.

13.2 Social Justice

The term "social justice" is not well defined. Some argue that it fundamentally

> rests on two overriding principles. First, social justice is viewed primarily as a matter of redistributing goods and resources to improve the situations of the disadvantaged. Second, this redistribution is not presented as a matter of compassion or national interest but as a matter of rights of the relatively disadvantaged to make claims on the rest of society. (Bankston 2010, p. 165)

B. Perry (✉)
School of Education, Charles Sturt University, Albury-Wodonga, Australia
e-mail: bperry@csu.edu.au

B. Perry et al. (eds.), *Transitions to School - International Research, Policy and Practice*,   175
International perspectives on early childhood education and development 9,
DOI 10.1007/978-94-007-7350-9_13, © Springer Science+Business Media Dordrecht 2014

Others suggest an increasing focus on "identity politics", moving away from the central notions of redistribution towards emphasis on recognition of identity:

> Many actors appear to be moving away from a socialist political imaginary, in which the central problem of justice is redistribution, to a 'postsocialist' political imaginary, in which the central problem of justice is recognition. With this shift, the most salient social movements are no longer economically defined 'classes' who are struggling to defend their 'interests', end 'exploitation', and win 'redistribution'. Instead, they are culturally defined 'groups' or 'communities of value' who are struggling to defend their 'identities', end 'cultural domination' and win 'recognition'. (Fraser 1997, p. 2)

Fraser (1997) promotes a critical approach to social justice that combines both recognition and redistribution. North (2006, p. 514) continues this argument, noting that

> The remedying of recognition injustices therefore does not require eliminating group differences, as suggested in the redistributive model, but instead revaluing them or reinventing conceptualizations of the human being that lead to oppression and domination.

As individuals strive for recognition within society, they become participants in many different relationships both within and outside of their "groups" or "communities of value". It is these relationships that provide the loci of social justice for the individual, the groups and all the people involved, for social justice is not something that can exist in isolation from society. Young (2011, p. 157) suggests that while 'Enlightenment' principles might declare that 'people should be treated as individuals, not as members of groups; [and] their life options and rewards should be based solely on their individual achievement', 'the very success of political movements against differential privilege and for political equality has generated movements of group specificity and cultural pride'.

While the notion of being treated as an individual and being free to choose one's own life is seductive, it is not particularly practical given that we all live in social groups that will be affected by our choices and which, in turn, will affect the wider society. Bronfenbrenner (Bronfenbrenner and Morris 1998) labels these social groups 'microsystems'. So, while individuals might like to be treated by society in ways that recognise and support diversity, there needs to be realisation that decisions made within society have a potential impact on all members of that society; for justice to be genuinely "social justice", benefits need to accrue beyond the individual level. Issues such as the needs, interests, rights and power (Blackmore 2006) of all involved need to be considered as we strive towards a socially just society.

The position I take in this chapter is that social justice is about treating all people with dignity and respect. It is about a community recognising and acknowledging injustices and the development of both appropriate and collaborative actions and processes to address these injustices for individuals or groups so that there is a degree of equality in the overall outcomes (Howard et al. 2011). It is about the establishment of strong, positive relationships based on social respect, personal regard, perceived competence and perceived integrity (Bryk and Schneider 2002).

13.3   Social Justice in Early Childhood

For the first time ever in Australia, there is a national curriculum framework for early childhood (Department of Education, Employment and Workplace Relations (DEEWR) 2009). While there is no definition given for social justice in this document, many of the aspects mentioned by the professional development participants introduced earlier and by those scholars advocating a recognition theory of social justice are apparent. For example, the document includes the following statements:

> Early childhood educators who are committed to equity believe in all children's capacities to succeed, regardless of diverse circumstances and abilities. (p. 12)

> There are many ways of living, being and of knowing. Children are born belonging to a culture, which is not only influenced by traditional practices, heritage and ancestral knowledge, but also by the experiences, values and beliefs of individual families and communities. Respecting diversity means within the curriculum valuing and reflecting the practices, values and beliefs of families. Educators honour the histories, cultures, languages, traditions, child rearing practices and lifestyle choices of families. They value children's different capacities and abilities and respect differences in families' home lives. (p. 13)

To honour and value as suggested here is not straightforward. It does require a consciousness and sensitivity, based on positive relationships and knowledge, when interacting with children and families. Many early childhood educators do not find this easy (Durand 2010). Most importantly, it requires the suspension of judgement about cultural practices that may be different from those used by the educators in their own families and communities (Rogoff 2003). Social justice in early childhood requires educators to deal with situations in which

> the beliefs, values, practices and socialisation goals for children are fundamentally different across the home and school microsystems. … we have to acknowledge that the children and families we serve don't start in the same place. They come from different places. They don't look the same. They don't act the same. They don't speak or use language in the same ways. (Durand 2010, p. 837)

While the quality and nature of interactions among early childhood educators and young children are important for the development of the children's identities within the diverse worlds in which they live and play (Brooker and Woodhead 2008), we must not forget that these same children are learning about social justice in practice, through these interactions.

> Children from very young ages internalize messages about power and privilege with regard to gender, race/ethnicity, class, sexual orientation, and language, which they perpetuate through their play and talk … classroom practices communicate and reinforce strong, subtle, and repeated social messages about what is and is not valued. (Hyland 2010, p. 82)

Early childhood education can play a critical role in the achievement of social justice. Success will depend on early childhood educators becoming critically aware of the historical and contemporary roles of education in further marginalising disadvantaged groups, realising the potential for them to play a major role in this marginalisation and acting to counter this potential (Schoorman 2011) through practices such as those outlined in Australia's national early childhood curriculum framework. Indeed,

> early childhood educators need to view themselves as leaders who possess insightful voices regarding the growth and development of all children, regardless of ability, race, class, gender, culture, or language. This type of leadership becomes increasingly important, as early childhood education does not exist in isolation from the broader world. (Dana and Yendol-Hoppey 2005, p. 191)

In the remainder of this chapter, the transition to school is considered as an opportunity for the enactment of social justice. How this opportunity plays out for all involved in the transition will determine whether the opportunity becomes reality.

13.4 Theoretical Foundations

The work on transition to school that Sue Dockett and I (and a number of other collaborators) have undertaken since 1997 began with investigations of the experiences and expectations of children, families and educators as they engaged in the transition to school. One of the key innovations in our work, particularly in the Australian context, was the emphasis we placed on listening to children as they explained their experiences. We established the theoretical foundations for our studies using the ecological model of Bronfenbrenner (Bronfenbrenner and Morris 1998) with its clear message that a child lives – and goes to school – within many different contexts, all of which impact on the child and are impacted by the child. As well, our research was designed to reflect the rights-based approaches established in the United Nations Convention on the Rights of the Child (United Nations 1989) and drew on commitments to strengths-based perceptions of children, where children are regarded as competent social actors who are experts on their own lives (James and Prout 1997; Rinaldi 2006).

Our understanding of transition to school is anchored in Rogoff's (2003) conceptualisation of transitions across the life span as times when individuals 'change their roles in their community's structure' (p. 150). 'This view reflects both individual and community influences on children's changing participation in activities' (Dockett and Perry 2012, p. 7) as children start school.

However, transition to school is not just about the child. Children prepare to start school from within a very wide variety of contexts, most of which involve family. Families come in all shapes and sizes but all influence, and are influenced by, the individuals who are in the group. All families have rights and responsibilities, derived from the grouping as well as the individuals that make up the family. All families have strengths which determine what is possible for them, as well as challenges that establish some constraints on their actions. Our theoretical foundation is strengths-based – we emphasise and build upon the strengths of families, while recognising, but not being bound by, their challenges (McCashen 2005; Saleebey

2006). In particular, we emphasise and build upon the strengths of children within these families.

Other important players in a child's transition to school include educators in schools as well as prior-to-school educators. These people also have rights and responsibilities derived from the professional role that they play in the transition process. These educators bring much power to the transition to school endeavour, both in terms of their ability to control transition practices and processes in their own institutions and through their professional education which often leaves them in a perceived position of knowing more about education than any of the other stakeholders in the transition exercise.

Power differentials abound as children start school. Very often, there is a clear power difference between educators on the one hand and families and communities on the other, in terms of knowledge about education. Sometimes, this extends to knowledge about children and their potential adjustment to school. This may be evident when some educators indicate that they do not need to access family knowledge about the child, or even information related to the children offered by prior-to-school educators, preferring instead to observe the child as they start school and find out for themselves (Dockett and Perry 2007a; Dockett et al. 2007). There can be a very strong belief that because school educators hold power in the settings to which the children are moving, they know best and that the structures within the schools are the most appropriate to determine the approach to transition used. Referring to this situation, Woodhead and Moss (2007, p. 40), note that

> … relationships between primary education and the early childhood sector are often one-sided. Schools and early childhood centres do not interact with each other sufficiently, often because ECEC [early childhood education and care] tends to be viewed as the weaker partner. This needs to change, and the educational role of the early childhood sector needs to be recognised.

For transition to school to be socially just for all, there must be 'a strong and equal partnership' (Woodhead and Moss 2007, p. ix) among all stakeholders.

Finally, the theoretical and practical position that transition to school is an opportunity for societies to enhance their social justice quantum has driven much of our work. In Australia, as in many other countries, children and families do not live in environments that provide equal opportunities and are not treated equally by school systems or, even, by individual schools or prior-to-school settings. Stereotypes abound as children start school. Children are judged on perceptions of their families' previous schooling (e.g. one boy was cautioned by a teacher who had taught the boy's mother that 'He needed to be better than her at school'). Some judgements are based on race (e.g. 'She is Chinese so she will do well' or 'Those kids come from [an Indigenous settlement], so they will not be ready for school') or socio-economic class (e.g. 'What can be expected from these kids; their families cannot support them properly' *or* 'The parents are just not interested in the kids'). The theoretical stance taken in our work is that transition to school must be seen as an opportunity to provide an excellent start to schooling for all children.

The Australian *Early Years Learning Framework* (DEEWR 2009) suggests that transition to school offers both opportunities and challenges and that children, families and educators all have roles to play in ensuring successful transitions between settings. However, the emphasis is on preparing the children 'to understand the traditions, routines and practices of the settings to which they are moving and to feel comfortable with the process of change' (DEEWR 2009, p. 15). The *Early Years Learning Framework* continues 'Early childhood educators also help children to negotiate changes in their status or identities, especially when they begin full-time school' and 'Educators work collaboratively with each child's new educators and other professionals to ensure a successful transition' (DEEWR 2009, p. 15). There seems to be a lot more emphasis on what the children are to become rather than on what they have been. Compare this with the following excerpt which highlights a different way of considering transition.

> For Aboriginal children, we not only use the term 'transition' which can imply a one-way journey towards something better, but also the term 'fire stick' period (an Aboriginal term for a stick that is kept alight to ensure the availability of fire). This highlights the way in which culture is not something to be left behind, but is an integral part of their lives. The 'fire stick' period is particularly difficult for young Aboriginal learners, who need to adjust to an extra range and layer of experiences, demands, and expectations relating to their cultural, language, and social skills. If these children are to succeed in the school context then they must know that it is safe and acceptable to move backwards and forwards between these cultures. ... Such terminology can be applicable to children from many cultural groups where the 'fire stick' period equates with the time needed for them to learn how to navigate between their home and school cultures. For young children beginning their school lives, it is critical that this time is framed in a climate of mutual trust and respect. (Simpson et al. 2001, p. 57)

These two perspectives on transition to school highlight the need for consideration of social justice issues within the context of such transitions. Bourdieu (1991) has described schools as institutions that are much more likely to reproduce existing social relations and inequalities than change these. Hence, schools are more likely to serve the interests of children and families who have similar values to those of the schools. In Australia, these values are still seen to emanate from white, middle-class society, the source of most teachers and educational administrators.

On the other hand, the "fire stick" philosophy places transition to school within a context of cultural relationships where children and families are valued for what they bring to the new setting and are encouraged to maintain those values as they develop those of the school. For this to happen successfully, schools need to change or adapt to the new entrants – both children and families – and seek to meet their needs, just as children and families make adjustments to the new setting. It is not assumed that in order for a successful transition to school to occur, the children and families need to change to fit in with the school. Such an approach requires the development of trustful and respectful relationships among all the players in the transition enterprise and a social justice perspective on transition to school.

13.5 Some Examples

The following four examples are taken from earlier work in which I have been involved (Dockett et al. 2011; Perry 2011). They will be used to illustrate the opportunities and challenges to a social justice approach that can occur during the transition to school process.

1. Julie was a single mother with five children – 4 older boys, two of whom were in primary school, and Maddy who was old enough to go to school. Julie suffered from a mental illness caused by a chemical imbalance. She felt that she was engaged with her children's school because she walked to the school gate every morning and every afternoon to deliver and collect her children. 'I would like to know more about the school but no one comes out to talk with me'.

2. In Queensland, a new curriculum framework (Department of Education, Training and the Arts 2007) has been introduced into Indigenous preschool classes in 35 communities. Among many other aspects, the framework emphasises the need for young children to develop:

   • Pride in their personal and cultural identities
   • Their first language as well as standard Australian English
   • Ability to actively participate in learning
   • Literacy and numeracy skills
   • An understanding of their roles, rights and responsibilities

   All of these are seen as building upon the children's strengths and preparing them for school. The Director of one of these preschools expressed her frustrations about the value of the approach once the children go to school 'Why are they failing in grade 1? Why aren't they listening in grade 1? Why isn't Gary [preschool child from 2 years ago], who always gets in trouble, being an active participant … Because he just showed us he can be a learner, imagining and responding, investigating environments. Why can't he do maths?'

3. Tess is a single mother with two children – Astrid in Year 3 and Damien about to start school. The family lives in a regional city without support from extended family. Tess is looking forward to being able to get a job once Damien starts school, both for her own sake and in order to bring in some extra money.

   Damien attends a local preschool and has had a tough time with his behaviour. He has been diagnosed with a conduct disorder, is on medication and is quite often disruptive both at home and preschool. The family does not have support from friends: 'Every time we visit anyone, Damien plays up and I get embarrassed. So, we just stay at home or go out to the local park when no one else is there'.

   Tess decided that teachers at Damien's new school, which is about 3 km from home, should know about his behaviour. She talked with the Principal and with the kindergarten (first year of school) teacher. They thanked her and told her that they would let her know about plans for Damien's school start.

For the first term of kindergarten, Damien is placed on a "partial enrolment". That is, he comes to school in the morning and is sent home at lunchtime. Tess needs to pick him up from the school. She also needs to be available during the time he is at school 'Just in case something goes wrong and we need to send him home'.

4. Sarah's son, Harry, had been diagnosed with Down syndrome. Harry was to attend the local mainstream school, hopefully with support from a teacher aide. To be eligible for this support, Harry needed to be assessed as having at least a moderate intellectual disability. As a result of assessment, he was judged to have a severe intellectual disability. While Sarah was pleased that this made him eligible for additional support, she was upset about the process and the label:

> ...for his whole life we've been trying to build him up and working on his strengths and everything and then all of a sudden it's the exactly opposite, you want him to perform badly and you don't want him to do this and you have to tell them about all of his weaknesses and so it's the exact opposite to what we've been doing for the last five years with him.

One must assume that all people involved in the process of a child's transition to school have the best interests of the child at heart. Parents want the best for their children, want them to learn at school and want them to be happy. Teachers want to have children at school who want to be there and display positive learning dispositions. Children want to learn at school, be with their friends and be happy. Administrators, bureaucrats and politicians want children to be successful at school, do well in national and international tests of literacy and numeracy and move towards being productive citizens. However, in spite of all the best intentions, do we sometimes make matters worse for the children and their families, especially for those who are positioned outside the mainstream?

Julie in Example 1 just wanted someone from the school to talk with her. She did not have the agency to commence the conversation and no one seemed to notice. (This is not a criticism of the school or its teachers. Rather, it is a criticism of a system in which such 'noticing' is constrained by the other duties required of teachers.) Transition to school is about building sound, trustful and respectful relationships (Dockett and Perry 2007a; Pianta and Cox 1999). In any relationship there are gradations of power. With transition to school, it is much more common for the locus of power to be with the school and its teachers than with the parents and children. Care needs to be taken in exercising this power, and, at times, it is necessary for those with power to take steps to ensure that those with less power are provided with opportunities to show their strengths and express their needs.

I have often heard the lament that schools seem to destroy many of the 'good things' that preschools develop in young children. While the situation is certainly not as one sided as this might suggest, there are questions that need to be raised about continuity and change as children start school. Prior-to-school settings, including children's homes, and schools have different purposes and different ways of achieving these purposes (Dockett et al. 2007). Children want school to be different from what they have experienced before. 'Children expect to engage in tasks that are different from those in prior-to-school settings and they expect to work rather than play in school' (Dockett and Perry 2007a, p. 55). However, if things are so different in school that a child moves from being proud and strong in his own identity to failing, what has been achieved through a quality early childhood programme? Example 2 reports a Director pondering this issue. Have things been made worse for Gary just as they are supposed to be better? Has the gap between Gary and the mainstream children widened? The chance that 'differences between early education and school may create new difficulties for children as they enter school' (Woodhead and Moss 2007, p. 30) must be avoided because we know such a chance will impact differentially on the most vulnerable within our societies.

The situation in which Tess finds herself in Example 3 provides evidence of unintended consequences of efforts to meet the needs of children and other players in the transition to school. The partial enrolment arrangement is designed to provide Damien with as successful a start to school as possible; to provide Damien's teacher with an opportunity to work with him over shorter periods of time so that conflict and tension can be avoided; and to provide the other children in Damien's class with a less stressful beginning of their schooling than might otherwise be the case. All of these people have a right to be treated with justice in these ways, but what about Tess and Damien? Is it reasonable for Tess to have to postpone even partial fulfilment of her needs in order to fit into the system's constraints? Is it just for her? Is it reasonable that Damien is missing out on valuable learning at the very beginning of his school career?

Sarah's anguish in Example 4 shows how bureaucratic processes can impact on the wellbeing of families as well as the children starting school. While no one will deny the need for equitable processes in the allocation of scarce resources, one wonders what might have happened in a family less confident in exercising their agency than this one. It seems unnecessary for a family to be placed in such an unenviable position, and it certainly impinges on the social justice quantum of the community involved.

13.6   Conclusion

There are many challenges and issues that arise from the theoretical foundations for researching transition to school that I have considered in this chapter. The first is to convince other researchers and practitioners that in a diverse society such as Australia's, the potential for breaches of social justice as children and families start school is high. There are many examples of expectations based on stereotypical views of children and their families becoming self-fulfilling prophecies. Often these occur around determinations of the readiness of children to start school. (For example, shouldn't we think it odd that all boys who are younger than five when they start school *or* all Aboriginal children *or* all children from low socio-economic status families are likely to struggle throughout their schooling?) A detailed commentary on readiness is outside the scope of this chapter, but many colleagues have already written on the social justice aspects of this concept (Bernard van Leer Foundation 2006; Dockett and Perry 2009; Graue 2006; Meisels 1999).

My stance on the strengths and agency of children as they start school has caused me to reconsider the appropriateness of my methodologies for researching with children in this area. In fact, the topic of researching with children has, in some ways, overtaken our work in transition to school. A social justice perspective that respects children's rights and recognises their strengths places in question many of the traditional research approaches that I have used in the past (Dockett et al. 2009; Dockett and Perry 2007b; Harcourt et al. 2011). As well, it means that researching only mainstream, generalised transition approaches and programmes – where Dockett and Perry began their transition to school explorations – is no longer adequate. Since, 1997, our transition to school research programme has expanded to include various groups in Australian society that are often described as vulnerable or disadvantaged, including Indigenous Australians (Perry 2011; Perry et al 2007), culturally and linguistically diverse families (Sanagavarapu and Perry 2005) and families with complex support needs (Dockett et al. 2009, 2011).

From 2009 to 2011, I evaluated the implementation of a preschool curriculum framework in Indigenous communities in Queensland (Department of Education, Training and the Arts 2007; Perry 2011). I believe that it is an excellent framework which recognises and celebrates the strengths and values of Indigenous children and families. Even over the brief evaluation period, however, I have seen and heard of many Indigenous children who have moved onto school following a successful preschool experience only to be confronted with unreasonable and unsupported expectations. As a result, these children are moving from seeing themselves as successful learners in preschool to seeing themselves as failures in the first year of school. Clearly, there is still much to be done to ensure that for all the stakeholders in transition to school, social justice is paramount.

Many challenges and issues arise from a social justice stance. None is more important, however, than the stance itself which 'necessitates a commitment to recognising and respecting the human rights of children whilst they are in school - including respect for their identity, agency and integrity' (UNESCO 2006, p. 2).

References

Bankston, C. L., III. (2010). Social justice: Cultural origins of a perspective and a theory. *The Independent Review, 15*(2), 165–178.

Bernard van Leer Foundation. (2006). A framework for successful transitions: The continuum from home to school. *Early Childhood Matters, 107,* 23–28.

Blackmore, J. (2006). Social justice and the study and practice of leadership in education: A feminist history. *Journal of Educational Administration and History, 38*(2), 185–200.

Bourdieu, P. (1991). *Language and symbolic power.* Cambridge, MA: Harvard University Press.

Bronfenbrenner, U., & Morris, P. A. (1998). The ecology of developmental processes. In W. Damon & R. M. Lerner (Eds.), *Handbook of child psychology: Theoretical models of human development* (5th ed., Vol. 1, pp. 993–1029). New York: Wiley.

Brooker, L., & Woodhead, M. (2008). *Developing positive identities: Diversity and young children.* Milton Keynes: Open University Press.

Bryk, A. S., & Schneider, B. (2002). *Trust in schools: A core resource for improvement.* New York: Russell Sage.

Dana, N. F., & Yendol-Hoppey, D. (2005). Becoming an early childhood teacher leader and an advocate for social justice: A phenomenological interview study. *Journal of Early Childhood Teacher Education, 26,* 191–206.

Department of Education, Employment and Workplace Relations (DEEWR). (2009). *Belonging, being and becoming: The early years learning framework for Australia.* http://www.deewr.gov.au/EarlyChildhood/Policy_Agenda/Quality/Documents/Final%20EYLF%20Framework%20Report%20-%20WEB.pdf. Accessed 5 June 2012.

Department of Education, Training and the Arts. (2007). *Foundations for success.* Brisbane: Department of Education, Training and the Arts.

Dockett, S., Einarsdóttir, J., & Perry, B. (2009a). Researching with children: Ethical tensions. *Journal of Early Childhood Research, 7*(3), 283–298.

Dockett, S., & Perry, B. (2007a). *Transitions to school: Perceptions, expectations, experiences.* Sydney: University of NSW Press.

Dockett, S., & Perry, B. (2007b). Trusting children's accounts in research. *Journal of Early Childhood Research, 5*(1), 47–63.

Dockett, S., & Perry, B. (2009). Readiness for school: A relational construct. *Australasian Journal of Early Childhood, 34*(1), 20–26.

Dockett, S., & Perry, B. (2012). "In Kindy you don't get taught": Continuity and change as children start school. *Frontiers of Education in China, 7*(1), 5–32.

Dockett, S., Perry, B., Campbell, H., Hard, L., Kearney, E., Taffe, R., & Greenhill, J. (2007). Early years curriculum continuity for learning project: Final report (Adelaide, Department of Education and Children's Services). http://www.earlyyears.sa.edu.au/files/links/final_lit_review.pdf. Accessed 6 June 2012.

Dockett, S., Perry, B., Kearney, E., Hampshire, A., Mason, J., & Schmied, V. (2009). Researching with families: Ethical issues and situations. *Contemporary Issues in Early Childhood, 19*(4), 353–365.

Dockett, S., Perry, B., Kearney, E., Hampshire, A., Mason, J., & Schmied, V. (2011). *Facilitating children's transition to school from families with complex support needs.* Albury-Wodonga: Research Institute for Professional Practice, Learning and Education, Charles Sturt University. http://www.csu.edu.au/__data/assets/pdf_file/0009/154899/Facilitating-Childrens-Trans-School.pdf. Accessed 3 May 2012.

Durand, T. M. (2010). Celebrating diversity in early care and education settings: Moving beyond the margins. *Early Child Development and Care, 180*(7), 835–848.

Fraser, N. (1997). *Justice interruptus: Critical reflections on the 'postsocialist' condition.* New York: Routledge.

Graue, E. (2006). The answer is readiness – Now what is the question? *Early Education and Development, 17*(1), 43–56.

Harcourt, D., Perry, B., & Waller, T. (2011). *Researching young children's perspectives: Ethics and dilemmas of educational research with children.* London: Routledge.

Howard, P., Cooke, S., Lowe, K., & Perry, B. (2011). Enhancing quality and equity in mathematics education for Australian Indigenous students. In B. Atweh, M. Graven, W. Secada, & P. Valero (Eds.), *Mapping equity and quality in mathematics education* (pp. 365–378). Dordrecht: Springer SBM NL.

Hyland, N. E. (2010). Social justice in early childhood classrooms: What the research tells us. *Young Children, 65*(1), 82–87.

James, A., & Prout, A. (Eds.). (1997). *Constructing and reconstructing childhood* (2nd ed.). London: Falmer.

McCashen, W. (2005). *The strengths approach.* Bendigo: St. Luke's Innovative Resources.

Meisels, S. (1999). Assessing readiness. In R. C. Pianta & M. Cox (Eds.), *The transition to kindergarten* (pp. 39–66). Baltimore: Paul H. Brookes.

North, C. E. (2006). More than words? Delving into the substantive meaning(s) of 'social justice" in education. *Review of Educational Research, 76*(4), 507–535.

Perry, B. (2011). Evaluation of the Implementation of Education Queensland's Pre-Prep Curriculum Strategy Foundations for Success in Cape York and Torres Strait Islander Communities. Brisbane: Education Queensland. http://deta.qld.gov.au/indigenous/pdfs/evaluation-implementation-foundations-for-success-17112011.pdf. Accessed 12 July 2012.

Perry, B., Dockett, S., Mason, T., & Simpson, T. (2007). Successful transitions from prior-to-school to school for Aboriginal and Torres Strait Islander children. *International Journal for Equity and Innovation in Early Childhood, 5*(1), 102–111.

Pianta, R. C., & Cox, M. (Eds.). (1999). *The transition to kindergarten.* Baltimore: Paul H. Brookes.

Rinaldi, C. (2006). *In dialogue with Reggio Emilia: Listening, researching and learning.* London: Routledge.

Rogoff, B. (2003). *The cultural nature of human development.* Oxford: New York.

Saleebey, D. (Ed.). (2006). *The strengths perspective in social work practice* (5th ed.). Boston: Pearson.

Sanagavarapu, P., & Perry, B. (2005). Concerns and expectations of Bangladeshi parents as their children start school. *Australian Journal of Early Childhood, 30*(3), 45–51.

Schoorman, D. (2011). Reconceptualizing teacher education as a social justice undertaking. *Childhood Education, 87*(5), 341–344.

Simpson, L., Clancy, S., & Howard, P. (2001). Mutual trust and respect. In S. Dockett & B. Perry (Eds.), *Beginning school together: Sharing strengths* (pp. 56–61). Canberra: Australian Early Childhood Association.

United Nations. (1989). *Convention on the rights of the child.* New York: United Nations. http://www.unicef.org/crc/crc. Accessed 5 August 2012.

UNESCO (United Nations Educational, Scientific and Cultural Organisation). (2006). *A Human-rights approach to education for all.* http://unesdoc.unesco.org/images/0015/001548/154861E.pdf. Accessed 2 August 2012.

Woodhead, M., & Moss, P. (2007). *Early childhood and primary education: Transitions in the lives of young children.* Milton Keynes: The Open University.

Young, I. M. (2011). *Justice and the politics of difference.* Princeton: Princeton University Press.

Chapter 14
Transition to School: Normative or Relative?

Sue Dockett

14.1 Introduction

It is the case that some children, in some contexts, find the transition to school problematic. It is also the case that many children find it a time of excitement and adventure, albeit tinged with some initial nervousness. The research focus on transition (to which my colleagues and I have contributed) has helped to identify the nature of some of the problems experienced by children, families, communities and school as children start school, as well as ways to assist in promoting a smooth transition. However, the time has come to reflect critically on the impact of much of this transitions research and to consider some unintended implications from this approach. In our focus on 'easing the transition' have we:

- Generated normative expectations, expecting that some children, but not others, will find the time of transition to school problematic?
- Positioned some children and families – particularly those considered vulnerable or disadvantaged – as necessarily needing support in order to meet these normative expectations?
- Sought to remove much of the risk and challenge children encounter as they start school?

The aim of this chapter is to explore these questions.

S. Dockett (✉)
School of Education, Charles Sturt University, Albury-Wodonga, Australia
e-mail: sdockett@csu.edu.au

B. Perry et al. (eds.), *Transitions to School - International Research, Policy and Practice*,
International perspectives on early childhood education and development 9,
DOI 10.1007/978-94-007-7350-9_14, © Springer Science+Business Media Dordrecht 2014

14.2   Political Interest in Transition to School

Political interest in managing transitions derives largely from broader economic and social agendas. For example, much of the interest in early childhood education stems from an investment perspective, emphasising the economic benefits of intervention in the early years, particularly when compared with the substantially increased cost of later intervention and remediation for children experiencing difficulties (Heckman and Tremblay 2006). In addition, calls to develop a competitive, globalised workforce underpin efforts to promote early education and engagement with schools and schooling. In particular, there is reference to investment in early childhood as 'the ultimate long-term investment', which results in 'better educated, more capable people for the workforce of tomorrow' (Harvard Business School 2008, p. 1).

These moves have been accompanied by concerns about social exclusion and disadvantage and the impact of these on people's ability to enter and remain within the labour market (Australian Government 2009, 2010). For example, a positive start to school education, leading to greater and ongoing connection with school, has been identified as a factor in disrupting cycles of social and economic disadvantage (Council of Australian Governments (COAG) 2009; Smart et al. 2008). Further, the connection between a positive start to school and overcoming disadvantage has been a core feature of the Australian government *Closing the Gap* strategy, which aims to halve the gap between educational outcomes for Indigenous and non-Indigenous Australians within a decade (Department of Families, Housing, Community Services and Indigenous Affairs 2009).

Underlying these policy approaches is the assumption that 'improved transition to school' leads to 'improved educational, employment, health and wellbeing outcomes' (COAG 2009, p. 4). This is coupled with the aim of reducing 'inequalities in outcomes between groups of children' (COAG 2009, p. 6). These commitments are underpinned by assumptions that the transition to school is problematic for particular groups of children and that more effective management of this transition will lead to improved outcomes. These sentiments are encapsulated in statements such as the following:

> In Australia, the transition to school is likely to be more challenging for children from financially disadvantaged families, Indigenous families, families with children who have a disability, and culturally and linguistically diverse (CALD) families. Children from these backgrounds are also less likely to attend an early childhood education and care service before they start school. (Rosier and McDonald 2011, p. 1)

> Children in low-income families are more likely to have poor developmental outcomes, make a difficult transition to school, and have reduced aspirations and to pass this risk on to their children in a cycle of intergenerational disadvantage. (COAG 2009, p. 33)

The most common strategy outlined to overcome these challenges involves managing transitions through transition to school programmes. While there is the potential for such programmes to recognise and respond to the complexity of transitions to school (Dockett and Perry 2007; Fabian and Dunlop 2007), many such programmes have a more narrow focus on preparing children for school and 'helping children settle into the school environment before they commence school' (Rosier and McDonald 2011, p. 9).

The argument outlined in this chapter does not deny the existence of marked inequities related to educational engagement and outcomes for different groups of Australian children. Nor does it seek to dismiss the importance of a positive start to school and the potential for transition to school programmes to promote successful transitions. Rather I argue for critical reflection on the ways in which such evidence has been transformed into general expectations that all children, families and communities with particular characteristics will face problems as they experience the transition to school. In urging critical reflection, I echo the calls of critical theorists (Giroux 2005; Petriwskyj and Grieshaber 2011) and proponents of children's rights (Woodhead 2006), who seek to shift the focus away from categorisations of children and 'universalising discourses of early childhood that regulate children's lives, notably expressed through "developmental norms" …[that] have been strongly shaped by goals and expectations for children's "readiness" for the school systems that dominate their childhood years' (Woodhead 2006, p. 34). At the very least, I argue that we need to consider what constitutes a "problematic" transition and a "nonproblematic" transition, who is expected to experience a problematic transition and the ways in which these expectations influence policy and practice. A definition of transition is needed in order to achieve this.

14.3 Defining Transition

Transitions occur across the life course as individuals 'change their role in their community's structure' (Rogoff 2003, p. 150). Educational transitions, such as the transition to school, involve changes in the identity and agency of individuals, as they engage in different educational contexts and adopt different roles. There may well be increased demands as children change roles, identities and settings, such as in the move to school. Indeed, Pianta (2004) describes the transition to school as a time when such demands increase and supports decrease. The definition of transition as changing roles and identities within different contexts is drawn from a number of theoretical perspectives, including bioecological theory, sociocultural perspectives, critical theory and strengths-based approaches.

Bronfenbrenner's (2005) bioecological theory described ecological transitions – times when individuals changed their role and/or environment – as developmentally significant because of their link to changed expectations. Within transitions research, bioecological theory affirms a focus on contexts and recognition of the importance of relationships and interactions across both contexts and time. This is encapsulated in the statement that 'transition to school is understood in terms of the influence of contexts (for example, family, classroom, community) and the connections among these contexts (e.g., family-school relationships) at any given time and across time' (Pianta et al. 1999, p. 4).

The defining properties of Bronfenbrenner's bioecological model are processes, people, contexts and time. In describing these elements, Bronfenbrenner and Morris (1998) noted the role of developmental processes between the individual and their contexts, the individual repertoire that each person brings to interactions and contexts, the nested system of contexts in which people engage and the impact of time, in multiple dimensions including the past, present and future. Within this model, microsystems, such as the family or school, consist of

> pattern[s] of activities, social roles, and interpersonal relations, experienced by the developing person in a given face-to-face setting with particular physical, social and symbolic features that invite, permit, or inhibit, engagement in sustained, progressively more complex interactions with, and activity in, the immediate environment. (Bronfenbrenner 1994, p. 1645)

From this theoretical perspective, transition to school recognises the importance of the individual within a range of social contexts and the importance of interactions with both people and contexts, over time.

As with bioecological theory, sociocultural perspectives of transition emphasise both individual and social elements. The processes of transition involve both individual and social experiences, actively constructed as individuals participate in social and cultural processes that, by their very nature, are communal events. Contexts overlap and individuals participate in many contexts (Corsaro et al. 2002; Rogoff 2003). Different contexts can constitute different communities of practice (Lave and Wenger 1991). As children start school, they are required to negotiate a set of practices that are unique to schools generally and the school they will attend specifically. This negotiation is influenced by children's prior membership of different communities (such as prior-to-school settings) and their experiences in crossing other community boundaries. In this sense, the term 'boundary' describes a situation where individuals are required to participate in practices that are associated with a new community of practice (Wenger 1998). Participation in different communities of practice is influenced by individual identities (Lave and Wenger 1991).

It is important to note that at the time of transition to school, both families and children can be required to navigate new communities of practice and negotiate changing identities. For example, children become *school students* (Griebel and Niesel 2003; Pollard and Filer 1999) and parents become *parents of a school student* (Dockett and Perry 2007). Brooker (2008, p. 8) notes that 'every transition into a new group challenges our sense of identity'. Problems can arise when individuals have to reconstruct their identity as they change contexts or communities, where what constitutes a viable identity in one context is not transferable to another (Pollard and Filer 1999). Children's identities constructed around school participation are deeply embedded in personal understandings of capability and maturity. For example, children often talk about starting school in terms of being 'big' and describe their role at school as 'learning to read and do numbers' (Dockett and Perry 2007). A range of emotions can be involved, as children feel both excited and nervous about how they will manage the changes in identity and what these changes mean in practice.

Each of the aspects of transition noted above considers children and families as active contributors to transition experiences and outcomes. Critical theory acknowledges that issues of power are central to interactions and expectations, influencing the ways in which these are framed and valued (Giroux 2005). For example, Petriwskyj and Grieshaber (2011, p. 81) note that critical theory 'attends to the unequal distribution of power according to social class, gender, race, disability, culture and language, and to the ways structural factors (e.g. low funding) and low expectations can impede the achievement of minority groups'. In relation to transition to school, critical theory underpins questions about who is expected to have a successful, or problematic, transition to school and how these expectations are enacted.

Agency, and the exercise of agency, changes at times of transition. Biesta and Tedder (2007) argue that agency is concerned with both the ways in which individuals engage in contexts and their ability to shape or reframe these contexts. Other views of agency consider structural factors – such as class, race, gender and socio-economic status – and the ways in which these shape expectations and experiences (Ecclestone 2009; Giroux 2005). In the case of transition to school, the recognition and exercise of agency is changed not only for children but also for families. Where there is substantial discontinuity and disconnection between prior-to-school environments (including home, prior-to-school settings and schools), there is the potential for transitions to be extended and precarious for both children and families (Heinz 2009). This can be seen in the time taken by children and families to feel comfortable within the new school environment and in the ways in which children and families position themselves and are positioned by others. Agency is an important consideration at the time of educational transitions, as it implies competence to undertake planning and make appropriate decisions (Heinz 2009). Children's perceptions of their own agency influence their transition to school; so, too, do the perceptions of others about agency. Judgements are made about children's agency such as their ability to make appropriate decisions within the school environment – as well as family agency – including what decisions the family has made about school and how they support children as they start school.

How children and families are positioned across the transition to school is a core feature of identifying the outcomes of transition. Underlying much of my current work (with Bob Perry) is a commitment to strengths-based approaches, recognising the strengths of children and families as well as the challenges they may face (Munford and Sanders 2003). Strengths-based approaches regard children and families as experts on their own lives, capable of exercising agency and achieving positive change (Saleebey 2006). Respect and collaboration are essential elements of strengths-based approaches – respect for individuals and families and a commitment to building collaborative relationships based on rapport and trust (Berg and Kelly 2000). This approach is summarised by Beilharz (2002, p. 4) as 'a way of working with people, based on social justice values, that recognises people's and communities' strengths and facilitates their application to achieve self-determined goals'.

These theoretical perspectives contribute to a definition of transition as a time of individual and social change, influenced by communities and contexts and, within these, the relationships, identities, agency and power of all involved.

14.4 Successful and Problematic Transitions

Defining what makes a successful transition to school is an interesting challenge, not the least because there are many different answers, often depending on who is asked to make the judgement. Children have identified successful transitions when they know the rules of school and have friends; parents have reported a successful transition when they and their children are comfortable in the school environment; and educators have focused on children's adjustment to the social and organisational elements of school as the keys to a successful transition (Dockett and Perry 2007). Problematic transitions are described as the opposite of these, with the result that children are described as unsettled, lonely or disengaged; parents feel disengaged or not valued; and educators describe children in terms of the problems they seem to present or the disruptions they seem to cause.

The potential for successful transitions is often linked to perceptions of school readiness: when children are considered "unready" for school, the changed context of school, the increased demands and changed practices of school, coupled with children's perceived lack of preparedness, flag transition as a time of difficulty. In one US study (Rimm-Kaufman et al. 2000), 46 % of teachers reported that half or more of their class were unprepared (unready) for starting school. Problems cited by teachers included children's reported inability to follow directions, lack of academic skills, disorganised home environments, difficulty in working independently, lack of preschool experiences and difficulty in working as part of a group.

Different theoretical perspectives promote different definitions of, and approaches to, readiness (Dockett and Perry 2002). Contemporary explorations of readiness recognise the importance of child, family, community and school factors (Dockett and Perry 2009). Despite this, many perceptions of readiness, and unreadiness, rely on normative constructions of children, their abilities and backgrounds. In many cases, these norms are derived from developmental discourses and stage theories (MacNaughton et al. 2007). Drawing on these perceptions, discourse and theories, it is possible to construct a checklist of expected or normal behaviours to be exhibited by children who are ready for school. Failure to demonstrate these, by definition, labels a child as not ready for school. Automatically, this positions the child, and often the family, according to perceived deficits and establishes the need for remediation of some form, in order to move the child from unready to ready.

Defining readiness in relation to a set of normative characteristics ignores the diversity and strength of children's backgrounds and experiences and has the potential to restrict children's rights to participate in education (Woodhead 2006). A contrasting argument holds that

> 'Lack of readiness' is not a problem of children being insufficiently skilled to learn at school, but instead is it where there is a mismatch between the attributes of individual children and families, and the ability and resources of the school and/or system to engage and respond appropriately. (Dockett et al. 2010, p. 1)

It is noticeable that certain groups of children are routinely identified as likely to be unready for school and hence to experience a problematic transition. Much of the current national and international agenda around promoting positive transitions to school is framed in terms of "closing the gap" between these groups of children and those judged more likely to make a successful start to school. In some cases, this involves the framing of transition programmes as interventions, aimed at improving children's readiness, which, in turn, is proposed as the means for smoothing the transition to school.

14.5 Managing Transitions

The aim of smoothing the transition to school is an admirable one. It focuses on the wellbeing of children and seeks to promote positive early engagement with school. Much research, policy and practice is directed towards identifying groups for whom the transition is likely to be problematic and trying to rectify this through the provision of additional or specialised support. Within this frame, it is possible to identify specific groups who require such support. Both in Australia and overseas, these groups include children whose first language is not the language of school instruction, Indigenous children, children with disabilities or developmental delays, children with additional health needs and children in vulnerable circumstances (Brooker 2002; Dockett and Perry 2005; Janus et al. 2007; McTurk et al. 2008; Petriwskyj et al. 2005; Rous et al. 2007; Smart et al. 2008).

In some instances, children who have not accessed prior-to-school services also fall into same category of needing additional support to make a successful start to school (Magnuson et al. 2004; Rosier and McDonald 2011). Other groups often regarded as needing additional support are those children described as young or just meeting the age cut-off date for school entry (Stipek 2002) and boys (Childs and McKay 2001).

There is a fine balance between providing appropriate support and a deficit approach which identifies specific groups of children (and their families) automatically, as having insufficient background, experiences, skills or knowledge to make a positive transition to school without expert assistance. A deficit perspective assumes that there is a normative[1] pattern of transition where, given specific

---

[1] This use of the term *normative* in relation to transition contrasts with Bronfenbrenner's reference to normative transitions as the predicted and expected transitions that will be experienced by the majority of people within a life course.

preparation and experiences, children will progress into school with minimal problems. Normalisation of transition also assumes homogeneity and equality in opportunities before school, and that all children will enter similar educational programmes and contexts (Meisels 1999). Yet, there is considerable evidence that children have diverse backgrounds and many different opportunities for learning, as well as access to different resources and experiences before school (Bradley et al. 2001; Siraj-Blatchford 2010). It is also clear that there is variation among schools and educational programmes, even when they are guided by the same curriculum.

Such diversity is often not captured in policy documents, which tend to represent transition as specific, 'discernable events, experienced in a linear sequence' (Ecclestone 2009, p. 19) and with predictable patterns and normative expectations. Often, normative expectations are framed by measureable outcomes, which are, in turn, linked to funding and quality assurance. All of these combine to 'narrow what it means to make a successful transition' (Ecclestone 2009, p. 19) and who is likely to make a successful transition. Normative expectations assume that a specific progression can be mapped out and, where problems are identified, these can be remediated along the way – in essence, eradicating transition problems.

Yet, such expectations can also create problems, including the following:

- Establishing a specific time frame for transition. Transition is often framed as a process that occurs before school begins, culminating in the first day at school. Many transition programmes operate on this time frame, consisting of a series of events in the lead up to school start. However, if transition is dependent on participation within a specific community, managing the new practices of that community and changing identities within a new community – in this case, the school – it must continue beyond the first day of school, well into the school year. For some children, constructing the identity of a school student, exercising agency and forming relationships within the school context will take considerable time. Nominating a specific cut-off point for transition will ensure that some children will never make a successful transition.
- Identifying transition as a set of activities to be delivered. Such activities may contribute to the transition process, but they are unlikely to be sufficient to embrace the range and nature of changes experienced by all children, or their families, as they start school. Enacting one set of activities for everyone making the transition assumes homogeneity in prior experiences.
- Nominating a set of 'best practices' in transition. While it may well be possible to suggest a range of practices that support transition, nominating any of these as suitable for all children, in all contexts, neglects the diversity that exists among young children as they start school, as well as the diversity of schools and educational programmes.
- Assuming that successful transitions can be quantified and measured, through strategies that establish targets for transition programmes, such as the number of participants, groups represented or measures of children's academic or social achievement on completion of the programme. Different groups will have different perspectives about what constitutes successful transitions. These perspectives are

not immune from external pressures, including pressure for improved educational outcomes and participation rates.

- Increasing focus on assessment as part of transition – in various guises, such as portfolios, statements, checklists, school entry assessments and measures of readiness. Assessment may be undertaken as a means of promoting continuity between settings – by establishing what children know and can do – but also has the consequence of generating a range of artefacts that, in turn, contribute to norms, by establishing what most children can do or know.
- Narrowing the focus of successful transitions, through assessment, has the potential to target specific skill or knowledge sets and to make the sort of comparisons that affirm the likelihood of poor transitions for certain groups. The narrow focus mitigates against a view of transition as a time of broad adjustment to a changed context and the changes in identity and agency that accompany this.
- Focusing on perceived deficits or problems, rather than recognising the strengths and competencies each child and family bring with them to school. This has the potential to position those with these perceived problems as passive – in the belief that things can only improve with the intervention of external experts, agencies or programmes.
- Eliminating challenges or difficulties in transition, with the potential consequence of diminishing participants' sense of efficacy in addressing these. The intervention of others to solve or remove problems, sometimes even before problems are identified, positions participants as unable to manage change themselves.
- Locating problems in transition within the child, or family, rather than the transition process, institutional structure or broader community and society. If there is a well-established transition programme and most children progress through this to make a successful transition to school, children who do experience problems can be considered abnormal, with any problems therefore located outside the programme and within the child or family.

Normative expectations of transition assume that children, families and schools are all motivated to engage in transition experiences. Such experiences are usually devised and delivered by experts. There may be specific programmes developed for certain groups. For some groups, there is a noticeable increase in the formalisation of transition support and an increased expectation that families and children will engage with such support. Those who choose to opt out are automatically considered to be disinterested, disaffected or disengaged with schooling.

14.6 A Critical Look at Transition

Regardless of how we define transition, we need to exercise caution in the ways we represent it. For example, representing transition as a time-limited process, occurring prior-to-school entry, promotes a linear progression that diminishes the importance of children developing roles and identities while participating in school. Further, Ecclestone (2009, p. 23) cautions that representing transitions as times that are 'unsettling, disruptive, daunting, anxiety-inducing and risky' contributes to the potential for generating 'normative assumptions about how to manage them'. For example, if we focus on the transition to school as a time of great anxiety for children, we expect children to be anxious and develop a range of resources and strategies to address this. We also then position children who are not anxious as unusual in some way. Similarly, if we expect that children from specific groups will find school unsettling and unfamiliar, we also set up expectations around appropriate ways to manage transition and what constitutes a normal transition for these children.

As one example, a school developed two transition programmes for children and families. One targeted Aboriginal children, and the other targeted all other children. There was a relatively small uptake among Aboriginal families for the transition programme designed specifically for them. School staff interpreted this as a sign of disengagement with education; Aboriginal parents said that they wanted their children to be treated like everybody else's children (Dockett et al. 2007).

Once a set of practices or procedures have been established, there is an expectation that children and families will respond by engaging in these. Failure to do so further adds to the perception of abnormality. However, engagement in these activities also confirms the expectations underpinning them and affirms participants as in need of such support.

While it seems reasonable to provide a range of support as children (and their families) make the transition to school, it is important to do so in ways that build on existing strengths, promote positive identities within school contexts, encourage the recognition and exercise of agency, embrace diversity and difference, recognise the importance of respectful relationships, promote a sense of value and belonging at school for children and families and reject notions of deficit or blame. Failure to do so sets up a situation of assumed incompetence. Formalising levels of support has the potential to stigmatise specific groups, labelling them as unable to manage the transition without such help. The presence of formal support also reinforces concerns that transition is a time of difficulty that needs to be eased or smoothed. In other words, it is not an experience that individuals or groups of individuals are expected to be able to manage on their own. Ecclestone (2009, p. 23) argues:

> the idea that people cannot deal with transitions without formalised help sits uneasily with the possibilities of creative risk, opportunity and change that transitions can create. It also erases the positive effects of difficulty, challenge and overcoming problems and risk, attributing 'problems' to particular groups so that people become a problem to be supported and managed more effectively; the combination of 'supporting and managing' only serves to mask the management.

In contrast, we can be challenged to consider transitions as times of opportunity, where children, families, educators and other stakeholders can build relationships and where transition experiences and expectations can be shaped by those involved. Support, where offered, can be relevant, contextual and changing as those involved change. Relevant support recognises the strengths of participants and builds their capacity to identify areas for ongoing development, whether they are adults or children. Identifying appropriate support can be achieved by working with people, rather than making decisions for and about them. Available support recognises the importance of changing identities, agency and context, but also acknowledges the impact of structural factors on the nature of transition experiences. While recognising that some participants may experience problems at times of transition, this view does not assume that problems will exist. In summary, appropriate support positions individuals as active participants, capable of identifying issues of relevance, proposing changes to address these issues and enacting potential solutions.

Considering transition to school as a time of opportunity rejects the focus on binary distinctions such as "ready" or "unready", replacing these with acknowledgement of children's rights to participate in education (Woodhead 2006). It challenges us all to move away from normative expectations in order to embrace transition to school as an opportunity for 'differentiated transition processes and ongoing pedagogic provision that capitalise on the lifeworld experience and strengths of all school entrants [and] offer opportunities for all children to feel valued and develop a sense of belonging' (Petriwskyj and Grieshaber 2011, p. 82).

14.7 Conclusion

I have argued that many current approaches to transition have generated a range of normative expectations and positioned some children and families as necessarily in need of support. In addition, approaches that seek to smooth the transition to school could well remove levels of challenge and mask the discontinuities that exist between prior-to-school and school settings, in a sense "papering over the cracks".

Does this mean that we should ignore efforts to facilitate a positive transition to school and dismiss efforts to bridge prior-to-school and school contexts? Such a response would be simplistic and ignore the significance of the transition to school. Somewhere between ignoring the importance of transition to school and assuming that any problems associated with it can be solved by intervening with specific transition programmes is an approach that acknowledges the relative and individual nature of transitions. No two people will experience transition to school in exactly the same ways; no one set of transition practices will ensure that every child and every parent feel comfortable in a school community. When we consider what makes a successful transition, we are making a relative judgement. However, in many instances, such judgements are treated as normative. We know that children have many diverse experiences prior to starting school. We know that children grow, develop and learn in different ways and at different rates, particularly in relation to the opportunities they are afforded. Why then do we expect children to start school with similar competencies and capabilities? Why do we expect children to experience transition in similar ways? What assumptions do we have about families and their role within the transition to school? How do we acknowledge discourses of power and inequality? Do we encourage all involved in transition to consider it a time of opportunity? How do we provide opportunities for all involved to reflect critically on their assumptions and practices, critiquing the labels and language used? Do we aim to engage a language of critique and possibility, moving towards 'pedagogical practices that not only heighten the possibilities for critical consciousness but also for transformative action' (Giroux 2005, p. 72)?

The definition of transition offered earlier in this chapter promoted transition as a time of individual and social change, influenced by communities and contexts and, within these, the relationships, identities, agency and power of all involved. This view recognises the social element of transition and accepts that children and families experience transition in different ways. Underpinning successful transitions is a focus on relationships, whether they be existing relationships such as those between parents and children or new relationships such as those between children and teachers. These relationships provide the contexts in which identities are constructed and assessed and where agency and power are recognised and exercised. Further, this view of transition suggests that it is possible to develop and offer supports for children and families, but cautions that the institutionalisation of that support has the potential to position individuals as passive and unable to manage transitions without such support. This view also recognises that the transition to school will be unsettling and challenging for some children. Most importantly, this view argues that children and families have the competence to manage such changes, particularly in a context of appropriate support that recognises the strengths and the diversity of experiences they already have.

References

Australian Government. (2009). National Indigenous reform agreement (Closing the Gap). http://www.socialinclusion.gov.au/Initiatives/Pages/closingthegap.aspx. Accessed 2 June 2012.

Australian Government. (2010). Social inclusion principles. http://www.socialinclusion.gov.au/SIAgenda/Principles/Pages/default.aspx. Accessed 10 July 2012.

Berg, I. K., & Kelly, S. (2000). *Building solutions in child protective services*. New York: Norton.

Beilharz, L. (Ed.). (2002). *Building community: The shared action experience*. Brisbane: Solutions Press.

Biesta, G., & Tedder, M. (2007). Agency and learning in the lifecourse: Towards an ecological perspective. *Studies in the Education of Adults, 39*(2), 132–149.

Bradley, R. H., Corwyn, R. F., McAdoo, H. P., & Garcia Coll, C. (2001). The home environments of children in the United States: Part 1. Variations by age, ethnicity and poverty status. *Child Development, 72*(6), 1844–1867.

Bronfenbrenner, U. (1994). Ecological models of human development. In T. Husen & T. N. Postlethwaite (Eds.), *International encyclopedia of education* (2nd ed., Vol. 3, pp. 1643–1647). Oxford: Pergamon.

Bronfenbrenner, U. (2005). The bioecological theory of human development. In U. Bronfenbrenner (Ed.), *Making human beings human: Bioecological perspectives on human development* (pp. 3–15). Thousand Oaks: Sage. Original work published 2001.

Bronfenbrenner, U., & Morris, P. (1998). The ecology of human developmental processes. In W. Damon & R. M. Lerner (Eds.), *Handbook of child psychology: Theoretical models of human development* (5th ed., Vol. 1, pp. 993–1029). New York: Wiley.

Brooker, L. (2002). *Starting school: Young children learning cultures*. Buckingham: Open University Press.

Brooker, L. (2008). *Supporting transitions in the early years*. Maidenhead: Open University Press.

Childs, G., & McKay, M. (2001). Boys starting school disadvantaged: Implications from teachers' ratings of behaviour and achievement in the first two years. *British Journal of Educational Psychology, 71*(2), 303–314.

Corsaro, W., Molinari, L., & Rosier, K. B. (2002). Zena and Carlotta: Transition narratives and early education in the United States and Italy. *Human Development, 45*(5), 323–349.

Council of Australian Governments (COAG). (2009). Investing in the early years – A national early childhood development strategy. http://acecqa.gov.au/storage/national_ECD_strategy. pdf. Accessed 11 May 2012.

Department of Families, Housing, Community Services and Indigenous Affairs. (2009). Closing the gap on Indigenous disadvantage: The challenge for Australia. http://www.fahcsia.gov.au/ sites/default/files/documents/05_2012/closing_the_gap.pdf. Accessed 7 June 2012.

Dockett, S., & Perry, B. (2002). Who's ready for what? Young children starting school. *Contemporary Issues in Early Childhood, 3*(1), 67–89.

Dockett, S., & Perry, B. (2005). Starting school in Australia is "a bit safer, a lot easier and more relaxing": Issues for parents from culturally and linguistically diverse backgrounds. *Early Years, 25*(3), 271–281.

Dockett, S., & Perry, B. (2007). *Transitions to school: Perceptions, expectations, experiences*. Sydney: University of NSW Press.

Dockett, S., & Perry, B. (2009). Readiness for school: A relational construct. *Australasian Journal of Early Childhood, 34*(1), 20–26.

Dockett, S., Perry, B., & Kearney, E. (2010). School readiness: What does it mean for Indigenous children, families, schools and communities? Closing the Gap Clearinghouse, Issue paper No. 2. http://www.aihw.gov.au/closingthegap/documents/issues_papers/ctg-ip02.pdf. Accessed 8 May 2011.

Dockett, S., Perry, B., Mason, T., Simpson, T., Howard, P., Whitton, D., Gilbert, S., Pearce, S., Sanagavarapu, P., Skattebol, J., & Woodrow, C. (2007). Successful transition programs from prior-to-school to school for Aboriginal and Torres Strait Islander children. http://www.cur-riculum.edu.au/verve/_resources/ATSI_Successful_Transition_programs_Report_Dec_2007. pdf. Accessed 2 April 2011.

Ecclestone, K. (2009). Lost and found in transition. Educational implications of concerns about 'identity', 'agency' and 'structure'. In J. Field, J. Gallacher, & R. Ingram (Eds.), *Researching transitions in lifelong learning* (pp. 9–27). London: Routledge.

Fabian, H., & Dunlop, A-W. (2007). Outcomes of good practice in transition processes for children entering primary school. Working paper 42. The Hague: Bernard van Leer Foundation.

Giroux, H. A. (2005). *Border crossings* (2nd ed.). New York: Routledge.

Griebel, W., & Niesel, R. (2003). Successful transitions: Social competencies help pave the way into kindergarten and school. In A-W Dunlop, & H. Fabian (Eds.), *Transitions: European Early Childhood Education Research Monograph Series, 1*, 25–34.

Harvard Business School. (2008). *Managing human capital: Global trends and challenges*. http:// www.hbs.edu/centennial/businesssummit/global-business/managing-human-capital-global-trends-and-challenges.html. Accessed 17 July 2012.

Heckman, J., & Tremblay, R. (2006). The case for investing in early childhood. http://www. thesmithfamily.com.au/webdata/resources/files/Heckman_Tramblay_Snapshot_April_2006_B4F68.pdf. Accessed 4 Aug 2012.

Heinz, W. R. (2009). Structure and agency in transition research. *Journal of Education and Work, 22*(5), 391–404.

Janus, M., Lefort, J., Cameron, R., & Kopechanski, L. (2007). Starting kindergarten: Transition issues for children with special needs. *Canadian Journal of Education, 30*(3), 628–648.

Lave, J., & Wenger, E. (1991). *Situated learning: Legitimate peripheral participation*. Cambridge: Cambridge University Press.

MacNaughton, G., Hughes, P., & Smith, K. (2007). Early childhood professionals and children's rights: Tensions and possibilities around the United Nations General Comment no. 7 on children's rights. *International Journal of Early Years Education, 15*(2), 161–170.

Magnuson, K., Meyers, M. K., Rouhm, C. J., & Waldfogel, J. (2004). Inequality in preschool education and school readiness. *American Educational Research Journal, 41*(1), 115–157.

McTurk, N., Nutton, G., Lea, T., Robinson, G., & Carapetis, J. (2008). *The school readiness of Australian Indigenous children: A review of the literature*. Menzies School of Health Research, School for Social and Policy Research, Charles Darwin University.

Meisels, S. J. (1999). Assessing readiness. In R. C. Pianta (Ed.), *The transition to kindergarten* (pp. 39–66). Baltimore: Paul H. Brookes.

Munford, R., & Sanders, J. (Eds.). (2003). *Making a difference in families*. Sydney: Allen & Unwin.

Petriwskyj, A., & Grieshaber, S. (2011). Critical perspectives on transition to school: Reframing the debate. In D. Laverick & M. Jalongo (Eds.), *Transitions to early care and education* (pp. 75–86). New York: Springer.

Petriwskyj, A., Thorpe, K., & Tayler, C. (2005). Trends in construction of transition to school in three western regions, 1990-2004. *International Journal of Early Years Education, 13*(1), 55–69.

Pianta, R. (2004). Going to kindergarten: Transition models and practices. In D. Whitton, S. Dockett, & B. Perry (Eds.), *Proceedings of the international conference, continuity and change: Transitions in education (CD rom)*. Sydney: University of Western Sydney.

Pianta, R. C., Rimm-Kaufman, S., & Cox, M. (1999). Introduction: An ecological approach to kindergarten transition. In R. C. Pianta & M. Cox (Eds.), *The transition to kindergarten* (pp. 3–12). Baltimore: Paul H. Brookes.

Pollard, A., & Filer, A. (1999). *The social world of pupil career: Strategic biographies through primary school*. London: Cassell.

Rimm-Kaufman, S., Pianta, R. C., & Cox, M. (2000). Teachers' judgements of problems in the transition to kindergarten. *Early Childhood Research Quarterly, 15*(2), 147–166.

Rogoff, B. (2003). *The cultural nature of human development*. Oxford: Oxford University Press.

Rosier, K., & McDonald, M. (2011). Promoting positive education and care transitions for children. Communities and Families Clearing house Resource Sheet. http://www.aifs.gov.au/cafca/pubs/sheets/rs/rs5.html. Accessed 19 May 2012.

Rous, B., Myers, C. T., & Stricklin, S. B. (2007). Strategies for supporting transitions of young children with special needs and their families. *Journal of Early Intervention, 30*(1), 1–18.

Saleebey, D. (Ed.). (2006). *The strengths perspective in social work practice* (5th ed.). Boston: Pearson.

Siraj-Blatchford, I. (2010). Learning in the home and at school: How working class children 'succeed against the odds'. *British Educational Research Journal, 36*(3), 463–482.

Smart, D., Sanson, A., Baxter, B., Edwards, B., & Hayes, A. (2008). *Home-to-school transitions for financially disadvantaged children: Summary report*. Sydney: The Smith Family and Australian Institute of Family Studies. http://www.thesmithfamily.com.au/site/page.cfm?u=105. Accessed 4 July 2012.

Stipek, D. (2002). At what age should children enter kindergarten? A question for policymakers and parents. *Social Policy Report, 16*(2), 3–16.

Wenger, E. (1998). *Communities of practice*. Cambridge: Cambridge University Press.

Woodhead, M. (2006). Changing perspectives on early childhood: Theory, research and practice. Background paper prepared for the Education for All Global Monitoring Report 2007, Strong foundations: early childhood care and education. http://unesdoc.unesco.org/images/0014/001474/147499e.pdf. Accessed 31 May 2012.

Chapter 15
Critical Theory and Inclusive Transitions to School

Anne Petriwskyj

15.1 Introduction

Traditional expectations of children's readiness for school are inconsistent with current definitions of inclusion that are framed by appreciation of the diversity of children's abilities and backgrounds as a reality and resource, rather than a deficit. Inclusion in Australia is defined not just by the placement of children with disabilities and children from culturally and linguistically diverse backgrounds in regular schools and ECEC centres, but by children's ongoing achievement and their sense of belonging and being valued. Therefore, contemporary constructions of transition to school as a collaborative process of supported change are being framed by theories that emphasise respect for diversity. Ecological and sociocultural frames have offered opportunities to consider broader stakeholder involvement in transitions and wider influences on children although their potential for supporting inclusive transitions has some limitations. Critical and post-structuralist theories offer an alternative frame of reference for interrogating current practices to identify ways in which children, families and communities are marginalised and to highlight more inclusive strategies for transition to school. This chapter considers these shifts in thinking and their application to transition practices that are more inclusive of the real diversity of children entering schools.

A. Petriwskyj (✉)
School of Early Childhood, Queensland University of Technology, Brisbane, Australia
e-mail: a.petriwskyj@qut.edu.au

B. Perry et al. (eds.), *Transitions to School - International Research, Policy and Practice*,   201
International perspectives on early childhood education and development 9,
DOI 10.1007/978-94-007-7350-9_15, © Springer Science+Business Media Dordrecht 2014

15.2   Theoretical Foundations of Inclusive Transition Research

While transition models based on ecological systems theory consider children within their family and community context, they do not account sufficiently for longer-term trajectories or the diversity of children's cultural background and social circumstances. Reliance on ecological theory has been criticised on the grounds that it may mask differences in individual and cultural experience and so oversimplify real complexities in the lives of children, families and communities (Vogler et al. 2008). Further, assumptions that the central place of the individual child in ecological theory is universally appropriate are open to debate. Such assumptions overlook the multiple priorities of families and communities in group-oriented cultures and divert attention from the role of culture on children's learning (Vogler et al. 2008). This is a key consideration for Australian refugee, immigrant and Indigenous children, families and communities whose cultural perspectives have not yet been accorded sufficient priority in the development of transition programmes (McTurk et al. 2011; Millar 2011; Sanagavarapu 2010).

Sociocultural perspectives take into account both the influence of the cultural context on children and the impact of children's participation in events as a means of negotiating transitions (MacNaughton 2003). Minimising the contrasts in expectations between contexts would offer greater continuity of experience and enhance children's self-confidence. Continuity of experience during transition to school involves continuity between both ECEC and school settings and between home and school. In the context of inclusion, home-school continuity requires sensitive negotiation of transitions to maintain children's learning and sustain their sense of self-confidence, as children from culturally diverse backgrounds may not understand the expectations or language of the school (Millar 2011; Sanagavarapu 2010). Relationships amongst stakeholders (e.g. amongst children, between children and teachers, families/communities and teachers, teachers in different settings) offer a secure base for more seamless transitions and for supporting continuity through shared understandings (Bowes et al. 2009; Dockett et al. 2011). However, the effectiveness of relationships and communication amongst stakeholders is dependent on mutual respect, trust and shared power. Critical and post-structuralist theories offer alternate frames for addressing power issues that are often invisible and for interrogating the assumptions that underlie transition practices.

Critical theories draw attention to the unequal distribution of power according to social class, gender, race, disability, culture and language and to the ways structural factors (e.g. category-targeted funding) and low expectations can impact on the outcomes of less powerful groups (McLaren 2007). In contrast to developmental and ecological perspectives, critical theories represent social behaviour as being organised around the group or community (e.g. local family community, community of learners in a school or centre) rather than the individual and conceptualise it as an ongoing conflict over power and resources (Giroux 2006). Critical theories identify inequalities in power relationships as a central concern and define diversity categories as social constructions that reinforce inequalities (MacNaughton 2003). Application of critical theories in transition research implies attention to participation rights, social rather than medical models of diversity and inclusive educational language.

15.2.1 Refocus on Participation Rights

Normative developmental notions about children reinforce stereotypes, rather than attend to children's right to a quality education. Re-conceptualisations of diversity move away from normative ideas that underpin categorisations of children to recognise the right to participation of all children (Woodhead 2006) and the role of social institutions such as schools in creating circumstances that enable children to succeed, regardless of their characteristics, abilities and backgrounds (McLaren 2007; Slee 2000). Thus, instead of learning difficulties or socio-economic background in school entrants being identified as risks or deficits requiring reme-diation, they would be reframed as indicators of a requirement for more equitable access to resources, more effective continuity of experience or more respectful recognition of child and family strengths (Dockett et al. 2011; Terzi 2005). This shift has refocused attention towards ready schools: that is, schools that are prepared for the reality of a complex range of school entrants (Graue 2006). Ready schools are not expecting children to enter as a homogeneous ready group, but address participation rights and the reality of diverse class composition through changed organisation, supportive transition practices, stronger relationships and more inclusive curriculum and pedagogy.

15.2.2 Reconsider Medical-Model Social Constructions

The inadequacy of traditional categorisations of groups within education (e.g. children with disabilities, gifted children, refugees, low socio-economic status) and their tendency to support marginalisation of groups are highlighted by critical theories. Such theories identify the ways in which socially constructed dis-tinctions between categories of difference, such as gender, race, social class and disability, draw attention away from the social impact of circumstances. Such cat-egorisations support a medical-model focus on children's deficits as a reason for failure to meet normative educational expectations rather than focusing attention on changes that might be made to improve education and social circumstances for these children, their families and communities. The focus on separate specialised categories fails to include the "in-betweens"; that is, the children who do not have a diagnosis but who are not progressing well across the transition to school. It also fails to recognise the multiple overlapping aspects of diversity that may exist within any group or individual and impact on their education. For example, a child might be gifted, Indigenous, female and belong to a particular regional community (Cronin and Diezmann 2002). These multiple identities all represent resources (not challenges) for transition, and no single category can indicate an appropriate transition process.

15.2.3   Reframe Educational Language

Post-structuralist theories draw attention to the limitations of both traditional structural ways of thinking (e.g. stage of development, category, readiness for school) and of cultural structures such as language. Taken-for-granted notions such as children being "at risk" are considered as social constructions and deficit labels that may serve to restrict or marginalise some children. Unexamined assumptions about categories (e.g. low socio-economic status, disabilities) are reconsidered from the perspective of the power imbalances and inequities that might be supported by such categorisation and language labels. Slee (2000) drew attention to the cultural politics of educational language and the importance of interrogating professional language as the first step to achieving social justice. Thus, deficit-focused categorical language such as "special needs" or "additional needs" comes under criticism for failing to acknowledge the strengths and resources a child with a developmental disability or language other than English may bring to an educational setting. Terms such as "readiness for school" imply deficit in those children who do not meet anticipated norms and may encourage approaches to these children that reinforce low expectations, negative interactions or disrespectful relationships with children, families or communities (Tayler 2011; Terzi 2005). Such terms, Slee (2000) and Smyth (2010) have argued, turn the cultural politics of academic failure back on those who educational services have failed: that is, the language serves to blame children, families and communities for any difficulties rather than directing attention to questioning educational practice and social conditions.

15.3   Implications of Critical Theory Frames for Policy and Practice

The value of these alternate theories for transition to school lies in their potential for prompting critical reflection by teachers, principals, policymakers and curriculum designers on unexamined biases and inequities and on considering more socially just and inclusive transition approaches. Changes to policies, curricula and pedagogies must be considered from the perspective of their positive support for transition of a range of children and their framing of respectful partnerships between teachers, children, families and communities so they share confidence in education programmes and transition processes.

15.3.1 Align Inclusive Curriculum Content

The development of national curriculum frameworks in Australia has offered opportunities to adopt contemporary theoretical perspectives, embed inclusive practices and frame transition to school as an important process. The national coverage of these documents has the advantage of reducing educational discontinuities for geographically mobile children and families who move across state borders within Australia. However, the two national curriculum documents focus differently on transition and inclusion. The principles of the *Early Years Learning Framework* (Department of Education, Employment and Workplace Relations (DEEWR) 2009) include equity and respect for diversity, and its definition of inclusion considers a wide range of child characteristics, abilities and backgrounds. It makes explicit the importance of shared responsibility between stakeholders and provision for continuity during transition to school. However, the Australian Curriculum for schools (Australian Curriculum, Assessment and Reporting Authority [ACARA] 2011) contains limited attention to transition to school and frames inclusion as cross-curricular priorities (e.g. Indigenous perspectives) and services for target groups (e.g. children with disabilities).

Alignment between the new Australian national curriculum documents would support more seamless transition to school and reduce unnecessary discontinuities that potentially interrupt the progress of some children. The shared use of learning outcomes in the *Early Years Learning Framework* for ECEC and the *Australian Curriculum* for schools represents an effort towards alignment, yet differences in content and emphasis are evident. The *Early Years Learning Framework* frames practice around play-based yet intentional pedagogies and holistic outcomes. In contrast, the *Australian Curriculum* is structured around skills and knowledge outcomes under subject categories (e.g. mathematics, history) and makes limited reference to pedagogies. Although Connor (2011) identifies some content coherence, pedagogic misalignment represents an area of potential discontinuity. Improved continuity between ECEC and schools could involve both more intentional teaching towards clear learning outcomes in programmes for younger children (e.g. DEEWR 2009) and incorporation of learning-oriented play in the early years of primary school (Petriwskyj 2010).

15.3.2 Form Equitable Partnerships with Stakeholders

Partnerships among teachers in sending and receiving settings to share information about children and about teaching would facilitate continuity and graduated change. Similar partnerships between teachers, families and communities offer valuable opportunities to enhance continuity of learning and draw upon local cultural resources. Continuity of approach between home/community and school offers more seamless transitions that sustain children's sense of confidence and self-worth. The importance of incorporating pedagogies that build upon the cultural capital that children bring while introducing them to the culture of schooling has been highlighted as a key avenue for assisting children from marginalised communities (Mills and Gale 2002). Pedagogies and policies based on critical theory seek to avoid blaming children, families and communities for difficulties in adjusting to the culture and academic demands of school (Giroux 2006; Smyth 2010). Critical pedagogy in early education involves critical reflection on Western European normative developmental assumptions, unequal power relationships with families and the underlying cultural frames for curriculum and pedagogy (Hyun 2007; Kilderry 2004). Early educators in Australia have been challenged to reframe practice around theories that go beyond traditional Western developmentalism and to transform pedagogies such that equity and the educational participation rights of all children are considered (Grieshaber 2009). Transition pedagogies, therefore, must be redesigned to ensure provision for the wide range of children, avoid stigmatising normative comparisons, demonstrate respect for all stakeholders and share power in decision-making. The challenge for teachers is to critically reflect on current practice, so that concerns about power and equity are examined and transition pedagogies redeveloped with, rather than for, diverse children, families and communities.

15.3.3   Develop More Inclusive Transition Processes

A shift from medical models of provision for diversity, focused on remediation of deficits, to social models, focused on provision of circumstances that support all children, frames the development of inclusive transition processes (Stephen and Cope 2003). In the context of inclusion policies, Australian transition studies have drawn attention to a wide range of separate diversity considerations such as gender, disability, cultural and linguistic experience, Indigeneity, social circumstances, giftedness, complex circumstances, rural location and refugee backgrounds (Boardman 2006; Cronin and Diezmann 2002; Dockett et al. 2011; MacDonald 2008; McTurk et al. 2011; Millar 2011; Tayler 2011; Whitton 2005). These studies have highlighted the real complexity of classrooms, the variation in family expectations and developmental provision and the individual nature of children's learning. Therefore, transition planning must include both structural changes (e.g. age of school entry, curricula, educational system organisation, ongoing support services) and pedagogic provisions (Dockett et al. 2011; Thorpe et al. 2005). Planning must consider pedagogic contributions to diverse children's successful school entry (e.g. alignment between settings, culturally respectful strategies, flexible learning environments, social supports such as buddy programmes). In addition, inclusive transition processes need to take into account the multiple forms of diversity existing within any individual child. Considering a child's transition to school in relation to a single category (e.g. disability) is inadequate, since it does not capture the richness of the child's multiple identities (e.g. gender, culture, social experience, learning style, specific abilities) and the consequent aspects of transition requiring deeper thought. Rather than emphasising individual readiness, transition planning should consider multifaceted processes that would support school entrants with a wide range of abilities and backgrounds and involve collaborative partnerships between ECEC, school, families and communities.

15.3.4 Attend to Multiple Overlapping Transitions

Interactions between transition to school and the multiple horizontal transitions that Indigenous children, and children with disabilities, itinerant family lifestyles, complex family circumstances or chronic illness make (e.g. regular classroom and learning support; school and hospital, school to school, more than one family home) also require more extensive consideration since these overlapping transition experiences impose additional pressures on children and families (Dockett et al. 2006, 2011; Henderson 2004; Shiu 2004). Home-school transitions include not only a single school-commencement change event but also the daily transitions to school that some children and families find challenging, resulting in compromised adjustment or school refusal (Thamirajah et al. 2008). An Australian school study of transitions showed that teachers made changes in both sending and receiving classrooms, considered ongoing cycles of transition from year to year and shared information amongst staff to improve continuity, yet they gave more limited attention to the equally important aspects of home-school continuity and overlapping multiple transitions (Petriwskyj 2010). Inclusive transition processes need to be non-stigmatising yet provide support to individual children and families in negotiating their changing circumstances and multiple transition experiences. Consultation with families and communities is essential to take local circumstances into account and cross-sectoral professional collaboration to coordinate ongoing provision of support services for those children and families who utilise them.

15.3.5 Use Strengths-Based Inclusive Language

In early childhood contexts, Davis et al. (2007) argue that the development of more socially just pedagogies requires transformation of discourses, as well as policies and practices, based on significant shifts in thinking about diversity. The naming of practices frames thinking about children's abilities, the potential contribution of children and families and the roles of teachers, schools and communities. Referring to "transition to school" rather than "readiness for school" directs attention to educational processes rather than the characteristics of children. Referring to "children with diverse learning rights" (Organisation for Economic

Cooperation and Development [OECD] 2006) or "children with diverse abilities and backgrounds" rather than "special/additional needs" highlights more positive aspects of diversity including those that may be less visible, such as giftedness, gender and geographic location. The adoption of a "strengths-based", rather than "deficit-based", discourse of transition supports the development of more equitable relationships and of practices that build on the personal and cultural resources children and families bring to school transition. Consideration of children's "transition capital" (Dunlop 2007) offers a more respectful incorporation of child perspectives and strengths into transition approaches, based on awareness of the ideas, abilities and experiences that children bring to the learning situation at school. For example, Australian Indigenous children, whose cultural experience supports the development of resilience and collaboration, may feel more confident if these personal cultural resources are celebrated and built upon during transition to school. Since the range of children's characteristics and background indicates that these transition resources will be individual and contextual, more nuanced transition strategies are required.

15.3.6   Address Power Imbalances in Relationships

Early educators whose work has been re-conceptualised using critical and post-structuralist theoretical perspectives have moved away from approaches framed by static notions of best practice (e.g. developmentally appropriate practice), to integrate multiple voices into dynamic decision-making and to consider the complex daily realities of children and their families (Soto and Swadener 2002). Involvement of families and communities in the development of transition processes offers an important avenue for ensuring that the range of perspectives are considered and for providing for the real, rather than assumed, requirements of children (Petriwskyj 2010; Tayler 2011). However, rhetoric about partnerships with families and communities may mask the power imbalances that often form part of these relationships. Davis et al. (2007) argue that the development of more socially just pedagogies requires self-conscious awareness of power in pedagogic decisions. If teachers position themselves as experts and families and communities as novices to be advised, then the power imbalance impacts on genuine partnership (Slee 2000; Smyth 2010). Respectful reciprocal relationships with families and communities form a key part of an inclusive transition approach within which the different kinds of contributions of families and communities to decision-making are accorded due respect and value. Critical perspectives have also drawn attention to the agency of children, through which children feel empowered to value themselves and others, and to have a voice in decisions that impact upon them directly (Kilderry 2004; McLaren 2007). This indicates that involvement of children in decision-making around transition to school would be fruitful, since they are the people most familiar with the realities of their transition experience.

15.3.7 *Critically Reflect on Transition Teaching Decisions*

Teachers' reflection on the effectiveness of their transition approach could be extended to incorporate critical reflection on whether transition practices were inclusive of the perspectives of a range of stakeholders. Critical reflection involves reconsideration of transition decision-making regarding whose voices were heard and who held power in decision-making, to assist teachers in reframing transition approaches so they become more inclusive. It should lead to transition action plans that encompass improved social justice and equity (DEEWR 2009; Grieshaber 2009). Ongoing professional learning for teachers (e.g. cultural education programmes to reduce home-school mismatch) would assist teachers to understand recent theories, inclusion and transition and ways to enact action plans arising from critical reflection. Critical reflection may identify children whose perspectives have been overlooked (e.g. gifted children) or transition practices that may marginalise some children or families (e.g. readiness testing).

15.4 Implications of Critical Theory for Research

Work based on critical theory examines the perspectives of groups outside the mainstream, asks whose interests are served by current educational approaches and seeks to identify more socially just alternatives for the least advantaged in the community (Mills and Gale 2002). In inclusive transition research, the voices of teachers, families, communities and the children themselves are important sources of information. In particular, the voices of groups beyond the majority social and cultural community are considered.

15.4.1 *Voices of Children*

Transition research has tended to consider evidence from adult stakeholders, but has not always attended to the voices of children themselves. Discrepancies between the views of children on their transition to school and those of adults have been identified (Dockett and Perry 2007; Thorpe et al. 2005) highlighting the value of researching the views of children, not just adults. In a study of preparatory/kindergarten education (Thorpe et al. 2005), interviews of children highlighted concerns that children held about transition to school (e.g. separation from family members, missing friends, feeling incompetent) and their preferences for schooling (e.g. active and outdoor activity, social interaction with peers, engaging learning environments). This evidence from children themselves offered insights into challenges children encountered or anticipated encountering (e.g. playground bullying) and potential enabling circumstances that could form part of a transition process (e.g. buddy programmes, gradual withdrawal of families, graduated change in pedagogy). Further research into the perceptions and preferences of children with diverse characteristics, abilities and backgrounds would extend current understandings of what constitutes helpful transition practice from their viewpoints.

15.4.2 Voices of Families and Communities

Research involving families and communities has drawn attention to the varying experiences of children who have not attended a high-quality ECEC programme because of illness, Indigenous lifestyle, rural isolation, family circumstances or family choice (Dockett et al. 2006, 2011; MacDonald 2008). The voices of families and communities are important sources of information in inclusive transition research, as they highlight the challenges confronted by groups whose concerns may differ from those of the majority. Australian families from culturally and linguistically diverse backgrounds (Millar 2011; Sanagavarapu 2010; Thorpe et al. 2005) have identified school adjustment concerns for their children, such as anxiety, peer problems, boredom and internalising behaviours, that teachers failed to note or identified as lack of school readiness. The families of children with disabilities have also identified exclusionary practices or limited consideration for the structural and attitudinal difficulties faced by these children during transition (Rietveld 2008; Walker et al. 2012).

Research with families and communities has tended to be focused on the views of parents, particularly mothers, rather than taking into account the wider constructions of *family* and *community* evident in cultures in which there is a communal responsibility for children. For example, in Australian Aboriginal contexts, family has a broader meaning than the Western nuclear family, so other kinfolk and community members such as Elders may be involved in shared decisions and support regarding transition to school. Further research into the perspectives of varying cultural and linguistic communities has the potential to offer alternate approaches to supporting transition. Framing research using critical theories would mean incorporating more culturally sensitive approaches to research that incorporate the voices of participants more effectively (Smyth 2010). Thus, co-researching with groups should be considered: that is, involving community members or other respected people as co-researchers.

15.5 Challenges and Issues Provoked by Critical Theory Frames

Two key challenges attend application of critical and post-structuralist theories to inclusive transition. The most difficult is that of the retention by stakeholders of traditional notions of children's readiness for school and accompanying understandings of diversity as deficit. Such notions infer a continuing reliance on developmental theory and a construction of inclusion as mainstreaming or integration; that is, expectations that homogeneous classes of school entrants will require only minor adjustments to the regular teaching programme. Thus, children's variations in characteristics, abilities or background are deemed to constitute a readiness problem requiring a remedial solution, rather than a reality requiring change in structural provisions and in transition pedagogies. The other challenge is the negotiation of competing agendas around school entry and subsequent outcomes and negotiation of shared approaches.

Notions of school readiness as a characteristic of children persist amongst teachers and in some public literature despite efforts to shift the focus to the shared responsibilities of families, children, schools and communities in transition to school (Dockett and Perry 2007, 2009). The persistence of readiness notions indicates reliance on traditional Western developmental stage theories, despite the lack of evidence of their relevance to non-European cultures (Grieshaber 2008). Stage theories imply deficits in children with delayed developmental progress or culturally diverse experience. Graue (2006) has criticised this emphasis on children's readiness and grade retention on the grounds that providing additional maturational time alone does not address the learning challenges some children face. Developmental stage theories may also incorrectly imply that gifted children do not require support or pedagogic variation or that accelerated timing of school entry is adequate provision for gifted children. In studies of transition in Australia, teachers consistently emphasised children's readiness for school, were unaware of gifted children and reported continued use of retention in grade or the use of remedial services for children who were deemed "unready" (Petriwskyj 2010). Such constructions have been supported by government literature for families, containing titles such as "preparatory" or highlighting the role of ECEC in readiness for school despite the *Early Years Learning Framework* (DEEWR 2009) presenting an alternate position.

These tensions draw attention to the second challenge – that of negotiating the competing agendas, pressures and voices in the debate around school entry and subsequent adjustment and achievement. In the context of inclusive policies, it is surprising to see two forms of readiness assessment – at an individual achievement level and a community level – in use in Australia because of accountability pressures. *Performance Indicators in Primary Schools* [PIPS] (Wildy and Styles 2008) assess individual readiness in reading, mathematics, vocabulary and phonological awareness. The *Australian Early Development Index* [AEDI] focuses on predictors of adult outcomes such as physical health, emotional well-being and communication skills to identify communities as "vulnerable" for allocation of support funding. Although these initiatives have value in addressing inequalities in community resourcing, they have been criticised for their potential to position groups as being in deficit (Agbenyega 2009). Differences from the norm are still likely to be constructed as family or community problems or child-related deficits requiring a remedial solution. Programmes to support school entry in the past have often been specifically preparatory or remedial, particularly for children from socially and culturally diverse backgrounds or for children with developmental delays. However, such approaches are not fully compatible with inclusive views of diversity as a resource (e.g. cultural contributions children bring from their home background, individual strengths of children) and of children and families as competent co-contributors to learning (Kilderry 2004; Tayler 2011). Research is required on effective ways to enact new thinking about diversity and transition in order to offer evidence on inclusive approaches.

15.6   Future Directions

Since traditional readiness notions are so persistent, research into alternate transition approaches is limited by the availability of examples of transformative practices. The development in Australia of schools utilising educational reform approaches such as *Productive Pedagogies* (Lingard and Mills 2003) offers opportunities to investigate whether such approaches are associated with improved continuity and whether children's outcomes are supported by such continuity. The finding in the Queensland school reform study that early years teachers deemed outstanding by peers adopted more Productive Pedagogies elements than other teachers and that there was a significant correlation between such pedagogies and children's outcomes (Lingard and Mills 2003) indicates that links are worth investigating. Since *Productive Pedagogies* emphasises inclusion, this research offers examples of strategies for transition that are informed by alternate theories and inclusive policies in practice. Clearer policy settings on transition to school that are linked to inclusive approaches would also reduce slippage between policy and practice.

Continuing transition evidence of concern linked to categories (boys, children in challenging home circumstances, Indigenous children, non-English speakers, children with disabilities) (Boardman 2006; Walker et al. 2012) indicates that transition approaches relying on structural provisions, school orientation and preparatory practices are insufficient. Policy revisions are required to attend to transitions into school and to clarify approaches that are respectful of the views of stakeholders and are consistent with inclusive policy. Research into teacher education, links between ECEC and schools, school-community relationships and differentiated transition approaches would inform more effective policy. While research into separate categories indicates perspectives that may have been overlooked, broader non-categorical research on diversity and transition is required to inform inclusive policy and practice on transition.

An additional avenue for research has arisen from the development of new national curriculum documents for prior-to-school and school settings. The limited linking of these documents on issues of content, transition and inclusion serves to heighten tensions between the sectors, potentially impacting on transition to school across Australia. This research area is important because of the potential impact on continuity of learning during transition between sectors. Policy revision is required to frame better pedagogic continuity and curricular alignment between ECEC and schools and between home/community and educational programmes, as well as across states of Australia. This indicates the value of a consistent transition to school policy that is non-stigmatising, reflects Australia's diversity and focuses on pedagogic strategising as well as on structural provisions.

References

Agbenyega, J. (2009). The Australian Early Development Index, who does it measure: Piaget or Vygotsky's child? *Australian Journal of Early Childhood, 34*(2), 31–38.

Australian Curriculum, Assessment and Reporting Authority. (2011). *Draft Australian curriculum Version 3*. http://www.australiancurriculum.edu.au/guide. Accessed 10 Oct 2012.

Boardman, M. (2006). The impact of age and gender on prep children's academic achievements. *Australian Journal of Early Childhood, 31*(4), 1–6.

Bowes, J., Harrison. L., Sweller, N., Taylor, A., & Neilsen-Hewett, C. (2009). *From childcare to school: Influences on children's adjustment and achievement in the year before school and in the first year of school*. Report to New South Wales Department of Community Services. http://www.community.nsw.gov.au/docswr/_assets/main/documents/research_childcare_school.pdf. Accessed 14 July 2012.

Connor, J. (2011). *Foundations for learning: Relationships between the early years learning framework and the Australian curriculum*. http://www.earlychildhoodaustralia.org.au/pdf/ECA_ACARA_Foundations_Paper/ECA_ACARA_Foundations)Paper_FINAL.pdf. Accessed 2 June 2012.

Cronin, R., & Diezmann, C. (2002). Jane and Gemma go to school: Supporting young gifted Aboriginal children. *Australian Journal of Early Childhood, 27*(4), 12–17.

Davis, K., Gunn, A., Purdue, K., & Smith, K. (2007). Forging ahead: Moving towards inclusive and anti-discriminatory education. In L. Keesing-Styles & H. Hedges (Eds.), *Theorising early childhood practice: Emerging dialogues* (pp. 99–117). Sydney: Pademelon.

Department of Education, Employment and Workplace Relations (DEEWR). (2009). *Belonging, being & becoming: The early years learning framework for Australia*. Canberra: Commonwealth of Australia.

Dockett, S., Mason, T., & Perry, B. (2006). Successful transition to school for Australian Aboriginal children. *Childhood Education, 82*(3), 139–144.

Dockett, S., & Perry, B. (2007). *Transitions to school: Perceptions, expectations, experiences*. Sydney: University of New South Wales Press.

Dockett, S., & Perry, B. (2009). Readiness for school: A relational construct. *Australasian Journal of Early Childhood, 34*(1), 20–26.

Dockett, S., Perry, B., Kearney, E., Hampshire, A., Mason, J., & Schmied, V. (2011). *Facilitating children's transition to school from families with complex support needs*. Albury: Research Institute for Professional Practice, Learning and Education, Charles Sturt University. http://www.csu.edu.au/research/ripple/publications/index.htm. Accessed 6 May 2012.

Dunlop, A.-W. (2007). Bridging research, policy and practice. In A.-W. Dunlop & H. Fabian (Eds.), *Informing transitions in the early years: Research, policy and practice* (pp. 151–168). Maidenhead: Open University Press.

Giroux, H. (2006). *The Giroux reader*. Boulder: Paradigm.

Graue, E. (2006). The answer is readiness – now what is the question? *Early Education and Development, 17*(1), 43–56.

Grieshaber, S. (2009). Equity and quality in the early years of schooling. *Curriculum Perspectives, 29*(1), 91–97.

Grieshaber, S. (2008). Interrupting stereotypes: Teaching and the education of young children. *Early Education and Development, 19*(3), 505–518.

Henderson, R. (2004). Educational issues for the children of itinerant seasonal farm workers: A case study in an Australian context. *International Journal of Inclusive Education, 8*(3), 293–310.

Hyun, E. (2007). Cultural complexity in early childhood: Images of contemporary young children from a critical perspective. *Childhood Education, 83*(5), 261–266.

Kilderry, A. (2004). Critical pedagogy: A useful framework for thinking about early childhood curriculum. *Australian Journal of Early Childhood, 29*(4), 33–37.

Lingard, B., & Mills, S. M. (2003). Teachers and school reform: Working with productive pedagogies and productive assessment. *Melbourne Studies in Education, 44*(2), 1–18 (Note: *Melbourne Studies in Education* has been re-named *Critical Studies in Education*).

MacDonald, A. (2008). Kindergarten transition in a small rural school: From planning to implementation. *Education in Rural Australia, 18*(1), 13–21.

MacNaughton, G. (2003). *Shaping early childhood: Learners, curriculum and contexts.* Maidenhead: Open University Press.

McLaren, P. (2007). *Life in schools: An introduction to critical pedagogy in the foundations of education* (5th ed.). Boston: Pearson.

McTurk, N., Lea, T., Robinson, G., Nutton, G., & Carapetis, J. (2011). Defining and assessing the school readiness of Indigenous Australian children. *Australasian Journal of Early Childhood, 36*(4), 69–76.

Millar, N. (2011). Korean children's cultural adjustment during transition to the early years of school in Australia. *Australasian Journal of Early Childhood, 36*(3), 10–17.

Mills, C., & Gale, T. (2002). Schooling and the production of inequalities: What can and should we be doing? *Melbourne Studies in Education, 43*(1), 107–128.

Organisation for Economic Cooperation and Development. (2006). *Starting strong 11: Early childhood education and care.* Paris: OECD.

Petriwskyj, A. (2010). Diversity and inclusion in the early years. *International Journal of Inclusive Education, 14*(2), 195–212.

Rietveld, C. (2008). Contextual factors affecting inclusion during children's transitions from preschool to school. *Australian Journal of Early Childhood, 33*(3), 1–9.

Sanagavarapu, P. (2010). Children's transition to school: Voices of Bangladeshi parents in Sydney, Australia. *Australasian Journal of Early Childhood, 35*(4), 21–29.

Shiu, S. (2004). Maintaining the thread: Including young children with chronic illness in the primary classroom. *Australian Journal of Early Childhood, 29*(1), 33–38.

Slee, R. (2000). Professional partnerships for inclusive education. *Melbourne Studies in Education, 41*(1), 1–15.

Smyth, J. (2010). Speaking back to educational policy: Why social inclusion will not work for disadvantaged schools. *Critical Studies in Education, 15*(2), 113–128.

Soto, L., & Swadener, B. (2002). Towards libratory theory, research and praxis: De-colonising a field. *Contemporary Issues in Early Childhood, 3*(1), 38–66.

Stephen, C., & Cope, P. (2003). An inclusive perspective on transition to primary school. *European Education Research Journal, 2*(2), 262–276.

Tayler, A. (2011). Coming ready or not: Aboriginal children's transition to school in urban Australia and the policy push. *International Journal of Early Years Education, 19*(2), 145–161.

Terzi, L. (2005). Beyond the dilemma of difference: The capability approach to disability and special educational needs. *Journal of Philosophy of Education, 39*(3), 443–459.

Thamirajah, M., Grandison, K., & De-Hayes, L. (2008). *Understanding school refusal: A handbook for professionals in education, health and social care.* London: Jessica Kingsley.

Thorpe, K., Tayler, C., Bridgstock, R., Grieshaber, S., Skoien, P., Danby, S., & Petriwskyj, A. (2005). *Preparing for school: Report of the Queensland preparing for school trials 2003/2004.* Brisbane: Queensland University of Technology and Department of Education, Training and Arts.

Vogler, P., Crivello, G., & Woodhead, M. (2008). *Early childhood transitions research: A review of concepts, theory and practice.* The Hague: Bernard van Leer Foundation.

Walker, S., Dunbar, S., Meldrum, K., Whiteford, C., Carrington, S., Hand, K., Berthelsen, D., & Nicholson, S. (2012). The transition to school of children with developmental disabilities: Views of parents and teachers. *Australasian Journal of Early Childhood, 37*(3), 22–29.

Whitton, D. (2005). Transition to school for gifted children. *Australian Journal of Early Childhood, 30*(3), 27–31.

Wildy, H., & Styles, I. (2008). Measuring what students entering school know and can do: PIPS Australia 2006–2007. *Australian Journal of Early Childhood, 33*(4), 43–52.

Woodhead, M. (2006). *Changing perspectives on early childhood: Theory, research and practice.* UNESCO Strong Foundations background paper http://unesdoc.unesco.org/images/0014/001474/147499e.pdf. Accessed 28 Nov 2010.

Part IV
Connecting Theory, Research, Policy and Practice

Chapter 16
Starting School: Synthesis and Analysis

Amy MacDonald, Wendy Goff, Kathryn Hopps, Cathy Kaplun, and Susanne Rogers

16.1 Introduction

At the 2010 Starting School: Research, Policy and Practice conference, higher degree research students were asked to consolidate the critiques of individual papers into an overview that could inform the ongoing development of the *Transition to School: Position Statement* (Educational Transitions and Change (ETC) Research Group 2011). This group of students—some now graduated—has undertaken a similar task in developing this chapter.

16.2 Considering Context in the Research

The preceding chapters offer insights into the importance of context in transitions and transitions to school research. Indeed, the chapters themselves and the research they represent are a lesson in context and demonstrate the impact of physical, social and political contexts on both the ways in which children experience transition and the ways in which transitions research is conducted.

A. MacDonald (✉) • K. Hopps • S. Rogers
Charles Sturt University, Albury Wodonga, Australia
e-mail: amacdonald@csu.edu.au; khopps@csu.edu.au; rogsr@bigpond.net.au

W. Goff
Monash University, Gippsland, Australia
e-mail: wendy.goff@monash.edu

C. Kaplun
University of New South Wales, Liverpool, Australia

Charles Sturt University, Albury Wodonga, Australia
e-mail: c.kaplun@unsw.edu.au

B. Perry et al. (eds.), *Transitions to School - International Research, Policy and Practice*,   219
International perspectives on early childhood education and development 9,
DOI 10.1007/978-94-007-7350-9_16, © Springer Science+Business Media Dordrecht 2014

A provocation raised in these chapters is the varied ways of considering context—both at the theoretical level and in more pragmatic ways. At the theoretical level, the predominant stance across many of the chapters is that of Bronfenbrenner's ecological model, with its nested spheres of influence and proximal processes each impacting upon children's transitions in diverse ways. As Murray (Chap. 4) explains, utilisation of an ecological model positions the child at the centre as an active agent in the transition process. Be it Turunen's (Chap. 11) consideration of macrosystem, exosystem and microsystem influences upon individuals' culturally framed biographical narratives of starting school; Murray's (Chap. 4) examination of the chronosystem and changes in perceptions and understandings over time (in this case, the first year of school); or Mackenzie's (Chap. 7) recognition of ecological influences upon emergent writing, the enduring influence of Bronfenbrenner's model of context is clear.

However, an important contribution made in this book is the theorising of transition *beyond Bronfenbrenner*. Petriwskyj (Chap. 15) encourages readers to consider how a critical theory perspective, with its interrogation of power relationships and its questioning of assumptions, may provide a more effective framework for supporting the diverse needs of *all* children during transitions and provide a more inclusive approach to the development of transitions programmes. A critical theory perspective on context shifts the emphasis away from Bronfenbrenner's notion of "child as central" to instead emphasise the centrality of the role of culture and the priorities of families and communities. Petriwskyj argues that this shift in emphasis enables transitions programmes to better support the needs of children and families from diverse backgrounds, including refugee, migrant, Indigenous, rural and remote, and other contexts often constructed as "disadvantaged". A critical theory approach to transitions shifts the focus away from the perceived disadvantage of these contexts to instead consider the resources, priorities and strengths of these communities during transition to school.

Also thinking critically about the theorisation of transitions in context, Graue and Reineke (Chap. 12) outline a critical constructionist perspective on transition, reflecting on how current positions on transitions and "readiness" have developed over time in response to social and cultural forces. This critical perspective on context-driven notions of readiness demonstrates how the perception of a child as "ready" for school is socially constructed in local communities, and how this perception is informed by the communities' different ideas about children, the role of schooling and the nature of development (Graue 1993). Indeed, as Graue and Reineke (Chap. 12) so candidly put it, 'as a result, one child will be ready on one side of town and not ready on the other'.

A counterpoint to Graue and Reineke's thinking is the notion that children and families need not be passive recipients of their contexts; rather, it is possible for them to be "agents" who actively shape transitions. As Dockett (Chap. 14) argues, 'the processes of transition involve both individual and social experiences, actively constructed as individuals participate in social and cultural processes that, by their very nature, are communal events'. Furthermore, children and families bring with them what Dunlop (Chap. 3) has termed "transitions capital". This notion has been informed for the most part by Bronfenbrenner's bioecological model—in tandem with a variety of other perspectives—because from Dunlop's perspective, 'the ecological systems theory works'.

Despite some views to the contrary, it seems the consensus is that the foundational elements of Bronfenbrenner's model—the acknowledgement that a child affects and is affected by the settings in which time is spent, the recognition of the importance of family, settings and community, the immediacy of interaction and interrelation between individuals and contexts—continue to have a core role to play in transitions research. Rather than move away from Bronfenbrenner entirely, Peters suggests researching and understanding transitions using a combination of ecological and sociocultural lenses, in particular, the notions of habitus, social and cultural capital as described by Bourdieu (1997), and Thomson's (2002) notion of "virtual school bags". This complementarity of theoretical perspectives allows examination of multiple factors which impact upon interactions between the individual and the environment and allows researchers to keep the "bigger picture" in mind when focusing on particular points bounded by time, place and culture. Einarsdóttir presents a similar blending of theoretical perspectives in her chapter, explaining how postmodern constructions of culture, time and space and an emphasis on complexity, irregularity, diversity and individual differences (Albon 2011; Dahlberg et al. 1999; Elkind 1997) cannot be separated from the social environment and Bronfenbrenner's notion that children are part of their environment; they are influenced by it, and it by them.

Despite some differences in how transitions and their contexts are theorised, there are some common themes across the research described in this book. In the next section, we explore these themes more closely.

16.3 Common Themes Across the Research

A key similarity across the chapters in this book is their recognition of theory as a tool for understanding children's experiences in transition. Although the chapters represent a diverse range of theoretical and conceptual bases from which to examine and understand transition, they are unified in their stance that theory is useful in determining what to research, how to research it and how experiences of children can be understood.

Another similarity which is clear from the previous section is the emphasis on context. All of the chapter authors agree that children's experiences must be considered, measured and understood with regard to the context, immediate and wider. Furthermore, there is agreement that transition should be understood "in context", and contextual factors which influence transition need to be identified and investigated. Social contexts are viewed as very important influences on children's transitions, and there is consensus that, as Lam, in particular, discusses in Chap. 10, transition contexts and practices are crucial factors affecting children's responses and adaptation. These include, but are not limited to, the individual, the systemic and the wider political contexts and practices that work in symbiosis to shape the transition to school. Harrison (Chap. 5) asserts that particular elements of social contexts such as student-teacher relationships in school classrooms 'are likely to have direct or indirect influence on children's experience of school transition' and further offers that these can be examined through statistical analysis in large-scale studies 'to explain children's different outcomes and developmental pathways through school'.

Across the chapters, the importance of relationships in transitions consistently emerges as a core theme. As outlined by Peters (Chap. 8), the underpinnings of successful and effective transitions to school have a central theme that recognises the experiences of the individual and the interactions that occur within the relationships that exist in home and school environments. Positive and respectful relationships form the basis for more positive, effective and successful outcomes in transition to school. Margetts (Chap. 6) argues that relationships form the basis of effective communication and transition programme design and suggests building collaborative partnerships between home, school and community to develop transition programmes which are relevant to the needs of the school community.

Another common thread across several of the chapters, namely, Harrison (Chap. 5), Lam (Chap. 10), Mackenzie (Chap. 7), is the examination of continuity— or indeed, *dis*continuity—of children's experiences from prior-to-school settings to school settings. Mackenzie asserts that transitions may be complicated by a mismatch between what happens in preschools and schools in regard to standards, curricula, assessment processes, teachers' beliefs and different pedagogical approaches. She argues that the shift from preschool to school may disrupt children's learning (Stephenson and Parsons 2007) and that the challenge for children is successfully to make the transition from the preschool environment where they have a great deal of agency to the tighter, more controlled, school environment. Lam suggests that the process of children adapting to the new environment is important to study, while Harrison, in a similar vein to Mackenzie, argues that it is what happens before school as well as at school that is important for transitions.

While there may be some who lament the differences between preschools and schools, Perry (Chap. 13) emphasises that prior-to-school settings, including children's homes, and schools have different purposes and different ways of achieving these purposes (Dockett et al. 2007). As Perry explains, children want school to be different from what they have experienced before and expect to engage in tasks that are different from those in prior-to-school settings. The challenge, though, is in determining how different these settings should be. Lam (Chap. 10) suggests that the gap should be just big enough so that it is suitably challenging for children and promotes ongoing learning, but not so big 'that a child moves from being proud and strong in his own identity to failing' (Perry Chap. 13).

A suggestion for supporting transitions "across the border" from preschool to school is provided by Peters (Chap. 8). She suggests that the key to successful transitions across the border lies in creating shared understandings (the "borderlands") in educational environments which support children's continued learning and enjoyment of school, and build and sustain a sense of belonging. Much like Perry (Chap. 13) and Petriwskyj (Chap. 15), Peters argues that a social justice perspective can assist in building these shared understandings by acknowledging the social and cultural capital of each child in their transition to school, thus creating the context for building shared meanings across prior-to-school and school contexts.

While social justice perspectives promote the notion of "ready schools"—that is, the schools being positioned as welcoming and accommodating of the unique strengths and needs of children and families—readiness of the child is still a discourse in transition influencing research and is a topic of discussion across several chapters in this book. With a growing awareness by governments of the importance of early years education comes a renewed interest in the "readiness" of children for school. This has been a persistent issue in the United States where, as Graue and Reineke (Chap. 12) describe, there has been strong emphasis on "readiness" since the early twentieth century. Harrison (Chap. 5) also describes the current emphasis on children being "ready to learn", particularly in the United States, which has resulted in research emphasising the identification of predictors of success so that preventative interventions can be employed. Lam (Chap. 10), in describing the Hong Kong context, discusses a similar emphasis on assessing children's "preparedness" and measuring children's adaptations. Einarsdóttir (Chap. 2) examines the Icelandic media's construction of "school readiness", and describes the advice provided by the media to parents to assist their children in preparing them for starting school—advice such as training children to be self-reliant and follow instructions and preparing children for reading and mathematics instruction.

Graue and Reineke (Chap. 12) describe a complementarity of readiness and transition, in that both are social and cultural constructs developed in local communities. However, within the US context, the positioning of "readiness" of some children—resulting from differences between values and social/community practices of middle-class white families and those of colour or economic poverty— meant deficit views and the establishment of interventions. Of some concern is that in looking across the chapters in this book and the international contexts they represent, cultural divides and resulting deficit views are evident in most of the developed world and are a growing phenomenon in Australia. As Perry (Chap. 13) suggests, 'in Australia, as in many other countries, children and families do not live in environments that provide equal opportunities, and are not treated equally by school systems or, even, by individual schools'. Children are judged on the perceptions of their families' previous schooling, their race or their socio-economic class. Such views impact directly on children and their families.

16.4   Implications for Research, Policy and Practice

A strong theme throughout this book is the argument that children's perspectives on transitions are important, but have been under-researched. Murray (Chap. 4) has emphasised the importance of children as active contributors in transition to school research but has also acknowledged that there are challenges inherent in this, namely, the question of how to engage children in transitions research in authentic and appropriate ways. Dunlop (Chap. 3) has asserted that children need to be at the centre of our thinking in relation to transition, and a challenge arising from this assertion is how to establish the central position of children in transitions research, policy and practice.

The *Transition to School Position Statement* described in Chap. 20 provides a means of achieving this, as it encourages transitions researchers, policymakers and practitioners to consider the opportunities, aspirations, expectations and entitlements of children during the transition to school. This child-focused discourse supports an inclusive approach to transition programme development and provides a moral imperative for all transitions stakeholders to consider the unique strengths and needs of individual children as they make the transition to school. Furthermore, the Position Statement reinforces Dunlop's notion that children are not just products but producers of their experiences—and that transitions are transforming. This is a crucial consideration for transition to school policy and programme design, in the sense that planning should, as Dunlop describes, occur with rather than for children and families. Graue and Reineke (Chap. 12) suggest that there is significant work to be done on incorporating the 'reciprocal funds of knowledge'—that is, the knowledge and practices that all families bring to their children's schooling.

Taking a slightly different (though complementary) perspective on the issue, Lam (Chap. 10) has suggested that future research, policy and practice around starting school needs to focus on what educators do to support children's transitions, that is, examining what teachers do in the new setting, as well as in the previous, that determines children's success (or otherwise) in adapting to the new educational environment. Harrison (Chap. 5), too, suggests that what happens in the school environment, including the teacher's pedagogy and the teacher's relationships with the children, is important and should be a focus of transitions research, policy and practice.

Graue and Reineke (Chap. 12), in considering the nexus between transitions research, policy and practice, have recommended the implementation of research collaborations of prior-to-school and school-based educators working with university personnel to inform starting school policy and practice. This suggestion by Graue and Reineke is in keeping with Peters' notion of constructing shared understandings and developing partnerships between educators in prior-to-school and school settings so as to better understand the borders that are crossed (Mulholland and Wallace 2000) and the borderlands (Britt and Sumsion 2003).

16.5   Recommendations for Development and Sustainability

Work presented in this book highlights that following children through the journey of transition to identify patterns which make children successful at adapting to the new environment is important for developing transitions research. Longitudinal studies present opportunities for sustained research on transitions—over time—as well as reflecting on both past, present and future transitions practices. Indeed, significant longitudinal studies such as the *Longitudinal Study of Australian*

Children (LSAC) (Department of Families, Housing, Community Services and Indigenous Affairs (FaHCSIA), 2012) present many opportunities for comprehensive, large-scale explorations of transitions, and the work carried out by Harrison, in particular, is testament to the possibilities these sorts of studies provide for transitions researchers. As Harrison (Chap. 5) describes, large-scale, longitudinal research studies have so far provided important information about children's transitions to school, and there is a need to continue this type of research to understand the complexities of the interactions between child, family, educator and school/early childhood setting variables that impact upon children's success at school. There are unanswered questions that longitudinal studies can address, particularly as they look at outcomes over time. Furthermore, the examination of existing data sets such as those generated from studies like LSAC promotes sustained research in this area with the accessibility to large amounts of data. This sort of meta-analysis enables researchers to explore contextual and temporal elements of transitions without some of the constraints of initiating new data gathering on these issues. Indeed, data mining is a sustainable approach to research which provides many opportunities for new modelling and theory building in this field.

Peters (Chap. 8) introduces the notion of "borderlands", and this provides an interesting area of development for transitions to school researchers. Considering perspectives on both sides of the preschool-school border in order to create shared understandings has the potential to better support children's transitions to school. Sustaining the key ideas presented in Peters' chapter will involve further exploration and understanding of the borderlands that exist between early childhood settings and school, with a focus on developing partnerships to assist families and children as they cross the border and negotiate the borderlands between these educational contexts. With Margetts (Chap. 6), Dockett (Chap. 14) and Perry (Chap. 13), Peters suggests that a social justice perspective on acknowledging and gaining the perspectives of those whose voices may not be sought or heard is important in researching experiences of transition to school to build social and cultural capital and develop shared understandings for all transition to school stakeholders.

Another area for development proposed by authors in this book is the use of historical perspectives on transition. The work of both Dunlop (Chap. 3) and Turunen (Chap. 11) illustrates how we can learn about the impact of transitions by "looking back". The historical implications of transitions are significant, and the experience of starting school may have a lifelong impact. Turunen's chapter, in particular, highlights how the examination of recalled transition demonstrates that starting school is a part of an individual's "life course" (Elder 1998). Starting school is, as Turunen describes, one of the key life events an individual experiences and might contribute to a person's identity and life trajectory. Turunen (Chap. 11) explains how recollections of starting school are event-specific knowledge that can become part of a person's self-defining memories; and 'the content of self-defining memories is associated with success in relationships or achievement, personal adjustment and levels of distress, and they arouse positive or negative feelings at the time of recall'. The message of Turunen's research is that there may be a lifelong impact of the transition experience, and further exploration of recalled and historical perspectives on starting school will make an important contribution to the transitions field of research.

Looking back on transitions also raises questions about the nature of the transition experience. Garpelin (Chap. 9) poses a question as to whether transition should be viewed as an individual practice or a social practice. Indeed, is transition a social practice that is individually experienced or is it an individual experience that is socially constructed and practiced? Further examination of Garpelin's provocation seems warranted.

16.6   Future Directions

The chapters in this book demonstrate that a considerable amount of significant research on transitions to school has been undertaken internationally, and this work should be celebrated. However, the chapters collectively also represent a call for further research in this area. Drawing on the preceding chapters in this book, the following would seem to be the key areas for consideration for future programmes of transitions research:

- Use of a variety of theoretical and conceptual frameworks to help understand children's experiences from a range of perspectives
- Examination of the features of home, early childhood service and school contexts that support children's transitions
- Amplification of children's and parents' voices in transitions research
- Development of a philosophy of transition
- Consideration of historical implications of transitions
- Continued exploration of large data sets to examine factors which impact on transitions
- Investigation of the influence of temperament characteristics and child-teacher relationships on outcomes for children's transitions
- Interrogation of transition policy and practice through the lens of inclusion
- Further reflection on how to define and assess a successful and effective transition to school for families and children

In addition to pondering future avenues for transitions research, we must also consider the policy and practice initiatives which might result from such research. Indeed, some examples of research-informed practice and policy are presented in the chapters which follow. In essence, the synthesis presented in this chapter provides the "bridge" between the *research* presented in Chaps. 1, 2, 3, 4, 5, 6, 7, 8, 9, 10, 11, 12, 13, 14, and 15 and the *policy* and *practice* in Chaps. 17, 18, 19, and 20

Acknowledgement   The authors would like to acknowledge the contributions of Leonie McIntosh in the early stages of development of this chapter. Her insights shared during the *Starting School: Research, Policy and Practice* conference in 2010 were integral to the early planning of this chapter and helped to inform the approach taken here.

References

Albon, D. (2011). Postmodern and post-structuralist perspectives on early childhood education. In L. Miller & L. Pound (Eds.), *Theories and approaches to learning in the early years* (pp. 38–52). Los Angeles/London: Sage.

Bourdieu, P. (1997). The forms of capital. In A. H. Halsey, H. Lauder, P. Brown, & A. S. Wells (Eds.), *Education, culture, economy and society* (pp. 45–58). Oxford: Oxford University Press.

Britt, C., & Sumsion, J. (2003). Within the borderlands: Beginning early childhood teachers in primary schools. *Contemporary Issues in Early Childhood, 4*(2), 115–136.

Dahlberg, G., Moss, P., & Pence, A. R. (1999). *Beyond quality in early childhood education and care: Postmodern perspectives*. London: Falmer Press.

Department of Families, Housing, Community Services and Indigenous Affairs (FaHCSIA). (2012). Growing up in Australia: The Longitudinal Study of Australian Children (LSAC). http://www.growingupinaustralia.gov.au/. Accessed 9 Aug 2012.

Dockett, S., Perry, B., Campbell, H., Hard, L., Kearney, E., Taffe, R., & Greenhill, J. (2007). *Early years curriculum continuity for learning project: Final report*. Adelaide: Department of Education and Children's Services. from http://www.earlyyears.sa.edu.au/files/links/final_lit_review.pdf. Accessed 3 July 2012.

Educational Transitions and Change (ETC) Research Group. (2011). *Transition to school: Position statement*. Albury Wodonga: Research Institute for Professional Practice, Learning and Education, Charles Sturt University. http://www.csu.edu.au/research/ripple/research-groups/etc/Position-Statement.pdf. Accessed 19 Oct 2012.

Elder, G. H. (1998). The life course as developmental theory. *Child Development, 69*(1), 1–12.

Elkind, D. (1997). The death of child nature: Education in the postmodern world. *Phi Delta Kappan, 79*(3), 241–245.

Graue, E. (1993). *Ready for what? Constructing meanings of readiness for kindergarten*. Albany: State University of New York Press.

Mulholland, J., & Wallace, J. (2000). *Restorying and the legitimation of research texts*. Paper presented at the annual meeting of the National Association of Research in Science Teaching, New Orleans.

Stephenson, M., & Parsons, M. (2007). Expectations: Effects of curriculum change as viewed by children, parents and practitioners. In A.-W. Dunlop & H. Fabian (Eds.), *Informing transitions in the early years: Research, policy and practice* (pp. 137–148). Berkshire: Open University Press.

Thomson, P. (2002). *Schooling the rustbelt kids: Making the difference in changing times*. Sydney: Allen & Unwin.

Chapter 17
The Wollongong Transition to School Experience: A Big Step for Children, Families and the Community

Tracey Kirk-Downey and Shabnam Hinton

17.1   Introduction

Wollongong is a highly multicultural city of 200 000 people, located between the mountains and the sea on the east coast of New South Wales (NSW), Australia, approximately 80 km south of Sydney. Children under the age of 5 constitute more than 7 % of the population. There are 55 primary schools and 94 prior-to-school education and care services within the city boundaries.

In 2003, transition to school was identified as a priority area for funding through the NSW State Government. To consider the opportunities this provided, initial meetings of early childhood professionals were held in Wollongong and the neighbouring Shellharbour local government area. These meetings resulted in the formation of the Illawarra[1] Transition to School Reference Group. Over the next 12 months, this group focused on goals, objectives and a funding application to Families NSW (the relevant state government authority) in order to support the network. Interim funding was provided by Wollongong City Council and the NSW Department of Education and Training.

---

[1] Illawarra is the name of the region containing both Wollongong and Shellharbour.

T. Kirk-Downey (✉)
Wollongong City Council, Wollongong, Australia
e-mail: TKirk-Downey@wollongong.nsw.gov.au

S. Hinton
Big Fat Smile, Wollongong, Australia
e-mail: shabnam.hinton@bigfatsmile.com.au

B. Perry et al. (eds.), *Transitions to School - International Research, Policy and Practice*,   229
International perspectives on early childhood education and development 9,
DOI 10.1007/978-94-007-7350-9_17, © Springer Science+Business Media Dordrecht 2014

17.2   Initial Progress

Funding was obtained to appoint a project officer (although it took a considerable time for recruitment), and it was decided that there would be two networks – Wollongong and Shellharbour – although both would have access to the project officer and undertake some activities jointly. Research was commissioned to survey early childhood educators in all schools and prior-to-school services covered by the networks about the current state of knowledge and practice around transition to school (Kirk-Downey and Perry 2006; Einarsdóttir et al. 2008).

This research provided direction for the reference group about where to focus their energy. In particular, it was ascertained that most schools were operating what they called "orientation" programmes and that these differed from school to school. Survey results indicated that the concept of "transition to school" was relatively new to most schools and that schools felt their orientation programmes were generally satisfactory. However, most schools and prior-to-school services had little or no contact with each other in relation to children moving from one environment to the other, and many prior-to-school services reported attempting to make contact with schools to ensure their children had a smooth transition but gaining little response.

There was an identified need for professional development for staff in both schools and prior-to-school services. As a result, a series of presentations and workshops were planned and undertaken during 2004 and 2005. The two networks took slightly different tasks at this stage, and what is reported here derives mainly from the Wollongong Network.

17.3   Becoming Established

The Wollongong Transition to School Network invited all schools and prior-to-school services in the local government area to become members of the network. The invitation outlined the aims of the network as developing a group of interested people who were willing to assist in promoting the importance of quality transition to school programmes that met the needs of each community and developing and supporting initiatives to assist schools and prior-to-school services achieve this goal. Over a period of several months, a network of more than 15 staff from public schools, Catholic schools, not-for-profit prior-to-school services, Wollongong College of Technical And Further Education, University of Wollongong, Illawarra Children's Services, Illawarra Area Child Care, NSW Department of Education and Training, and Wollongong City Council was formed.

Workshops were implemented during 2004 and 2005 and included both research- and practice-based materials on the following topics:

- What is transition to school?
- Children's voices in transition to school.

- Transition versus orientation.
- Transition to school in a community with very low prior-to-school attendance.
- Using children's portfolios for transition to school.
- Understanding children's friendships.
- The NSW Curriculum Framework.[2]
- Transition to school and parent mentoring.
- Key learning areas.
- Brain research and the NSW Curriculum Framework.
- Indicators of progress in transition to school.
- Aboriginal transition to school.

In addition to these professional development workshops, the Wollongong Network undertook a variety of other initiatives and activities, including the following:

- Regular monthly meetings to discuss local issues regarding transition to school
- Providing feedback on *Guidelines for Effective Transition to School Programs* and *Indicators of Progress* matrix[3] (Dockett and Perry, 2006) and encouragement for schools and prior-to-school services to use these
- Strategic planning leading to a Wollongong Network Action Plan
- As a result of the work on the *Indicators of Progress* matrix, the network identified community involvement as an area for future development. This led to initiatives such as:

  - The mascot Billy Backpack
  - The introduction of the School Starters Picnic
  - Wollongong City Council's Kids Garden Groove – a children's festival held in the Wollongong Botanical Gardens – at which the network held a stall to promote the importance of transition to school and provided information to parents and children on how to assist their children make this transition successfully
  - Transition to school stalls at shopping centres and other community events

- Promotion of the NSW Department of Education & Training Starting School information booklets and posters (NSW Department of Education and Training 2003)
- Development of a Wollongong Transition to School brochure

A number of these activities led the way in transition to school practices in Australia. Details of some of these initiatives are provided below.

---

[2] At the time, this was the early childhood education curriculum framework used in NSW settings.

[3] Both the *Guidelines for Effective Transition to School Programs* and the *Indicators of Progress* matrix derived from the Starting School Research Project (Dockett and Perry 2006). The *Indicators of Progress* matrix outlines different levels of attainment for each of the Guidelines and encourages groups to map their current practice as well as planning for improved transitions practice.

17.3.1   School Starters Picnic

The School Starters Picnic grew out of discussion at one of the regular monthly meetings about how to increase community awareness and participation in transition to school programmes. It was decided to organise a picnic, inviting all children in the local government area who were starting school the following year. Corporate sponsorship provided special hats for all the children who attended. These hats were a major attraction for the children as they designated them as special 'school starters'. Information bags were provided, containing materials for children, such as writing pads, pencils as well as relevant information for parents about helping their child make the transition to school. Activities at the picnic were run by schools and prior-to-school services. As well, local community groups and performers provided some gym fun activities, live music, bubble blowing and arts and crafts. All activities were free and the day finished off with a sausage sizzle run by various community groups. The picnic has always been supported by the Wollongong Lord Mayor, who attends and, in opening the picnic, typically describes the importance of school transition. The School Starters Picnic is regarded as a major event by the entire network and by the local community. The first picnic in 2005 was attended by about 60 people. The numbers have increased steadily considerably over the years with more than 400 people now attracted to the event every year.

The purpose of the School Starters Picnic is to raise awareness of the importance of a positive transition to school and to show that the City Council and the community support this important time for children. The parents and children love the picnic and line up for photos. The parents are hungry for information and keen to talk about their child starting school. The School Starters Picnic is a special event and can be quite emotional. It is a key plank in the Wollongong Transition to School Network's agenda (Figs. 17.1, 17.2, and 17.3).

17.3.2   Starting School in Wollongong School Brochure

While the Wollongong Transition to School Network promoted materials from a number of sources, it was decided that individual schools in the network might like to develop their own brochures featuring their own children, uniforms and routines. A generic brochure (Fig. 17.4) was developed by the network, and schools were invited to insert photos relevant to their particular context. Many schools took up this initiative with excellent results, judging from feedback from prior-to-school settings and families.

17.3.3   Big Schools Parents Expos

Initial research identified the potential to bring a stronger community aspect to local transition to school programmes. As a result, the network decided to implement parent meetings in public, non-school venues, inviting all primary schools in a local

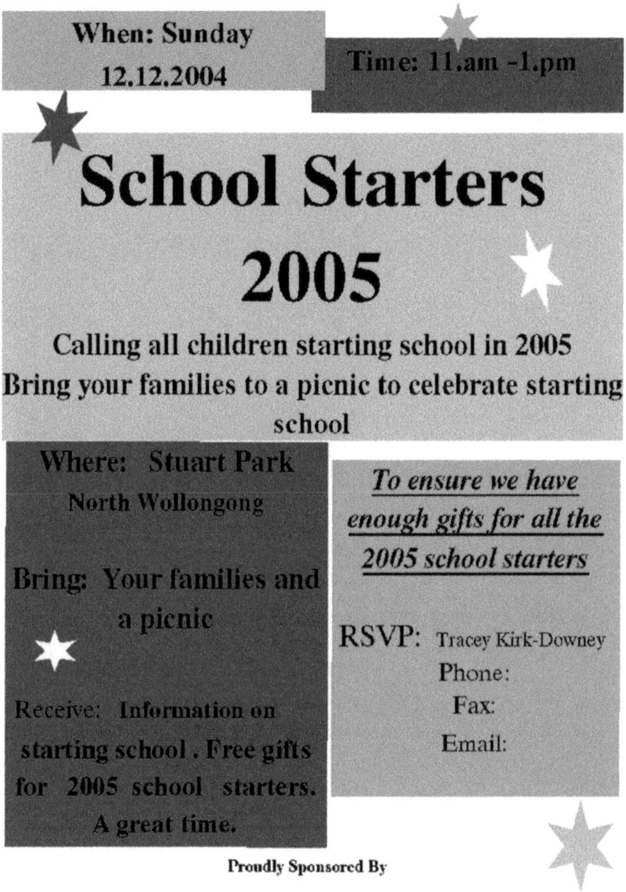

Fig. 17.1 Our first invitation went out to every school, prior-to-school service, doctor's surgery, community centre, library and various other child-focused organisation in the Wollongong area, (©Tracey Kirk-Downey, Children and Family Services Coordinator, Wollongong City Council)

district to present information about their school, display their school in a positive light and meet parents. The specified objectives of the Big School Expos were to:

- Reach as many parents as possible, particularly those whose children did not attend a prior-to-school service
- Have teachers and schools come to the one non-school venue, thereby making it accessible for parents whose images of school were not positive
- Allow parents to have access to all the schools in their area at the one venue
- Provide support for parents to fill out enrolment forms, ask questions, look at uniforms and talk about policies and practices in schools
- Achieve a coordinated approach to transition to school with everyone getting the same message

The expos were held in the first half of the school year, with parents and families targeted if they had a child starting school in the following year. Wollongong was

Fig. 17.2 Lord Mayor at the
first School Starters Picnic,
(©Tracey Kirk-Downey,
Children and Family Services
Coordinator, Wollongong
City Council)

Fig. 17.3 Positive media coverage began with the first picnic and has continued ever since,
(©Hank Van Stuivenberg, Fairfax Media)

Starting School In Wollongong

2006

Things parents and children can do together to prepare for school.

1

✧ Talk to each other about why children go to school.

✧ Talk to each other about what you think school will be like.

✧ Visit the school together - as part of the organised orientation and by yourself – after contacting the school.

✧ Both you and your child talk with adults and children who already go to school.

✧ Be reasonable in the expectations you build up in your child about starting school: once you start, keep going – it is not just for one day; get excited about uniforms but do not go overboard; do not suggest that your child will learn to read the first day.

✧ Both you and your child should get to know the teachers who will be taking Kindergarten when your child starts school.

✧ Encourage your child's early childhood educator to send your child's records on to the Kindergarten teacher.

✧ Tell the Kindergarten teacher what you know about your child.

✧ Make sure your child is comfortable in getting to school and home again, whatever this means in your circumstances.

2

✧ Give your child access to other children in a variety of setting such as visiting the library for story time sessions.

✧ Get involved in sporting clubs such as little athletics, swimming, soccer, cricket, etc.

✧ Encourage your child to play with and use pens, paper, paint, water, balls, etc. Through play, young children learn naturally. Play activities provide opportunities for your child to explore, interact and solve problems.

✧ Set a time to read to your child and talk about what might happen next in the story.

✧ Access a variety of facilities such as parks and public toilets with your child

✧ Encourage questioning and curiosity.

✧ Have an up-to-date immunisation record for your child.

✧ Make learning a fun and pleasurable experience, not a chore.

3

✧ Parents never stop being educators.

✧ Teachers and parents are active and sensitive observers, initiators and participators in this most distinctive and significant year of schooling.

✧ Parents and teachers are partners in enhancing the child's experiences.

> **For further information contact:**
> • Your prior to school service
> • Early Learning Program Coordinator Department Education and Training Illawarra and South Coast Region 42249219
> • Your local school

This brochure is an initiative of Illawarra Families First,
Wollongong City Council and
Wollongong Transition To School Network

4

Fig. 17.4 Starting School in Wollongong generic brochure, (©Tracey Kirk-Downey, Children and Family Services Coordinator, Wollongong City Council)

divided into five districts and an expo held in each in community centres and service clubs. The Big School Expos were scheduled for evenings to facilitate participation by working parents.

All primary schools in each district were sent invitations to attend and bring enrolment forms, school uniforms and anything else they would like, to show parents about their school. Local community speech and occupational therapy, and nutrition units also attended with displays and presentations for parents.

Each expo began with input from a transition to school researcher on the importance and content of a good transition to school programme. This was followed by a teacher presentation on some very practical things parents can do to help their children make a positive transition to school. A speech therapist spoke on the importance of getting the children's eyes and hearing tested and encouraging parents to arrange an assessment if they had any concerns about their child's speech. Following a time for questions, parents were free to visit the displays organised by the schools they were considering for their child, meet staff (often including the principal), and ask questions. Parents also received a bag of information about transition to school from the network.

Parent feedback on the Big School Expos was that they appreciated having the opportunity to meet some of the staff from the school their child would attend and also valued the opportunity to talk in a relaxed atmosphere and ask questions about enrolment procedures, uniforms and other detailed matters.

17.3.4 Billy Backpack

Perhaps the most amazing achievement of the Wollongong Transition to School Network is the development of Billy Backpack. Billy is the mascot for the network and has done marvellous work in the community to establish the transition to school as an important process and something to be celebrated. Even the design of Billy Backpack was seen as a community event, highlighting the importance of transition to school. The objectives for this network initiative were to:

- Involve the broader community in the Transition to School Network by engaging school age children
- Create a character who could be identified with transition to school by children, families and communities throughout the Illawarra region
- Celebrate children's creative and imaginative talents through the design of the mascot
- Provide Illawarra children with a *'sense of ownership'* of the character

The Transition to School Network ran a competition involving all the local primary schools. Information about the competition asked children to design a character to represent transition to school in the region. Local business and local, state and federal government organisations were involved in the process through sponsorship and membership of the competition judging panel. Wollongong City Council provided a marketing team to develop a design brief that would transform the selected design into both a logo and a mascot for the transition network.

Hundreds of entries were received and the judging panel chose the top ten. Wollongong City Council held a reception for these children and their parents and teachers with the members of the panel. All ten children received their drawing back in a frame with a certificate, and the top three finalists received gift certificates for their schools for a local bookshop and a gift voucher for themselves from a local

Fig. 17.5 The winning entry in the design a mascot competition, (©Tracey Kirk-Downey, Children and Family Services Coordinator, Wollongong City Council)

Fig. 17.6 Mitchell Prior, designer of Billy Backpack, on Billy's debut at the 2005 transition to school picnic, (©Liz Depers, Intern, Wollongong City Council)

electrical retailer. The winning entry (Fig. 17.5) was announced and there was a celebratory afternoon tea. Not only was this a wonderful culmination to the competition but it also received much media attention, further celebrating the importance of transition to school.

Using this design, Billy Backpack came to 'life' as a mascot (Figs. 17.6 and 17.8) and as a highly recognisable logo (Fig. 17.7).

Fig. 17.7 Billy Backpack
logo (©Tracey Kirk-Downey,
Children and Family Services
Coordinator, Wollongong
City Council)

Fig. 17.8 Billy Backpack and members of the Wollongong Transition to School Network at the
2005 transition to school picnic (©Tracey Kirk-Downey, Children and Family Services Coordinator,
Wollongong City Council)

17.4 Setting a Strategic Direction

The first few years of the Transition to School Network had achieved many important
initiatives that had raised the profile of starting school in the Illawarra region.
However, strategic planning was needed to ensure that the network continued to
flourish. This was a major task during 2005 and was a critical process in the success
of the project as it gave all clear directions in which to head and also gave each of

the Shellharbour and Wollongong networks the freedom to develop initiatives that reflected the communities in which they worked.

The strategic plan was developed in answer to the following key questions:

1. How can schools and prior-to-school services build on existing transition to school programmes?
2. How can we ensure that Aboriginal children have a successful transition to school?
3. How can we ensure that children who do not experience a prior-to-school setting have a successful transition to school?
4. How do we improve parent and community knowledge about the importance of a successful transition to school?
5. How do we promote and extend our Transition to School Networks?

The strategic plan was implemented and has been evaluated and reviewed each year. Both Shellharbour and Wollongong networks have used the strategic plan to develop a Local Action Plan.

17.5 Consolidation and Expansion

The Illawarra Transition to School Network is dedicated to promoting an optimal transition for children entering formal schooling by providing current research-based information, available avenues of practical support across the Illawarra and links to related resources for children, parents and families and educators in both prior-to-school settings and schools. Networks were established in Wollongong, Shellharbour (including Kiama), Nowra[4] and for transition to school for Aboriginal children. Since 2009, all activities have been coordinated by Big Fat Smile (formerly Illawarra Children's Services).

17.5.1 Website Development

The Transition to School website (http://www.transitiontoschool.com.au/) was launched in 2006 by the NSW Minister for Community Services. The high-profile launch raised awareness of the overall Illawarra project, the website and the importance of a successful transition to school.

The website was set up to achieve several objectives:

- To promote transition to school to the broader community
- To provide a place for parents and families to find up-to-date information about transition to school in their local community

---

[4] Shellharbour, Kiama, and Nowra are cities south of Wollongong.

- To provide a forum for parents and staff to share their transition to school experiences and programmes

The website offered unprecedented access to starting school information and resources for children, parents and educators. It was the first of its kind in the sector and rapidly became a popular tool within the Illawarra and beyond.

17.5.2   Voices of Children Starting School Project

During 2007, Wollongong City Council – as key drivers of the network – sought to enact the commitment to children's participation in transition to school planning. Children had been involved in the design competition for Billy Backpack, but the network was keen to extend children's participation beyond this. The *Voices of Children Starting School* project provided an opportunity to achieve this. It also provided yet another way to develop further the relationships between prior-to-school services and schools in the Wollongong area.

A successful application for funds was developed and invitations were sent to all schools and prior-to-school services in the Wollongong area seeking expressions of interest from those wishing to participate in the project. These expressions of interest had to come from clusters of at least one school and at least one of its feeder prior-to-school settings. Very few details were given in the call for expressions of interest beyond that the project was about prompting children's participation in transition to school.

Several expressions of interest were received and educators from the chosen schools and related prior-to-school services were invited to a meeting to discuss the project brief. Much to the horror of some of the participants, the brief was very 'BRIEF'. The overall aim of the project was to review and improve the transition to school programme that currently existed in the cluster, and the instructions given to the participants were as follows:

- The schools and prior-to-school services in their area had to work together.
- They had to take on board some of the children's ideas and thoughts.
- Children had to be involved in the implementation of the programme.
- They were to document their processes.
- They had to present their process and outcomes at a forum to other schools and prior-to-school services and include children in their presentation.

Some of the educators were concerned that they were not told how exactly how they might undertake the project. They were told that they could go about this project differently in each cluster, so long as all of the above instructions were covered. A time limit of 3 months was set before the final presentation and celebration day.

The outcomes of this project were outstanding, with all educators reporting the significant strengthening of relationships between the school and prior-to-school services in their area. They all reported that the children had come up with ideas, issues and thoughts that the educators had never considered and their input and participation was invaluable.

There were many tangible products from the project including books, DVDs, PowerPoint presentations, social stories and the final presentations by children and educators to about 90 people at the Wollongong City Council. Other reported outcomes arising from the involvement of children included the following:

- More inclusive transition to school programmes.
- Stronger relationships between the children starting school with the current first year of schoolchildren.
- Significant improvements in transition to school programmes stimulated by the many great ideas generated by the children.
- Children having a sense of ownership of and commitment to the transition to school programme.
- The children developed skills in planning, implementing and evaluating a transition to school programme as well as developing and delivering a presentation to a large audience.
- Increased self-esteem in the children.
- Vibrant and flexible transition to school programmes that were responsive to the needs of the children and families.
- Strong, cooperative and mutually respectful relationships between the two educational sectors.

For further information concerning this innovative project, see Perry and Dockett (2007, 2011).

17.5.3   State Forum on Transition to School

Towards the end of 2007, the Illawarra Transition to School Network was privileged to host the 2007 State Forum on Transition to School. Some 120 participants travelled from across NSW and interstate to participate with presentations from children involved in the *Voices of Children* project, high school students, helpers from the School Starter Picnics, Indigenous educators and university researchers. The forum was also an opportunity for each region of the network to celebrate their achievements and to discuss variations across NSW in transition to school processes and funding.

17.5.4   Starting School Booklet

In 2008, a resource for parents and educators, titled *The Starting School Booklet*, was developed (Illawarra Transition to School Network 2008). The booklet was able to be individualised for each school in the Illawarra. It has been translated into several languages and contains information about starting school, offers tips to parents and doubles as an orientation booklet for school starters. The booklet has been reproduced and updated annually since the initial version and continues to assist parents and educators across the region.

17.5.5 Professional Development

From its inception, professional development has been a strong focus for the network. For example, a workshop exploring notions of resilience attracted 400 educators and parents. Another set of very successful workshops for educators and parents around child health and physical development in the lead-up to school highlighted a need for the project to work more closely with the Area Health Service. This has resulted in strong partnerships with the South Eastern Sydney & Illawarra Health Service which continue to the present day.

17.5.6 Other Developments and Change

Although popular as events, evaluations of the School Starter Picnics and Big School Expos showed that they were not reaching those families that would benefit most and particularly those families in the typically hard-to-reach categories – Indigenous families, families from a culturally and linguistically diverse background and families with a child who had not attended a prior-to-school service. With the intention of extending the programme's reach to all families, events were trialled in shopping centres. This proved very successful in ensuring contact with all families, in sharing important information and in creating awareness of the benefits of preparing for the transition to school. For example, five Shopping Centre Expos were held in 2009. Local schools were invited, along with health professionals (dental, paediatric and speech pathology). This partnership with health professionals assisted with early intervention and parents were able to access advice free of charge and in a non-threatening environment. Free entertainment and activities for the children offered great incentives for parents to attend. Shopping centre events continue to be the best means so far devised of reaching 'hard-to-reach' families.

School Starter Picnics initially raised awareness about the importance of a successful transition to school. This was positively reinforcing for many middle class families, but did not connect with other families that would benefit most from the project's services. Over time and with a variety of new connection points in place so that all families can be reached, the picnics have become celebrations rather than channels solely for distributing information.

In 2008, a 6-week Koori[5] playgroup was established, leading up to the inaugural Koori School Starters Picnic. These activities were conducted in partnership with

---

[5] 'Koori' is a term used by some Indigenous Australians as a generic descriptor of Aboriginal people living in certain areas, including the Illawarra region.

the local Aboriginal Cultural Centre and the Aboriginal Child, Youth and Family Strategy (NSW Government 2011). Transition to school for Aboriginal children has been a major project for the network and continues to be so.

In 2012, the programme continues with the focus of informing parents and educators in a number of settings such as prior-to-school services, TAFE colleges and universities. Events at smaller, suburban shopping centres are now included in the programme of annual events.

The Transition to School website and Starting School Booklets have been revamped to include more relevant information and up-to-date research. Recognising that social media offer a fast, effective, low-cost and popular channel for many families, a Facebook page has been introduced.

Much work has been done to foster community partnerships that can encourage and facilitate links to families in the target group. One very successful initiative has been the introduction of Centrelink parenting workshops. These workshops are targeted at parents with children aged 4 and 5 and cover a range of topics including child health, development and socialisation.

17.6 Building a Sustainable Future

The Illawarra Transition to School Network has come a long way since its initial days in 2004. Transition to school is now seen as a community event in Wollongong and the other Illawarra areas. Inevitably, as the network has diversified and come under the governance of an organisation rather than a group of enthusiasts, some of the ideals informing those enthusiasts have had to be reconsidered. Nonetheless, there are many achievements and many forms of recognition for the Transition to School Network.

The work has become known nationally and internationally. For example, the network attracted prior-to-school and school educators from New Zealand who shared how they approached transition to school and then were enthralled to hear the network's achievements in the field. The New Zealand visitors attended a Starting School picnic. On their return home, they began developing plans for their own picnics and made other changes to their approach. The Wollongong Network also took some of their ideas and approaches, and several services and schools included them in their programmes. International publications (Kirk-Downey and Perry 2006; Kagan and Tarrant 2010; Perry and Dockett 2011) have reported aspects of the work of the Wollongong Transition to School Network.

There are a number of reasons why the Wollongong Transition to School Network has achieved so much and will continue to do so. Firstly, there is the ongoing strength of support from the Wollongong City Council through both its Children's Services Coordinator and its Lord Mayor. The involvement and commitment from the Lord Mayor and his personal and organisational support has helped display the importance of transition to school within the community. His agreement to encourage the Council's Children's Services Coordinator to run with the project, especially in the first 2 years, meant that there was an on-the-ground 'driver' for the project. Secondly, the model of having local people making local decisions about the transition programmes in their community was critical. However, it would not have worked without passionate teachers and other staff from both schools and prior-to-school settings who were creative; were willing to think outside the square; had a strong connection with, and understanding of, their community; were willing to step outside their safety zones and take risks; were content to be challenged and take on new ideas; were able to learn about each others' teaching environments; and showed respect for each others' skills and talents. Thirdly, finding a champion in each setting or school is critical to the success of the programme. This champion does not have to be the principal – it can be a teacher or a parent. There were many people in our network who went into the school at which their child was about to start and offered to organise a picnic for the new school starters and help out with the transition to school programme. Several schools have made significant changes in their programmes as a result of this 'championing'.

These amazing people created something quite special from very little. Billy Backpack is now famous; he has his own song and CD; he has his own Facebook page and is highly sought after both locally and elsewhere – he is very well travelled!! Billy is a transition to school 'rock star'. The children LOVE him and he creates excitement wherever he goes. All this because we had an environment where new ideas were encouraged and nothing was impossible. We had a formula that worked well and from that first meeting of our Wollongong Network, we went from strength to strength achieving many great things that made a difference for many children starting school in our community.

17.7   Final Words

The Wollongong Transition to School Network has been the most rewarding project I have ever worked on. The relationships formed during that time with the amazing people in the network have been long standing, and we love to reminisce when we see each other. There are now champions for transition to school all over the Illawarra as they have moved schools or gained promotions and taken with them their commitment for ensuring children have the best start to school possible.

The programme was a slow burn and sometimes very frustrating because it seemed that things were not happening fast enough, but it was all worth it and we are all very proud of the outcomes we have achieved over the years. Whilst some things have gone by the wayside and no longer happen, some things have remained. We have learned the following:

- Every school and prior-to-school service needs a champion for transition to school and a leader that is supportive.

- Programmes with a strong child focus that value parents and educators as partners work the best.
- Programmes that foster strong relationships with parents, educators and children and encourage commitment to and participation in the school have the most beneficial impact.

The Network has made a difference for many children, families and educators as children start school. We can be very proud of what we have achieved and need to continue with the good work.

Appendix

This poem was inspired by the John Lennon song 'Imagine' and the ways in which Carter and Curtis (2010) have used it to inspire visionary thinking about the ways we want education (or in this case, transition to school) to be. It has been written by Margaret Gleeson and Michele Kicks, in collaboration with the Wollongong Transition to School Network.

A.1   *Imagine a Transition Program*

Imagine a transition program
Where children are respected and their feelings are important
Where children's voices are heard and their questions explored
Where learning is motivated by children's sense of wonder and their capacity for joy
And the magic of childhood infects families, teachers and educators

Imagine a transition program
Where the measures of success are smiles on children's faces and their eagerness to return
rather, than the number of worksheets they bring home
Where play and collaboration are recognised as primary vehicles for learning
Where children are active participants in their learning rather than passive recipients
And the importance of developing positive relationships is not overlooked

Imagine a transition program
Where cultures are valued and respected and influence the life of the classroom
Where the strength and capabilities of children are recognised and valued
Where their individuality is celebrated and allowed to shine
Where their eagerness to meet this new challenge is nurtured
Where they feel competent and confident in themselves as learners
Where children can attempt challenges without fear of the consequence of failure
And are valued as contributing members of the school community

Imagine a transition program
Where families are recognised as the child's first and most important teacher
Where the doors of prior-to-school settings and classrooms are always open

Where the strong foundations of early childhood are recognised and built upon
And the collaboration between families, teachers and educators focuses on the best interests
of the children

Imagine a transition program
Where the mixed feelings of families are seen as valid and can be shared
Where it's okay to cry and tissues and tea are always on hand
Where parents can linger and feel supported by mentors
And the hopes of families for their children are translated into the goals of teachers
Where families, teachers and educators form close partnerships
Where this important step for families is acknowledged, families are supported
and barriers are broken down
Where families are empowered to ask questions and voice opinions,
Where feedback is viewed as a chance to grow and improve

Imagine a transition program
That evolves in response to research and best practice
That is personalized by each school and its community
That is embraced as an essential component of the whole school
Where buddies share the excitement of school starters
Where the wider community acknowledges the significance of transitions
And their positive contribution to community wellbeing

Imagine a transition program
Where teachers have the time and resources to be creative
Where teachers have strong networks for collaboration and support
Where their hearts and minds are nourished through professional development
Where their passion and commitment to children is embraced and infectious

Imagine a transition program
Validated by the Government through the provision of resources!

References

Carter, M., & Curtis, D. (2010). *The visionary director* (2nd ed.). St Paul: Redleaf Press.

Dockett, S., & Perry, B. (2006). *Starting school: A guide for educators*. Sydney: Pademelon Press.

Einarsdóttir, J., Perry, B., & Dockett, S. (2008). Transition to school practices: Comparisons from Iceland and Australia. *Early Years, 28*(1), 47–60.

Illawarra Transition to School Network. (2008). Starting school booklet. http://www.transitiontoschool.com.au/downloads/early_childhood/00051_TTS_School%20starters%20book_web.pdf Accessed 6 Oct 2011.

Kagan, S. L., & Tarrant, K. (2010). *Transitions for young children: Creating connections across early childhood systems*. Baltimore: Paul H. Brookes.

Kirk-Downey, T., & Perry, B. (2006). Making transition to school a community event: The Wollongong experience. *International Journal of Transitions in Childhood, 2*, 40–49. http://extranet.edfac.unimelb.edu.au/LED/tec/pdf/journal2_pract_kirkdowney%20and%20perry.pdf. Accessed 22 Jan 2012.

NSW Department of Education and Training. (2003). Starting school with a smile. http://www.schools.nsw.edu.au/media/downloads/languagesupport/start_sch_smile/sch_smile_eng.pdf. Accessed 21 Oct 2011.

NSW Government. (2011). Aboriginal child, youth and family strategy. http://www.community. nsw.gov.au/docs_menu/for_agencies_that_work_with_us/our_funding_programs/acyfs.html. Accessed 24 July 2012.

Perry, B., & Dockett, S. (2007). Voices of children starting school. Wollongong: Illawarra Transition to School Network. http://www.transitiontoschool.com.au/downloads/research/ Voices%20of%20children%20in%20starting%20school%20-%20Bob%20Perry%20and%20 Sue%20Dockett.pdf. Accessed 9 Aug 2012.

Perry, B., & Dockett, S. (2011). 'How 'bout we have a celebration?' Advice from children on start- ing school. *European Early Childhood Education Research Journal, 19*(3), 375–388.

Chapter 18
Transitions, Inclusion and Information Technology

Bronwyn Glass and Margaret Cotman

18.1 Introduction

Transitional actions are recognised internationally as being a vital component underpinning quality practice in early childhood and primary education (Dockett and Perry 2007; Dunlop and Fabian 2007; Hartley et al. 2012; Margetts 2007; Peters 2010) with the emphasis in both settings firmly embedded in the importance of building a feeling of belonging and a feeling of being valued. Peters believes that successful transitions enhance children's engagement in the learning process and their view of themselves as learners by building a strong bridge from the existing funds of knowledge from home and from their early childhood setting to the new primary school setting. As well, when there is a commitment to a climate of inclusion, attention to transitional actions becomes even more vital. Attention to detail, focus on the individual and an openness to different or new possibilities lead to the path to success (Glass et al. 2008). There are numerous ways in which transitionally inclusive actions can take place between an early childhood setting and a primary school. In this study, Skype was chosen as the preferred method for interactions between kindergarten and school. Skype is a free application that can be added to computers for the purpose of written, verbal and video communication using a voice over the Internet programme (VoIP), that 'converts voice signals into data streams that are sent over the Internet and converted back to audio by the recipient's computer' (EDUCAUSE 2007).

B. Glass (✉)
Botany Downs Kindergarten, Botany Downs, New Zealand
e-mail: bronwynglass@gmail.com

M. Cotman
Lucknow School, Havelock North, New Zealand
e-mail: margaret.cotman@gmail.com

B. Perry et al. (eds.), *Transitions to School - International Research, Policy and Practice*, 249
International perspectives on early childhood education and development 9,
DOI 10.1007/978-94-007-7350-9_18, © Springer Science+Business Media Dordrecht 2014

This Skype project arose from the commitment of two teachers wanting to make a difference to children's transition to school, and in particular the transition from Botany Downs Kindergarten to Botany Downs School. Botany Downs is a sessional kindergarten, with 45 children attending the morning session and 45 children attending the afternoon session. The kindergarten shares a back boundary with Botany Downs Primary School and looks out onto the playing field. The children can see their siblings at play or they can gather at the fence to say hello. Many of the kindergarten children move on to Botany Downs School, yet children exit to as many as eighteen local primary schools. Botany Downs Kindergarten has a commitment to inclusion and a strong community base, enriched by a wealth of parent involvement.

Prior to the Skype initiative, a number of transitional and inclusive actions were embedded in the kindergarten programme. For example, the children and teachers would attend assembly at Botany Downs School at least once a term, visit the school library a couple of times a year, attend Jump Jam (an aerobics programme designed for schoolchildren) a couple of times a year and attend some special events at the school. It was a relatively formal relationship mostly initiated by the kindergarten head teacher (Glass et al. 2009).

Many transitional actions take place daily at kindergarten. When the children arrive at kindergarten in the morning, they put their photograph up beside the primary school they are going to attend. The children then sign in and put their name on their magnetic board and their photo beside the tidy up job they will do for that day. In the book area, the kindergarten has books with photographs provided by most schools telling of the activities and expectations of new entrant children at their school. Every 6 months the teachers take photographs of children who will be going to the same school so that children and their families can make connections with other children and families going to the same school, and these photographs are placed in each child's portfolio.

Botany Downs School caters for children from Years 1 to 6 and has an enrolment of around 500 students. As is traditional in many New Zealand primary schools, preschool children visit a teacher's class for a morning session once a week in the month leading up to starting school. On these visits, kindergarten children take part in the regular classroom programme alongside the schoolchildren getting to know the children, the teacher and becoming familiar with the school and classroom environment. One particular child's visit strengthened the commitment to build a stronger meaningful relationship with the kindergarten.

On one such morning a sunny and enthusiastic boy from Botany Downs Kindergarten visited the classroom. He was the younger brother of a girl the Room 9 teacher had previously taught and had talked about being in "Miss Cotman's class" like his sister from the age of three. On that particular morning visit he explored the classroom and animatedly asked questions about school. He already had his school uniform and was wearing it every chance he could. Just 48 hours after this school visit the kindergarten and school communities were in immense shock after learning that this beautiful young boy had passed away and would never attend his first day at school. We were all the poorer for that, and we became even more aware that there were no certainties in tomorrow.

The following week the Room 9 teacher attended the Learning@School conference in Rotorua as part of a school-wide professional development focus in Information Technologies. As a result of these two experiences, the teacher developed a vision to strengthen the relationship between the school and the kindergarten at this difficult time, and she realised that information technology could be the tool. Soon after the conference she arranged to meet with the head teacher of Botany Downs Kindergarten and proposed using the 'voice over the Internet programme' (VoIP) Skype as a way to develop a closer relationship between the two communities.

18.2 The Skype Project

From the floating of an idea, a path forward emerged. The teachers recognised that the success of the Skype project would depend on the ease of operation and it sitting comfortably within existing curriculum programmes in both settings. What was the vision for this project? How would it be introduced? How would it be managed and how would we measure success? Two members of the Skype teaching team had Skyped privately and two had no previous experience of Skyping. The kindergarten often Skyped with children and their families when they were on holiday in other parts of the world or they had moved away from Botany Downs. While most were very successful, one concerning case remained embedded in the minds of the teachers.

> A four year old had moved to England with her family. With a view to continuing the personal contact with the family it was decided that they would Skype. After much attention to differing time zones, the moment arrived to Skype. There was a sharing of news and photographs, and introductions to family. A couple of weeks later the kindergarten received an email to say that the child had been very distressed after the call. She wanted to come back to New Zealand to be with her friends.

This was a cautionary tale that led to a commitment to do no harm in the Skype project.

18.2.1 The Vision

The vision that drove this project was to strengthen relationships between children, teachers and communities of Botany Downs Kindergarten and Botany Downs School.

18.2.2 The Planning

The Room 9 teacher came to the kindergarten for what was to be the first of many planning meetings with teachers at Botany Downs Kindergarten. The Skype team (three teachers at Botany Downs Kindergarten and the Room 9 teacher from Botany

Downs School) were deeply committed to making the Skype project a success and recognised that the initial planning would be crucial to the success of the project. It was decided that:

- The children, teachers and parents would visit each other's settings to establish context.
- They would Skype at 10:20 a.m. on a Thursday morning for twenty minutes.
- They would project the images onto a big screen.
- They would use external microphones and speakers.
- The whole class would be involved in each setting.
- They would start every session with a greeting in Māori as is customary in NZ.
- They would alternate who started the Skype session each week.
- They would evaluate by email after each session to begin with.
- Success would be determined by the quality of subsequent relationships.

18.2.3   Validating the Project

The school timetable 'was already tight' and so the Skype project was required to fit into the existing classroom programme. The Year 1 (called Room 9) class timetable included daily oral language sessions, and so once a week Skype became the medium for oral language learning. The Room 9 teacher had to consult with other classroom teachers. At the time, several classrooms were receiving new entrant students, and organisational questions arose. Why should one class of children in the school have this experience? Would five-year-olds arriving from the kindergarten expect to be placed into that classroom?

18.2.4   The Project Begins

At the first meeting it was decided that the project would begin with visits to each other's classrooms so that introductions could be made in context and the children would not be distracted by the environment. After attending assembly one Friday morning, the kindergarten class of 45 children, teachers and accompanying parents followed Room 9 back to their classroom. As everyone squashed into the classroom, it was an opportunity to compare classroom and class size, check out the environment that they would be seeing in the background on Skype and meet the Room 9 Skype participants. Many of the children in Room 9 had attended Botany Downs Kindergarten and some had siblings currently attending. Room 9's teacher welcomed the kindergarten children to their space and each of the schoolchildren introduced themselves. The following week the children from Room 9 came to the kindergarten where the same introductory processes took place.

These visits were an opportunity to introduce the children to the technologies that they would be using in the Skype project. The teachers turned on the data projector and the webcam so the children were able to see themselves as they would appear on Skype.

The first Skype sessions required a steep learning curve for teachers and children alike. The teachers in both settings had to deal with sound and visual challenges, and the children had to learn how to speak into a microphone and how to position themselves in front of the webcam. The initial response from the children was to talk excitedly to each other about who they were seeing on the forefront and background of the screen and wave to their friends. While this was a delightful response, it proved to be quite a distraction to the processes of talking and listening. Upon reflection the teachers decided to have a couple of sessions at other times during the week they called *open Skyping* where the children were able to talk to each other freely and wave to their heart's content. For some children this process allowed them to experiment with the possibilities of Skype and build upon inter-class relationships.

Choosing which children would share during the Skype session was a point of discussion amongst the teachers. It seemed logical that children closest to going to school should get preference so that closer links could be forged as transition to school approached. If these children who were nearly five did not have news on that day, they could share happenings at kindergarten or lead a song. At school, the Room 9 teacher kept a class list and recorded when each child shared to ensure every child had an opportunity.

18.2.5 A Typical Skype Session

A typical Skype session would start with the children greeting their buddy class with Kia Ora, a Māori greeting. Two or three children in each setting would be chosen to share their work on Skype that week. The kindergarten children would share their work, news items, new songs or upcoming events. The children in Room 9 often shared pieces of schoolwork (e.g. writing, poems, artwork, handwriting). Often the children would sing waiata (songs) together or teach each other action songs. Here are some examples of the sharing:

> From kindergarten Lauren took the opportunity to share a tomato from home. When her Mum had cut their tomato open they had found that the seeds were already growing inside the tomato. The children could see the seeds growing and share Lauren's delight in the discovery.

Lauren's sharing required that the teachers initially focus the camera on Lauren, then position the tomato so that the seeds growing inside the tomato could be seen on the screen. As the teachers used the built-in camera in the computer, it required the tomato to be held up to the computer for good vision. It was a disjointed way to present the news item. This experience prompted teachers to use a separate webcam that allowed more flexibility in planning and capturing events.

Annaliese was excited to show the kindergarten children her new school shoes and held her foot up to the camera. "These are my new school shoes," she said.

Annaliese had only been at school a couple of days, and it was evident that her new school shoes were very important to her. It was a short, animated, excited, relevant sharing. Annaliese was beaming with pride.

Liam read the short story he had written at school.

Liam is a really quiet child who said very little when he was at kindergarten. There was huge pride in seeing him read his story to the kindergarten children, a great role model for the kindergarten children.

18.2.6 Creating Possibilities

For all situations in which challenges arise, the kindergarten teachers encourage the children to engage in possibility thinking (Cremin et al. 2006). Through reflection the children identified new possibilities for the use of Skype and helped problem solve when there were difficulties.

A number of the children from Room 9 come into kindergarten at the end of the day to meet their parents as their parents come in to kindergarten to collect their siblings. On one occasion Mia lamented that she would not be able to Skype that week as Skype day fell on a teacher only day. As she processed what she was saying she came upon an idea. "I know," she said, "We could Skype from home." What a great idea. A time was fixed with her Mum and Mia Skyped the kindergarten children from home, sharing what she was doing on her day off school.

On another occasion as the kindergarten was trying to Skype they discovered the school network was down. By chance they discovered that the ex-chairperson of the kindergarten committee was online … so they Skyped her. Without batting an eyelid she listened to the children's news, asked questions and offered engaging comments. It was a fabulous animated Skype session with a difference.

As the time came for Jake to leave kindergarten and go to school he became quite fixated upon the fact that he was going to a different school and would no longer be part of the Skype process. After watching and listening to his despair over a number of days the kindergarten teachers had an idea. Why not set a time for Jake to Skype kindergarten from home each week after school? And so it came to be. Every Tuesday afternoon the teachers at kindergarten would huddle around the computer and listen to Jake's school and family stories. In return we would share what was happening at kindergarten, who else had left and gone to school and outings we had been on. In a few weeks Jake's need to Skype had been fulfilled and the Skype sessions came to a natural conclusion.

Further opportunities for the use of Skype as a collaborative transitionary opportunity emerged during the year. Some of these are outlined below.

18.2.6.1 School Assembly Collaboration

Each week at Botany Downs School, a class is responsible for the organising and facilitating of assembly for the whole school in the school hall. As Room 9's turn approached, the classroom teacher had the idea of presenting items together with the kindergarten and their Year 5/6 buddy class for the assembly. As the kindergarten was strengthening their skills in waiata, it was decided that three Māori waiata would be presented. There were many challenges around setting times and finding a place for such a large group to rehearse their items, and so the three groups of children rehearsed via Skype. When the day arrived there was a flawless performance although the children had never once rehearsed face to face.

18.2.6.2   Franklin the Turtle Turns Five

The kindergarten turtle Franklin is a most popular member of the kindergarten community. Pets are renowned for their ability to smooth transitions (Donowitz 2002), and Franklin is instrumental in settling children as they transition into Botany Downs Kindergarten. Each year there is great excitement as his birthday is celebrated in fabulous style. As the preparations were discussed with Room 9 via Skype, a plan was hatched. In the next Skype session, the kindergarten children would invite Room 9 to come over and join in Franklin's 5th birthday celebrations. There was much anticipation and preparation on both sides 'of the fence' in the lead-up to the birthday celebrations. In New Zealand, most children leave their early childhood setting and start school when they turn five… so where was Franklin the day after his birthday? At school, of course! The Room 9 children and teacher documented his time at school, adding a page to Franklin's portfolio so the children at kindergarten could revisit the event.

18.2.6.3   The Ghostbusters Movie Premiere

Through their emergent curriculum, the kindergarten children had been pursuing their fascination with Ghostbusters and had ventured into the field of movie making. With the movie in the can, a red carpet premiere event was organised for the community of Botany Downs. Room 9 was invited via Skype to attend the event. Upon arrival at kindergarten, they joined the kindergarten children in drawing and cutting out their money, queuing to purchase their ticket from the ticket office and positioning themselves for good viewing beside the red carpet. After the viewing, they were able to partake in a Ghostbusters-themed morning tea before returning to class.

18.2.6.4   Occupations

As part of the school curriculum, Room 9 studied occupations. The children were invited to think of their future career path and write a letter to someone who was employed in their occupation of choice. A letter came to the kindergarten asking what does a kindergarten teacher do? This was answered with an outline of the diversity of kindergarten teaching, returned by post and shared in class and on Skype.

18.2.6.5 The Elections

As the time for the general elections in New Zealand drew near, the children in both settings were studying the finer points of electioneering, voting and electing a government to power. The teacher in Room 9 decided to hold Fairy Tale Elections in her classroom, and the children chose fictional characters as their candidates – Little Red Riding Hood, The Woodcutter, The Big Bad Wolf and Rapunzel. The Year 1 children developed manifestos for each candidate and made posters and voting papers. They explained their upcoming election to the kindergarten children via Skype. The kindergarten children received their voting papers via email. The completed forms were returned by special delivery mail to Room 9. The Big Bad Wolf's win was celebrated via Skype.

18.2.6.6 The Disco Invitation

On another occasion the kindergarten children shared that there would be a disco at kindergarten on Friday night and invited Room 9 to join the kindergarten children if they wished. For the first time, schoolchildren with no affiliation to the kindergarten other than through the Skype project attended the disco.

18.2.6.7 End of Year Picnic

By the end of the year, there was a strong connection between the kindergarten and Room 9. These links prompted the organisation of a joint picnic on the school field complete with shared food and games. The kindergarten children were allowed to bring a school lunch. It was a natural interaction with familiarity.

18.2.7 Other IT Interaction

At the same time as the Skype project was in progress, the kindergarten and Room 9 maintained their own blog sites where they posted comments about the learning in their setting. As a result of the Skype project, Room 9 added a link to the kindergarten's blog page on their own blog, and so Room 9 children were able to read the kindergarten's blog page during class time and at home. The kindergarten children would look at Room 9's blog during their group time giving further insights into life at Botany Downs School.

18.2.8 Insights from Children

Teachers interviewed a number of the children involved in the Skype project. Their comments had very similar themes.

Kathleen I like seeing the kindergarten each Friday after library. I saw all different people that I don't know but then I saw Mia's sister. I like sharing stories from my folder cause I like the kindy seeing what I am doing at school and I liked finding out what they were doing.

Connor I like getting to talk to Bronwyn because it's fun. I like telling everyone about the election and the score. I made something and Miss Cotman put it up outside our class. I like to see the kindergarten. I like listening with what they say. I like the news.

Mia I like that you get to meet your friends that you haven't seen for ages. I get to see people from around the world when I Skype. I saw Bronwyn and the kindy kids. Sometimes when my sister is there I get to see her.

Stacey I like to see all the kids that are my friends and also my old teachers. It's fun because we get a turn to talk. I get to see my old kindy and that's nice.

The children valued the connections made to their past and their memories.

Oliver It was cool cause I liked it talking to the kindy. I talked about the spider. It's a chart I brought in from Australia. I saw the children. I liked their songs.

18.3   Challenges

The Skype project was exciting and opened many doors of communication. However, it was not without its challenges. EDUCAUSE (2007) talks about Skype not being as stable as other forms of communication, and the teachers in this project would attest to that. Most challenges centred around viewing and sound. The desire to project the images onto the big screen multiplied the challenges. The teachers found that the microphones on the computers were not sufficient to pick up the sound of individual children's voices so they moved to an external microphone and speakers. If the child speaking sat too close to the speakers, there would be feedback through the speaker system and the talking was impossible to listen to. As well, teachers experimented with the use of headphones. The sound was so much clearer for those in the 'other' classroom; however, for the children in the speaker's classroom, there was a loss of interest as they could not hear the verbal responses from the other members of the listening class. Room 9 remedied this by only plugging in the microphone plug on the headset. The teachers experimented with a mixture of both options, but this was complicated by the need to readjust the settings in Skype for each format.

As the challenges occurred, the teachers would endeavour to sort them out at the time and then debrief with the Skype team later in the day. They felt that it was important for the children to see teachers role modelling the disposition to persist with challenges and problem solving and observe that in practice.

From time to time the teachers at kindergarten were approached by a concerned parent stating that their child was not going to be in Room 9 or attend Botany Downs School and could we Skype with the class or school their child would be attending. We decided early on that there would be only one Skype experience at this point in time. It would not be possible to Skype with all eighteen schools, especially as most schools had more than one new entrant class. It was assumed that, just as with the experience of attending assembly, children would be able to generalise what they were seeing and hearing to their own setting as they transitioned to school.

With a class of 45 kindergarten children, it was vital to have contingency plans in place and to work as a team as timing and challenges were sorted out. A song or two to fill in the gap, a discussion about who they might see or a prediction about what Room 9 might share were all strategies employed to fill in the gaps. Room 9 also had to employ poems and songs to fill in these moments.

There were a couple of occasions early on where the kindergarten, not so used to structured routines, forgot to Skype. It was just that the programme was busy and the time just passed. Fortunately Room 9 phoned a reminder. From then on, the teachers set a reminder on a phone so this would not happen again. While the delayed Skype sessions worked well after the hiccup, the teachers in both settings felt a little frazzled rushing to get everything set up for the session.

18.4   Discussion: Implications for Practice

The process of using information technology as a transitionary and inclusive experience offered opportunities to enhance relationships, support children's sharing of knowledge about school and expanding children's multiliteracies as they entered school.

18.4.1   Relationships and Inclusion

Skype started out as addition to existing transitional inclusive actions. Little did we know that it would become much more. It became a development of relationships: a depth of connections between children and children, children and teachers and teachers and teachers. As the project evolved, so did the relationships. The children were eager to see children they had seen previously. When the children from both classes met together face to face, there was an eagerness to be together to share, show each other around, mentor and enjoy each other's company. The Room 9 teacher noticed that children who had recently started school came up to her in the school playground, seeking her out because they knew her. Having some knowledge of the children before they transitioned to school started the new entrant relationship on a new level. Room 9 children were able to prepare for the children starting, tapping into the interests they had shared on Skype. Peters (2010) found that knowing made children feel valued and gave them a sense of belonging as they navigated the landscape of transition to school. 'Relationships can empower the new entrant in their new role as a school pupil' (Hartley et al. 2012, p. 55).

18.4.2   Sharing Knowledge and Problem Solving

Skype opened the doors of discussion with the kindergarten children and between kindergarten and Room 9 children. The children became the holders of the knowledge. On more than one occasion, children could be heard explaining Skype and the experience of Skyping. The children could also be heard engaging in conversations about which class they were going to go to and who their teacher would be. Knowledge is a powerful factor in the feeling of self-worth. Dockett and Perry (2007) recommended the use of what if games so that children could gain understanding of the school setting. Skype enabled a similar problem solving sharing, enhancing children's sense of competence and confidence about school. The teachers felt that it was important the children see their teachers as problem solvers and that sometimes things do not go as planned but there are other ways the same result can be achieved. Most importantly, the children could see that their teachers do not give up.

18.4.3   Multiliteracies

There was a tremendous amount of pride felt by the teachers at kindergarten as the schoolchildren stepped up to the microphone and read the stories they had written at school. What great role models these children were. The children at kindergarten could see the literacy possibilities that come to be at school. However, literacies in contemporary early education go beyond print literacies to incorporate information technologies (Zevenbergen 2007). Skyping is just one of the technologies that these children are exposed to in their daily lives. They already use and understand many of the literacies associated with these technologies. Teachers have a choice to join the children in their technological world and explore the possibilities, building on the children's own lived experience in the family and community (Glass et al. 2008). The Skype project was an addition to internal blogging and podcasting in both settings – a tool for meeting and enhancing the objective of building transitional actions and emerging multiliteracies.

18.4.4   Things to Do Differently

Of all the challenges that the participating teachers identified, they would sort out the sound quality issues before starting the project. Sharing clearer information regarding the details of available information technology quality (e.g. Internet speed, video quality) emerged as important to the smoothness of the Skyping process. Teachers also reflected that they would supply each other with lists of the children's names so that they could greet the children properly and in a manner that was personal, so children felt a sense of belonging.

Sustaining a project across staffing changes emerged as a barrier to continuation of the project. However, its success indicated the value of re-establishing effective relationships between kindergarten and Year 1 teachers. Perhaps sharing the project with other Year 1 teachers may have permitted other teachers with less information technology experience to engage in the project in subsequent years.

18.4.5 Where to Next?

Although the Skype project drew to a close, while it operated, it successfully bridged the divide between kindergarten and school and in turn created a whole new community of learners with a life and vitality all of its own. As Room 9's participating teacher left Botany Downs School, the Skype project drew to a close. The teachers discussed whether they would continue the project with this teacher's new class in Havelock North but decided that it was possible but would not have the same strength of connection that existed at Botany Downs because of the lack of physical proximity. It would alter the notions of inclusion and transition. It would take another teacher at the school to commit to the programme and at the point of writing this has not happened. Nevertheless, it was a hugely successful experience building reciprocal relationships for the children and teachers involved. Perhaps there will be other possibilities.

References

Cremin, T., Burnard, P., & Craft, A. (2006). Pedagogy and possibility thinking in the early years. *Thinking Skills and Creativity, 1*(2), 109–119.

Dockett, S., & Perry, B. (2007). *Transitions to school: Perceptions, expectations and experiences.* Sydney: University of New South Wales Press.

Donowitz, L. (2002). Pet therapy. *The Pediatric Infectious Disease Journal, 21*(1), 64–66.

Dunlop, A.-W., & Fabian, H. (Eds.). (2007). *Informing transitions in the early years: Research, policy and practice.* Maidenhead: McGraw-Hill.

EDUCAUSE. (2007). Educause learning initiative. www.educause.edu/eli. Accessed 25 Mar 2012.

Glass, B., Baker, K., Ellis, R., Bernstone, H., & Hagan, W. (2008). *Documenting for inclusion: How do we create an inclusive environment for all children?* (Early childhood folio, Vol. 12). Wellington: NZCER Press.

Glass, B., Baker, K., Ellis, R., Bernstone, H., & Hagan, W. (2009). Inclusion at Botany Downs kindergarten: Centre of innovation 2006.2008. Final research report. The Centre of Innovation Programme. http://www.educationcounts.govt.nz/__data/assets/pdf_file/0004/75028/Botany-Downs-Kg-COI-FINAL-report.pdf. Accessed 10 April 2012.

Hartley, C., Rogers, P., Smith, J., Peters, S., & Carr, M. (2012). *Crossing the border: A community negotiates the transition from early childhood to primary school.* Wellington: NZCER Press.

Margetts, K. (2007). Preparing children for school benefits and privileges. *Australian Journal of Early Childhood, 32*(2), 43–50.

Peters, S. (2010). *Literature review: Transition from early childhood education to school.* Wellington: Ministry of Education. http://www.educationcounts.govt.nz/publications/ece/78823. Accessed 8 April 2012.

Zevenbergen, R. (2007). Digital natives come to preschool: Implications for early childhood practice. *Contemporary Issues in Early Childhood, 8*(1), 19–29.

Chapter 19
Building Connections Around Transition: Partnerships and Resources for Inclusion

Marge Arnup

19.1 Introduction

Gippsland is a rural region of Victoria, Australia. Located in the south-east of the state, it has a population of approximately 230 000, dispersed throughout large and small towns, farms and allotments. In this region, over 3000 children start school annually at one of 165 government or non-government primary schools. The Department of Education and Early Childhood Development (DEECD), Gippsland, is responsible for the operation of all government schools in the area. During the period of the project (2004–2009), DEECD was responsible for establishing and maintaining connections across a number of government initiatives operating in the area, all of which were designed to enhance outcomes for young children. Various projects operated under the auspices of local, state and federal government and included *Best Start* (DEECD 2007), *Communities for Children* (Edwards et al. 2009), *Neighbourhood Renewal* (Latrobe City Council 2009) and *Municipal Early Years Plans* (Municipal Association of Victoria 2006). Several of these projects promoted the importance of a positive start to school. This was matched by interest across the early childhood field, with some school communities reporting that up to 30 % of children arrived at school with significant additional needs not identified prior to school entry.

Through the DEECD, a project officer was appointed to work collaboratively with early childhood services, schools, government and non-government agencies, parents and the broader community to develop strategies to promote children's successful transition to school. A key role was to establish links across projects, with the aims of enhancing transition to school practices for children with additional needs, increasing opportunities for preschool children to engage in activities to

M. Arnup (✉)
Early Childhood Educator, Rural Victoria, Australia
e-mail: marge_arnup@bigpond.com

B. Perry et al. (eds.), *Transitions to School - International Research, Policy and Practice*,   261
International perspectives on early childhood education and development 9,
DOI 10.1007/978-94-007-7350-9_19, © Springer Science+Business Media Dordrecht 2014

support their literacy development and building partnerships between DEECD and the wider community. This project had two major outcomes: collaborative partnerships and, through these, the development of resources and strategies that were responsive to local needs.

19.2 Network Partnerships

19.2.1 Why the Partnership Approach?

Leading transition to school researchers acknowledge the importance of partnerships between children, parents and educators (Centre for Equity and Innovation in Early Childhood 2008; Dockett and Perry 2006; Fabian and Dunlop 2006; Peters, 2010).

In implementing the project, it was hypothesised that the establishment of a local network of practitioners representing the range of early childhood, education and family services would support strategic and collaborative planning that would result in the provision of programmes to address local transition needs. Local networks could also provide a vehicle to build relationships, share knowledge and understanding of the range of services and programmes operating and build opportunities for future learning and development. Further, it was believed that children, families and professionals would benefit from the increased collaboration and cooperation among services promoted by the networks.

The importance of collaboration across services and supports has been highlighted by Dockett and Perry (2006). Seven of their ten *Guidelines for Effective Transition to School Programs* incorporate the importance for partnerships through:

- The establishment of positive relationships between children, parents and educators
- The involvement of a range of stakeholders
- Strong planning and evaluation
- Flexibility and responsiveness
- The need for mutual respect
- Reciprocal communication among participants
- The need to account for local community context and the needs of individual families and children within that community

19.2.2 How Did the Networks Operate?

Like transition, local community networks were not "one size fits all". Some networks were created with the sole purpose of supporting transition to school; other networks met to address issues across the broader early childhood service system, with transition to school as a priority issue. Networks were town, district or municipality based, with memberships ranging from 10 to 40. The more isolated areas had smaller networks whose membership was drawn predominately from preschool educators and school staff with a focus solely directed towards school transition. Networks servicing large towns and municipal regions had a larger membership base representative of a broad range of education, children and family services. The DEECD project officer initiated the majority of the networks while consolidating or supporting those networks already functioning.

Meetings of the local networks were facilitated, in collaboration with local government and community agencies providing children and family services. These networks met at least once per term. The initial meeting utilised an invitation to the broad range of staff involved in services for children aged from birth to 8 years, including maternal and child health staff, childcare educators (home-based, centre-based and out-of-school hours care), preschool (administrators and educators), school (principals and/or teachers), allied health staff (speech therapy, occupational therapy, psychology), disability support services, cultural support services (including those supporting Indigenous families) and other family services organisations.

Invitations were sent collaboratively under the combined banner of key organisations and projects operating in each local area—asking people to come together to:

- Develop a shared vision
- Provide better opportunities and improved outcomes for children, parents and professionals
- Support networking and professional learning for staff
- Improve the local service system

A positive response to the concept of networks was always received. People were most willing to come together, driven by a desire to see improved outcomes for children, opportunities to meet with and learn from others and/or to be informed of the many changes and opportunities available in birth-to-8-year services. In all networks, the steps taken were:

- Establishment of a local network open to all professionals providing services for children from birth to 8 years
- Identification of shared issues and concerns
- Agreement to work towards shared goals
- Meeting regularly (minimum of once per term)
- Brainstorming ideas to achieve goals
- Creating timelines
- Implementing strategies
- Reviewing, evaluating and refining practices

These steps reflect the cycle of transition recommended by Dockett and Perry (2006).

A successful early action was the brainstorming of local transition to school issues for children, parents and professionals with network members. This was beneficial as it provided a forum for participants to recognise their shared beliefs, provided an opportunity to develop a shared understanding of terms and identified possible barriers to establishing positive collaboration in the future.

The operation of the Gippsland networks reflects the ecological model of transition described by Dunlop and Fabian (2002). This model is based on Bronfenbrenner's ecological theory and highlights the nature and importance of connections across and between different systems, as children start school. (A revised version of this model is discussed by Dunlop in Chap. 5 of this volume.)

19.2.3 Common Transition Issues Identified by Networks

When discussing the transition needs of children, families and professionals, it became most apparent that:

- Confusion existed around the terms orientation and transition—most people when talking about transition were describing orientation experiences only.
- Families, service providers and educators lacked information and resources to guide their practices, particularly when supporting children with additional needs associated with developmental delay, disability and cultural diversity.
- Therapists working with children prior to school entry often were a neglected resource.
- There was a need for creativity and new approaches to engage with families whose children did not participate in playgroup, childcare, preschool or school orientation activities. This was raised as an issue particularly when children who had not attended prior-to-school services started school with needs, such as developmental delay that had not previously been identified.
- There was no shared understanding of the concept of school readiness between families and educators in prior-to-school settings and schools.
- Early childhood and school educators had limited knowledge of each others' needs or practices. For example, many early child educators were unaware of the need for the majority of school enrolments to be received 3–4 months in advance to permit whole school planning.
- There was limited knowledge of curriculum across the preschool and school settings, with the result that discussions about continuity were hampered.
- Educators reported being time poor and needing support and resources in order to be better equipped to enhance current transition practices.
- Transition planning focused on individual schools rather than the local community.
- School familiarisation was often the only focus of transition planning.
- There was a tendency to overlook engagement with other professionals and services who worked with families whose children were making the transition to school.

Addressing these issues became the springboard for network goal setting and strategy implementation.

19.2.4   Network Achievements

A broad range of achievements were attained across the many networks including:

1. Forums, which served to:

   - Develop shared understandings of school readiness between parents and early childhood/school/community services professionals
   - Provide transition to school information for parents, including forums specifically for families with children with disabilities and/or developmental delay and for Indigenous families
   - Promote shared understandings of school transition between parents and early childhood/school/community services professionals

2. Resources, including:

   - Resources for sharing with parents, including school transition brochures and early childhood literacy and numeracy information sessions, brochures, DVDs and activity packs
   - Service directories for professional networking, planning and supporting children and families
   - Transition directories for families—listing all local early childhood services and schools, addresses, contact details, transition coordinators and any deadlines for enrolments

3. Community collaboration and planning through:

   - The development of transition protocols for individual communities (agreeing when and how enrolments would be sought and when orientation activities would commence)
   - Information sharing and joint planning at community level to support children with additional needs as they made the transition to school
   - Development of an information template for sharing individual child information between home, prior-to-school settings and schools
   - Local enrolment campaigns aimed to get information to families who were not accessing prior-to-school services
   - Central enrolment initiatives on behalf of all local schools
   - The generation of transition programmes for Indigenous families and children to encourage timely school enrolment, participation in transition activities, identification of developmental delays and to support schools be culturally inclusive
   - Provision of playgroups in schools for families not accessing other programmes

4. Professional learning opportunities to:

   - Foster shared understanding of early childhood literacy, oral language development and the implications for literacy learning
   - Foster the identification of children at risk of language development delay

- Discuss and foster shared understanding of early childhood and school curriculums for those working with children from birth to 8 years
- Facilitate participation in transition research activities to inform future practice

19.2.5 Network Benefits

The establishment of transition networks created many positive benefits for local communities. Networks led to early childhood professionals learning about other services and programmes that could support their own work with children and families and identified potential partners to enhance transition practices. For example, many schools had tended to overlook childcare services, particularly home-based childcare when promoting transition activities within the community. Local networks provided knowledge of, and the opportunity to meet and talk with, childcare providers.

Local networks also provided a reason for people to meet together. While individuals supported the concept of collaboration and networking, their own priorities, workloads and lack of opportunities had been barriers to meaningful networking. Having someone to facilitate and lead a network that was adequately resourced assisted in gaining and maintaining commitment to the network.

Feedback from network members indicated that they saw benefits in the opportunity to meet staff from other sectors, visit other schools and early childhood services, access professional learning and be an influence for positive change. Comments from participants included:

> My understanding is much broader now – transition doesn't just affect kindergarten and school but also families and other agents.
> This has given me more hope that we can all work out a better system for our children and families.

The Gippsland networks became a powerful tool for engaging local people in strategic projects and taking responsibility for planning and delivering transition programmes in their community that resulted in improved outcomes for children, families and professionals.

The collaborative partnerships developed through the networks were seen as an important factor in contributing to successful planning and provision of transition programmes. While this was evident in the DEECD project, it is also evident in research, such as that undertaken within the *Better Beginnings, Better Futures Project* in Canada (Corter and Peters 2011, p. 2), which identified the benefits of community partnerships in promoting:

- Increased levels of activities and programmes for children in the community
- Increased visibility of projects in communities over time
- Joint planning and delivery of services and/or activities with other agencies

- Increased funding for programmes
- Changes in attitudes and practices of service providers
- Increased collaboration among partner agencies

19.2.6 Lessons Learnt: Networking

Based on experiences throughout the project, the following factors have been identified as contributing to effective transition networking:

- Understanding of the value and commitment to networking from school leadership, service managers, government agencies and others managing staff and programmes
- Collaboratively planning for partnerships including early childhood, school and community services representatives coming together to plan and promote the establishment of a network
- Leadership and facilitation of the network, where someone is responsible for the organisation and ongoing management of the network
- Drawing on the expertise of local people and services to plan, coordinate and champion networks
- Clear articulation of the network purpose
- Ensuring personal contact with services to explain and promote the network concept—emails and letters are not enough
- Shared identification of goals, timelines and responsibility for implementing strategies
- Some actions achieved within the first 3–4 months
- Strong leadership and administrative support, with all potential network members receiving invitations to and notes from all meetings
- Creation of an environment where all parties feel their opinions are heard and respected
- Scheduling of meetings outside of contact time with children
- Alternating meeting venues amongst the range of services, schools and agencies involved in the network
- Provision of food, drink and name tags at all meetings
- Scheduling informal networking/information sharing time prior to or immediately after meetings
- Adequate resourcing
- Activities to support professional learning of the network participants held in the early stages of the group's development. This can help participants feel that they belong and that the network is beneficial for them personally

Advice for those developing transition networks (Astbury 2009, p. 21) includes:

Being patient, taking a personalized approach and recognizing that individuals and agencies are often at different stages in terms of their understanding of transition and readiness to adopt new strategies.

In keeping with other recommendations from Astbury (2009), it has been important to:

- Foster shared understandings and agreement on values and goals
- Ensure that networks are broad based including families, early childhood education and care, schools, community agencies, maternal and child health care services as well as any of the relevant stakeholders or community members
- Prepare, monitor and evaluate local action plans
- Ensure that power is equally distributed and balanced among partners (decision-making should not rest solely with one agency/person)

19.3   Resources for Supporting Children with Additional Needs

In addition to the local networks described above, an additional network to support children with disabilities and/or developmental delay also operated across the Gippsland region. Known as the Gippsland Early Childhood Intervention Advisory Network (GECIAN), this network was established in 2002 as a partnership between early intervention service providers and DEECD, with a charter to develop and implement an integrated service system for families whose children experienced disabilities and/or developmental delays. Working parties were formed to address service collaboration, strategic planning and early childhood/school transitions.

The "transition" working party began in earnest in 2005. Using the partnership model, it drew its membership from a broad range of service providers. Parents were also represented. Facilitated by the DEECD project worker, the activities of this group and the other aforementioned networks were interlinked.

After extensive local research and a literature review, it was determined that strategies were needed to:

- Provide timely information to families
- Establish procedures to ensure collaboration between the early childhood, education and community services sectors
- Establish procedures and practices to meet the needs of all children, not only those who were identified as having a disability or developmental delay
- Ensure information was provided to early childhood, schools, community services and all others managing or providing services to children from birth to 8 years
- Ensure families received timely information about eligibility for disability supports once their child was no longer eligible for early intervention services
- A "best practice resource kit" to:
- Assist professionals to develop a shared understanding of the range of service families may use;

- Provide access to resources available for sharing with families and to further professionals reading
- Showcase procedures that supported effective transition and the implementation of consistent best practice through all early childhood services and primary schools

was deemed the most effective and practical way to address the needs identified in Gippsland.

While the development of a resource was supported, several issues needed to be addressed in order to make sure that any resource was relevant and useful within the network. The first priority was to develop a set of agreed terminology for use within the resource. As in other parts of the world (Broström 2002; Fabian and Dunlop 2006), anecdotal evidence from the existing local networks and the diversity of working party membership indicated that, while people used the same terms, there was not a shared understanding of what those terms meant.

The second issue is related to the focus of the resource. It was perceived that early childhood educators would be most likely to use the resource if it related to a range of educational transitions, rather than just the transition to school. It was decided to address transitions *into* early childhood services as well as transitions into school.

Anecdotal evidence also indicated that staff new to a service/school or to the process of transition needed practical support and information to be aware of the many issues to be addressed when planning and supporting transition. This was particularly true for therapists, foster care staff and services supporting cultural diversity. However, the importance of embedding practice with theory was recognised, and as a consequence, the resource was to have both theoretical and practical components.

To support the development of linkages between services a section referencing the full range of services and supports available, contact details and information on protocols for sharing information were included in the resource.

19.3.1   Shared Understandings: Transition Terminology

In general terms, it was acknowledged that transition involved:

- The psychological process people go through to come to terms with a new situation
- A gradual process which takes differing amounts of time for different people
- Starting with endings (Bridges 1995).

In keeping with the definition used in *Transition: A Positive Start to School Initiative* (DEECD 2008), school transition was defined as a process that involves children, families, early childhood services, schools and the broader community. It is not a single activity; it is a range of strategies, approaches and practices that occur during the year before and the year of entry into primary school.

19.3.2 Shared Understanding: Best Practice

The GECIAN transition working party agreed that the following actions would be considered best practice in supporting the transition to school of children with additional needs:

- Family members have the information they need as decision makers and feel confident that all options have been considered.
- Family members are involved in developing a plan that meets their needs and the needs of their child.
- Family and staff from the sending and receiving settings jointly develop transition plans.
- Sending and receiving settings work cooperatively.
- Any services that may be needed by the children and the family after transition to the next setting are organised before the move occurs.
- Planning to be undertaken with sufficient time to achieve all steps and minimise stress for families.
- Time to prepare the child for any difference in the next setting.

The term "additional needs" was deemed to be inclusive of children with disability and/or developmental delay, cultural diversity (with an emphasis on Indigenous children) and those living in foster care situations.

19.3.3 Professional Resources: Best Practice Transition Kit

Initially the focus of the working party was on producing a school transition guide and a parent information resource specific to the Gippsland area. As these were completed, it became apparent that guides were needed for childcare and preschool and that these resources needed to be packaged in a way that made them easily accessible to all relevant parties.

Consisting of a large folder with sections dedicated to childcare, preschool and school transitions, a trial version of the kit was produced in 2007. The information included had been sought from parents, practitioners across Gippsland and key personnel from childcare, preschool and school sectors, including government departments, Catholic Education Office, the Independent Schools Association and other peak organisations. People from each sector were invited to working party meetings where information was exchanged. Ongoing communication with peak organisations representing parents, early childhood services and schools also assisted in the identification of what information needed to be included in the kit. The DEECD project worker was responsible for collating, editing and preparing information for review and endorsement by the working party representatives of government departments and those services featured in the kit, prior to publication.

Feedback such as the comment below from a member of the working party inspired the working party to move from pilot to final edition.

> This is an excellent resource kit and is a valuable tool for teachers and parents at every step in the transition process. All childcare, Maternal and Child Health Services, Kinders, and Schools should have a copy on their shelves as soon as possible.

The final kit contained sections relevant to:

- Transitions into childcare, preschool and school
- Children from Indigenous and other culturally diverse backgrounds
- Supporting children in child protection (foster care)
- Linking with other professionals
- Professional reading, other resources and space for readers to add their own resources in time

Each section contained pertinent transition information for professionals working within the sector or wishing to learn about the sector, a list of resources available in the community (other staff, services, printed material) and benchmark guides to relevant transition practices.

The information for the final edition (Gippsland Early Childhood Intervention Advisory Network (GECIAN) 2009a) covered 134 pages. This factor, combined with a limited budget and a desire to keep all information current into the future, led to the production of the kit online and in CD format. These formats allowed readers to go directly to sections or pages of relevance. To promote awareness and use of the kit, small folders containing a CD, step-by-step guide to using the CD, print copies of *Best Practice Transition Guides* and a booklet providing a guide to parents/carers of children with a disability and/or developmental delay were distributed at network meetings. There were also presentations to explain the content of the resource and how it worked. The kit was distributed widely to all early childhood education and care services, schools, local government and all Gippsland services promoted in the kit.

19.3.4   Professional Resources: Best Practice Guides

Best practice transition guides were included in the kit to provide a benchmark for families and professionals supporting transition to childcare, preschool and school. Additional guides specifically to support children in foster care make the transition to preschool and school were also included in the kit.

The *Best Practice Guide: Transition to School* (Fig. 19.1) identifies tasks, services and people involved in transition. The guide aims to promote discussion, planning and implementation of a cycle of transition activities within local networks. It showcases the range of people who may be involved in transition, tasks to be completed and timelines.

Best practice guide
Transition to School

	P	S	EC	SS
TERM 1 TASKS:				
Appoint a staff member to oversee the transition process		✔	✔	✔
Convene meeting, inviting all local Junior Schools, Kindergartens, Child Care Services, Pre School Field Officer, Specialist Children's Services, School Support staff any other Early Intervention Staff. (Consider joining with any 0-8 year's network that already meets.) **Purpose:** Review previous year transition activities (what worked, what didn't) and plan for current year transition activities. Determine how, when and who will provide information to parents/carers and professionals re: Making a successful transition to school; Choosing a school; Supporting children with additional needs; School Orientation & Open Days dates.	✔	✔	✔	✔
TERM 2 TASKS:				
Confirm Dates & Procedures for Enrolment, Orientation Days & Prep Information Night. Share with transition network members and families		✔	✔	✔
Attend information sessions re Program for Students with Disabilities funding processes for current year. DEECD, Catholic Education Office and Association Independent Schools Victoria all host sessions. Update knowledge of current protocols eg. Sharing Our Journey.		✔	✔	✔
Identify children with high level needs so relevant discussion, action and assessment can be undertaken to meet DEECD, CEO & AISV Student with Disabilities funding guidelines.	✔	✔	✔	✔
1st Joint Student Support Group Meeting (related to high level needs child including those in Child Protection). **Purpose:** To undertake the funding application process.	✔	✔	✔	✔
Provide information to Parents of children with high level needs (this may be 1:1 or professionals may work collaboratively to host a meeting to provide a range of information including school options, enrolment and funding applications processes, planning for transition). Encourage parents/carers/guardians to contact and visit schools.	✔	✔	✔	✔
Networking: Organise time release for prep teachers to spend a session observing the new children in their early childhood setting. Arrange opportunities for Kindergarten teachers. Childcare workers and other carers to visit the schools.		✔	✔	✔
TERM 3 TASKS:				
2nd Joint Student Support Group Meeting (related to high level needs child) - early - mid term 3. **Purpose:** To identify goals, strategies and timelines to familiarise the child with school **August: DEECD Schools - Identify any facilities modifications required and make application to Regional Office**	✔	✔	✔	✔
Liaise with school re planning & support for non funded "at risk" children. (i.e. children whom are ineligible for Disabilities funding but will need additional support to succeed).	✔	✔	✔	✔
TERM 4 TASKS:				
Complete Transition Learning & Development Statements and Sharing our Journey templates. Forward to schools.	✔	✔	✔	✔
Host orientation days for all incoming prep students and prep information sessions for parents/carers.	✔	✔	✔	✔
3rd Joint Student Support Group Meeting (high level needs child). Purpose: review set goals and identify goals for commencing school.	✔	✔	✔	✔
Joint Planning & Support Group Meeting for non-funded "at risk children". Purpose:- identify strengths, interests and learning needs and set goals for commencing school.	✔	✔	✔	✔
TERM 1 TASKS following year:				
Monitor progress of high level and "at risk" children through Student Support Group Meetings. **Ensure liaison with School Nursing Program and School Welfare Officer where appropriate. Ensure children with identified disabilities/developmental delay are linked to DHS Disability Services where appropriate.**	✔	✔	✔	✔

P   Parent
S   School - Primary, Special, Independent, Catholic.
EC   Early Childhood - Kindergarten, Childcare, Family Day Care, Maternal Child Health
SS   Specialist Services - Early Intervention Services, Child Protection.
Child First (Family Information Referral & Support Team) Community Health & Allied Services (e.g. Speech & Occupational. Therapist, Psychologist) Pre School Field Officer (PSFO), Koorie Early Childhood Field Officer, Koorie Pre School Assistant Inclusion Support Facilitator (ISF) School Support Staff, Primary School Nurse, DHS - Disability Services

DHS   Department of Human Services
DEECD   Department of Education and Early Childhood Development
CEO   Catholic Education Office
AISV   Association Independent Schools Victoria

Document prepared by Gippsland Early Childhood Intervention Advisory Network 2009 & adapted from the *Passing the Baton* 2000

Fig. 19.1 Best Practice Guide: Transition to School (Reproduced with permission (GECIAN 2009a), Copyright owned by the State of Victoria (Department of Education and Early Childhood Development). Used with permission)

19.3.5 Professional Resources: Moving to School

The resource also included a booklet entitled *Moving to School* (GECIAN 2009b) which aimed to support parents of children with a developmental delay and/or disability. It provided families with information relating to:

- School options
- Enrolment and planning for educational support
- Transition suggestions
- Parent support services
- Other support services

19.3.6 Resource: Benefits

A wide range of anecdotal feedback from users of the kit identified a number of benefits, including:

- Focus on addressing the needs of local children, parents and professionals
- Parents receiving timely information to support decision-making for their children's early childhood and school transitions
- Parents and professionals working collaboratively to provide information to assist educational planning and the use of appropriate strategies to support the transitions of children with additional learning needs
- The development of shared understandings of transition and school readiness between parents, early childhood, school and community services professionals
- Increased provision of positive practices that support the successful transitions of children with additional needs.

19.3.7 Lessons Learnt: Resources

The provision of easy to access *transition to school* information is desired by families, early childhood, school and community services professionals supporting *all* children transitioning to school. There is an even greater demand for information and resources to support the transitions of children with additional needs. This was the gap the GECIAN resource aimed to fill.

19.3.7.1 Families

Families with children with disabilities and developmental delays were most interested in what educational options were available to their children, timelines to be met and recommended actions to support a successful transition to school.

These parents often reported feeling hurt when receiving information that detailed a list of skills and attitudes perceived as necessary for making a successful start to school. They were already aware that their children would be severely challenged at school, by not having achieved developmental milestones regarded as the norm for their age. The concept of *schools being ready for the child rather than the child being ready for school was* highly regarded by these families. (This concept has emerged in recent years from the National School Readiness Indicators Initiative in the United States and draws on Bronfenbrenner's ecological systems theory. This concept implies that schools are ready to meet the educational needs of all individual children. For more information see Rhode Island Kids Count (2005)).

Indigenous families had a much higher engagement in transition programmes when these were respectful and supportive of cultural differences and were jointly facilitated by an Indigenous community member. In one service, staff reported that because of the transition programme, all eligible Indigenous children had attended on the first day of the school year. In previous years this had not been the case. Parents also reported feeling comfortable about participating in transition programmes because they had support from a community member.

19.3.7.2 Professionals

Feedback from professionals indicated that resources being sought included templates for sharing information, guides for action and timelines, strategies to access resources for families and other professionals who may assist children with additional needs and access to current research and evidence.

Providing resources for both transition "into" and "from" early childhood services assisted in engaging early childhood services in transition to school planning and building trust and respect. Utilising local "transition champions" to participate in the development of benchmark guides ensured local needs were addressed and assisted in the readiness of the community to use the guides. For example, one of the working party groups reported that children with physical impairments often started school without ramps and other building modifications to assist mobility. The school transition guide highlights the timeline for submitting funding applications for building modifications. It was also the case that the resources were particularly well received when it was noted that they had been developed specifically for Gippsland, by people who worked in the area. Network meetings proved an effective tool to showcase, discuss and advocate for the use of the resources.

When making recommendations for resources for school policy and implementation, Astbury (2009, p. 38) identified the need for:

> the provision of clear information (e.g. resource kits, templates, manuals, and research evidence) on how to develop local transition programs, complete transition statements and implement promising practices. This could be followed-up with training as well as technical assistance where required to provide early childhood educators, schools and community agencies with the necessary knowledge, skills, and confidence to implement enhanced transition processes and practices.

These elements are reflected clearly in the GECIAN kit.

19.4   Conclusion

In summary, a number of implications for future planning and policy development can be gleaned from the Gippsland experience. These lead to recommendations that:

- Governments, schools and services consider embedding the role and place of networking into transition to school policy and practice
- Broad-based networks servicing early childhood, schools, community services and families be established in local communities to plan, implement and evaluate transition to school practices
- Early childhood services, schools and community services allocate funding to support effective networking and the implementation of transition plans
- Networks be utilised as a means to promote available resources
- Resources that:
  - Provide transition to school information for families and professionals
  - Benchmark transition practices and timelines
  - Promote access to locally relevant networking, planning and support information
  - Provide coordinated supports for children with additional needs
  - Are based on relevant research and evidence

be readily available to all families and professionals supporting transitions into early childhood services and schools.

References

Astbury, B. (2009). Evaluation of transition: A positive start to school pilots. Centre for Program Evaluation Report. The University of Melbourne. http://www.eduweb.vic.gov.au/edulibrary/public/earlychildhood/learning/transitionevaluationreport.pdf. Accessed 5 June 2012.

Broström, S. (2002). Communication and continuity in the transition from kindergarten to school. In H. Fabian & A.-W. Dunlop (Eds.), *Transitions in the early years: Debating continuity and progression for children in early education* (pp. 52–63). London: Routledge Falmer.

Bridges, W. (1995). *Managing transitions.* Cambridge, MA: Da Capo Press.

Centre for Equity and Innovation in Early Childhood. (2008). Literature review. Transition: A positive start to school. Melbourne: University of Melbourne. http://www.eduweb.vic.gov.au/edulibrary/public/earlychildhood/learning/transitionliteraturereview.pdf. Accessed 24 July 2012.

Corter, C., & Peters, R. (2011). *Integrated early childhood services in Canada: Evidence from the Better Beginnings, Better Futures (BBBF) and Toronto First Duty (TFD) Projects.* Encyclopedia on Early Childhood Development. Toronto: Centre of Excellence for Early Childhood Development. http://www.child-encyclopedia.com/documents/Corter-PetersANGxp1.pdf. Accessed 7 June 2012.

Department of Education and Early Childhood Development. (2007). Best Start program overview. Department of Human Services. State Government of Victoria. http://www.eduweb.vic.gov.au/edulibrary/public/beststart/best_start_overview_14032007.pdf. Accessed 4 Aug 2012.

Department of Education and Early Childhood Development. (2008). *Transition working party principles and definitions.* Melbourne: Department of Education and Early Childhood Development.

Dockett, S., & Perry, B. (2006). *Starting school: A handbook for early educators.* Castle Hill: Pademelon Press.

Dunlop, A. W., & Fabian, H. (2002). Conclusions. In H. Fabian & A.-W. Dunlop (Eds.), *Transitions in the early years: Debating continuity and progression for children in early education* (pp. 146–154). London: Routledge Falmer.

Edwards, B., Wise, S., Gray, M., Hayes, A., Katz, I., Mission, S., Patulny, R., & Muir, K. (2009). *Stronger families in Australia study: The impact of Communities for Children.* Canberra: Australian Government Department of Family, Housing, Community Services and Indigenous Affairs.

Fabian, H., & Dunlop A. W. (2006). Outcomes of good practice in transition processes for children entering primary school. Paper commissioned for the EFA Global Monitoring Report 2007, Strong foundations: early childhood care and education. http://www.scribd.com/doc/50601340/null. Accessed 6 July 2012.

Gippsland Early Childhood Intervention Advisory Network. (2009a). Best practice transition kit. http://www.gecian.org.au/3/17181/17181.html Accessed 11 July 2012.

Gippsland Early Childhood Intervention Advisory Network. (2009b). Moving to school. http://www.gecian.org.au/3/17181/18520.html. Accessed 11 July 2012.

Latrobe City Council. (2009). The year 8 report: Latrobe Valley neighbourhood renewal, 2002–2009. http://www.latrobe.vic.gov.au/WebFiles/Council%20Services/Community%20Development/00112%20LV%20Neighbourhood%20Renewal%20Report%20-%20Full%20Draft%20sml.pdf. Accessed 11 July 2012.

Municipal Association of Victoria. (2006). Municipal early years plan initiative. http://www.mav.asn.au/policy-services/social-community/children-families/municipal-early-years-planning/Pages/default.aspx. Accessed 4 July 2012.

Peters, S. (2010). Literature review: Transition from early childhood education to school. Ministry of Education New Zealand. www.educationcounts.govt.nz/publications. Accessed 5 July 2012.

Rhode Island Kids Count. (2005). School readiness indicators initiative. www.GettingReady.org. Accessed 18 July 2012.

Chapter 20
Research to Policy: Transition to School Position Statement

Sue Dockett and Bob Perry

20.1 Introduction

In October 2010, 14 researchers from seven countries met in Albury, New South Wales, Australia, to explore their research and current directions in transitions research. They exchanged information with six research higher degree students who were also investigating specific aspects of transition; 35 policymakers representing local, state and national organisations with direct responsibilities for transition to school; and approximately 100 practitioners, employed in both prior-to-school and early years of school settings.

One of the aims of this transitions conference was to synthesise the wide range of transitions research, policy and practice into a position statement which would, in turn, inform and guide future research, policy and practice in the area of transition to school. While the conference was undertaken in Australia, the contributions of research participants from Australia, New Zealand, Iceland, the United Kingdom, the United States, Sweden and Hong Kong ensured that the discussions encompassed issues and approaches of international relevance and significance. In addition, the involvement of both practitioners and policymakers promoted a focus on not only the research but the ways in which it was, and could be, interpreted and applied. Collaborative involvement in the development of a position statement offered the opportunity for researchers, policymakers and practitioners to generate a common language around issues related to transition, consider ways in which research could influence policy and practice and create pathways such that issues of transitions policy and practice could generate new approaches to research.

S. Dockett (✉) • B. Perry
School of Education, Charles Sturt University, Albury Wodonga, Australia
e-mail: sdockett@csu.edu.au

B. Perry et al. (eds.), *Transitions to School - International Research, Policy and Practice*,   277
International perspectives on early childhood education and development 9,
DOI 10.1007/978-94-007-7350-9_20, © Springer Science+Business Media Dordrecht 2014

20.2   Research, Policy and Practice

The everyday worlds of practitioners, policymakers and researchers are often far removed from each other. The contexts in which they work have been described as different cultures (Cadigan 2012). Yet there are regular calls for research to be utilised in both policy and practice and for research to be built upon professional knowledge.

The ways in which research influences policy and practice, and the ways in which issues within policy and practice inform research, are often not well understood. In some instances, there has been the assumption that 'researchers should produce high-quality research, make it clear and accessible, and then practitioners should apply it to their work' (Tseng 2012, p. 4). Embedded assumptions in this linear model are that the research that is generated is closely linked to practice and policy and is usable in these contexts and that policymakers and practitioners are users of the research that is produced. Recent investigations of the ways in which research is accessed and used indicate the flawed nature of these assumptions (Nutley et al. 2007; Tseng 2012).

Rickinson et al. (2011, p. 5) outline a more complex model, describing user engagement with research in terms of 'knowledge exchange processes that involve different players, are multi-directional and have strong personal and affective dimensions'. This model emphasises the importance of relationships and interactions as those who engage in research and those who engage with research 'bring their own experience, values, and understanding to bear in interpreting research and its meaning for local contexts' (Nutley et al. 2007, p. 305). This approach recognises practitioners, policymakers and researchers as experts in their own fields and provides opportunities to promote both the application of research and input from policy and practice to 'ongoing problem formulation and data analyses within research projects' (Rickinson et al. 2011, p. 24).

Interactions between researchers, policymakers and practitioners are required if research is to have an impact on practice and if issues relevant to policymakers and practitioners are to become the focus of research. The importance of linkages in promoting the exchange of knowledge and ideas across these groups has been highlighted (Amara et al. 2004; Lavis et al. 2003), leading to the conclusion that research is most likely to be adopted and used by those who have been involved in its development and/or interpretation (Easton 2012; Lomas et al. 2005).

Developing genuine interactions and ongoing conversations between practitioners, policymakers and researchers requires both relationships and a common means of communication. Relationships act as the conduits for the sharing of information – as practitioners and policymakers turn to researchers to translate or interpret research in ways that are relevant for them and as researchers respond to the ways in which research impacts on policy and practice (Tseng 2012). Communication about research has often involved the development of research briefs or research summaries. Though useful, these rely on the unidirectional sharing of information. Effective communication across groups of researchers, policymakers and practitioners can require the generation of new ways of naming and talking about particular issues. This was one of the aims underlying the development of a position statement about transition to school.

20.3   Position Statements

Position statements offer a clear statement of a position on an issue, particularly when varying or controversial opinions exist. They act as a form of advocacy, arguing for a position that is supported by research and/or professional practice. Position statements are often developed and adopted by organisations and professional groups as a means of interpreting research and sharing it in a form that is readily available and accessible to practitioners and policymakers. The most effective position statements are developed through processes of consensus, where there are opportunities to canvass 'diverse perspectives and areas of expertise related to the issue and … opportunities for members and others to provide input and feedback' (National Association for the Education of Young Children [NAEYC] n.d.). The *Transition to School Position Statement* provided a focus for sharing a wide range of research; recognising the expertise of all involved – practitioners, policymakers and researchers; generating a document that outlined a common position; using language that was relevant and meaningful for all involved; and outlining a path for the development of research, policy and practice into the future.

20.4   Diverse Perspectives of Transition to School

As the contributions to this book attest, there are many views related to transition to school. There is consensus about the importance of a positive start to school, with research from around the world indicating that a positive start to school is linked to later positive educational and social outcomes (Alexander and Entwisle 1998; Dockett and Perry 2007; Dunlop and Fabian 2007; Margetts 2007; Peters 2010). However, there is considerable diversity about what constitutes a positive start to school, how this might be achieved and what it looks like in practice for all involved. Further, there is a range of ways in which transition in general, and the transition to school in particular, is theorised and conceptualised. The commitment to promoting a positive transition to school, as well as recognition of the diverse perspectives, approaches and issues that surround it, has provided the impetus for the development of the position statement.

In Australia, as in other countries, an increasing focus on children's readiness for school has emerged, coupled with perceived pressure to push down school curriculum to prior-to-school settings. Anecdotally at least, such pressures are related to the increased focus on national testing (Dockett et al. 2007). The same trends have been reported in the United States and the United Kingdom (Fisher 2010; Wesley and Buysse 2003).

At the same time as an increased focus on children's readiness, there is evidence that many children start school without having accessed high quality early childhood programmes or other services that support their optimal growth, development and learning. This situation gives rise to concerns that children are not well prepared for school and that they will not obtain maximum benefit from engagement with school. For example, the recent roll-out of the Australian Early Development Index (AEDI) in Australia (Centre for Community Child Health and Telethon Institute for Child Health Research 2009) indicates that significant numbers of Australian children are considered to be "developmentally vulnerable" across at least one developmental domain at the time they start school. In many instances, these children are considered to be "unready" for school.

In much public commentary, the conflation of research related to readiness and the transition to school has meant that transition is often described in terms of the characteristics of individual children. While broad definitions of readiness have been promoted (Ackerman and Barnett 2005), there remains a focus on children's readiness, rather than on ready schools, families or communities. The focus on transition – as a broader construct – reflects efforts to direct research, policy and practice away from a deficit approach (as is indicated by definitions of readiness or "unreadiness") towards strengths-based approaches (Saleebey 2006) that acknowledge the knowledge, understandings, skills and abilities of all involved in the transition to school.

20.5 Developing the Position Statement

Fourteen researchers from seven countries working in the area of transition to school met in 2010 to share their research perspectives and to collaborate in the initial development of a draft position statement on transition to school. Six higher degree students researching specific elements of transition also participated in this collaboration. These researchers engaged with a range of policymakers with responsibilities at local, state and national levels and a group of approximately 100 practitioners, primarily educators employed in prior-to-school services and schools. A modified Delphi method was employed to generate a position statement that reflected consensus among these participants.

Since their development in the 1950s, Delphi methods have been used across a variety of fields – including education – to generate consensus from experts around a specific topic or issue, particularly where there is contradiction or controversy (Baumfield et al. 2012; Pollard and Pollard 2004; Vernon 2009). Franklin and Hart (2007, p. 238) note that

> in selecting a Delphi approach, researchers are interested in collecting the judgements of experts on a particular topic to (a) document and assess those judgements (Stewart 2001), (b) capture the areas of collective knowledge held by professionals which is not often

verbalised and explored (Stewart & Shamdanasi 1990) and (c) force new ideas to emerge about the topic.

Delphi methods provide a structured framework for accessing and filtering the information contributed by a range of experts, through an iterative cycle of questioning, feedback and refinement of views. Several different types of Delphi methods have been identified, as well as a number of variations (Day and Bobeva 2005; Powell 2003). The core features of Delphi methods are the expert panel, iteration with controlled feedback, statistical group response and anonymity (Vernon 2009). Variations in the ways in which these elements are adopted or adapted lead to the many different applications of Delphi methods. For example, several studies have included a group meeting as part of a Delphi approach (Baumfield et al. 2012; Heimlich et al. 2011).

The development of the *Transition to School Position Statement* reflected some, but not all, of these elements and is therefore considered to be an example of a modified Delphi approach. Elements that were critical to the development of the position statement were the involvement of experts and the iterative process of seeking input and providing controlled feedback. As the position statement was developed through face-to-face meetings, anonymity was not possible, and the need for statistical responses related to elements of the draft statement was replaced with further consultation. Indeed, it was considered important for the identity of at least the group of expert researchers to be known and associated with the final statement, as this enhanced the credibility and perceived relevance of the final statement.

While there are many variations of the Delphi technique, each typically consists of three phases (Dutta et al. 2010):

Stage 1: Harnessing the expertise of an identified group of experts in order to explore an issue
Stage 2: Understanding how the group of experts views the issue
Stage 3: Establishing consensus where the information gathered is analysed and provided back to the experts for review and potential agreement

These stages guided the development of the position statement and are outlined below.

20.5.1 Stage 1

A group of experts was identified and invited to participate. Part of the rationale for involving experts was to draw on the latest possible evidence, including that which had not yet been published. Experts included researchers, policymakers and practitioners – each with an interest and/or involvement in some aspect of transition to school. The purposive selection of transition to school researchers identified 20 international researchers who had recently researched and/or published in the area, whose work reflected diverse perspectives and experiences, and who were considered to have credibility in the research area (Vernon 2009). Fourteen experts from seven different countries accepted the invitation to be involved. Research expertise was supplemented by six research higher degree students whose substantive research focus involved aspects of transition to school. As in other studies using Delphi approaches in education (such as Rice 2009), groups of policymakers and practitioners also provided expert advice. All participants attended a meeting hosted by the Educational Transitions and Change research group in Albury, Australia, in October 2010.

20.5.2   Stage 2

Several strategies were used in order to understand how the group of experts viewed transition to school:

- Each of the expert researchers was invited to write a paper outlining their current research approach to transition to school, exploring the theoretical foundations of their work and implications of this for policy and practice.
- These papers were submitted before the Albury meeting and each paper was reviewed by two members of the expert panel.
- During the Albury meeting of the research experts, these reviews – but not the papers – were presented to the group. Open discussion followed these presentations.
- At the conclusion of the presentations, the research students synthesised the papers, presentations, review comments and discussion. This synthesis was shared with the group of researchers as a means of prompting the identification of elements to be incorporated in a draft position statement.
- A draft position statement was developed to reflect this synthesis and the consensus from the group. This draft was returned to the group for refinement and modification.
- The draft statement was shared with the policymakers' group, which consisted of 35 representatives of local, state and national organisations and government departments.
- During a series of workshop sessions, small groups of policymakers worked with researchers, sharing their expertise, commenting on the draft, suggesting revisions and reviewing the content.
- The draft statement was shared with a group of approximately 100 early childhood practitioners. A further series of workshop sessions provided opportunities for practitioners to share their expertise and suggest revisions and refinements of the statement.

20.5.3   Stage 3

Several of the latter strategies in Stage 2 paved the way for the focus of Stage 3, where the information gathered was used as the basis for establishing consensus. All of the information gathered from the various expert groups was recorded, collated and analysed. The draft statement was amended to reflect consistent suggestions. The inclusion of the workshop sessions provided opportunities for individuals to share views, raise concerns and make suggested changes. As a result, there was a great deal of consistency in the suggestions made. After modification of the draft statement, a further two rounds of consultation with the group of research experts were undertaken before full consensus was attained.

The *Transition to School Position Statement* (Educational Transitions and Change (ETC) Research Group 2011) was launched in August 2011. It has been included as an Appendix to this chapter and can be downloaded from http://www.csu.edu.au/research/ripple/research-groups/etc/Position-Statement.pdf.

20.6   Consensus About Transition to School

The Delphi approach resulted in a document that refocuses and repositions attention to transition to school. The following statements, taken from the document, outline this:

> The position statement reconceptualises transition to school in the context of social justice, human rights (including children's rights), educational reform and ethical agendas, and the established impact of transition to school on children's ongoing wellbeing, learning and development.
>
> Transition to school is taken to be a dynamic process of continuity and change as children move into the first year of school. The process of transition occurs over time, beginning well before children start school and extending to the point where children and families feel a sense of belonging at school and when educators recognise this sense of belonging.
>
> Transition to school is characterised by:
>
> - opportunities
> - aspirations
> - expectations
> - entitlements

The *Transition to School Position Statement* aims to promote increased recognition of the important role of transition to school and ongoing engagement in education and to provoke changes in the ways in which transition to school is researched, represented in policy and enacted in practice. It has been developed as an aspirational document, targeted to all concerned with the education, care and wellbeing of young children, their families, educators and communities. It is presented as a "living document" to be used and updated as appropriate. While its initial formulation represents the context in which it was developed – Australia – it is an international document to be adapted for different audiences and different contexts. To this end, a number of the expert group of researchers have already adapted the research overview section to reflect their contexts and translated the core elements into a number of languages.

20.7 Limitations

While the Delphi approach used to produce the Transition to School Position Statement proved to be a very effective means of engaging a wide range of experts and harnessing their collective wisdom, as a process it also has a number of limitations. By outlining the processes used in some detail, we aim to provide a clear overview of the ways in which the experts were chosen, the data were generated and consensus was reached. Dissemination of the position statement in Australia and internationally suggests that it has relevance and resonance in a number of different contexts. Such transparency is important in determining the credibility and applicability of the statement produced, which in turn, contributes to the validity of the document (Day and Bobeva 2005).

Experts who participated in this process were not randomly chosen, and it is clear that they represent a selection of those whose work encompasses transition to school, whether it be research, policy or practice, or a combination of these. The strength and applicability of the position statement largely depends on how it is adopted and used in a range of contexts and by a range of people.

The position statement reflects a concerted effort by those who engage in research and those who engage with research to share their expertise and to collaborate in ways that promote the transfer of research to policy and practice and the incorporation of professional knowledge into research directions and agendas. In offering new ways of conceptualising and communicating about transition to school, the position statement encourages continued conversations among all stakeholders as they promote a positive start to school for all involved.

Preamble

Worldwide recognition of the significance of the early childhood years for later development and wellbeing and the importance of investing in high quality early childhood education (OECD, 2006) has promoted a great deal of interest in transition research, policy and practice. This trend is seen in Australia, particularly in COAG commitments to early childhood education (Commonwealth of Australia, 2009b), including the *Early Years Learning Framework* (Commonwealth of Australia, 2009a). These commitments are being enacted at the same time as the Australian curriculum is being developed and implemented. It is timely to consider the transition to school as the point at which different contexts, systems, curricula, philosophies and approaches meet. Beginning school is also a time when all involved have responsibilities to promote a positive transition.

The importance of a positive transition to school has been emphasised in research around the world. It is well established that a successful start to school is linked to later positive educational and social outcomes. Children who have a positive start to school are likely to regard school as an important place and to have positive expectations of their ability to learn and succeed at school (Alexander & Entwisle,

1998; Dockett & Perry, 2007; Dunlop & Fabian, 2007; Margetts, 2007; Peters, 2010).

A successful transition to school is marked by children's positive approach to school and a sense of belonging and engagement. Families have critical roles to play in supporting positive transitions, as do educators*, health and other professionals, as well as communities. Societies benefit when children and families view school as a positive place to be and when education is regarded as valuable, relevant and attainable. A positive start to school, leading to greater and ongoing connection with school, has been identified as a factor in disrupting cycles of social and economic disadvantage and in promoting resilience among young people (Commonwealth of Australia, 2009b; Smart, Sanson, Baxter, Edwards, & Hayes, 2008).

This position statement has been developed by a group of national and international transition to school researchers who have been working in the area over the last 20 years. An overview of the researchers' seminal research is included at the end of this document. The authors have been assisted in this task by a wide range of educators and policy makers, who have reviewed the document and enhanced it through their constructive criticism.

*The term educators includes teachers in school and prior-to-school settings, as well as other adults with the responsibility for the care and education of young children in these settings.

Purpose

This position statement has been developed as an aspirational document targeted to all concerned with the education, care and wellbeing of young children. This includes policymakers, educators, health and other professionals, families and communities. The position statement reconceptualises transition to school in the context of social justice, human rights (including children's rights), educational reform and ethical agendas, and the established impact of transition to school on children's ongoing wellbeing, learning and development. These principles support a range of educational entitlements around the transition to school.

This position statement has been developed as an aspirational document targeted to all concerned with the education, care and wellbeing of young children.

The position statement is based on national and international understandings of the importance of the transition to school. It provides a strong basis for action for government, organisations and individuals as all strive for policies and practices that support the best possible start to school for all children and their families.

The statement is underpinned by the importance of:

- understandings of all children as competent, capable and creative, who have already learned a great deal before they enter school, regardless of their context or backgrounds;

- acknowledging and supporting children as active participants in their own transition and learning;

- recognising and valuing the strengths of all involved in transitions to school;

- genuine partnerships involving reciprocal, responsive, respectful relationships;

- critically reflecting on established policies and practices and their underlying assumptions; and

- curriculum and pedagogy relevant to children's characteristics, interests and circumstances.

In this document, transition to school is taken to be a dynamic process of continuity and change as children move into the first year of school. The process of transition occurs over time, beginning well before children start school and extending to the point where children and families feel a sense of belonging at school and when educators recognise this sense of belonging. This means that transition may occur over a longer period of time for some children.

Transition to school is characterised by:

- opportunities;   - expectations;

- aspirations;   - entitlements.

Opportunities

Opportunities are afforded to children when they are recognised as competent and capable, when their cultural heritage and histories are respected, and when they are supported in their approaches to new and challenging situations and interactions. The transition to school provides opportunities for children to continue shaping their identities and to extend their existing knowledge, skills and understandings through interactions with adults, peers and family. Children are well placed to respond to these opportunities when they feel secure, valued and respected for who they are and the histories they bring – when they feel a sense of belonging at school. The transition to school provides opportunities for children to become citizens within school communities and to experience the rights and responsibilities associated with this.

Transition to school provides opportunities for families to collaborate with educators and other professionals in ways that strengthen and support each child's ongoing learning and development. It provides opportunities to reflect on children's attainments and to share responsibilities for future achievements.

Children are well placed to respond to these opportunities when they feel secure, valued and respected for who they are and the histories they bring – when they feel a sense of belonging at school.

 Transition to School   1   Position Statement

The transition to school is an opportunity to establish and maintain positive, respectful collaboration between home and school contexts that sets a pattern for ongoing interaction. Families have opportunities to build links for their children between prior-to-school and school experiences.

During the transition to school, educators have opportunities to build relationships with children, families and communities that provide the basis for effective learning and teaching interactions. Educators have opportunities to share their own expertise, while recognising the expertise of others, as they communicate and make connections with children, other educators, families and communities. The transition to school is a specific opportunity for prior-to-school and school educators, and the systems in which they are employed, to work together and to draw support from each other.

Educators have opportunities to share their own expertise, while recognising the expertise of others, as they communicate and make connections with children, other educators, families and communities.

Community recognition and support for transition to school marks this transition as an important life event. Transition to school affords opportunities for communities to celebrate children and families and to demonstrate the value of early education as well as respect for those involved in this endeavour. The transition to school is an opportunity to strengthen the community identity of schools and prior-to-school settings and the place of these institutions within communities.

Aspirations

As they start school children are enthusiastic learners, keen to extend their learning in a safe and friendly environment. They seek to maintain existing friendships and build new friendships as they engage in play and learning. They hope that school will be an enjoyable context which supports their developing autonomy and their active engagement in learning. Children want their learning to be recognised and valued in both process and product.

Families aspire to positive educational outcomes for their children, as well as continuity between the early childhood settings – at times of transition and beyond. They would like their children to be happy and successful at school, to have friends and be respected and recognised as individuals within the various groups of which they are members. Families also aspire to contribute to their children's education through the development of trusting, respectful and reciprocal relationships.

Educators aspire to the development of strong partnerships with families, other educators, professionals and communities as part of strong and supportive educational environments in the first year of school. They want children to learn to their full potential in an inspiring, challenging and supportive environment.

Communities aspire to provide ongoing support and resources to promote children's positive engagement in school and to reap the social, cultural, educational and economic benefits of education that are regarded as valuable, relevant and attainable. Communities also aspire to provide the support, resources, services and living conditions that promote the wellbeing of children and families. Communities with strong social networks and access to resources that can be mobilised to support children and families are well positioned to promote positive transitions to school.

Within educational organisations and systems, policy makers aspire to all children engaging in positive educational trajectories and achieving sound educational outcomes. This is based on commitments to reducing inequalities in educational access and outcomes. Strategies to achieve positive educational outcomes for all include continuity of curriculum and pedagogy and strong coordination between the prior-to-school and school sectors.

Educators aspire to the development of strong partnerships with families, other educators, professionals and communities as part of strong and supportive educational environments in the first year of school

 Transition to School 2 Position Statement

Expectations

Transition to school is a time of changing expectations for all involved.

Children and families start school with a range of expectations about what school will be like and what it means to be a school student or parent of a school student. Children start school expecting to learn and to be recognised as learners. They expect to encounter challenges and to be supported in their approaches to these. Children expect to engage with their friends, family and community at school and about school. Children seek continuity of support as they encounter change as they start school: changes in themselves, their environments and their interactions.

Children and families start school with a range of expectations about what school will be like and what it means to be a school student or parent of a school student.

Families expect that their knowledge of their children will be respected at school. They expect that their children's educators will draw on this, as well as their own expertise and that of other professionals, to create the best possible learning environments for their children. Families expect to contribute to their children's education, and may seek guidance from educators about how partnerships can operate effectively. Families expect children's safety and wellbeing to be central features in decisions about educational provision. They expect schools to recognise the strengths their children bring, as well as to be responsive to their diverse learning needs. Families expect to be advocates for their children, and to be supported in this by the advocacy of other professionals.

Educators expect to engage with children, families, other educators and professionals in the creation of positive learning and teaching environments during the transition to school. They expect appropriate support and resources to create challenging learning environments for all children. Educators expect to work with children, families and other professionals to recognise children's strengths and to provide appropriate support. They expect appropriate professional recognition and regard for their roles in promoting each child's learning, development and wellbeing during the transition process.

Communities expect schools to be sites where children are regarded as competent and capable learners, experience a sense of belonging, and enact the rights and responsibilities of citizenship. Effective schools attend to the wellbeing of all involved, generate positive and respectful learning environments and have regard to the communities in which they are located.

Within educational systems and organisations, there are expectations that all children will benefit from education. Further, education is identified as a major force for reducing inequality and disadvantage and promoting long-term social and economic productivity.

Policy makers within educational organisations and systems expect that specific programs will be required to promote educational engagement and attainment for all children. One key area for such focus is the transition to school.

Entitlements

All children are active participants in their transition, entitled to access high quality education that is respectful of, and responsive to, their existing competencies, cultural heritage and histories.

High quality education builds upon these competencies by creating educational environments that provoke, recognise and celebrate each child's learning potential. These environments acknowledge the central roles of families and communities in children's educational outcomes. There is potential for transitions to school to provide a site for the enactment of these entitlements from the very beginning of children's school careers.

Families are entitled to be confident that their children will have access to education that promotes equity and excellence and that attends to the wellbeing of all children. Families are entitled to be respected as partners in their children's education.

High quality education builds upon these competencies by creating educational environments that provoke, recognise and celebrate each child's learning potential.

 Transition to School   3   Position Statement

Educators are entitled to professional regard and respect for their work with children, families and communities during the transition process. They are entitled to levels of professional support and resourcing that facilitate the creation of the best possible learning and teaching environments for all children, and to opportunities for ongoing professional development and critical reflection, both individually and collaboratively.

Communities are entitled to be regarded as essential contributors to children's education, and to have a major role and place within education institutions. Policy makers are entitled to expect that education systems will work towards alignment and continuity, providing necessary supports and provocations to promote high quality education for all.

Communities are entitled to be regarded as essential contributors to children's education, and to have a major role and place within education institutions.

Educational systems and organisations are entitled to expect that educators, families and communities will be active contributors to the wellbeing, learning and development of young children.

Recommendations

This position statement has been developed as a call to action for all with an interest in the wellbeing, development and learning of young children. This includes policymakers, educators, health and other professionals, families and communities. In urging individuals, groups, communities, organisations, systems and governments to recognise the importance of a positive transition to school for all children, we recommend the development of processes, practices and policies that incorporate the following:

1. Recognition of transition to school as an integral component of quality educational provision.

2. Commitment to equity and excellence in the development of transition programs, evident in the engagement of children, families, professionals, educators and community members in the implementation of relevant, appropriate and meaningful approaches.

3. Approaches to ensure that all children, families and communities have access to appropriate support across the processes of transition.

4. Focus on the competencies, strengths and achievements of children and families as they make the transition to school.

5. Acknowledgement of the central role of relationships in positive transitions and opportunities for those involved to build and maintain these relationships.

6. Recognition of children's active roles in shaping their transition experiences and the importance of consulting them about transition.

7. Enactment of the principles of family engagement in education, based on trusting, respectful and reciprocal relationships.

8. Appropriate support for educators whose roles encompass transition to school, including support for the development of curriculum and pedagogy that supports positive transitions, opportunities for critical reflection on policies and practices and appropriate professional development.

9. Recognition of the transition to school as an opportunity to build positive connections between the many systems and sectors that engage with young children and their families.

10. Acknowledgement of the major roles in transition played by those outside school systems, including prior-to-school educators, special educators and other professionals, families and communities.

11. Opportunities for systems and sectors to define transition approaches and to consider constructive alignment of curriculum and pedagogies across educational contexts.

12. Ongoing commitment to the entitlements of all children, families and educators in positive transitions to school.

This position statement has been developed as a call to action for all with an interest in the wellbeing, development and learning of young children.

  Transition to School   4   Position Statement

References

Alexander, K. L., & Entwisle, D. R. (1998). Facilitating the transition to first grade: The nature of transition and research on factors. *Elementary School Journal, 98*(4), 351-364.

Commonwealth of Australia. (2009a). *Belonging, being, becoming: The early years learning framework for Australia*. http://www.deewr.gov.au/EarlyChildhood/Policy_Agenda/Quality/Pages/EarlyYearsLearningFramework.aspx

Commonwealth of Australia. (2009b). *National quality framework for early childhood education and care*. http://www.deewr.gov.au/Earlychildhood/Policy_Agenda/Quality/Pages/home.aspx

Dockett, S., & Perry, B. (2007). *Transitions to school: Perceptions, expectations, experiences*. Sydney: University of NSW Press.

Dunlop, A-W., & Fabian, H. (Eds.) (2007). *Informing transitions in the early years: Research, policy and practice*. London: OUP/McGraw Hill.

Margetts, K. (2007). Preparing children for school: Benefits and privileges. *Australian Journal of Early Childhood, 32*(2), 43-50.

OECD. (2006). *Starting strong II. Early childhood education and care, Executive summary*. http://www.oecd.org/document/63/0,3343,en_2649_392632 31_37416703_1_1_1_1,00.html

Peters, S. (2010). *Literature Review: Transition from early childhood education to school*. Wellington: New Zealand Ministry of Education. http://www.educationcounts.govt.nz/publications/ece/78823

Smart, D., Sanson, A., Baxter, B., Edwards, B., & Hayes, A. (2008). *Home-to-school transitions for financially disadvantaged children: Summary report*. Sydney: The Smith Family and Australian Institute of Family Studies. http://www.thesmithfamily.com.au/site/page.cfm?u=105

Authors

The authors of this statement are leading researchers in the field of transition, from Australia and around the world. Individually and collectively, they have conducted high quality research on the transition to school over many years, published widely in prestigious academic journals, addressed learned forums, informed professional practice and provided input for policy. Their work has formed the basis of advice for various levels of government, educational organisations and systems and provided the framework for approaches to transition in their respective countries, as well as internationally. The researchers and key publications are listed below.

Professor Sue Dockett, Murray School of Education, Charles Sturt University.

http://www.csu.edu.au/faculty/educat/murrayed/staff/dockett_sue.htm

Dockett, S., Perry, B., & Kearney, E. (2010). *School readiness: what does it mean for Indigenous children, families, schools and communities? Issues Paper 2*. Canberra: Closing the Gap Clearinghouse.

http://www.aihw.gov.au/closingthegap/documents/issues_papers/ctg-ip02.pdf

Emeritus Professor Aline-Wendy Dunlop, University of Strathclyde, Scotland.

http://www.strath.ac.uk/humanities/courses/education/staff/dunlopaline-wendyprof/

Dunlop, A-W., & Fabian, H. (Eds.) (2007). *Informing transitions in the early years: Research, policy and practice*. London: OUP/McGraw Hill.

Professor Jóhanna Einarsdóttir, Faculty of Education, University of Iceland, Iceland.

https://uni.hi.is/joein/

Einarsdóttir, J. (2010). Children's experiences of the first year of primary school. *European Early Childhood Education Research Journal, 18*(2), 163-180.

 Transition to School   5   Position Statement

Professor Anders Garpelin, School of Education, Culture and Communication at Mälardalen University, Sweden.

http://www.mdh.se/ukk/staff/sqa/agn02

Garpelin, A. (2004). Accepted or rejected in school. *European Educational Research Journal, 3*(4), 729-742.

Professor Beth Graue, Department of Curriculum and Instruction, University of Wisconsin, Madison, USA.

http://www.wcer.wisc.edu/people/staff.php?sid=472

Graue, E. (2006). The answer is readiness - Now what is the question? *Early Education and Development, 17*(1), 43-56.

Associate Professor Linda Harrison, Charles Sturt University.

http://www.csu.edu.au/faculty/educat/teached/staff/harrison_l inda.htm

Harrison, L., Clarke, L., & & Ungerer, J. (2007). Children's drawings provide a new perspective on linkages between teacher-child relationship quality and school adjustment. *Early Childhood Research Quarterly, 22,* 55-71.

Dr Mei Seung (Michelle) Lam, Assistant Professor, Department of Early Childhood Education, Hong Kong Institute of Education, Hong Kong.

https://oraas0.ied.edu.hk/rich/web/people_details.jsp?pid=9863

Lam, M. S., & Pollard, A. (2006). A conceptual framework for understanding children as agents in the transition from home to kindergarten. *Early Years: An International Journal of Research and Development, 26* (2), 123-141.

Dr Noella Mackenzie, Murray School of Education, Charles Sturt University.

http://www.csu.edu.au/faculty/educat/murrayed/staff/macken zie_noella.htm

Mackenzie, N.M (2008) Becoming a writer: Can we predict how children will engage with the writing process at school entry? *Journal of Reading, Writing and Literacy, 3*(1), 1-19.

Associate Professor Kay Margetts, Melbourne Graduate School of Education, The University of Melbourne.

http://www.edfac.unimelb.edu.au/cgi-bin/public/staff_profile.cgi?id=3921

Margetts, K. (2009). Early transition and adjustment and children's adjustment after six years of schooling. *European Early Childhood Education Research Journal, 17*(3), 309 – 324.

Dr Elizabeth Murray, School of Teacher Education, Charles Sturt University.

http://www.csu.edu.au/faculty/educat/teached/dubbo/staff/lib bey_murray.html

Murray, E., & Harrison, L. J. (2005). Children's perspectives on their first year of school: Introducing a new pictorial measure of school stress. *European Early Childhood Education Research Journal, 13,* 111-127

Professor Bob Perry, Murray School of Education, Charles Sturt University.

http://www.csu.edu.au/faculty/educat/murrayed/staff/perry_b ob.htm

Dockett, S., & Perry, B. (2007). *Transitions to school: Perceptions, expectations, experiences.* Sydney: University of NSW Press.

Dr Sally Peters, Department of Human Development and Counselling, University of Waikato, New Zealand.

http://edlinked.soe.waikato.ac.nz/staff/index.php?user=speters

Peters, S. (2010). Literature review. *Transition from early childhood education to school.* Wellington: Ministry of Education.

Dr Anne Petriwskyj, Faculty of Education, Early Childhood, Queensland University of Technology.

http://staff.qut.edu.au/staff/petriwse

Petriwskyj, Anne (2010) Who has rights to what? Inclusion in Australian early childhood programs. *Contemporary Issues in Early Childhood, 11*(4). 342 352.

Dr Tuija Turunen, Murray School of Education, Charles Sturt University; University of Lapland, Finland.

http://www.csu.edu.au/faculty/educat/murrayed/staff/turunen _tuija.htm

Turunen, T. A. (2011). Memories about starting school. What is remembered after decades? *Scandinavian Journal of Educational Research.* (In press).

Research students

Several research higher degree students made invaluable
contributions to this Position Statement:

Wendy Goff, Charles Sturt University

Kathryn Hopps, Charles Sturt University

Cathy Kaplun, Charles Sturt University

Amy MacDonald, Charles Sturt University

Leonie McIntosh, University of Western Sydney

Susanne Rogers, Charles Sturt University

The development of this statement has been facilitated
through funding support from the following organisations;

Charles Sturt University, Australian Government Department
of Education, Employment and Workplace Relations, The Ian
Potter Foundation, NSW Department of Education and
Training – Western Region, South Australian Department of
Education and Children's Services, Victorian Department of
Education and Early Childhood Development – Hume Region
& Regional Express.

The opinions expressed in this document are those of the
authors and do not necessarily reflect the opinions of the
funding bodies.

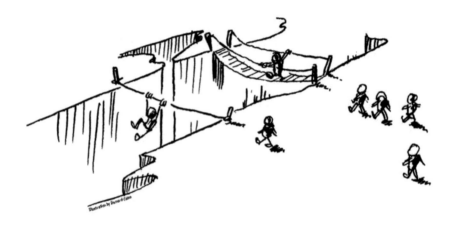

Illustration by Dulani & Cato

ISBN 978-1-86467-231-2

Suggested Citation: Educational Transitions and Change (ETC) Research Group. (2011). Transition to school: Position statement
Albury-Wodonga: Research Institute for Professional Practice, Learning and Education, Charles Sturt University.

Imagecorp Pty Ltd

References

Ackerman, D., & Barnett, W. (2005). Prepared for kindergarten: What does readiness mean? NIEER policy report. http://nieer.org/resources/policyreports/report5.pdf. Accessed 12 Mar 2012.

Alexander, K. L., & Entwisle, D. R. (1998). Facilitating the transition to first grade: The nature of transition and research on factors. *Elementary School Journal, 98*(4), 351–364.

Amara, N., Ouimet, M., & Landry, R. (2004). New evidence on instrumental, conceptual, and symbolic utilisation of university research in government agencies. *Science Communication, 26*(1), 75–106.

Baumfield, V. M., Conroy, J. C., Davis, R. A., & Lundie, D. C. (2012). The Delphi method: Gathering expert opinion in religious education. *British Journal of Religious Education, 34*(1), 5–19.

Cadigan, K. (2012). Commentary on the uses of research in policy and practice. *Social Policy Report, 26*(2), 17–19.

Centre for Community Child Health, & Telethon Institute for Child Health Research. (2009). A snapshot of early childhood development in Australia: Australian Early Development Index (AEDI) national report, 2009. Canberra: DEEWR. www.rch.org.au/aedi/media/Snapshot_of_Early_Childhood_DevelopmentinAustralia_AEDI_National_Report.pdf. Accessed 12 Mar 2012.

Day, J., & Bobeva, M. (2005). A generic toolkit for the successful management of Delphi studies. *The Electronic Journal of Business Research Methodology, 3*(2), 103–116.

Dockett, S., & Perry, B. (2007). *Transitions to school: Perceptions, expectations, experiences.* Sydney: University of NSW Press.

Dockett, S., Perry, B., Campbell, H., Hard, L., Kearney, E., & Taffe, R. (2007). Early years learning and curriculum. Reconceptualising reception: Continuity of learning. http://www.earlyyears.sa.edu.au/files/links/final_lit_review.pdf. Accessed 9 May 2012.

Dunlop, A.-W., & Fabian, H. (Eds.). (2007). *Informing transitions in the early years: Research, policy and practice.* London: OUP/McGraw Hill.

Dutta, A., Kundu, M., & Chan, F. (2010). The conduct of socially valid investigation by culturally diverse researchers: A Delphi study. *Rehabilitation Education, 24*(3–4), 113–122.

Easton, J. (2012). Commentary on the uses of research in policy and practice. *Social Policy Report, 26*(2), 19–20.

Educational Transitions and Change (ETC) Research Group. (2011). *Transition to school: Position statement.* Albury Wodonga: Research Institute for Professional Practice, Learning and Education, Charles Sturt University. http://www.csu.edu.au/research/ripple/research-groups/etc/Position-Statement.pdf. Accessed 19 Oct 2012.

Fisher, J. (2010). *Moving on to Key Stage 1.* Maidenhead: Open University Press.

Franklin, K. K., & Hart, J. K. (2007). Idea generation and exploration: Benefits and limitations of the policy Delphi research method. *Innovative Higher Education, 31*(4), 237–246.

Heimlich, J. E., Carlson, S. P., & Storksdieck, M. (2011). Building face, construct, and content validity through use of a modified Delphi: Adapting grounded theory to build an environmental field days observation tool. *Environmental Education, 17*(3), 287–305.

Lavis, J. N., McLeod, C. B., & Gildiner, A. (2003). Measuring the impact of health research. *Journal of Health Services Research and Policy, 8*(3), 165–170.

Lomas, J., Culyer, T., McCutcheon, C., McAuley, L., & Law, S. (2005). Conceptualising and combining evidence for health system guidance. http://www.chsrf.ca/other_documents/pdf/evidence_e.pdf. Accessed 7 Oct 2012.

Margetts, K. (2007). Preparing children for school: Benefits and privileges. *Australian Journal of Early Childhood, 32*(2), 43–50.

National Association for the Education of Young Children (NAEYC). (n.d). Position statements. http://www.naeyc.org/positionstatements. Accessed 1 Dec 2012.

Nutley, S., Walter, I., & Davies, H. (2007). *Using evidence: How research can inform public services.* Bristol: Policy Press.

Peters, S. (2010). *Literature review: Transition from early childhood education to school.* Wellington: Ministry of Education. http://www.educationcounts.govt.nz/publications/ece/78823. Accessed 8 May 2012.

Pollard, C., & Pollard, R. (2004). Research priorities in educational technology: A Delphi study. *Journal of Research on Technology in Education, 37*(2), 145–160.

Powell, C. (2003). The Delphi technique: Myths and realities. *Journal of Advanced Nursing, 41*(4), 376–382.

Rice, K. (2009). Priorities in K-12 distance education: A Delphi study examining multiple perspectives in policy, practice, and research. *Educational Technology & Society, 12*(3), 163–177.

Rickinson, M., Sebba, J., & Edwards, A. (2011). *Improving research through user engagement.* London: Routledge.

Saleebey, D. (Ed.). (2006). *The strengths perspective in social work practice* (5th ed.). Boston: Pearson.

Stewart, D. W., & Shamdanasi, P. N. (1990). *Focus groups: Theory and practice. Applied social research methods series*, Vol. 20. Newbury Park, CA: Sage.

Stewart, J. (2001). Is the Delphi technique a qualitative method? *Medical Education, 35*, 922–923.

Tseng, V. (2012). The uses of research in policy and practice. *Social Policy Report, 26*(2), 1–16.

Vernon, W. (2009). The Delphi technique: A review. *International Journal of Therapy and Rehabilitation, 16*(2), 69–76.

Wesley, P., & Buysse, V. (2003). Making meaning of school readiness in schools and communities. *Early Childhood Research Quarterly, 18*(3), 351–375.